D1104738

For a complete selection of our "Underwater World of Alaska Sportfish" series of instructional videos and books, including "Underwater Secrets of Catching Trophy Halibut, Rockfish and Lingcod" refer to our website:

www.AlaskaAngler.com

How To Catch Trophy
HALIBUT

How To Catch Trophy
HALIBUT
Proven Tips, Techniques And
Strategies Of The Experts

Christopher Batin
& Terry Rudnick

Photos by Christopher and Adela Batin
and Terry Rudnick
Illustrations by Karen Farrell

Published by Alaska Angler Publications
Fairbanks, Alaska

How To Catch Trophy Halibut: Proven Tips, Techniques and Strategies Of The Experts is part of the *Alaska Angler Sportfishing Library*™, a series of books that provide you with the advanced information necessary for you to experience unparalleled success in your sportfishing pursuits.

Cover photo: Galen Daily with a 316-pound Homer halibut. Photo by Chris Batin.

How To Catch Trophy Halibut: Proven Tips, Techniques And Strategies Of The Experts, ©Copyright 1996 by Christopher Batin and Terry Rudnick. All rights reserved. No part of this book may be reproduced in any form or by any electronic or mechanical means including information storage and retrieval systems without permission in writing from the publisher, except in the case of brief quotations embodied in critical reviews and articles.

Published by Alaska Angler® Publications, P. O. Box 83550 Dept. TR, Fairbanks, Alaska, 99708, (907) 455-8000.

First Edition, December 1996

Book and cover design: Adela Ward Batin
Typography and production: Award Design, Fairbanks, Alaska
Illustrations: Karen Farrell, Intelligraphics

Library of Congress Cataloging in Publication Data
Batin, Christopher—
    How to catch trophy halibut: proven tips, techniques and strategies of the experts.

    Includes appendix.

    1. Fishing--Alaska. 2. Halibut.
    3. Halibut fishing--Washington. 4. Halibut fishing--Oregon.
    5. Halibut fishing--British Columbia.
    6. Halibut fishing--California. 7. Pacific halibut fishing.
  I. Rudnick, Terry.   II. Title.

SH691.H3B37 1996   96-083949

ISBN 0-916771-15-6

Produced in the State of Alaska
Printed in the United States of America

You can obtain any Alaska Hunter® or Alaska Angler® book in print by ordering directly from the publisher. See order form in the back of this book, or for our complete catalog of books and publications that help ensure your success in the Alaska outdoors, send $1 to Alaska Angler/Hunter Publications, P.O. Box 83550, Dept F3, Fairbanks, Alaska 99708 (907) 455-8000.

Dedication

To the Pacific halibut,
one of the Almighty's greatest
sportfish creations.
We celebrate your existence
with this book.

Halibut Crest—adapted from designs used by Tlingit, Tsimshian and Haida Indians.

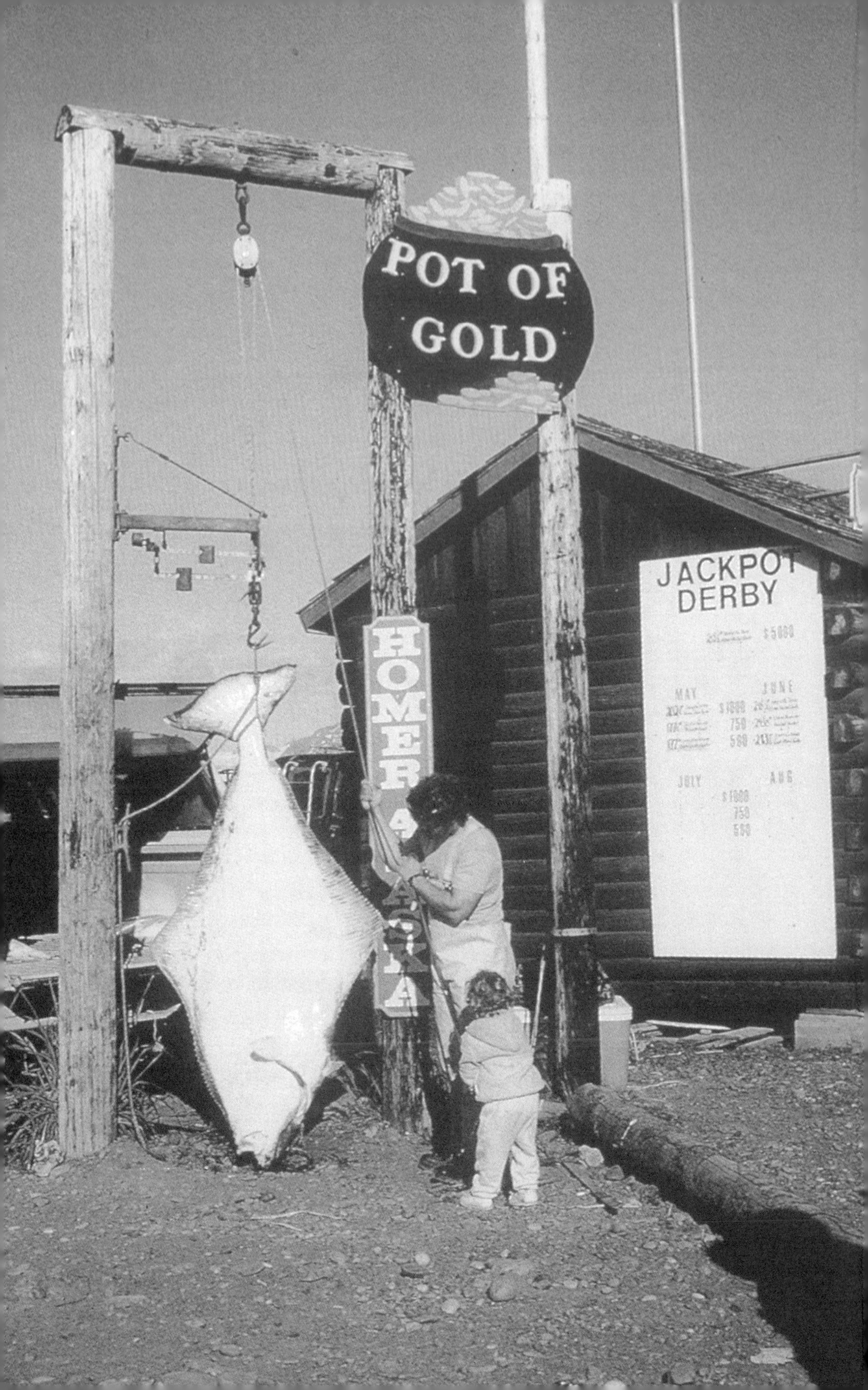
POT OF GOLD
HOMER
JACKPOT DERBY
MAY
JUNE
JULY
AUG

Table of Contents

A halibut derby angler and son weighing a 230-pound halibut caught from Lower Cook Inlet.

Special Section
Halibut Fishing Hotspots And Tips

Craig and Eddie Battisfore of Modesto, California, teamed up to boat this 203-pound halibut, caught from Kashevarof Passage, near the north end of Alaska's Prince of Wales Island.

Introduction

Pacific halibut fishing is skyrocketing in popularity from Alaska to California. Why? In both cases the answers are the same: fun and culinary investment. Halibut is not only a prime eating fish, but also a single fish can fill your freezer with enough of the flaky, white meat to last the entire year. With halibut currently selling for over $4 a pound, it's no wonder that all categories of anglers—from fly fishermen to bait casters—are finding that a day trip for halibut more than pays for itself. And of course, catching fish that can reach weights of 400-plus pounds is a challenge offered by few other North American bottomfish. Critical fish stocks along the Pacific coast also benefit from halibut fishing's popularity. For instance, The Alaska Angler® staff has identified a growing trend among anglers who spend a week or more at a "full-service" lodge. Rather than take home rainbow or salmon fillets, they schedule a day or two of halibut fishing to acquire fish for their freezer. This action is to be commended, as it allows utilization of a currently plentiful saltwater species in lieu of limited numbers of slow-growing freshwater sportfish.

As a reader of this book, you are obviously looking for ways to experience this growing and exciting fishery and perhaps the thrill of catching a 200-pound or larger barn-door for yourself. If so, you've come to the right place.

Study the information in this book, and you'll receive the equivalent of a Ph.D. in halibut fishing. *How to catch Trophy Halibut* contains the combined knowledge of guides, outfitters, biologists and their decades of halibut fishing experience. All this is yours...for the reading.

You'll also benefit from the experience of Terry Rudnick and myself. Terry and I work as full-time outdoor writers and editors. Together, we have over 40 years of halibut fishing experience covering the entire Pacific Northwest and Alaska.

In writing this book, we felt it was important to provide you with not only biological and scientific insights, but also specific how-to and where-to-go information that will minimize the costly mistakes every angler makes afield. For the do-it-yourself angler, we point the way to hotspots. And for the guided angler, our advice should spare you the horrid experience and lost dollars of booking a trip with a fly-by-night operator.

How to catch Trophy Halibut is more than a book: It is your personal reference guide to halibut fishing success. When you prepare tackle, keep it at your side as an ever-ready reference. With use, this book will become a trusted and valued friend; a must-have companion on all your halibut fishing excursions from that week-long charter in Alaska to a day trip off the Oregon or California coast.

I believe that with knowledge comes responsibility. Please, do not use the knowledge in this book to rape our stocks of Pacific halibut. Use it to interact with the fish, its environment, and appreciate the true wonder of the Almighty's creation known as the Pacific Ocean, and its denizen of the deep, the halibut. Terry and I promise that the result of your actions will last for generations.

In Closing

You are more than a fishing license number to us. You are a valued reader and friend in the sport of Pacific halibut fishing. Terry and I care about your success on the water, and hope that you will write us with your experiences, proven tips and techniques. You can reach us at POB 83550, Fairbanks, Alaska 99708.

Until either Terry or I can meet you or talk to you in person, the best of success in all your trophy halibut fishing adventures. Now if you're ready, turn to Chapter 1 and allow us to introduce you to the Pacific halibut.

Chris Batin, Editor, The Alaska Angler®
Co-author, *How to catch Trophy Halibut*

Halibut Life History And Biology

An Alaska-grown Pacific halibut is a super heavyweight slugger with a division and honor all its own. For instance, the fish has stamina beyond belief. Adults can travel more than 2,000 miles and to depths of 1,800 or more feet. They've also been known to sink boats, break arms and legs and snap 120-pound Dacron as if it were sewing thread.

Despite its power, such a fish isn't born ready to do battle. Rather, its beginning is meek and mysterious, one that is aptly suited for the lifestyle Mother Nature gave it.

Description And Scientific Name

Halibut belong to a family of flounders called *Pleuronectidae*. These symmetrical, torpedo-shaped fish exhibit heavily pigmented backs and white to yellowish-gray bellies. Anglers have no difficulty identifying a mature halibut from other flatfish: Flounders and soles rarely reach weights of up to 500 pounds attained by Pacific halibut. Identification of flounder and similar-sized halibut (fish smaller than 10 pounds) however, requires closer examination.

Flounders are compressed laterally and, except in the larval stages, have both eyes on one side of the head. Like halibut, the eyed-side is pigmented and the underside is white.

Halibut usually are dextral, that is, both eyes are on the right side. Pigmentation varies from olive to black or dark brown with lighter, irregular markings or blotches that often are similar to the color pattern of the ocean floor. In Alaska's Cook Inlet, this coloration can vary greatly from dark to light gray with white "starbursts". This protective coloration makes the fish less conspicuous to predators and prey. The left or blind side

Halibut migrations into shallow water in late spring and summer allow anglers to catch fish on light tackle. This halibut was caught on an eight-ounce jig fished within 100 yards of a western Cook Inlet shoreline.

faces the ocean bottom and usually is white, and on older fish is sometimes covered with barnacles, scars and external parasites.

Here's an interesting question that is always asked at one of my Advanced Alaska Fishing Techniques seminars: "Are the eyes ever found on the white side of the halibut?"

Although rare, anglers occasionally hook into what is called a reversed halibut, a genetic variation where the eyes are found on the left rather than right side of the halibut. Estimates indicate about 1 in 20,000 halibut are reversed.

Here are a few more halibut variations you might see one day:

Ambicoloration describes a condition when the normally white side of the halibut shows pigment or color, either entirely or partially. This is a rarity. In one survey of 3,941 halibut, ambicoloration was found on 18 fish. And even more rare is an entirely white or albino halibut.

Other identification features? The average width of a halibut is about one-third its length, and it is longer overall than most other flatfishes. The mouth is extremely muscular and relatively large, extending to below the lower eye, and nearly symmetrical. Larger fish have sharp teeth lining the perimeter of the lower and upper jaws.

At first touch, the scales on a halibut are difficult to detect. The skin is smooth to the touch. Rub your hand from the tail to the head, and you'll notice tiny scales that are well-buried in the skin. Also note that the lateral line makes a pronounced arch above the pectoral fin.

Taxonomy

The derivation of the name halibut is cause for debate and discussion among lexicographers, outdoor writers and fisheries scientists. The fanciful versions claim the name was derived from the word, "halybutte" in Middle English, meaning the fish to be eaten on Christian holy days, a long-standing tradition that bans the eating of meat on Fridays and Holy Days of Obligation. New Englanders say the name was derived from "Haul-a-boat" which aptly describes the size and power the Atlantic halibut can exhibit once hooked.

The most accepted derivation of the name seems to have originated from the Scandinavians, who named the Atlantic halibut, "halleflundra" meaning "a fish that can be found in deep holes." The scientific name for Pacific halibut is *Hippoglossus stenolepis*, a name derived from the Greek hippos (horse), glossa (tongue), steno (narrow), and lepis (scale).

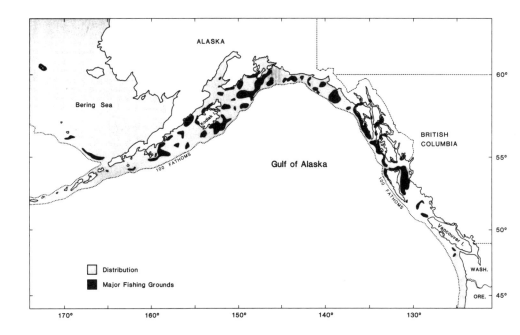

ALASKA

60°

Bering Sea

BRITISH
COLUMBIA

55°

Gulf of Alaska

100 FATHOMS

50°

Vancouver I.

WASH.

Distribution

Major Fishing Grounds

ORE. 45°

170°   160°   150°   140°   130°

According to the International Pacific Halibut Commission, the name was proposed in 1904 by Russian scientist, P. J. Schmidt, whose identifying criteria distinguishes the Pacific halibut from the Atlantic halibut, *Hippoglossus hippoglossus*, by anatomical differences such as the shape of the scales, length of the pectoral fin, and the shape of the body.

North American distribution of Pacific halibut and major sport and commercial fishing grounds. (Map courtesy IPHC).

In 1936, another Russian, M. F. Vernidub, claimed that the differences between the Atlantic and Pacific halibut did not warrant the designation of separate species and suggested the name *Hippoglossus hippoglossus stenolepis* for Pacific halibut. However, North American scientists have detected some serological and other morphological differences between halibut from the Pacific and those from the Atlantic. The name suggested by Schmidt is the one most commonly accepted.

Distribution And Migration

Pacific halibut are found throughout the coastal and deepwater regions of the North Pacific Ocean. They have been recorded along the North American coast from Santa Barbara, California to Nome, Alaska and also occur along the Asiatic Coast from the Gulf of Anadyr to Hokkaido, Japan. Halibut are demersal, meaning they live on or near the bottom, and prefer water temperatures ranging from 35 to 41 degrees Fahrenheit. Although halibut have been taken on commercial

17

fishing gear as deep as 3600 feet, most of the sport-caught fish are caught during the spring, summer and fall when they are at depths from 10 to 500 feet.

Halibut move from deep water along the edge of the Continental Shelf to shallower banks and coastal waters during the summer. Most return to deep water in the winter. This seasonal movement also is associated with winter spawning and summer feeding. Halibut undergo coast-wide migration that may involve distances of hundreds of miles. These movements have been documented by tagging experiments conducted by the International Pacific Halibut Commission (IPHC).

The IPHC has tagged over 350,000 halibut since 1925 and over 35,000 tagged fish have been recovered. A reward is paid for tags that are returned to IPHC. Most of the tagging experiments have been conducted in the summer and most of the recoveries also occur during the summer when fishing is at its peak. Although extensive summer-to-summer movements have been recorded, most of the recoveries take place within 60 miles of the release area. Data from tagging experiments in which halibut were tagged or recovered in the winter are limited, but the results show that summer-winter movements are more extensive than those between summers, and that the predominant direction of movement may differ substantially between the two seasons.

The distance and direction of the migrations also may differ with the size and age of the fish. According to IPHC biologists, emigration has been observed from all regions, but few recoveries of adult halibut released in the Gulf of Alaska have been made in the Bering Sea. An example of the distribution of tag recoveries from a Bering Sea experiment in 1959 is shown on page 19 (chart courtesy IPHC).[1]

Halibut occasionally migrate great distances and several have been recovered over 2,000 miles from their point of release. These fish were tagged in the Bering Sea or near the Aleutian Islands and recovered at points from Cape Flattery, Washington to Cape Mendocino, California. One of the fish was recovered two years after being released; the others were recovered in five or six years. The longest migration was from Atka Island in the Aleutian Islands to Coos Bay, Oregon, a distance of 2,500 miles. Another halibut released southeast of Cape Navarin, Soviet Union, during a joint Soviet-IPHC experiment in 1975. The fish was recovered in 1977 near the Shumagin Islands in Alaska, a distance of 1,000 miles.

Juvenile halibut, those under seven years old, also migrate

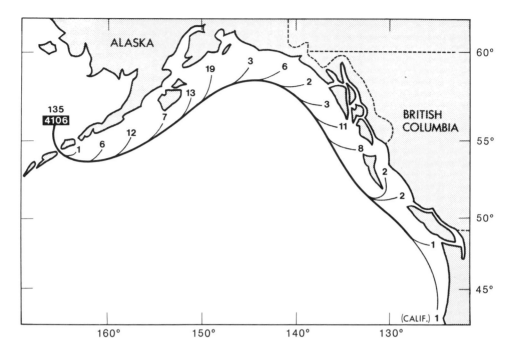

ALASKA

BRITISH
COLUMBIA

60°

55°

50°

45°

135
4106

19   3
13   2
        6
7   3
12   11
6   1
8
2
2
1
(CALIF.) 1

160°   150°   140°   130°

long distances, apparently counterbalancing the northwesterly drift of the eggs and larvae. Larger fish migrate as well, but have a much smaller home range. These juvenile and adult movements result in net migrations of an easterly and southerly direction in the Gulf of Alaska This complex pattern of movements indicates that the halibut stocks are interrelated and that intermingling is extensive. After all is said and done, there is, however, only one known genetic stock of halibut in the North Pacific.

Recoveries of tagged halibut in the Bering Sea. The number of fish tagged is shown in the black box. (Map courtesy IPHC).

Reproduction And Development

Halibut maturity varies with sex, age, and size of the fish. Females grow faster, but are slower to mature than males. Most males are mature by the time they are eight years old, whereas the average age of maturity for females is about 12 years. The oldest recorded female was 42 years old and the oldest male 55 years of age.

From November to March, mature halibut concentrate on spawning grounds along the edge of the continental shelf at depths from 600 to 1,500 feet. Spawning occurs annually. The major spawning sites include Cape St. James, Langara Island (Whaleback), and Frederick Island, Goose Islands, Hecate Strait and Rose Spit off the British Columbia coastline. Off the Alaska coast, sites include Yakutat, Cape Suckling, Yakataga, Portlock

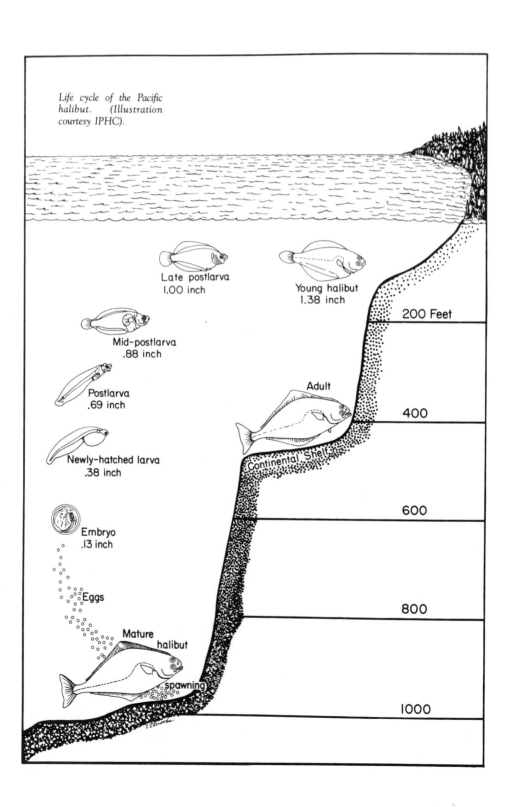

Life cycle of the Pacific halibut. (Illustration courtesy IPHC).

Late postlarva
1.00 inch

Young halibut
1.38 inch

Mid-postlarva
.88 inch

Postlarva
.69 inch

Newly-hatched larva
.38 inch

Embryo
.13 inch

Eggs

Mature
halibut

spawning

Adult

Continental Shelf

200 Feet

400

600

800

1000

Bank, Cape Ommaney, Cape Spencer, Cape St. Elias and Chirikof Island. Spawning concentrations also occur in the Bering Sea. In addition to these major grounds, there is reason to conclude that spawning is widespread and occurs in many areas, although not in as dense concentrations as in the above-mentioned areas.

The number of eggs produced by a female is related to her body size. A 50-pound female will produce about 500,000 eggs, whereas a female over 250 pounds may produce four-million eggs.

The free-floating eggs are about three millimeters in diameter when released and fertilization takes place externally. Developing ova generally are found at depths of 300 to 600 feet, but occur as deep as 1,500 feet. With optimum water temperature, the eggs hatch in 15 days. Newly hatched larvae are heavier than the surface sea water and drift passively in deep ocean currents. As the larvae grow, their specific gravity decreases and they gradually move towards the surface and drift to shallower waters on the Continental Shelf. The life cycle of halibut is depicted on page 20.

Postlarvae may be transported many hundreds of miles by the Alaskan Gyre which flows counterclockwise in the Gulf of Alaska and westward along the Alaska Peninsula and Aleutian Islands. Some of the larvae are carried into the Bering Sea. The velocity of this current may exceed one mile per hour in certain coastal areas, but overall speeds of three to five miles per day are the norm.

Halibut larvae begin life in an upright position with an eye on each side of the head. Nutrition is obtained from a yolk sac, which is absorbed during the early postlarval stage. Then the young fish must begin feeding on small planktonic organisms. When the larvae are an inch long, an extraordinary transformation or metamorphosis occurs: As the fish grows and flattens, the left eye moves over the snout to the right side of the head and pigmentation on the left side fades. When the young fish are about six months old, they have the characteristic adult form and settle to the bottom in shallow, in-shore areas. The survival of young halibut is affected by the environment and the abundance of year classes varies accordingly. Juveniles from one to three years old generally remain in relatively shallow inshore waters and usually are not caught by the commercial setline fishery. With increasing age, many juveniles move to deeper waters and migrate in an easterly and southerly direction, reciprocal to the passive movement

*Growth and early develop-
ment of halibut. (Photo
courtesy IPHC).*

NEWLY-HATCHED LARVA (Stage 1)

Showing prominent yolk sac.

Approximately 9 mm in length.

POSTLARVA (Stage 3)

Yolk sac has been absorbed.

Approximately 16 mm in length.

POSTLARVA (Stage 7)

Approximately 21 mm in length.

POSTLARVA (Stage 9)

Showing the beginning of eye migration.

Approximately 25 mm in length.

YOUNG HALIBUT

Adapted to bottom life.

How to Catch
Trophy Halibut

Approximately 35 mm in length.

of eggs and larvae. Juveniles tagged in the Bering Sea and the western Gulf of Alaska have migrated as far south as British Columbia, Washington and Oregon, suggesting they may have been spawned in this general area. During the migratory phase, many of the young halibut are taken on a limited nature by sport anglers and as an incidental catch in trawls that are used to catch other species of groundfish.

Food And Feeding

Halibut are strong swimmers and carnivorous feeders, eating almost any animal they can catch. Larval halibut feed on plankton. Halibut one to three years old are usually less than 12 inches in length and feed on small crustaceans and fish. As halibut increase in size, fish become a more important part of the diet. The species of fish frequently observed in stomachs of large halibut include cod, sablefish, pollock, rockfish, sculpins, turbot, and other flatfish. Halibut often leave the bottom to feed on pelagic fish such as sandlance, salmon and herring. As a result, many anglers catch fish at mid-depth at slack tide. Being white on the blind or bottom side is a color adaptation that allows halibut to blend in with the sky and to escape detection from bottom-feeding predators, killer whales and sharks, and to a lesser extent, sea lions.

Halibut also favor octopus, crabs and clams, as well as an occasional smaller halibut, although stomach analyses indicate that cannibalism is uncommon. While crabs with a carapace width of seven inches have been found in the stomachs of halibut, biologists indicate that halibut do not appear to be a *primary* predator of crab. Many sport anglers who fish the shallower, in-shore waters may from time to time differ with this assessment. I have observed—along with many halibut skippers out of Homer and Deep Creek—the sight of fresh-caught halibut regurgitating handfuls of crab. These fish were caught from the shallower depths where crab are plentiful. In these areas, a crab bait or jig works well, and is discussed in the section on leadhead jigs. For more details on stomach analyses and what halibut eat, turn to Chapter 9.

Age And Growth

Halibut are the largest of all flatfish and are among the larger species of fish in the sea. Halibut from the Atlantic and the Pacific can reach lengths of over nine feet and have been reported to weigh 700 pounds. These weights, however, have not been thoroughly documented. An eight-foot-long, 33-year-

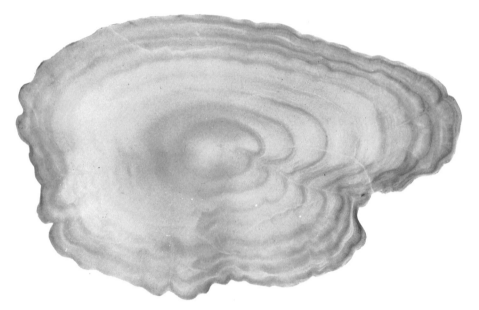

Otolith from a halibut in its ninth year. Photographed on a dark background, the wide, white bands are the opaque summer zones; the dark bands are the translucent winter zones. (Photo courtesy IPHC)

old Pacific halibut female that weighed 375 pounds with its head and viscera removed, or 500 pounds live weight, has been documented by biologists. This fish was caught in the Bering Sea in 1974 by the commercial fishing vessel THOR. Two other specimens weighing 500 pounds have been authenticated, one from Petersburg, Alaska and the other from Sakhalin Island, near Japan.

Anglers catch 300-pound halibut each year; rod and reel-caught halibut over 400 pounds are rare in the annual sport harvest.

Sport anglers often think the commercial fishing boats catch all the big halibut, because they fish deeper, more remote waters. Consider the facts: The North American catch of Pacific halibut, caught mostly by longline gear, consists of individuals chiefly from 10 to 200 pounds. The average size in the commercial catch is between 30 and 40 pounds. Therefore, anglers, be proud of any halibut you catch over 40 pounds; ecstatic over 80-pound-plus fish; and euphoric over a 200-pound behemoth.

Here's another tidbit regarding size: Few males reach 80 pounds and nearly all halibut over 100 pounds are females. IPHC studies have shown that female halibut grow faster and live longer than males and that both males and females are growing slower now than they did a few years ago. For example, in the 1970—1980 period, 10-year-old male and female halibut in the Gulf of Alaska were on the average 38 and 46 inches long and weighed 20 and 37 pounds, respectively. In the 1920s and again in the early 1990s, the same fish would have averaged 29 and 32 inches long and weighed eight and ten pounds, respectively. The fluctuation in the growth rate since the 1920s

How to Catch
Trophy Halibut

is assumed to be the result of changes in general circulation of the North Pacific, population density and/or other environmental conditions. Halibut growth has important biological and management implications because stock biomass and fecundity are related to the growth rate.

A recent report by the IPHC reveals that the average age of Pacific halibut stocks is either relatively stable or slightly decreasing. Recent catch statistics show that halibut from nine to fourteen years old comprised 67 percent of the total commercial harvest. The percentage of fish under nine years old in the commercial catch increased in 1995, possibly indicating a strong year class entering the fishery. This is good news for sport anglers, because older fish mean larger fish. On the reverse side, an abundance of older fish means failed age classes of fish.

There are safeguards in place to help prevent overharvest. IPHC biologists sample the commercial catch and obtain age and length information from about 40,000 halibut each year. This information is used to assess the condition of the resource. For example, the number of fish at each age in the catch indicates the relative strength of individual year classes. Over a succession of years, individual year classes can be traced throughout their life and the rate at which their numbers decrease is an indication of their mortality rate. The increase in length with successive age provides a measure of the growth rate of the fish. Strength of year classes, mortality rates, and growth are essential items of information for determining stock condition and implementing any conservation measures. According to the International Pacific Halibut Commission, the number of halibut in Alaska's offshore waters have increased dramatically since 1980, but have since begun to taper off after reaching record abundance in 1987. Stocks currently show a decline, which is expected to continue in upcoming years. Biologists say this is normal, considering the cyclic nature of halibut and increased fishing pressure via commercial and sport fishing the last decade.

Halibut are in good health, and sport anglers have never had it better throughout the Pacific Northwest. Improved technology in tackle and equipment components, more charter services and information allow anglers to pursue these fish from a foundation of knowledge rather than luck. This book is about providing you with that knowledge. But before we tell you how to catch them, turn to Chapter 2 for an overview of several unforgettable moments in halibut fishing.

If you don't have a scale, or intend to release fish, you can accurately estimate the weight of a halibut with a tape measure. Measure the distance from nose to tail, and refer to the accompanying length-weight chart on the opposite page. (Chart courtesy IPHC).

Weighing Halibut With A Tape Measure

Most anglers have read or heard about formulas—some of them quite complex—for determining a fish's weight by making certain measurements and calculations. Luckily for halibut anglers, there's an easy way to estimate the weight of a catch by taking a single measurement of the fish's overall length.

The International Pacific Halibut Commission has weighed and measured more halibut over the years than most of us will ever see, and they compiled that length-to-weight information into a simple conversion chart. Any fish, of course, may weigh more or less than the "average" for its length, and those differences seem to become more acute with larger fish, but this length/weight table is a whole lot better than nothing when it comes to establishing the weight of a barn door when there isn't a scale to be found within 20 miles! (See chart on opposite page).

You can determine the age of your halibut by cutting out the otolith, a calcareous or stone-like growth in each internal ear that serves as a hydrostatic or balancing organ. As the fish grows, these otoliths also grow and the size of halibut can be estimated from the otolith's length or weight. Each year, alternating opaque (summer) and translucent (winter) rings are deposited on the otolith. The annual growth rings are called annuli and are counted (much like rings on a tree) to determine the age of the fish. The oldest age recorded for a halibut is 42 years for females and 55 years for males. Most halibut in the North American commercial setline catch are eight to 15 years old.

How to Catch
Trophy Halibut

Pacific Halibut
Length—Weight Relationship

Length (Inches)	Weight (Pounds)	Length (Inches)	Weight (Pounds)
21	3.6	61	114.8
22	4.2	62	121.1
23	4.9	63	127.5
24	5.6	64	134.2
25	6.4	65	141.1
26	7.2	66	148.2
27	8.2	67	155.6
28	9.2	68	163.3
29	10.3	69	171.2
30	11.5	70	179.4
31	12.8	71	187.8
32	14.2	72	196.5
33	15.7	73	205.5
34	17.3	74	214.8
35	19.0	75	224.3
36	20.8	76	234.1
37	22.7	77	244.3
38	24.8	78	254.7
39	27.0	79	265.4
40	29.3	80	276.5
41	31.7	81	287.8
42	34.3	82	299.5
43	37.0	83	311.5
44	39.9	84	323.8
45	42.9	85	336.5
46	46.0	86	349.5
47	49.3	87	362.8
48	52.8	88	376.5
49	56.5	89	390.6
50	60.3	90	404.9
51	64.3	91	419.7
52	68.5	92	434.8
53	72.8	93	450.3
54	77.4	94	466.2
55	82.1	95	482.5
56	87.1	96	499.1
57	92.2	97	516.2
58	97.5	98	533.6
59	103.1	99	551.5
60	108.9	100	569.7

Data in this chart provided by the International Pacific Halibut Commission.

[1]Illustrations in this chapter courtesy IPHC. 1987. The Pacific Halibut: Biology, Fishery and Management. International Pacific Halibut Commission Technical Report Number 22.

CHAPTER 2

Halibut Lore And Battles

Throughout the history of the Pacific Northwest, halibut and other marine animals were an integral part of the folklore of coastal Indian tribes and were commemorated in totem pole carvings or painted on the fronts of community houses. The following excerpt is from *Tsimshian Mythology* by F. Boas, Bureau of American Ethnology, Annual Report, 1909-1910, U. S. Government Printing Office.

"On the following day three of their young people went out in a canoe across the inlet; and when they reached the foot of a steep cliff, behold! A large halibut came up, opened its mouth, and swallowed the canoe with the three persons—two princesses and one prince. The people on the other side saw it. Therefore two of their brave men went to kill the monster who had devoured their prince and their princesses. They crossed the inlet in their canoe, having their large knives tied to the right wrist. As soon as they reached the foot of the steep rock, a halibut came up, opened its mouth, and swallowed the canoe with the two brave men; but as soon as the halibut had swallowed them, they cut it inside with their knives. They cut up its intestines until it died. Then the supernatural halibut felt the pains in its stomach, jumped out of the water, and struck the water with its tail. It swam around the inlet, and finally ran ashore and died there. Then those who had remained alive went down to the beach, and saw that the great supernatural halibut was dead. They cut it open, and saw the two canoes and five persons. Then they sang their mourning song.

"Halibut was an important part of the diet of several Pacific Northwest tribes. Natives caught halibut with hook and line from large canoes, paddling as far as 20 miles from shore. The technique of these fishermen was well developed and very efficient. They caught

Subduing a trophy halibut at boatside can be an exciting, fun-filled moment, yet wrought with danger. Several shots from a .410 may be required to subdue a large fish. Wildly flopping fish can throw gaff hooks and harpoon heads. Enjoy the thrill of it all, but remember safety first.

halibut with hooks made of branches of red or yellow cedar, attached to fishing lines of braided cedar bark up to 360 feet long. Devilfish (octopus) was used as bait.''

Legend and myth aside, there is a moral to the story: All sportsmen should be aware of the dangers in handling a large halibut in a small boat. Halibut are powerful and have been known to smash objects with their tails. The following tragic story is from the *Alaska Empire*, Juneau, Alaska in August, 1973:

Fisherman Killed By Halibut

A man killed by halibut!

Alaska State Troopers investigated one of the most unusual deaths to occur in Alaska this year.

The body of Joseph T. Cash, 67, of Petersburg was found lashed to the winch of his troller after a 150-pound halibut had apparently broken his leg and severed an artery when he hoisted the fish aboard his boat while fishing alone in the vicinity of Eagle Point on Kupreanof Island.

Cash's customary way of landing a large halibut was to gaff the fish with a shark hook attached to a ten-foot length of half inch thick rope.

From evidence gathered at the scene, Cash hauled it aboard (and) it apparently flopped and in so doing crippled the elderly man.

When falling to the deck, Cash cracked three ribs on his left side. Based on information obtained from friends, Cash had a horror of being injured or killed and being washed overboard to become 'crab bait'. Consequently, he crawled to the winch and tied himself to it.

After his death the partially sunk trolling boat washed ashore and was found by men from another fishing boat. Crewmen of the boat found the old fisherman as indomitable in death as he was in life. His head and chest were still above water with the gaffed halibut at his feet.

Old Man And The Sea, Northern Style

Gordon Newhouse of Edmonds, Washington, was 82 years old and fishing the cold waters off Petersburg, Alaska, for the 40th consecutive year when he went one-on-one with one of the largest Pacific halibut ever to qualify for inclusion on the International Game Fish Association's line-class record list.

Newhouse was fishing with Petersburg resident Ed Hagerman in September of 1986 when the pair decided to visit a favorite halibut spot in Thomas Bay, which enters Frederick Sound several miles north of Petersburg. Hagerman had just released a small fish when something inhaled Newhouse's herring bait and moved off for parts unknown. After a couple of long runs the barn door settled to the bottom and stayed there, and it took the veteran angler an hour and 15 minutes to move it, then another 30 minutes to coax it to the side of the boat.

After breaking the sturdy handle of a gaff, the pair used a shark hook with a rope attached to gain some control over the monster, but it was still far from being subdued. That's when Hagerman's son, who had been fishing in a nearby boat, motored over and helped the two anglers drag their prize into the boat. (Authors' note: Whether boating the fish was a good idea is open to argument, but they got away with it).

Back at the docks in Petersburg, Newhouse's monster halibut measured six feet, 10 inches from nose to tail and weighed in at a whopping 344 pounds. A few months later it was certified by the IGFA as the men's 50-pound-line-class world's record.

The All-Night Fight

The angler's name was Ken, but his last name and home town have been lost in the re-telling of his story. And it's too bad that happened, because his tale is more than a memorable one. It's an epic story of man versus halibut, of a legendary battle which probably should never have taken place but which could have gone either way.

We heard the story from Curtis Currie, the guide with whom Ken was fishing that unforgettable night in July of 1991, and Duff McDowell, a second fishing guide who was running another boat when the halibut hit but joined Currie and his client to lend a hand.

Ken and his guide were trolling for chinook salmon in Campania Sound, at the south end of British Columbia's Douglas Channel, when a good fish popped the line off the downrigger. The time was about 7:30 p.m., and Ken's tackle consisted of a single-action Daiwa 275 reel, 11-foot fiberglass rod and 20-pound monofilament line. By 8 o'clock, both angler and guide agreed that the fish at the business end of that line wasn't a salmon!

The limber mooching rod and light line were no match for the huge fish, and by the last light of dusk no one on board the little 17-foot boat had gotten a look at it. By that time, though, there was little doubt that Ken's opponent was a big halibut.

Ken applied as much pressure as his light tackle would allow, and several times during the night he brought the fish up to where the bead chain connecting line to leader was in sight. One of those times the giant fish came up to within a foot or two of the surface, and in a flashlight's beam it looked nearly as large as the boat. Stacy Beard, a third guide who joined the others during the course of the battle in the hope that his experience landing big halibut might be helpful, got a good look at the monster and estimated that it was over 400 pounds, perhaps as big as 500.

Just as the fish was nearly brought to within harpoon range on several occasions, so did it almost earn its freedom a number of times during the night. At one point the angler told the guides that he was nearly out of line, and when they trained the flashlight's beam on the reel there were only three or four wraps of monofilament remaining on the spool.

Although he steadfastly refused to let anyone else play his fish or even touch the rod, Ken grew more and more weary with each passing hour. Sometime between 1 and 2 a.m., he actually fell asleep and let the rod slip from his hands. Miraculously, it dropped about a foot, hit the gunwale railing and bounced right back into his hands! He snapped back to attention and continued the fight.

The line became caught and could easily have snapped on at least two occasions during the night, once when it wrapped around a stern cleat and once with it wedged behind a button snap. Through all that, however, the line held the huge fish.

About 4 a.m. the sky started turning pink over the hills to the east, and those on board the little boat thought that at last they would have a chance to bring the big halibut within striking range. Then, with the halibut about 40 yards straight down, the line suddenly parted, and the battle between two worthy adversaries ended as quickly as it had begun. Other boats carrying eager and well-rested anglers were heading toward them in the dim light as Ken fell onto a seat and reeled the limp monofilament onto the reel. A new day of fishing was about to begin, but there was little chance it could match the drama of the night that had just ended.

Halibut One-Pound Shy Of Record

John Lucking, owner and operator of the M/V Suzanne Marie in Unalaska, couldn't have asked for a better way to end the 1995 sport fishing season. Ken Stuckey, first assistant engineer aboard the Sea-Land Anchorage, caught a 439-pound halibut on September 15, Lucking's last scheduled charter of the year. According to the Alaska Department of Fish and Game,

Stuckey's fish is the largest halibut weighed on an official scale in 1995. The all-time state record is 440 pounds, set in 1978. Stuckey's fish toppled the local record of Unalaska's Mike Golat, who caught a 395-pound halibut three months earlier.

At first, Stuckey thought he had hooked the bottom or snagged some discarded commercial fishing gear. A major tug-of-war battle ensued for the first half-hour, straining the 130-pound line.

As soon as Stuckey eased the fish to within inches of the surface, Lucking harpooned the fish in the gills, which caused the halibut to thrash wildly at boatside. Soon, gaffs were buried into the head and shoulder, and six men heaved the gargantuan flatfish over the side and into the boat.

Unalaska: Where World-Record Halibut Are Abundant

What do you do when you've hooked a world-record halibut from your 18-foot skiff and forgot your harpoon? Do what Mike Golat of Unalaska did, bring along an engineer!

What started off as a slow night of fishing turned into the longest night of the year.

Fishing just off Hog Island in Unalaska Bay, Mike Golat hooked into something big. Really big.

"My first thought was that I caught a sea monster," Golat said. "The problem of getting the fish into the boat became apparent when I brought it to the surface. It was well over 350 pounds, and we concluded a gaff into the head would only incite the beast."

Golat, an Environmental Compliance Coordinator for the City of Unalaska, and Tom Regan of Washington-based Regan Engineering, failed to lasso the barn-door sized bottomfish. This is where Regan's engineering background paid off. Obviously, a beast this size required special handling to avoid grievous bodily harm.

According to Golat, "Regan did a quick calculation of the tensile strength of the line and the weight of the fish, and concluded the line would hold, if we were careful. After much pondering, we decided to tow it to the nearest beach."

The two men towed the fish a half mile to Devil Fish Point, weaving in and out of kelp beds and rocks, until they found a landing point. Once on the beach, they used the nearest rock to pummel the massive brute so it could be loaded into the boat, weighed and photographed. The fish weighed 395 pounds and is the current IGFA, all-tackle, world-record halibut.

A week earlier, Golat took another consultant fishing in Unalga Pass. Bill Steigers, an air quality consultant from Denver, hooked and fought with four enormous but unseen halibut, resulting in two broken hooks, two broken 110-pound-test lines, and one very sore mainlander.

Golat said he only recently started fishing in the Unalaska/Dutch Harbor area. His prior halibut experience came fishing in Homer where he caught a 123-pounder. "I thought that one was great!" he said.

Mike Golat, left, caught this 395-pound halibut with the help of Tom Regan, right. The pair was fishing out of Dutch Harbor in late June.

3,000 Pounds Of Halibut!

It was truly the quiet before the storm.

The day, June 14, 1994, started out like many others along the Alaska coastline, with anglers in search of trophy fish.

Bob Candopoulos and Stephen Babinec of Saltwater Safari Company in Seward have spent years pioneering the Seward halibut fishery. They know it's all part of the job to find fish, and on some days it happens faster than others. By mid morning, Candopoulos had only a few runt-sized halibut to show for the effort of 14 anglers.

The outlook was gloomy.

The guests—all members of the wedding party of Eric and Carrie Laudon—were ready for a workout. The boat was also ready, equipped with top-of-the-line tackle and equipment. The seas were relatively calm. Weather good. And the area...well, Bob and Steve had been spreading the word that Seward is the place to consider if you want to catch trophy halibut. Now the responsibility was on their shoulders to either put up or shut up.

As he piloted the M/V Legend along the outer edge of Montague Island, Bob scanned the sonar unit's screen. What he saw numbed him with excitement: A school of baitfish near adjacent holding structure. He ordered his clients to "drop 'em down."

How to Catch
Trophy Halibut

The rest is history.

Captain Bob's 12 fishing clients (two others became seasick and did not fish) eventually hooked and landed over 3,000 pounds of halibut that included five fish weighing 265, 257, 246, 250 and 215 pounds, and seven weighing 183, 179, 174, 156, 146, 107, and 100. Several "small" fish from 60 to 90 pounds rounded out the catch. Using a 410 shotgun, Bob went through a box of 25 shells to dispatch the larger fish. A few of the larger flatties required two or more shots to "coax" them into submission before the crew grunted and heaved them onboard.

The clients were mostly newcomers to halibut fishing, with several having caught only panfish in their lifetimes. Bob's crew—Mike Moriarty, Carson Stevens and Jeff Barney—compensated for their guests' inexperience. They anticipated problems and kept the big fish, often several on at once, separated from the other lines in the water. Fish were gaffed, shot and hoisted on board in assembly-line fashion.

The surroundings weren't too shabby either. Scenic Montague Island borders the deep waters of the Gulf of Alaska. Salmon follow the current lines into nearby bays and shallow-water flats surrounding the island; ideal ambush spots favored by big halibut. The peak of the pink migration was taking place, and the halibut and huge ling cod caught that day were stuffed with the four to six-pound salmon.

The only problem came when Captain Bob saw that the amount of fish being hauled onboard exceeded his 2,000-pound fish hold. Undeterred, he stacked fish around the boat so he could get it on step to make the trip back to Seward.

As he entered the Seward Harbor, Captain Bob couldn't resist making a few "braggadocio" tours around the harbor, to show off the catch, before calling it a day.

Was this a fluke, a once-in-a-lifetime catch? Several weeks later, the M/V Legend and M/V Legacy brought in sport-caught halibut loads of 2,200 and 2,400 pounds. While catches like this don't happen every trip, the success rate caused lots of heads to turn and recognize this sleeping giant of a halibut fishery.

In the past, Seward may have sparked memories of the "folly" of its namesake, but anglers now realize there is nothing frivolous about Seward's position as one of the state's top halibut fishing ports.

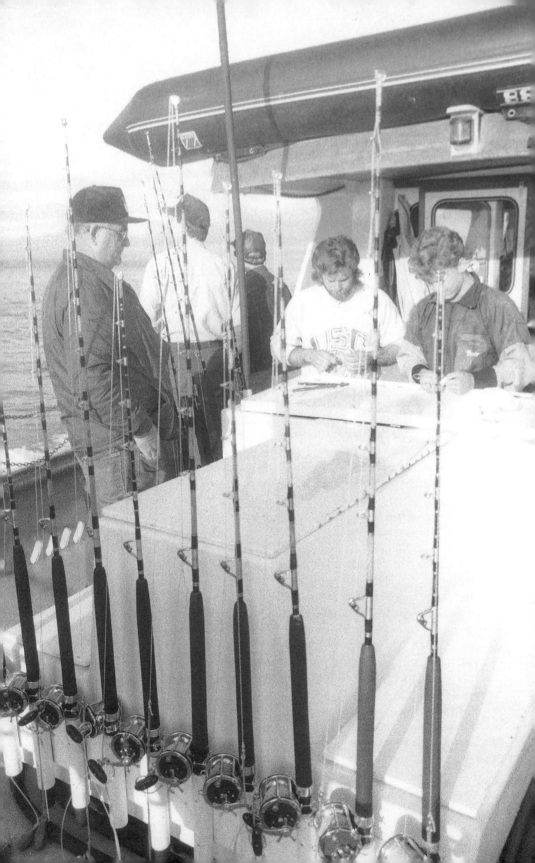

CHAPTER 3

Rods, Reels And Line

As recently as a decade ago, most people who fished for Pacific halibut did so with large, cumbersome reels, heavy-action rods with roller-tips and thick-diameter braided Dacron or high-test monofilament line. In certain situations, such tackle may still be the best way to go, but more and more anglers these days realize they have plenty of options on the halibut grounds, including the option of fishing very light tackle under certain conditions. If you're in the market for a halibut outfit, you have plenty of good choices.

Rods And Reels

Some anglers feel that, because of the Pacific halibut's potentially monstrous size, big, high-capacity reels and heavy-duty rods are prerequisites for successful halibut fishing. There's some validity to that philosophy if you specifically target big fish in areas where big fish are likely to be found. If your dream is to catch a 200-pounder and you don't want to bother with anything smaller, using heavy tackle might increase your chances of landing that fish of a lifetime if and when it comes along.

The reality of halibut fishing, however, is that most productive halibut-fishing spots have hundreds of smaller fish for every 200-pounder available, and unless you use extremely big baits or lures to discourage the smaller ones, you have to "mess" with some of them whether you want to or not. Wrestling with a few small halibut on heavy tackle wears you out almost as much as wrestling with one big flatfish, because the tackle itself takes strength, coordination and practice to use effectively. Large saltwater reels and husky, roller-tip rods

Heavy combinations such as these 6/0 Penn reels, stout boat rods and 80-pound braided Dacron line have their place in halibut fishing, especially if you fish deep water and must use large sinkers and heavy jigs to reach bottom. Such is the case around the entrance to Alaska's Cook Inlet, where you might find yourself fishing in 300 feet of water in a heavy tidal flow. These rods, reels and rigs are used there, by charter anglers out of Homer.

weigh several pounds, and just holding such a combo all day can take its toll on you.

And, all one has to do is skim through the listings of men's and women's line-class world records in the IGFA record book to realize that it's very possible to whip big halibut on incredibly light rods, reels and lines.

Before anyone jumps to the conclusion that we're bad-mouthing heavy tackle for halibut, we're not. In fact, fishing deep water, strong current, or a combination of the two may require the use of such gear to fish effectively. If you're trying to fish a spot that's 300 feet deep and the tidal flow is 10 knots, you may have to use 32 to 48 ounces of sinker or lure to reach bottom, and we recommend you don't even attempt it with your favorite steelhead rod and reel! Even if the halibut you're catching at those depths are small, you need heavy tackle to reach them.

Luckily, though, there are many productive halibut spots from Kodiak, Alaska, to Newport, Oregon, that are much shallower than 300 feet. Many, in fact, are less than half that depth, and if you know where and when to look you may find halibut in 20 or 30 feet of water. In those shallow-water situations, much lighter rods and reels will usually do the job just fine, allow you to have more fun with the fish you hook, and probably be a whole lot easier on your hands, wrists, elbows, shoulders and back.

The term "light," however, shouldn't be misinterpreted to mean "flimsy," "worn-out" or, especially, "mismatched." Any halibut, hooked at any depth, can be a tough customer, and the salty environment in which it's found can be very tough on cheap, poorly built rods and reels. Just as importantly, if the line, the action of the rod and the reel's drag system aren't a good match, light-tackle fishing for any species can be a nightmare.

Co-author Chris Batin and I have hooked and landed Pacific halibut in shallow water (depths of 60 feet or less) on spinning outfits that most anglers would likely associate with panfish or trout rather than with halibut fishing. Would you believe six-foot, medium-action rods, six- and eight-pound monofilament?

That tackle was used in areas where there seemed to be many small halibut—five to 15-pounds—and few, if any, large ones. Using 25-pound-test monofilament shock leaders so that there was little chance of "chew-offs," the light outfits handled those mini-hallies just fine and provided great sport.

The problem, though, was getting solid hook-sets so that the fish stayed attached all the way to the top. The mouth of a 10-pound halibut is almost as tough and hard to penetrate with a hook point as the mouth of a 150-pounder, and it's not easy to do with light, stretchy monofilament and a wispy little rod that was built for pan-size fish. Even using needle-sharp barbs and imparting a hookset with all the force the light line would allow, we were lucky to bring one hooked fish in three all the way to the surface.

Most of our ultralight halibut fishing experiences have been with artificials, either leadheads or metal jigs, and it's safe to suggest that a higher percentage would have stayed hooked had we been fishing with bait and therefore letting them take it longer before setting the hook. Of course, using bait and hooking halibut deeper can present other problems, especially when you're hooking and releasing a lot of small fish.

You will lose some halibut if you fish light or ultralight tackle for them, either because of break-offs or failure to get a solid hook-set. You'll increase your odds of success, however, if you match rod, reel and line. Use a light line with too stiff a rod and you'll be breaking off almost every fish you hook, and you'll have a similar problem if you spool 200 yards of light monofilament on a reel whose drag isn't smooth enough for the job. If the rod and the reel fail to absorb some of the shock of a lunging halibut, the line takes all the abuse, so you'd might as well fish light line with your bare hands as fish it with a rod and reel combo that's too heavy for the job.

Light-tackle halibut fishing, of course, isn't for everyone, but if you pursue such freshwater fishing activities as flippin' for largemouth bass, trolling for walleyes, or if you like to pull plugs or back-bounce bait for river chinook salmon, there's a pretty good chance you have at least one rod-and-reel combination that's adequate for shallow to mid-range halibut fishing. Keep in mind that we're not talking about an outfit that will allow you to crank 250-pounders from 350 feet of water with any kind of consistency, and realistically, how often do you expect to find yourself in that situation?

The rod for this moderate-range halibut fishing can be as short as seven feet and as long as eight, maybe 8½ feet. If you plan to fish artificials more than bait, you'll want a fairly stiff action, at least medium-heavy and probably heavy or even extra-heavy action—something that will lift and drop a four to 16-ounce jig in water as deep as 150 to 200 feet. Using a soft-action rod for this kind of fishing is counterproductive

Serious halibut anglers know the strategic advantages of using the right reel for the size of halibut they are pursuing. The lightweight, two-speed Shimano with a lever drag can handle a variety of rigs and fish. A standard Penn with an oversized speed handle or T-bar is ideal for fast cranking a heavy rig from extreme depths. The bar also helps to eliminate cramped hands and forearms during prolonged fights.

because you'll wear out your arm without moving the jig up and down, and if the jig isn't moving it isn't going to attract as many halibut.

While the jigging rod's action should be heavy, its weight should be light. Added rod weight means added strain on the arms, shoulders and back during a day-long jigging stint, and a few ounces can make a lot of difference. Graphite offers greater strength at lighter weight, so it's a good choice for the jigger in that regard.

If you do more bait fishing than jigging with artificials, you can get by with a softer-action rod, but remember that you need enough backbone to set the hook, so leave the noodle rod at home, even if you fish nothing but bait! Both the bait and lure fisherman will benefit from using a rod with a fairly long butt, which allows you to fish more comfortably and provides more leverage for hook-setting and pumping table-top halibut from the depths.

Finding a revolving-spool reel that matches well with your medium-range halibut rod shouldn't be much of a problem. With at least a half-dozen reel manufacturers building a wide range of sizes with a wide range of options, you can find at least one (and probably several) that have what you want. While we should point out that a few halibut anglers actually prefer spinning reels, most West Coast saltwater anglers like revolving-spool reels, and they certainly provide better line control and less line-twist in most situations.

How to Catch
Trophy Halibut

Since boat fishing for halibut tends to require little or no casting, the main qualities you want to think about in a reel are spool capacity, gear ratio, drag system, weight, whether or not it has a level-wind, left-hand or right-hand retrieve, resistance to the harmful effects of saltwater and, of course, those sometimes hard-to-define qualities of "toughness" and dependability. If you're like almost everyone else, price may also be an important factor in your final decision.

The level-wind reel you use to throw plastic worms for bass might do the job, or maybe you're better off using the same reel you're already using for saltwater salmon fishing. Then again, the best reel for you and your medium-range halibut fishing might be something in-between those two extremes, so this could be a great excuse for buying a new reel!

Some situations simply call for heavy tackle, especially those instances when you're gunning for big fish in deep water, so it's a good idea to equip yourself with at least one stout, "traditional" halibut outfit.

So-called "meat rods" for heavy-duty halibut fishing range in length from five feet to as long as eight feet or more, but in recent years an ever-growing number of anglers are turning to the shorter "stand-up" type rods so popular with big-game anglers in warmer parts of the world. These powerful sticks range from five to six feet long and are equipped with long butt and fore grips for added leverage. Used with a fighting belt and kidney harness, they help provide an angler with enough lifting power to move a small house, which, of course, makes them a logical weapon for barn-door halibut.

The action of a deep-water/big fish halibut rod may range from heavy to pool-cue, which makes sense when you consider the fact that it may be called upon to work three or four-pound sinkers along the bottom all day. The rod may not even bend noticeably most of the time it's in use, until it's needed to coax a 200-plus-pounder up from the depths.

When you're out shopping for a heavy-duty halibut rod, consider these features:

Weight—Similar rods can vary by several ounces, and that can make a big difference in fatigue factor where the angler is concerned.

Composition—Some heavy-action rods are still made of thick-walled fiberglass, others of thinner, lighter glass, still others of graphite or graphite composite. The glass rods may be more durable, but graphite will be lighter.

41

Guides—They may be aluminum oxide, they may be ceramic, maybe stainless steel, but if they appear cheap and spindly, they probably are! Check for quality wrapping as well as stout guides. If you're going to use braided Dacron or any of the new-technology lines (NTLs)—inclusive of braided gel-spun polyethylene or Kevlar lines—you might consider a roller tip to help ensure against the line cutting grooves in it.

Deep-water halibut anglers often use reels as large as 6/0, which will hold enough large-diameter line for virtually any halibut-fishing situation you're likely to encounter, even at depths as great as 600 to 700 feet. Such reels might be considered overkill by many anglers, since fishing at those extreme depths isn't all that common and a reel that large is certainly cumbersome and unwieldy.

A smaller, 4/0 reel has enough line capacity and muscle for the vast majority of the deep-water situations you're likely to encounter in halibut country. Even if you hedge your bets by using something like 80-pound Dacron line, the 4/0 will hold enough of it to allow fishing in several hundred feet of water. This smaller, lighter reel is also more manageable.

Some of today's bigger reels are equipped with a level-wind arm, but most don't have that accessory, and all but the most inexperienced angler is better off without it for deep-water halibut fishing. It's often the first thing to malfunction on a big-game reel, and it usually gives up the ghost at the worst possible time. Braided line is especially hard on a level-wind reel, actually sawing right into it as the bar spreads line back and forth across the reel spool. That's exactly why most anglers are blessed with more than enough fingers to hold the foregrip of a fishing rod; we can use the "extras" to guide line evenly onto a reel.

What about gear ratio? It's a subject that many anglers don't fully understand, but it's important to the person trying to catch big halibut in deep water. A higher ratio will put line back on the reel more quickly as you reel, which can be important if you crank your bait or lure up and down through the water column dozens of times a day, which is common in halibut fishing. When you hook a big halibut, however, a lower gear ratio works to your advantage, putting line back on the reel with less effort on your part

Fortunately, some of today's newer breed of reels offer both high-gear ratios for faster light-load retrieves and lower gears for power-cranking big fish. These two-speed reels cost more than comparable reels without the feature, and they're also

heavier, but they offer a real advantage to halibut anglers who spend a lot of time plying deep waters for husky barn doors. If price is no object, perhaps the best reel on the market for barn-doors is the Shimano Tiagra, with its two-speed function and pre-lubricated graphite drag washer.

A quality drag system is also a must for heavy-duty halibut fishing. Some reels, quite frankly, aren't up to the task, so do some comparing before you make your choice. While the more conventional star-drag style is still popular, the newer lever-drag systems allow for easier adjustment in mid-battle. By the same token, it's easier to tighten or loosen the lever-drag by accident as well as by design, which can lead to lost fish before you know what happened.

We've used everything from Ambassadeur 5001 reels with 14-pound mono to the impressive Triton two-lever drag series reels. The Triton features a high-speed 4:1 gear ratio which is a must-have for deepwater fishing, and crunches down to 1.7:1 for that barn door that refuses to budge.

Line

Take a close look at the reels of anglers on the halibut grounds these days and you might see as many as four distinctly different kinds of line on those reels: monofilament, braided Dacron, single-strand wire and any of the new "super braid" or "new technology" lines of braided Spectra or Kevlar. Wire line has

A fighting harness or gimbal belt is a must-have item for battling large fish. A model that includes a back support and harness that connects to your reel will greatly reduce muscle fatigue and stress.

very few advocates these days and offers even fewer advantages, but the other three have their places in the halibut angler's arsenal.

Monofilament, of course, is what many anglers consider "standard" for every kind of fishing. You can buy it almost anywhere, it's available in a wide range of strengths, it's easy to work with, it holds a knot well and it's relatively inexpensive. It comes as no surprise, then, that thousands of halibut have been caught on mono over the years, and for shallow to medium-depth halibut fishing it's pretty good stuff. If you do most of your halibut fishing in 75 to 150 feet of water, you can probably use mono and fish happily ever after.

Anglers fishing with monofilament, though, start to have problems at depths of more than about 150 feet. The line's stretch—which in shallow water provides a shock absorber against the hard charges of powerful fish—makes it hard to feel bottom at great depths, hard to detect a strike and hard to get a solid hook-set into a hard-mouthed denizen of the deep.

Monofilament will stretch up to one-third its length or more, and it's easy to understand the problem when you think about fishing in 240 feet of water with an extra 80 feet of stretch in your line. Working a 16-ounce jig along the bottom can be an exercise in futility, and we mean "exercise," since you'll get plenty of it while trying in vain to lift the jig far enough off the bottom to attract any attention from nearby fish. If one does take your offering and you happen to notice in time, you had better plan on cranking down as fast as you can, setting the hook with a long sweep of the rod, cranking down again, setting again, cranking down a third time, setting again, and maybe you'll get the hooks in deep enough to do the job.

Braided Dacron, on the other hand, has substantially less stretch, so its popularity among deep-water halibut anglers is understandable. Using Dacron, you can set the hook into a big barn door at 350 feet and feel reasonably certain that you did, in fact, really set the hook. Braided Dacron also is a little smaller in diameter than many monofilaments of the same test, which would mean less line drag in the water, except that the braid's rougher exterior provides more surface, catches more water and therefore negates much of the advantage of its smaller diameter.

One problem, at least for some anglers, is that some of the more popular monofilament knots don't work as well with braided line, so many halibut are lost to knot failure. Braided line also tends to flatten out with use, losing some of its strength and developing the nasty habit of digging into itself on the reel spool.

A new generation of braided fishing lines has taken the angling world by storm in recent years, and these new super braids are well-suited to the needs of most halibut anglers. Most are made of braided strands of gel-spun polyethylene, which is sold in this country under the brand name Spectra. This material—like the Kevlar being used in Stren's version of a super braid—is much stronger for its diameter than the Dacron and nylon from which the traditional braids are composed, so the end product is a thin, braided line whose breaking strength is much higher than anything we fishermen ever used before.

Advantages of the new technology braided lines to the halibut angler are many. Its extreme thinness means that you can fish 50-pound-test line with the diameter of only 10- to 15-pound monofilament, greatly reducing line drag in the water and allowing you to get a lot more high-test line on your reel, all of which is extremely beneficial to deep-water anglers. Because they're braided, these lines have almost no stretch and are extremely limp, greatly adding to their sensitivity. We have fished five-ounce metal jigs in 300 feet of water with 50-pound lines of braided Spectra and felt the sharp tap of the lure bouncing bottom every time we lifted and dropped the rod tip! The fact that we could even get a jig that light to the bottom at that depth says something about these super braids, but the fact that we could actually feel them hitting bottom at that depth says it all about this new breed of braided lines.

Not only does their lack of stretch increase the sensitivity of these new technology braids, but it greatly enhances their value when it comes to setting the hook into a halibut's tough jaw. You may remember our description earlier in this chapter of what it's like trying to sink the hooks while fishing deep water with stretchy monofilament, but that problem is all but eliminated with the new braids (or even the older, larger braids, for that matter). When you crank down on the reel and raise the rod that first time, you're actually making serious progress in getting that hook point embedded in a barn door's snout.

The first of the new super braids were available only in larger test sizes, 50-pound and heavier, which is fine for most halibut fishing. After all, when you can fish 80-pound line that's smaller in diameter than the 25-pound mono you have on your salmon reel, what's to complain about? Some manufacturers, though, got busy putting this new technology to broader use, and you can now buy braided lines with breaking strengths covering nearly the full range of possibilities. Fenwick has been especially responsive to the increased need for super braids, offering its Iron Thread braid in sizes from six to 130-pound tests. As with virtually any product, though, there are some drawbacks to go along with all of the NTLs' advantages. One is cost. The braiding process is slow and expensive, so you'll pay several times as much for these lines as you'll pay for an equivalent spool of premium-grade monofilament. Another problem is that, with the exception of Berkley's Ultra Max, these braided lines are hollow, so they flatten out on the reel spool and dig in, sometimes resulting in major catastrophes for anglers. The brute strength and lack of stretch in these lines is also tough on tackle, as anglers use their normal fishing techniques with line that's anything but normal. Broken rods are quite common, especially among first-time users of these super lines, and more than a few reels have also been destroyed by anglers fishing these thin lines the same way they would fish monofilament of the same diameter.

The most serious problem with the new generation of braided lines, however, is in its ability to hold a knot. Some anglers claim that 20 to 40 percent of the line's strength is lost at the knot, and even most manufacturers concede that there's no sure cure to knot failure with braided Spectra, braided Kevlar and other materials these lines are make of. Knots are tough to tie and they tend to slip, due mostly to the materials themselves and the way they're braided. It could be argued that losing 20 to 40 percent of the line's strength at the knot is okay when the line is already three or four times as strong as mono of the same diameter, but you will want to get all you can out of these lines, so it's important to tie the best knots possible.

Two knots that have proven themselves better than most others for use with braided Spectra are the Palomar Knot and the Trilene Knot, both of which are pretty well known among anglers and are relatively simple knots to tie. Both require running two strands of line through the eye of the hook, swivel or whatever you're tying to, an important factor in maintaining knot strength whether you're using monofilament or the new braided lines.

With every major line manufacturer in the country hopping on the super braid band wagon, the quality and variety of line available to anglers just keeps getting better, and halibut anglers will certainly be among those to benefit. Halibut anglers generally fish heavier lures, fish deeper, and hook larger fish than the vast majority of anglers anywhere in the world, so a super-strong, super-fine, low-stretch fishing line is just what the fish doctor ordered. The popular Spiderwire braid has already replaced Spectra 1000 with newer Spectra 2000, the base fiber which is reportedly even stronger for its size than the original.

Other improvements and lines will no doubt be forthcoming. Let's hope rod and reel manufacturers can keep up by building tackle that's tough enough to handle this new generation of "halibut line."

Palomar Knot

The Palomar Knot is a general-purpose connection used in joining fishing line to swivels, snaps, hooks and artificial lures. The double wrap of line through the eyelet provides a protective cushion for added knot strength.

1. Double the line and form a loop three to four inches long. Pass the end of the loop through hook's eye.

2. Holding standing line between thumb and finger, grasp loop with free hand and form a simple overhand knot.

3. Pass hook through loop and draw line while guiding loop over top of eyelet.

4. Pull tag end of line to tighten knot snugly and trim tag end to about 1/4".

Art Courtesy of Berkley Trilene

Trilene ® Knot

The Trilene Knot is a strong, reliable connection that resists slippage and premature failures. This knot can be used in joining line to swivels, snaps, hooks and artificial lures. The knots unique double wrap design and ease of tying consistantly yields a strong, dependable connection.

1. Run end of line through eye of hook or lure and double back through the eye a second time.

2. Loop around standing part of line 5 or 6 times. Thread tag end back between the eye and the coils as shown.

3. Tighten knot with a steady, even motion without hesitation. Trim tag end leaving about 1/4".

Art Courtesy of Berkley Trilene

Line Tips All Anglers Should Know

Replace your line every year or every other year, depending on its condition. If you are fishing from a charter boat where they provide the rod, reel and line, first take time to strip all your line off the reel during a tidal flow or before rigging up. I remember one operator out of Homer who was too lazy and cheap to respool worn line. When the angler complained that his line was frayed, the skipper stripped off half the line and knotted on some new line. The angler didn't know any better...until a big halibut nearly spooled him, which was soon followed by a parting of company at the skipper-tied knot. Moral: It's false economy to change only half your line, and always, always, check charter-boat provided tackle before fishing.

If you must join two sections of line, always use a blood knot or a double surgeon's knot. Next, fine-tune that knot. Super Glue® the tag ends or whip finish the knot on leader rigs and coat with Pliobond. This will increase knot strength and minimize wear and guide/roller damage caused by unwhipped knots passing through your guides.

Double Line It

Aside from knotted mainlines, the leader is where most halibut are lost. There is almost no reason to lose a fish because of a frayed or weakened leader. Unfortunately, because of inexperience, impatience or impracticality (on party boats with 12-plus anglers fishing) skippers don't use a double leader. A double leader is especially important when you're fishing a slip-sinker/swivel set-up, perhaps the most common bait rig used in Alaska.

If you are pursuing trophy fish under IGFA rules, a double leader is permitted and recommended. Here's why:

When you use an improved clinch, Palomar or Trilene knot, you have anywhere from 80 to 100 percent of the line's break strength. Most knots, as well as how they are tied, generally weaken monofilament to some degree. Worse-case scenario, your line drops to 80 percent or less of its rated strength. Now double the leader and you increase two-fold its resistance to abrasion and shock.

Many skippers use a single clinch knot on heavy mono and Dacron because it's easier to tie. Unfortunately, the single, tag end of Dacron under the pressure of several halibut or snags will eventually pull apart, resulting in lost fish. We discovered how to eliminate this problem in Hawaii one year while reading

How to Catch
Trophy Halibut

CORKSCREW SWIVEL
BEFORE CINCHING, PASS SWIVEL
THROUGH TAG END OF LOOP.

PREVENTS KNOT
AND LINE SLIPPAGE

Jim Rizzuto's book, "Fishing Hawaii Style." Jim offers this tip:

When using a clinch knot, use a double line when tying. With the tag end, pass it around the swivel before cinching, and this prevents the tagged end from slipping through and weakening the knot.

Using a stranded wire leader with light tackle may restrict the action of your bait in the water. With small or lightweight baits, a natural drifting or fluttering action is critical for success. On larger jigs and big baits that catch barn-doors, action is generally imparted by the angler, and a wire leader is worth considering because it resists bite through and abrasion.

Stephen Babinec of Saltwater Safari Company showed me how they rig their jigs and baits with black, plastic-coated stranded wire and 120-pound monofilament line.

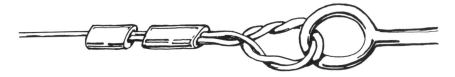

Babinec creates his wire and mono leaders each day on the way to the fishing grounds. The leaders incorporate special metal sleeves applied with a crimping tool. Babinec creates a Flemish eye in one end of a wire leader that connects the eye of the leadhead jig to a stinger hook that is inserted into a soft plastic bait or twister tail (see illustration). Ensure the tag end does not protrude from the sleeve. A protruding tag end can fray and cause painful puncture wounds, which can lead to serious infection or gury poisoning. Remedy this problem by using a second sleeve, or double back the tag end into the sleeve (which requires a larger sleeve).

As Babinec demonstrated, it's important not to crimp too tightly and damage the wire leader and weaken the sleeve. Slow, steady pressure is all that's required for a good crimp.

To prevent clinch knot slippage during big-fish battles, don't cut the tag-end loop of your knot. Instead, pass the swivel through the tag end of your loop before cinching. Use a drop of Super Glue® on braided line knots where the tag ends are cut.

When creating heavy wire or mono leaders, avoid using a single-strand loop. Create a Flemish eye with a crimping tool and one or more metal sleeves. Ensure the tag end is covered by a sleeve.

49

How to Fish the New Technology Lines (NTLs)

Line Selection: Select a line test based on the Dacron or similar line and tackle you are currently using. Remember, conventional Dacron and monofilament is three to four times thicker than comparable pound-test NTL. Spiderwire in 130-pound test has the diameter of 25-pound mono.

Colors: Of the new technology lines, co-author Chris Batin prefers Spiderwire. Spiderwire is available in Moss Green, Slate Gray and White. Some NTLs cannot be colored, so the color is applied to the line externally. These color coatings may fade in time. Markers easily refresh the color. Use a permanent felt-tip marker with a split end to custom color the last few feet of your line. We often use a dark green marker to color the 20 feet of line before the lure so it blends in with the bottom surroundings. This simple technique also offers a visual cue to you and the deckhands when a halibut nears the surface.

Loading Your Reel: Load your reel under tension. It is important to pack a NTL evenly and tightly across the spool to avoid "dig in." If you fail to do this on 100-pound or greater line, you risk losing your equipment if you snag bottom and can't break free.

Knots: While most popular knots may work with a NTL, anglers have experienced some serious problems with many common knots used with monofilament. The double uni-knot is one of the strongest. The Palomar knot is also recommended, and the surgeon's knot has proven suitable for joining NTLs to shock leaders. Some anglers add a touch of Superglue to the finished knot for added insurance.

Drag Set: Set your drag well below your usual setting. With a NTL, there is virtually no stretch to the line. Your rod and reel are your only shock absorbers. Many anglers getting acquainted with a NTL will fish with a lose drag, and use thumb pressure when additional drag is needed. They'll thumb down at the hookset, and ease off the spool as the fish surges. If you try this, be careful not to "fry" your thumb.

Sensitivity: NTLs dramatically improve the "feel" of fishing with either bait or jigs. Conventional monofilament lines can stretch as much as 35 percent when wet. In comparison, Spiderwire and Berkley's Gorilla Braid stretch about three percent.

When fishing 30 fathoms or deeper, it was, at one time, imperative to use circle hooks to consistently hook halibut.

Spiderwire is one of several "new technology" lines that is three times thinner than comparable monofilament line at the same test strength. The thinner line, with minimal stretch, is 12 times stronger than steel, and creates less drag in the water.

Now you can use jigs or J hooks at these depths with no loss in hooking efficiency. None of this waiting for the halibut to swallow the bait before slowly tightening the line. When you feel the slightest bump on your line, set the hook.

Hookset: The great strength of a NTL, coupled with its lack of stretch, means you can apply an unbelievable amount of energy into your hookset. It is very easy to break a rod with these lines. While a solid hookset is required for deepwater halibut, it is now unnecessary to keep hammering them with successive, "cross-their-eyes" hooksets. In the hands of an experienced hook-setter, once is usually enough.

Be Careful: Due to the high strength and ultra small diameter of a NTL, use extreme care when attempting to break off. Never try to pull or break a NTL with your teeth, fingers, hands or feet. Severe lacerations may result. If you must break a NTL, tie on to something solid (not your rod or reel), and pull carefully until the line breaks or the hook bends.

What You Can Expect: A NTL provides you with the opportunity to become an extremely successful halibut angler, provided you know the basics of hooking, fighting and landing fish. It's even more critical that you master these basic skills in order to maximize the full benefits offered by the many brands of new technology lines currently on the market.

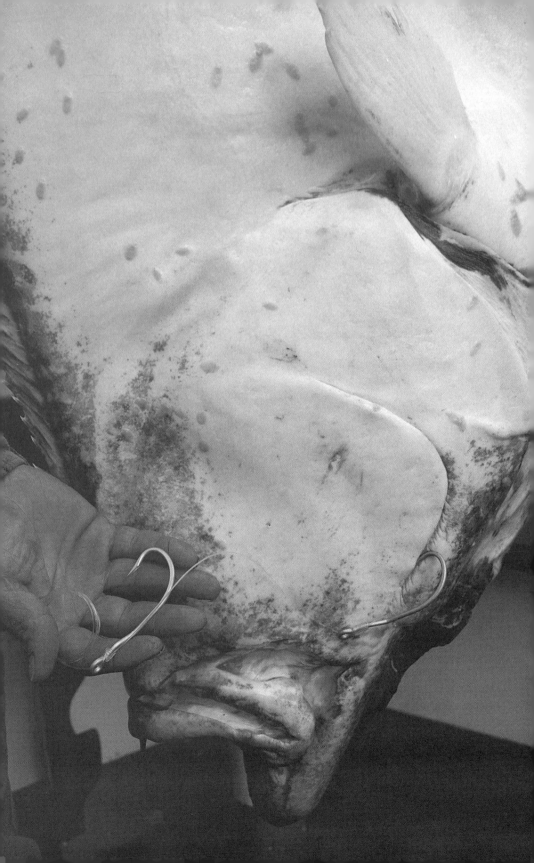

CHAPTER 4

Hooks: The Critical Link

Coastal Indians, the first halibut fishermen in this part of the world, had few choices when it came to selecting the proper hook for catching a halibut. The "right hook" was whatever an Indian fisherman could fashion by hand, using only bone and wood, and lashing the crude instrument together with natural fibers. That these hand-made creations worked at all is testimony to the ingenuity of these early fishermen, but it's also a safe bet that many an early bone-and-wood halibut hook was reduced to splinters by angry fish that were just too big and too tough for the "technology" of the day.

Today's halibut angler, of course, doesn't have to make his or her own hooks because there are plenty available in any well-stocked tackle shop that we might happen to visit. There are so many choices, in fact, that you may have trouble deciding which style and size is right for halibut. Because a fish hook is the primary link between you and that brown-and-white monster cruising the depths, "Which hook is best?" is a pointed question that merits further study.

Hooks For Bait Fishing

If you want to start a good argument, find about a dozen halibut anglers from different places along the Northwest coast and ask them which hook is better, the circle hook or the J-style hook? The conversation will get lively in no time, with advocates from both camps stubbornly extolling the virtues of their favorite hook style.

The fact is that each has its strengths and weaknesses, and the answer to which is better depends on how you fish.

It may come as a surprise to many that the circle hook, now

This 100-pound-plus halibut inhaled a whole herring fished on a tandem-hook rig featuring a pair of size 9/0 Tru-Turn J-hooks. These Perma-Steel hooks hold up well to the saltwater environment, but that also means they won't rust away if a halibut breaks off and escapes with the hooks stuck in its mouth.

The right hook for halibut depends on surrounding structure and current flow, water depth, bait or lure, and equipment you are using. Some of the most popular styles include the Mustad O'Shaughnessy (standard and extra short shank), Beak, XXXS Salmon, Tru-Turn, Kirby Sea, Shark and Circle with straight or off-set points.

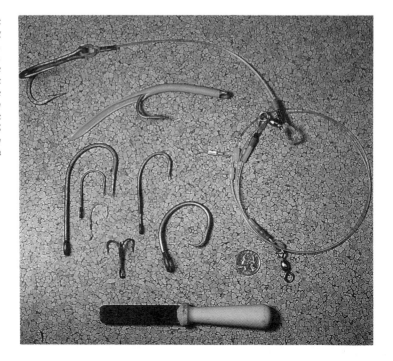

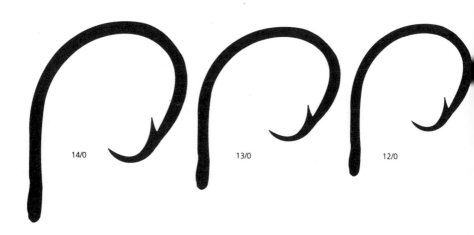

14/0   13/0   12/0

Illustration courtesy Mustad/North America

How to Catch
Trophy Halibut

considered standard equipment in many Alaskan halibut sport fisheries, is a relative newcomer to the scene, first appearing in the commercial halibut fishery in the early 1980s. Bob Trumble of the International Pacific Halibut Commission says the change-over from J-hooks to circle hooks revolutionized the commercial fishery, causing such an increase in the long-line catch that biologists at first wondered if halibut stocks had exploded.

But no, the circle hook simply turned out to be much more effective than the traditional J-hook for long-line fishing, as tuna fishermen had known for years; once a halibut had the hook stuck where it belonged, there was little chance of escape.

Word of the commercial fishery's success with circle hooks soon spread to the sport-fishing community, and some of today's anglers have never used anything else.

Patience is a key to success with circle hooks, and that's why they drive the eager-beaver-type halibut angler crazy. The fish must have time to fully inhale the bait and swim off with it before the hook is set or there's a good chance the hook will not stick where it's supposed to, and that is around the halibut's lip. Because of the hook's design, with the turned-in point nearly touching the hook's eye, there really aren't many places in the fish's anatomy that the hook can stick, so it either wraps around the lip, grabs part of the gullet, or doesn't grab at all.

Because the key to using circle hooks effectively is patience, they're best-suited to deep-water halibut fishing, where you let your bait soak and give the fish plenty of opportunity to move off with the bait before doing anything about it.

Even if you wait the required time—from a few seconds to as long as a minute or more—there's a chance the circle hook won't find its mark, especially if the hook is too small for the size of the lips you happen to be dealing with. A smaller—say, size 6/0—circle hook may have too small a "bite" to encircle the lip of a really big halibut, so it slips through without grabbing. By the same token, if you're using 14/0 or 16/0 hooks and the fish are running small, they may have trouble getting the hook into their mouths, which can be good or bad, depending on whether or not you want to land a lot of small halibut that day. Matching the proper hook size to the size of the bait and the size halibut you're targeting, then,becomes more important when using circle hooks than when using J-hooks.

Once a circle hook does wrap around the lip of its victim, it's usually there to stay, and that's what endears it to its most

The outfit chosen by this halibut angler isn't particularly heavy, including a 4/0 reel and 50-pound braided line, but it provided enough horsepower to haul this 225-pound Alaska halibut from about 130 feet of water.

staunch advocates. Unless the line breaks or the fish actually tears its own lip off with a powerful run, a halibut can turn somersaults, cartwheels, even turn itself inside out without becoming unhooked.

Another advantage of a circle hook is that, since a high percentage of fish are hooked in the lip, it's easier to release the halibut unharmed. The J-hook may stick in a gill, in the tongue, gullet, even the eye, all of which can result in a mortally wounded fish. Deep-hooking is always a problem for bait-fishermen, and there's a much higher risk of it with J-hooks than with circle hooks. In places like Homer, Alaska, where dozens of boats each day hook and release dozens of halibut each—almost all of them with circle hooks—the charter skippers claim they save hundreds of small halibut that would perish if they used J-hooks. They also save valuable fishing time removing hooks only from lips and not from other, internal parts of a halibut's body. (For complete details on fishing circle hooks for halibut, see Chapter 5, Bait Rigs And Methods For Success).

The standard, J-style hook is probably better suited to the fishing style and patience level of most halibut anglers, and is the more commonly used hook in Oregon, Washington and British Columbia waters. Unlike the circle hook, the J-hook is designed to stick wherever it gets the chance, which offers definite advantages—and certain disadvantages—to the angler who uses it.

J-hooks, of course, are readily available throughout Halibut Country, in a wide range of sizes, with many variations on the standard theme. Whatever finish, weight, shank length or size you want for your particular bait-fishing needs, you probably can find it in a J-hook.

Because a J-hook will stick in a halibut's lip, tongue, throat, the roof if its mouth or wherever it's pointed when the hook is set, anglers using them tend to enjoy a higher percentage of hook-ups on halibut of all sizes, under all kinds of conditions. Once the fish has the bait in its mouth, you stand a good chance of hooking it with a J-hook, whether or not you have the patience to wait for the "right moment."

While fishing circle hooks in tandem would offer no real advantage, using a couple of J-hooks several inches apart on the leader does increase your chances of sticking at least one hook in a halibut's mug.

Most halibut anglers, in fact, prefer tandem-hook rigs for their bait fishing, and the rig most often used is nothing more than

How to Catch
Trophy Halibut

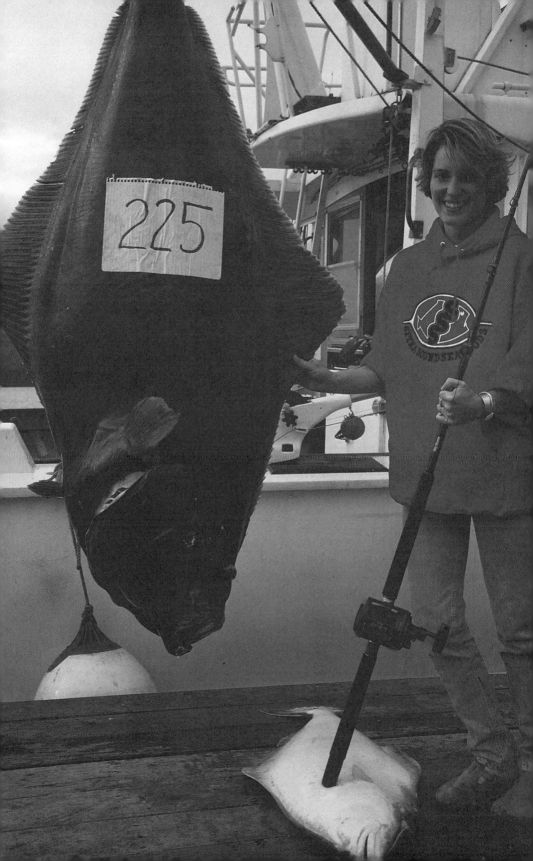

an up-scaled mooching set-up like those so commonly used for salmon.

A single hook, though, especially if it's a large one, should serve you well when bait fishing for halibut. I like to thread a single hook up through the mouth and snout of a large herring, go back through the same hole a second time to form a loop, then seat the hook into the side of the bait fish back near the tail. To put more or less roll on the bait, all I have to do is snug-up or lengthen the leader between the loop and the hook to put more or less arc in the herring.

J-hook sizes commonly used for Pacific halibut range from about 5/0 to 12/0. Size of the bait and size of the halibut you're targeting are important factors in determining the size hook or hooks you might want to use. You're likely to miss more strikes and even straighten out a hook or two if you go with size 5/0 Mustad hooks in foot-long horse herring baits in an area known for its 150 to 250-pound barn doors. A hook of size 8/0 or larger might be better suited to those fishing conditions. At the other extreme, if you're fishing small squid baits for 25-pounders along the Oregon or Washington coast, a 10/0 hook would not only be overkill, but might even cost you a few hook-ups. We like a hook to be big enough that its point and barb stick well out of the bait's side, but not so big that most of the entire hook is outside the bait!

One thing that some anglers fail to consider when selecting hooks is whether they want a light-wire hook, an extremely heavy gauge hook or something in-between. It's usually easier to stick a lighter hook into a halibut's kisser but it's also easier to straighten one during the course of battle or have it mangled and broken in the fish's vise-like jaws. A heavy hook, on the other hand, can be difficult to set, even if you keep its point razor-sharp, because its heavy wire is too thick for good penetration.

Hooks For Artificial Lures

Besides the lure's size and color, the biggest dilemma facing anglers who fish metal jigs for halibut may be deciding whether to use single or treble hooks on their lures. There's no pat answer to the question.

Most manufactured jigs come out of the package equipped with a lone treble at the end of the lure. Since these jigs are also popular among salmon anglers, at least in some areas of the Northwest, most of these trebles are fairly light, and big halibut have been known to pulverize them in a matter of seconds. Stronger, heavier trebles are an option, and some anglers use them to replace the fine-wire hooks installed by the manufacturers. But when these heavier trebles hang up on the bottom, as trebles seem to enjoy doing, there's a greater chance of breaking the line and losing an expensive jig than of straightening the hook and getting the lure back. The stronger, heavier hooks may also be harder to sharpen and certainly take a great deal more force to stick into a halibut's jaw.

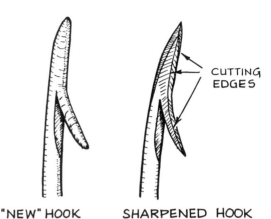

"NEW" HOOK   SHARPENED HOOK

A simple yet often overlooked way of increasing your halibut catch is to sharpen your hooks. Use a file to create razor-like cutting edges. A hook is ready to fish when it will stick into your thumbnail under light pressure.

Some anglers feel that single hooks are the best alternative.

"A single hook simply stays stuck in a fish's mouth better, and it's much easier to remove once you get the fish in the boat, whether you want to release it or put it in the fish box," says Pete Rosko, developer of the popular Crippled Herring jig, which was designed to carry a single siwash hook and is still made that way.

We agree that a single hook, once it's stuck firmly into a fish's mouth, may hold better than a treble. Two or three points of the treble hook may pierce two or three different parts of the mouth, allowing fish—especially big, powerful fish—to work one point against the other until all have straightened or pulled loose. That hook-pulling leverage is eliminated when there's only one hook point stuck in the fish, increasing the odds that it will stay there.

Anglers who do much of their halibut fishing over hard, "grabby" bottom like the single hook for another reason: it's a little less likely to snag the bottom, and fewer bottom hang-ups mean fewer lost lures and less fishing time wasted.

Fewer hook points to catch bottom, however, also means fewer hook points to catch fish, and some anglers argue that a single hook is only one-third as likely as a treble to stick when they set the hook. That might be true if the gap—that distance between the hook point and the shaft of the hook—were the same on the single as on the treble, but smart anglers know that when they use a single hook on a halibut jig it should be of a substantially larger size than a treble used on the same lure. That gap between point and shank is what determines a hook's size, but on a treble hook the shank is in the middle, with three points jutting out away from it. The overall "bite" of a treble, then, is substantially wider than a single hook in the same size. When using a single hook, the bite and the gap are the same, so you must use a larger hook if you want the same bite that the original treble had.

If you decide to put a single siwash, for example, on a jig that's currently equipped with a 5/0 treble, you would be wise to try something in the 7/0 or 8/0 range.

When fishing artificials for halibut, you're better off with a hook that's a little too big than one that's a little too small. This is especially true with lures that have only one hook, such as a leadhead or slab-type metal jig. You need a hook with enough gap to extend out past the edge of the lure and any bangles that might be hanging off it. If the hook is too small, the lure itself acts as a sort of deflector, keeping the point from coming into contact with the fish's mouth when it strikes.

Some hooks are made of materials that withstand the harshness of the saltwater environment, while others seem to melt before your eyes after only minutes of exposure to salt water and salt air. Bronze hooks go fast when used in the salt, as do the points of nickel-plated hooks that have been touched up with a file or hone. Stainless steel and Perma-Steel hooks hold up much better against the salt, and may be used for days with little or no sign of corrosion.

The problem with these saltwater-resistant materials, though, is that if you leave a hook in a halibut's mouth, whether by design or by accident, it's likely to stay there a long time, possibly causing serious injury and death to the fish.

Think about those pros and cons when selecting hooks, whether for bait fishing or to go on your favorite halibut jigs.

Whatever the specifics of the hook you select, keep it sharp. Unlike a few years ago, some of today's hooks come out of the box already sharp enough to fish, but never take such quality for granted. And, even if a brand-new hook does come from the box with a sharp point, don't expect it to stay that way through several hours of fishing. Get in the habit of checking hook points every time you bring your bait or lure to the top, and be especially thorough in your examination after playing a fish or experiencing any kind of bottom hang-up.

A three-sided "chisel" point works well for halibut, because it slices sharply into the skin and provides maximum penetration of the hook point. The idea is to create three flat surfaces, each meeting the other two at a razor-sharp edge that cuts like a hot knife through butter.

How to Catch
Trophy Halibut

FILE STROKE
FROM BARB TO POINT

POINT SHOULD STICK
INTO THUMBNAIL USING
LIGHT PRESSURE.

SHARPEN INSIDE
CUTTING EDGE

SHARPEN BOTH SIDES

LIGHTLY SHARPEN
OUTER EDGE

The easiest way to create this triangular point is with a small file, first flattening the outside of the point, then filing inward from both sides until all three flat sides meet at sharp edges. File toward the point, not only because it helps to create a sharper hook, but because it's a whole lot safer!

A file works better than a hone on large halibut hooks, and a file with a handle is the safest to use. Those Luhr Jensen hook files with the yellow plastic handles work very well for sharpening big hooks, and they fit easily into a tackle box or pocket. Keeping one in your shirt or jacket pocket while fishing is as good idea, because it's handy every time you bring up your line, so there's no excuse for not touching up those hook points regularly.

Hook Sharpening Tips: With a file or electric hook sharpener, create a sharp, inside cutting edge from tip to barb. Flat file the sides to create secondary cutting edges followed by sharpening the outside edge and point of the hook. Depending on your sharpening style, you should have a hook with four to six cutting edges. Create a long, thin, sharpened point for thin-wire hooks and deepwater fishing using bait; opt for a shorter point for hooks used on lures. A long, thin point grabs tissue found deep inside the mouth, and penetrates easily. A short point resists bending and is best suited for penetrating hard bone and cartilage found in and around the outer jaw, where most lure anglers hook their fish.

CHAPTER 5

Bait Rigs And Methods For Success

Catching big halibut on bait is easy...if you pay attention to details and assemble the right tackle components to match the conditions you will face. Let's review each major component of a bait rig, various types of rigs, and how to fish them.

Leaders

Halibut leaders run the gamut from simple to complex. Some anglers clip off a section of Dacron or new-technology mainline for their leader. Others prefer to use a two to three-foot length of 80 to 500-pound-test monofilament either knotted or crimped. Still others prefer mono-coated, seven-strand wire. Whatever you decide, have several pre-tied for the day's fishing, complete with sharpened, crimped or tied hooks on leaders attached to corkscrew or Sampo ball-bearing swivels. Avoid fishing with a white Dacron or Spiderwire leader. Instead, marker-color them in either green, black or brown, or use tinted monofilament.

Herring is a popular halibut bait, yet can be easily torn off the hook. Frozen herring stays on the hook longer. Best is a whole herring attached to a hook via mono harness, as shown in this chapter.

Below: When using Spiderwire or thin monofilament for your main line, a four to six-foot heavy-duty leader allows the skipper to maintain control of the fish at boatside. Author Chris Batin uses this leader rig for both lure and bait fishing. Components include 500-pound mono, corkscrew swivel with crimped ends, and stainless-steel swivel.

Sliders

Many charters will tie up a bait rig, and run the main line directly through the eye of a 20-ounce sinker. This is a quick and easy way to weight a standard and popular bait rig that has caught countless halibut. The only way this rig can be improved upon is by using a slider.

A slider is a hollow sleeve that clips onto the mainline. On the sleeve is a hanging clip to which a weight is attached. With a slider, you can adapt to any depth, tidal or water conditions within seconds. Increase or decrease the amount of weight with a simple flick of the snap. Standard slip-sinker rigs require cutting the main line to change weights, and retying your line. A slider rig also allows a quick switch from bait to jigs, or, if you snag bottom with the weight, the slider hook pulls open. You only lose your weight rather than leader, hook and swivel.

Swivels

Always carry a selection of heavy-duty swivels that serve as stops and/or connectors. Purchase stainless steel, and the best you can afford. Brian Butts, president of Sampo Swivels, advises anglers to avoid the cheap brass snap swivels that break at about half the pound test of similar size stainless steel swivels. His words are on target: We've had brass barrel swivels pop open on us, while we've yet to experience a failure with a Sampo or other stainless steel swivel. You'll pay a few cents more for a Sampo, but consider it must-have insurance on a trip that may already be costing you a hundred or more dollars. One of the great mysteries of the fishing world is why anglers will spend hundreds of dollars on rods, reels and day charters, only to scrimp on their swivels. This is false economy, and you must avoid its temptations.

Corkscrew swivels are superior for halibut fishing because they won't open up during battle as will snap-lock swivels. Veteran halibut anglers prefer Sampo ball bearing swivels with welded end rings. Avoid brass and barrel swivels, which can often break far below their rated strength.

Here are a few additional tips to help you understand, choose and use the right swivel.

• For trophy halibut, use a corkscrew swivel to attach your mainline to the leader or rig. When fishing is hot, changing leaders or switching from bait to a jig is a 10-second chore, compared to the minutes it takes to retie a new rig.

• A quality, ball-bearing swivel greatly eliminates line twist when you "walk the bait" or where heavy currents will tumble and rotate the bait.

• Avoid the cheap, clip-type swivels. A large halibut shakes its head with such force that it can quickly pop open a standard swivel. If you must fish a cheap snap swivel, crimp down the snap before fishing.

• Many light-tackle anglers prefer the Berkley Cross-Loks and have used them for many years with excellent results. Others prefer the McMahon type of swivel.

• Choose a swivel with a break-strength slightly greater than the rated break-strength of the line, but avoid overkill. It's unnecessary and a waste of money to use 300-pound-test swivels with 100-pound-test line.

Weights

Choosing the right weight depends on the type of fishing you plan to do. There are many types of lead weights used for halibut fishing. The preferred weight for deepwater fishing from boats is either a cannonball, teardrop or bank sinker. Their oval-round shapes sink quickly, and in heavy current, they roll easily along bottom.

If you're using a bait to create and fish a scent field, you want the weight and rig to stay in place. This is when a triangle or pyramid sinker is best because it digs into the mud or sand.

In southeast Alaska, where anglers deep-troll for king salmon and halibut, an in-line or keel sinker fished near bottom is frequently used to catch both species. While this rig catches fish, serious halibut anglers catch larger and more fish by using a rig specifically for halibut, and not fish "a rig for all species."

Our advice is to carry a selection of teardrop, cannonball, bullet and pyramid sinkers in your tackle box. In most areas, expect to fish weights from one to 20 ounces. Forty ounces of weight is required for deep water and heavy tidal flows.

Check the eye of the sinker before use. File smooth any sharp edges. On those with a wire eye, minimize wear and tear on your line by attaching the sinker to a plastic slider.

Anglers need several types of weights to effectively fish a variety of water. The most popular include teardrop, ball, pyramid, and keel. Slip-sinker rigs use a slider to attach weight to the main line. Carry the above types in weights from one to 20 ounces.

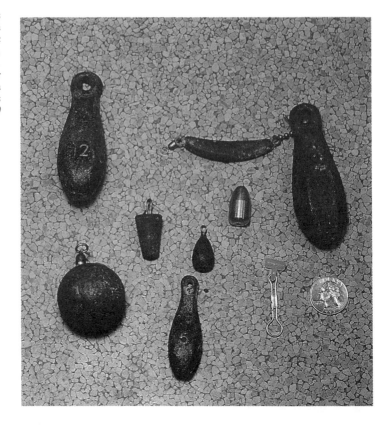

Hooks

Many anglers prefer using circle hooks when fishing bait, especially if they are catching and releasing fish. The trick here is to allow the fish at least 5 to 15 seconds to orient the bait in its mouth.

If you want to keep fish, chances are you're better off using J hooks, especially if you are prone to fishing shallow water and setting the hook quickly. The mortality rate with J hooks is usually greater than with circle hooks. Hook choice here, except in extremely deep water where circle hooks have the advantage, is a matter of personal preference and fishing style. See the chapter on hooks to learn the pros and cons of each, or read on to see how to fish a circle hook.

How to Fish a Circle Hook Effectively

1. Never attach a circle hook to a jig or lure. A circle hook is for bait fishing only. Use it with a variety of slip-sinker and fixed-weight rigs shown in this book.

2. Big halibut exhibit two behaviors when it comes to bait: Barn-doors will grab the bait and swallow it; smaller fish will grab it and run, stop to taste it, spit it out, reingest it and proceed to chomp on it like a snake swallowing a mouse.

3. **Refrain from a "cross their eyes" hookset when fishing a circle hook.** The fish will set the hook, automatically, as long as you give it plenty of time to ingest the bait before **SLOWLY** tightening your line.

4. Here's why and how a circle hook works, and the reason for the above admonition.

Take a close look at the circle hook. See how the point rolls in and is slightly offset? When the fish runs with and/or swallows the bait, the slight resistance of the water against the line pulls the hook and bait against the inside corner of the halibut's mouth or gullet. The flesh is pressed onto the gap or point of the hook, which also rotates the hook. Additional pressure causes the point to rotate, burying the barb into the bone and cartilage of the fish's mouth, or thick lining of the gullet. Once so hooked, the fish rarely escapes, and then only from the line breaking or as a result of angler or deckhand error in landing or dispatching.

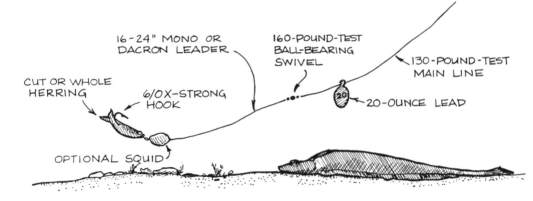

16-24" MONO OR DACRON LEADER

160-POUND-TEST BALL-BEARING SWIVEL

130-POUND-TEST MAIN LINE

CUT OR WHOLE HERRING

6/0 X-STRONG HOOK

20-OUNCE LEAD

OPTIONAL SQUID

A slip-sinker rig can be used with a variety of line tests and baits. This configuration is a favorite for big fish in deep water.

Best Bait Rig For Trophy Halibut

The slip-sinker rig is the most popular terminal rig for halibut. For trophy fish, this rig consists of a 2/0 to 12/0 hook crimped or tied to a 16 to 24-inch-plus length of 120 to 500-pound-test mono, wire or braided leader. Tie on a matching pound-test X6R Sampo or similar stainless steel ball-bearing swivel. Depending on current flow, attach a pyramid or teardrop sinker from 8 to 40 ounces onto a slider or your mainline of 80 to 120-pound test (use less weight in areas with minimal tidal fluctuation).

This type of slip-sinker rig allows you to sense the slightest strike, and doesn't alarm the fish when it inhales the bait, as the line passes through the eye of the weight.

Bait Fishing Tips

Catching large halibut is a science, and both novice and veteran anglers can't receive a more scientific education than that provided by some of the halibut skippers operating out of Alaska's coastal cities. I've spent several hundred hours under the tutelage of Frank Kempl, one of the early pioneers of the Homer halibut fishery. Kempl, who has since retired, landed more 100 to 300-pound-plus halibut in the late 70s and early 80s than most skippers read about in a lifetime. The techniques he used then are still being used by halibut skippers and anglers along the Pacific Northwest coast.

Kempl stresses that the proper bait is of paramount importance for large halibut. Herring is his favorite, and it must be firm, with shiny scales and a uniform shape, never soft, mushy or waterlogged. If obtainable, ''starved herring'' are undoubtedly the best. Kempl says this is a name for specially conditioned herring kept in huge vats without being fed for several days to a week. The starved herring have utilized their body fat to survive, thus becoming firm and extremely streamlined. They are then electroshocked and carefully packaged, preventing damage to their scales. The end product is a prime herring bait no trophy halibut can pass up.

Kempl likes to maintain the bait's appearance by keeping the herring frozen before and during use. He fishes it on a special slip-sinker rig that is rather simple to tie (see illustration).

When fishing this rig, here are a few tips to keep in mind:
• Ensure the swivel does not pass through the eyelet of the weight or become hung up in any way.
• Next, attach your leader of single or double line (Bimini twist) to the swivel. Either crimp or use a Trilene, Palomar or other knot for securing the line to the swivel, and to the heavy-duty, 9/0 or 10/0 hook.
• Now run the barb through the operculum of the herring, turn the point toward the tail of the fish, and bury the shank of the hook into the mid-section of the bait. Some skippers sew on the herring, while others run the hooks under the skin.
• If using half herring, bury the hook into the midsection of the piece, with only the point of the hook protruding from the other side. This is important as a halibut usually grabs a baitfish by its midsection. Upon feeling the sticky point or metal, a halibut will exhale the herring faster than you can react.

A herring fillet—properly cut and rigged—can provide better action than an entire fish. Thread the fillet onto the hook in two places. First insert the hook into the thickest part of the fillet. Reinsert the point facing the thinner or tapered end. Herring pieces should be cut diagonally for better action. Insert the hook into the head and gills on a front piece, and twice into the thick tail section.

CUT-BAIT RIGS

THREAD HERRING FILLET ONTO HOOK IN TWO PLACES IN THICK PORTION OF BAIT.

CUT LARGER HERRING DIAGONALLY

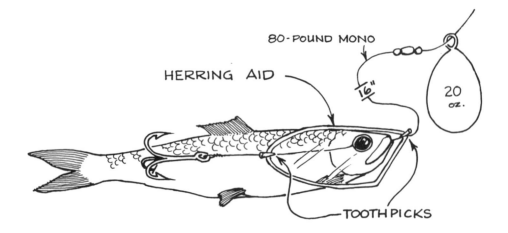

80-POUND MONO

HERRING AID

16"

20 oz.

TOOTHPICKS

A Herring Aid, modified with 80-pound mono and an extra-strong treble, is an excellent rig to use when drifting in fast current. The herring will spin and rotate above bottom, enticing fish to strike.

Herring Aid For Halibut

At times, large halibut can be picky about herring, especially if ol' Clampjaw has several hook/leader combos hanging from its trophy maw. Under these conditions, Terry and I prefer our herring to spin lazily in the current. And there's no better way I know of to accomplish this than a technique I discovered while trolling for king salmon off Alaska's Deep Creek Wayside.

It was an incoming tide, and the kings were out a bit farther than usual: about 200 yards from shore. I rigged up a Herring Aid with a large, nine-inch horse herring, added a three-ounce weight, and began trolling in a zig-zag pattern. I hadn't trolled more than 100 feet when my rod slammed down, and stayed down!

I motored around, thinking that I was hung on an old commercial fish net. Then I felt the fluttering sensation that signals only one thing...big halibut! I took an easy half hour to wrestle the 80-pound fish to the surface. As the fish neared the boat, I slowly reached for my .410 shotgun. Just as I was ready to shoot the fish, it shook its head twice across the 17-pound leader and broke free.

Two weeks later, while loading the boat for a halibut trip, I remembered what that lunker had been trying to tell me. So instead of tying on a standard 9/0 hook, I threaded the plastic Herring Aid onto an 80-pound-test leader and a number 8/0, extra-strong treble, and sweetened the rig with the largest herring in the bait box. My rig looked formidable, and it brought a few laughs from my fishing buddies. Later that afternoon, with a 52 and an 83-pound halibut in the boat, I had the last laugh. I finally succumbed to a variety of bribes and rented out the rig to my once-doubtful buddies. Since then, I've found this rig works best when drifting with 6 to 10 ounces of lead, or anchored in moderate tidal flows with 16 ounces of weight.

MOOCHING HERRING

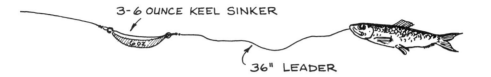

3-6 OUNCE KEEL SINKER

36" LEADER

Mooching Herring

When using whole bait herring for halibut, a popular rig among southeast Alaska skippers is a mooching rig similar to the one described above, consisting of a three to six-ounce keel sinker tied to the main line, to which is attached a 36-inch leader and herring impaled on 3/0 hooks. Troll this rig slowly near bottom or jig lightly, and be prepared to catch salmon or halibut.

More Bait Fishing Tips

No matter what method you use, fishing during slack tide requires the bait to be lowered to the bottom slowly and then raised up about a foot. Occasionally hitting bottom whenever the boat rocks from a swell is a good indication that your rig is staying within this strike zone. I lift the bait slowly every 10 to 20 seconds to impart added appeal and to prevent the crabs from stripping the hook.

When the tide is running full bore, your rig will seldom stay on bottom, even with 40 ounces of weight. This is when you must "walk the bait." Once you feel the current lift the sinker off bottom, slowly strip out or free spool line while lifting the tip of your rod to a 70-degree angle. Stop. Thumb down on the spool and slowly lower your rod. Walk your weight along bottom by tapping your rod as you would hammer a nail, lowering the rod as the current takes line. When your rod is horizontal to the water's surface, the current will again lift your weight off bottom, at which time you will repeat the above procedure.

After you've "walked" the bait about 60 yards, reel in and check the bait. Using this technique with 40-ounce weights during a full-bore tide is one of the most exhausting ways to fish for halibut. But it is usually the only way to catch halibut under these extreme conditions.

In areas with minimal tidal fluctuations, anglers often must contend with smaller fish and other bait thieves. An added enticer that is also a bait-thief deterrent is threading a walnut-size chunk of octopus or squid onto the line ahead of the herring. Even if thieves steal your herring, your rig will still remain appealing to halibut, as I've yet to find a bait thief that can remove a piece of octopus from a hook. Also, the feeding frenzy of the thieves around the octopus can attract larger halibut which simply move in, scatter the pip-squeaks and inhale the bait.

Big Baits Produce Big Fish

Salmon/Fish Heads

Stomach analyses of large halibut have shown they like big baits. And to catch big halibut, you can't be wasting valuable time hooking "chicken" halibut. Under these circumstances, "the bigger the bait, the bigger the fish" theory holds true.

An effective method for catching trophy halibut is to bait up with a whole salmon head. Millions of salmon migrate through prime Pacific Northwest halibut grounds, and Belugas and killer whales leave plenty of remains after their ambushes through the salmon schools. I've found that fishing an entire pink or sockeye salmon head near the bottom during heavy tidal flows, and at least four feet off the bottom during slack tide, will catch trophy halibut. Of course, a salmon head is usually large enough to keep the smaller 30 to 50-pounders off the hook, so don't expect much action. But when you do get a strike, you can bet your fishing buddy a king crab dinner that the halibut will near or exceed 80 pounds.

Visit any of the numerous salmon canneries along the coast to obtain more salmon head baits than you can carry away.

Salmon heads make excellent bait. Insert a 12/0 or larger hook into the jaw, running it up and out through the skull. Many anglers insert the hook through both gill covers when bait thieves are plentiful.

MAIN LINE

INSERT THROUGH GILL COVER

PINK, SOCKEYE SALMON HEAD RIG

Horse Herring

If you want to catch small halibut, use parts of a herring. If you want a chance at a large fish, use large, foot-long horse herring.

I was fishing for halibut with Stan Stephens Charters out of Valdez. It was in mid-July, several months after the infamous Exxon Valdez oil spill.

My partner, Jeff Schuler, had never caught a fish larger than a 10-inch trout, and he jumped at the chance to pursue halibut. He also jumped at the chance to catch the first fish. When an 84-pound halibut nailed his whole herring and proceeded to nearly pull him over the railing, it was all I could do to keep the tears of laughter away. His face was locked in amazement. So was mine, when the halibut surfaced and cleared the water in one jump. Schuler went wild, and I stood by ready to grab his coat, just in case he started slipping over the side. After 15 minutes of battle, I gaffed the halibut and brought it aboard. At that moment, there was not a happier angler than Schuler. He decreed that the spill didn't affect the halibut fishing in the least.

Big halibut prefer big baits, and an entire herring, when rigged properly, will catch halibut when they ignore lures and bait chunks. With the hook in the rear, a slight curve in the bait produces a slow roll while a sharp curve produces a tight roll.

Cod/Pollock Strips

Some anglers will use cuts of herring on the above rigs to first catch cod or pollock, a favorite halibut food. (For the sake of convenience, as both species are similar, I'll refer to both under the generic term, cod).

Cod are plentiful in flat, muddy bays or deepwater haunts.

WAYS TO RIG WHOLE HERRING

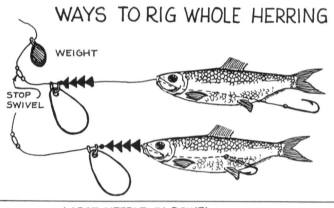

WEIGHT

STOP
SWIVEL

LARGE NEEDLE IN DOWEL

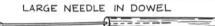

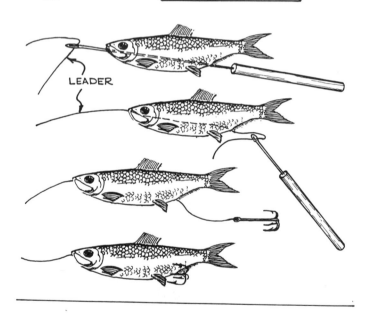

LEADER

Various ways to rig whole
herring or other baitfish.

How to Catch
Trophy Halibut

Experienced halibut skippers will often use their sonar units to search for huge schools of cod. They know that big halibut are almost always lurking nearby, waiting to grab an easy meal.

Chuck Crabaugh of Cie Jae Ocean Charters convinced me how effective cod is in catching big halibut. He catches a cod and fillets it into large strips of 2.5 inches wide by 12 to 14 inches long. He splits the tail, and leaves the skin attached and impales this on a slip-sinker bait rig described earlier. This rig was responsible for over 1,000 pounds of halibut caught the day I fished with Crabaugh and his guests near Cook Inlet's Barren Islands, and I'm certain it has caught many more halibut since.

The only problem I've experienced with using cod strips is in first finding the bait fish. This can be hit or miss. To ensure success, I always toss a few frozen cod belly strips (from a previous trip) into the cooler with my other bait, in case cod are scarce.

Here are a few final tips for fishing cod strips:
- Fish the cod with the skin side toward bottom.
- Once the flesh becomes washed out, replace with a fresh fillet or belly strip, or douse with herring or shrimp oil.
- Once a fish takes the bait, give the halibut LOTS OF SLACK and PLENTY OF TIME to take the entire bait into its mouth. Patience is a must to successfully using cod strips to catch big halibut.

In closing, use the fish you kill. And save the cod you don't use. They make good eating.

Create a cod strip by taking a fillet from a cod. Start half-way back and cut through the fillet and skin, creating a V-tail. Round edges and insert hook into uncut section. Fish skin-side down.

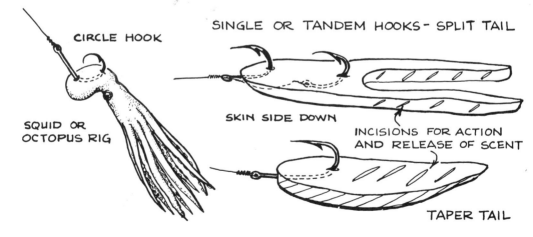

CIRCLE HOOK

SINGLE OR TANDEM HOOKS – SPLIT TAIL

SQUID OR OCTOPUS RIG

SKIN SIDE DOWN

INCISIONS FOR ACTION AND RELEASE OF SCENT

TAPER TAIL

Live Bait

Some anglers will catch a live cod or pollock, impale a 10/0 hook through both lips, clip the tail fin, and fish it slightly off bottom. Again, such a bait rig is for big fish, and don't expect lots of action from 30-to 50-pound halibut. You can, however, expect to catch LARGE fish!

A flutter at line's end is a sure sign you've hooked a halibut. If you hook a fish that doesn't flutter when hooked chances are it's a cod, Irish Lord, greenling or insignificant other. If so, don't horse it up. Instead, ease it off bottom. After cranking it up a few feet, lower it to bottom and jig it a few times. Often, a big halibut will home in on the distress actions of the hooked fish, and will quickly grab it. You'll either catch a halibut, or the cod will shake lose, allowing you to crank up your rig with less effort.

In either case, give the fish time to grab the bait, stop to reingest it head first and move off again before setting the hook.

Cod and similar-sized bottomfish are favorite foods of large halibut. This fish can be filleted or used as-is as bait on a slip-sinker rig.

Increase Your Halibut Catch
With Downriggers and Bait

Lower Cook Inlet and Kachemak Bay may be one of the best halibut fisheries off Alaska's coast, but they certainly don't earn high marks for being the easiest to fish. Fishing the 60 minutes of relatively slack tide is usually fun and productive, and that's where it ends. For the next five hours, the angler is forced to fish for halibut during strong tidal flows with a heavy-duty rod and reel and up to 40 ounces of weight to get the bait to the bottom. Fishing such a rig quickly fatigues the strongest of anglers.

The ideal situation would be to get your bait down to the fish with little, if any, weight attached to your fishing line. You stick the rod in the rod holder, and when it starts bucking from a strike, set the hook and play the fish. No more jigging, "walking the bait" or strained muscles. Impressed? So was I when I did that very same thing off the shore of Deep Creek many years ago.

The device that I used was a Speedtrol downrigger, but any quality downrigger will work. Used by anglers for deepwater trolling for salmon and trout, the downrigger consists of a large spool filled with wire cable. A steel arm with a pulley attached to the tip runs the cable from the spool out over the edge of the boat and into the water. Attached to the end of the cable is a 200-pound-test snap swivel. A seven-pound lead weight is attached to the swivel. A quick disconnect mechanism is positioned near the lead weight. The angler's line from his rod and reel is attached to this quick disconnect.

The operation is simple. The seven-pound downrigger weight takes the angler's line and bait directly to the bottom, and keeps it there. Because of the heavy lead weight, there's little belly in the wire cable, even in strong tidal flows. The fishing rod is placed in a rod holder mounted near the downrigger.

With a downrigger, there's no need to hold the rod. The angler trolls or drifts the rig over productive halibut structure, all the while watching the rise and fall of bottom structure on a sonar unit, so as to avoid snagging bottom. When a halibut sees the bait, it grabs it and swims off, triggering the quick disconnect. The angler can then fight the halibut without any cumbersome lead weight and resulting fatigue associated with deep water and heavy tidal-flow fishing. On that first down-rigger fishing trip nearly 21 years ago, my largest fish was 38 pounds. While I was pleased with my catch, I was more excited about the new possibilities downrigging for halibut offered.

But there's more to downrigger fishing for halibut than meets the eye. Here are a few pointers to get you started:

Most any medium-weight tackle will work with a downrigger. Most anglers like to use their king salmon rigs. They find that a halibut hooked on this type of rod will put up a more spectacular battle than one dampened by 40-ounces of weight. I use a 7½-foot, heavy-action salmon rod and level-wind Ambassadeur 7000 filled with 30-pound-test line. However, if you're intent on catching halibut for the freezer rather than sport, consider a new technology line such as Spiderwire that exhibits minimal stretch at all depths, which allows for a better hook-set after the fish has taken the bait.

How you fish your bait off a downrigger is an important consideration. Because you can't jig the bait, it's important for the bait to have its own action. Use a whole herring and rig it with two, 6/0 salmon hooks connected in series. Adjust the bait so that it maintains a wide, lazy roll.

I prefer fishing the herring three to four feet behind the downrigger weight. At peak tidal flows, the current is strong enough to keep the bait spinning above bottom, which entices the halibut to strike. Right before slack tide, move the bait six feet or more from the weight and troll as slowly as your outboard will allow.

If you're plagued by small halibut and bait thieves, a huge bait such as a salmon head, belly strip or cod strip is the only way to go. You may have less action, but the big fish results are worth the wait.

You can increase the effectiveness of your downrigger presentation by using a sonar unit. By first graphing the bottom, it's possible to set up drifts over areas that are migration routes for big halibut making their way into shallow-water feeding areas. These are usually in the form of wide channels running the length of the shoreline, or muddy, sandy areas near rock bottom or kelp beds. Scouting beforehand also forewarns me of any kelp beds or sudden changes in depth that can easily entangle a downrigger weight or cable.

Once I find a migration route, I'll motor to the head of a channel and fish the length of it. As a general rule, halibut won't chase a bait very far during peak tidal flows. If I find a fishy-looking area that should be fished longer, I'll fire up the outboard and hold the boat against the current, allowing the bait to spin in a tantalizing manner in front of the halibut. I guarantee very few halibut will look the other way.

When a halibut does take your bait, be ready to set the hook.

If your hook is honed needle sharp, at the most the point of the hook has buried itself into the fish's mouth. You need to set the hook several times to ensure the barb is buried. I prefer to set my release lever to release at five pounds of pull. This is usually enough to deter any bait thieves, yet light enough to prevent a big halibut from spitting out the bait due to an unnatural feel.

When a halibut springs the quick disconnect, have someone reel up the downrigger weight while you ensure the hook is set. I lost three halibut one year after they swam into the wire cable and sheared the monofilament line. Keep the fish on the bottom until the downrigger weight is above it.

Downrigger fishing for halibut is a sport that's still in its infancy. But I'm convinced of its effectiveness in the hands of anglers who take the time to learn how to use it. Give it a try this summer. If you don't like it, you can always use the downrigger to fish for deepwater lake trout in the summer, or suspended silver salmon in August. And with opportunities like that, you can't lose.

A dodger and herring is an excellent rig for drifting or trolling for halibut during heavy tidal flows. A Number 7 Skagit special spinner ahead of a herring bait is another excellent rig. Both require heavy-duty rod, reel and line to fish effectively.

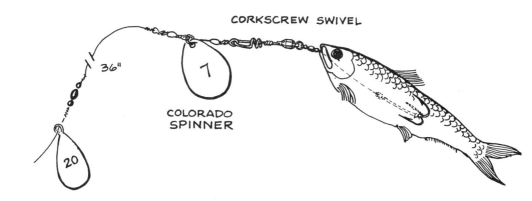

CORKSCREW SWIVEL

36"

7

COLORADO
SPINNER

20

Halibut Caller is a device that creates a powerful scent field that has proven effective in waters from Dutch Harbor to Prince of Wales Island. For best results, attach it to a swivel on a bait rig, or as a trailer on a jig.

Specialized Bait Enhancers

Baited Spinners
And Hootchie Skirts

Terry and I have obtained much of our halibut fishing knowledge from experience, as has Nick Dudiak, veteran halibut fisherman and sport-fish biologist in Homer. He believes that hootchie or plastic skirts on a baited hook give the angler an added advantage. Once a halibut follows the scent into an area, he says, their sense of sight takes over. A hootchie or plastic skirt on a baited hook provides added appeal.

"Whether you use scent or bait, the plastic hootchie will pick up and hold that scent for a period of time," Dudiak says. "Thus, if the halibut steals the bait, the skirt will have enough fish oil on it to draw another strike. Without the skirt, the angler would be fishing a bare hook."

Dudiak catches halibut on a regular basis by incorporating vibration, visual appeal and scent. He's had very good success fishing a large spinner/hootchie combo off a lead weight. He also baits this rig with herring. The rig pulsates along bottom, and big halibut "really smash it" he said.

Improve Any Bait With Halibut Caller

Halibut Caller is a new and effective bait scent system manufactured by Glen Graham of Anchorage. This mix of fish attractants, oils and scents enhances the effectiveness of any bait by creating a super-concentrated scent field (see Chapter 10 for explanation of scent fields and how important they are in attracting halibut).

I've had halibut target my bait to the exclusion of others, probably because of the intense scent field created by this tubular scent device that lasts for hours.

The caller has a fluorescent pink wick that triggers halibut into a feeding frenzy by imitating the action of shrimp and squid. This visual stimuli is further enhanced by the see-through canister that contains the wick.

Halibut Caller is easy to use. Open the canister, and the patented, time-release method of delivery allows the scent to disperse slowly. It's attached to your mainline swivel, so it doesn't interfere with your bait. It's that simple.

Glen handed samples out on the Kenai Peninsula for the last two summers. Now, because of the demand, stores continually sell out. Reports of large catches resulting from Halibut Caller have Glen working hard to manufacture sufficient quantities. Halibut Caller also works exceptionally well with artificial lures. I attach the call to my mainline swivel or directly to my jig hook. See page 357 to order Halibut Caller.

Bait Fishing Tips For Big Halibut

When using bait for big halibut, it's imperative to:
• Keep your rod tip down, in anticipation of a pickup, moving it to the horizontal or ¾ vertical position only when "tapping" to find bottom, or to tighten line to ascertain a pickup.
• Your lead weight should tap bottom every three to five seconds. A tap every 20 to 30 seconds, as suggested by some skippers, is fishing too high. Tapping bottom frequently is your guarantee the bait is rotating slightly above fish-holding structure, drifting in a natural manner and within easy sight and ambush of a halibut. Remember that halibut like to ambush prey. Yet during heavy tidal flows, they will not chase a bait that is very far off bottom. Off-bottom or mid-depth fishing is best at slack tide. At this time, a jig is the lure most favored by experienced halibut anglers.
• When you have a strike, lower your rod tip, dropping your lead weight to bottom. If you continue to maintain a tight line, the halibut can't inhale the bait, grabs at or misses it, resulting in a missed strike. Next, free spool or strip out line, allowing the fish to run with or "chomp" on the bait. I have a saying, "The larger the bait, the longer the wait."
• After a count of five to 10, or when you feel weight at the end of your now-tightened line, engage your bail and crank in the slack, all the while keeping your rod tip pointed at the fish. If you're using a J hook, set the hook with a full sweep of your rod. At the apex of your hookset, keep your rod tip high, but not vertical. Don't bring the rod tip past 65 degrees, because a sudden surge could snap the rod tip held past this angle. Allow the initial surge of the fish to help bury the hook. If the halibut hesitates, even for a few seconds, crank down quickly and set the hook again.
• With circle hooks, allow the line to tighten until you feel

the weight of the fish, engage the bail and apply steady pressure, allowing the curved point of the circle hook to grab a piece of jaw and bury itself. Either way, hang on for a tug-of-war that can last an hour or more.

• Of all the big halibut I've seen lost, more than half have been due to the angler trying to horse the fish after the hookset. The crankdown should be smooth and easy, with the upward pump of the rod equally controlled, smooth and slow. Any major resistance followed by a sudden absence of such is indicative of the fish thrashing or shaking its head. DO NOT continue pumping the fish. Maintain tension. There is usually enough stretch in the line to absorb the shock. Hold the fish in place until activities stop, then continue pumping slowly. Your drag should already be preset. Don't touch it! If you need a temporary increase in drag to budge a stubborn fish, use thumb pressure on the spool. This will keep you safe, especially at boatside. Should the fish sound 30 fathoms at the "speed of light," a slightly tightened drag will pop a new as well as frayed line.

• Ease the fish to the surface. When you see color, call for a deckhand or gaffer. NEVER break the surface of the water with any part of the fish. To do so is asking for a major sounding. Keep the fish at least a foot below the surface, and allow the skipper to guide the fish to gaff, gun or harpoon.

• Obey the commands of the deckhand, skipper or person who will handle the fish. Temporarily place curiosity aside. Stand away from the railing where the deckhand and skipper are maneuvering the fish to gaff. Step back, all the while preparing yourself to jump forward with rod extended should the deckhand miss the fish with the gaff, and the fish sounds. You'll have your sight picture and victory of accomplishment once the fish is onboard.

• Gaffing or harpooning is the last, critical step. Bury the point of the gaff (if you're doing the honors) directly behind the head, on the non-stomach side of the halibut. Place the gaff point between the flat spines. (Next time you fillet a halibut, take note of the location of these spines. The spines act as a stop for the gaff or harpoon). Likewise, ram the harpoon tip between these spines.

• When shooting halibut, it is best to shoot the fish in the brain or spine. Ensure you are far enough behind the mouth area with your shot placement. Some hooks are buried deep, and shooting has severed many a line or lure. Also, shooting a fish disqualifies it for IGFA record purposes.

Proven Method For
Preventing Seasickness

If you're one of those who gets seasick in your own bathtub, despair not. I know you've tried the pressure band, scopolamine patch and oral medication, and nothing seems to work. Here's a cure: try a combo of drugs tested by NASA and the Coast Guard: Promethazine (an antihistamine) and Ephedrine (a decongestant, available over the counter). Separately, the drugs have side effects. However, when taken together they cancel out each other's negative side effects and provide a remarkably effective remedy for sea sickness, with minimal drowsiness. Consult your doctor first, and advise him of your intentions. He'll need to give you a prescription for the promethazine. Take 25 milligrams of each about two hours before you depart.

CHAPTER 6

Fishing With Phonies

Leadhead Jigs

In the hands of an experienced halibut angler, a leadhead jig is the most effective lure available for trophy halibut. Optional and myriad dressings permit you to turn a standard jighead into a realistic imitation of a crab, herring, pollock, octopus, squid or other forage food preferred by halibut.

If you don't already know, it is to your advantage to learn how to fish leadheads. In the hands of an expert fishing the right conditions, a leadhead can outfish herring, metal jigs and bait because its weight and configuration allows precise depth and lure control.

Like any other rig or lure, jigs have their optimum range. They are most effective in depths up to 30 fathoms when using Dacron line, and double that with the new technology lines. You can use jigs during slack tide, and when the tide is running full bore. You can walk them or fish them stationary. You can enhance their appeal by adding bait, and change colors in seconds. The disadvantage of jigs is that you'll lose a few to rocky bottoms and kelp beds. While losing leadheads can be expensive, many anglers view the resulting take of a big fish is more than worth the expense.

Jigs can be effectively used in nearly every halibut fishing situation you'll encounter in the Pacific Northwest. In bays indirectly affected by heavy tidal action, an eight-ounce jig with fluorescent orange and yellow skirt with an Uncle Josh Off Shore Big Boy pork rind teaser will produce fish when all else fails. When fishing in 300-foot depths near the Continental Shelf with Spiderwire, 24-ounce jigs will now hook fish in areas

Leadheads with plastic, curl-tail bodies work well in most areas, provided the head is heavy enough to keep the lure hanging vertically. The leadhead's single hook rides above the lure, helping to avoid hang-ups. These plastics also appeal to large lingcod, which are also found in rocky structure.

where only circle hooks and bait were once king. Jigs keep fishing when other anglers are cranking up stripped bait rigs. Indeed, if I had to choose one lure that has caught more halibut for me than any other, it would be a leadhead jig.

Types Of Jigs For Halibut

The first leadheads I ever used for halibut were Sebastes jigs designed by Seattle photographer, angler and author Doug Wilson and his fishery biologist partner Fred Vanderwerf. The streamlined, bottom-weighted head has an action especially suited for halibut fishing. I approached Doug about six years ago in Seattle with a sad story of having lost my last Sebastes jig. I had used the eight-ounce leadhead to catch all types of bottomfish, and couldn't find a replacement anywhere. Doug took pity on me, smiled and handed me a box filled with various size Sebastes. Again, my catch rate skyrocketed. This story proves that when a halibut angler has confidence in the right leadhead for halibut, and knows how to fish it, there is not a more effective fish-catching combination on the water.

And therein lies the secret to success: not any one jighead is good for all conditions. There are many types of leadheads from which to choose. They include:

Roundhead: Most common. Effective when fished by itself, with hootchies, plastics or bait. Versatile.

Bullet: Commonly found in sporting goods stores, and available in a variety of weights for shallow and vertical jigging. Sinks quickly. The center-balanced types are best for vertical jigging. For trophy halibut, purchase those with XXS single hooks and reinforced eyelets.

Forward-Balanced or Banana Jig: Another type of tapered jig that dives through the water easier than broad-headed jigs.

Arrowhead: Streamlined after its namesake, and a favorite to use with plastic tails and hootchies.

Mushroom: Generally available only in smaller sizes, the leadhead on this lure imitates a gumdrop or mushroom cap. Ideal for attaching soft plastic shrimp tails and light-tackle fishing for halibut.

Rolly Polly or Halibut Jig: Oversized, center-balanced jig that is fast sinking, and used to fish bait and hootchie/plastic attractors in deep water or heavy current.

Stand-up: Maintains a near vertical attitude when you "walk" or drift it along bottom with the current, or jig it directly on bottom. Rarely hangs up on rocks or weeds because the hook rides up with the bait as the jig rests on bottom. It works well in keeping a whole herring or similar-sized bait above bottom, making the jig easier for the fish to see. Heavier slab or strip baits cancel out this stand-up effect. Difficult to find in larger sizes.

Trolling Jigs: Plastic baits with the lead weight or head buried inside the lure. These usually are rigged with a single, 7/0 or larger single siwash hook and run from six inches to over a foot long. Most commonly found in squid and minnow-imitating models. Excellent for vertical, deepwater jigging or drifting.

Jighead Color

Jigheads come in a variety of colors and finishes, from unpainted to rubberized, plastic-coated models. Simply put, I've caught halibut on them all. I tend to favor a fluorescent red or orange head because of its high visibility, followed by a black head with a huge yellow or fluorescent eye with black pupil.

There have been times when a contrasting head color and hootchie skirt was the key combination to my success, while other anglers using unpainted jig heads were experiencing poor or no results. At other times I've caught plenty of fish on unpainted jig heads, or on jigheads so gouged and hammered from impacting rock bottom all day that I was surprised they still stayed together, fish after fish!

Swivels And Leaders

When connected to a swivel, your jig will dance and flip enticingly. Also, when action is shot and a fish damages a jig, a snap swivel makes the switchover a 10-second chore, compared to the 50 or more seconds required to cut the line and retie directly to the lure.

If for no other reason, use a swivel to eliminate line twist when "walking the jig" in heavy currents. The swivel will save you money in lost jigs, line and fish.

I prefer the corkscrew type of snap swivels and have used them for many years with excellent results. Choose a wide-loop swivel with a break strength rated slightly higher than the break-strength of the line. The swivel is a potentially weak link, and I've had charter-boat-supplied cheap brass swivels equipped with snap rings separate on me. Always use the solid ring, stainless-steel variety. As mentioned previously, stainless-steel, ball-bearing swivels by Sampo are best, but expensive.

One final tip I mentioned in the bait chapter, and is worth repeating here as well. Avoid the common clip-type of snap swivel. A big halibut shakes its head with muscle-jarring force. Add the weight of a 16 to 24-ounce jig to this, and you have a combination of factors that can pop open a standard swivel in a split second. Using these cheap swivels is false economy.

You may want to use a clear mono leader when fishing a jig. A big halibut might shy away from a white line leading directly to your jig. Why take chances? Color your line with a permanent ink marker if tying direct to the jig swivel, or switch to a mono leader of 120-pound-or-greater test. Darryl Dossett, skipper of the Grand Aleutian out of Dutch Harbor, has landed hundreds of lunker halibut. He convinced me of the advantages of the clear mono rig when using jigs. He also says a clear mono rig allows him, as a skipper, to handle and maneuver the halibut for gaffing, harpooning and shooting. He says the thinner Dacron and braided lines of the same pound test can cut an ungloved hand as quickly and deeply as a razor. His rig is shown in this chapter.

Experience is the best guide in choosing the right jig type for the conditions you'll encounter in your immediate area. The following jig types and rigs have worked exceptionally well for us over the last several decades of fishing Alaska and Pacific Northwest waters. Use them as described, or modify them to match the conditions you'll find in the waters you fish.

Floating Jig Rig For Tidal Flows

Floating jigs have been used for years in the freshwater angling world, but the rig has yet to catch on in Alaska halibut fishing. It's easy to understand why. Many anglers get wide-eyed when switching from a size 6 floating jig to a 10/0 floating jig that covers the palm of your hand and part of your wrist. I switch over to this rig in extremely snag-filled tidal rips before I lose too many leadheads.

When I wanted to experiment with this technique, stores or catalogs didn't stock floating jigheads large enough for trophy halibut. I had to learn to create my own, and surprisingly, the process is extremely simple.

First, take an oversized jig hook, and place it in an arrowhead type jig mold. Next, fill the mold with aerosol foam, the type used to weatherproof houses. Allow to dry and sand down. It doesn't have to look pretty. Paint it if you so desire. Attach a hootchie and small scent ball or bait, as shown in the floating jig illustration. The jig—which can be fished with a wire

FLOATING JIG RIG

MAIN LINE

HALIBUT SKIN

spreader to prevent line tangling—will float above snag-covered bottoms, bouncing and darting around naturally in the current. Floating jigs are ideal for light to medium tidal flows, but use caution when fishing them while anchored during slack tide, as the jig often floats up and entangles with the main line or other lines nearby.

To combat this:
- Shorten your leader to three feet or less.
- Lower your rig slowly to bottom.
- If you cast out the jig, tightline your spool to flatten out or flip over the jig prior to it hitting the water.
- A drift or tidal flow will straighten out the jig, and you can walk it or bottom bounce it with the current. When a fish takes the jig, strike immediately.

You might try running a double line from a leadhead eyelet to a floating jig. While one roots along bottom, the other trails overhead and behind.

Expect your lead weights to snag bottom. Terry and I favor a wire breakaway attachment tested at about 60 to 70 percent of the break-strength of the main line. You'll lose the sinker, but save your floating jig head and rig.

A frozen herring is an ideal bait to use with a floating jig head. The six-inch variety is best because it's lightweight, and difficult to rip off the hook until it has thawed. The frozen herring appears occupied, trying to swim off with this huge bait (the jig head). As a predator that prefers to ambush its prey, the halibut waits for this type of scenario: an easy meal.

Batin's Floating Hal with attractor tail is extremely effective when fished from an anchored location during mild to medium-strength tidal flows. When adding bait, increase the size of the foam head to keep the rig floating over bottom. Use with a wire spreader to prevent tangles with the main line.

Rig it as shown and hold on.

If you're in an area with plenty of bait thieves, use chunks of octopus or squid. One chunk often lasts an entire morning of fishing.

Here's a tip I've found extremely effective: Instead of impaling the octopus on the jig hook, thread a small chunk, or for added appeal, a seven-inch length of a smaller tentacle onto the mainline above the jig, as an added enticer in case a bait thief rips off the herring. The rig will still catch fish, even with the herring missing.

Jigs and Grub Tails

Soft plastic grub tails are perhaps some of the most effective artificial "sweeteners" you can add to a leadhead. A grub-tail jig consists of a standard jighead with a plastic tail that moves or undulates when jigged, retrieved, or held stationary in current. The tail's life-like swimming action entices halibut to capture what appears to be an unsuspecting baitfish swimming by.

A variety of tail configurations exist. I prefer the flattened tail that rotates upwards counterclockwise, or the elongated, paper thin tails that twitch enticingly in the slightest current. Carry at least a couple dozen of these tails in a variety of colors, as halibut chew them to bits during the long "pump and grunt" journey from ocean bottom to boatside.

Rigging a twister tail leadhead with a stinger hook will increase your hookups. Use a long needle or rifle-cleaning rod to insert 120-pound-test black wire through the tail, as shown here. Use a Flemish Loop to attach the leader to the jig eye.

Shrimp Tails

While shrimp tails don't have the delicate swimming action of a grub tail, they do exhibit a flipping action typical of a shellfish swimming for cover. The larger tails are resistant to tears and fish bites, and offer a more "meaty" appearance.

Halibut Success Secret

If your soft plastic bait is suffering from massive lacerations from the ravages of halibut teeth and muscular jaws, perform immediate field cauterization. Here's how:

• Prep the area by first drying it inside and out.
• Use a lighter to melt the area around the cut or tear.
• Hold together until the plastic cools.
• Set aside for a few minutes, thread on, and fish aggressively.

On the 20-ounce and larger jigs, a thicker-bodied jig is a must. My personal preference is a thick shrimp tail that has grub tail appendages, offering the best of both mass and action. For deepwater halibut, consider the luminescent varieties which add a unique, visual appeal.

Because these 24-ounce jigs can be a mouthful, even the strongest halibut, when flaring its gills, can't create a vacuum strong enough to inhale a jig fished on a tight line. Thus, a halibut swims up and grabs it by the tail. You feel a take, set the hook, and retrieve a jig with half the tail missing.

Here's the prescribed course of action for fishing jigs with long grub tails.

On the standard 24-ounce jighead, the hook is four inches from the jighead, to which is attached a 12-inch hootchie or tail. Rig up a stinger hook, using plastic-coated steel wire. Anchor one end to the jig eye with a Flemish Loop, running the wire through the plastic bait before crimping on a 9/0 hook near the end of the fleshy part of the tail. Even though the main body of the lure will be stiffened somewhat by the wire, insert the stinger hook an inch or so before tail's end so the tail can undulate effectively. Place it at the very end of the tail, and you'll catch lots of small halibut and Irish Lords.

PLASTIC SQUID

A plastic squid/slip sinker rig. Attach a scent ball to the line at the hook's eye. This cotton material holds paste scents such as Smelly Jelly for up to a half hour, doubling the effectiveness of the rig.

Hootchies

Perhaps the least expensive and most readily available plastic add-on component for a leadhead is a hootchie. I'm not talking about the six-inch variety used for salmon, but rather, the 12-inch and longer hootchies used in saltwater trolling and deep-sea fishing. They come in a variety of colors to match the prevalent forage item in the area you'll be fishing.

In reviewing my logs and tackle box, here are the colors I've found most effective in my halibut fishing endeavors, and why:

Yellow or green to imitate cod or kelp greenling, and pearl white to resemble general forage fish;

Red, orange, light pink, fluorescent orange and red translucent for squid or shrimp;

Silver fleck to imitate herring, sandlance and other baitfish;

Luminescent for murky water, tidal rips, cloudy days, night fishing and fishing off the Continental Shelf.

These recommendations are simply the colors I'll thread onto the leadhead first. If they don't offer the visual stimuli necessary to induce a strike, I'll start experimenting with other colors such as lime green, purple, chartreuse, fuschia, fluorescent pink, and other hi-vis colors.

Batin's Halibut Bouncer is a super-effective lure that imitates tentacled prey favored by Pacific halibut. See page 357 to order Halibut Bouncer.

The action of a hootchie-skirted leadhead comes from jigging it aggressively in the water, causing the tentacles to undulate. I'm going to reveal a secret dressing for a jig that I have used for nearly a decade, and have yet to see used commercially in Alaska waters. Graduates from my Advanced Alaska Fishing Techniques seminars say it doubles or triples their catch rate. They call it Batin's Halibut Bouncer, and I pass it on to you free of charge:

Obtain an orange and a red 10-inch or larger saltwater hootchie, with a 1.5-inch or larger diameter. Insert together to make one hootchie of red and orange.

Thread the hootchie backward onto the jig, so the cone is facing the rear of the jig, rather than the lead head. This causes the tentacles to flare out from the body, and increases the effectiveness of the lure 100 fold. Insert a white grub tail onto the hook. To hold the hootchie in place, slip on a small rubber band over the hootchie base where it comes in contact with the barbed color of the jig or grub tail, or tie it down with some elastic cord or mono. Anchoring the skirt in this manner helps prevent the fish from tearing off the hootchie, plus the skirt remains in place during aggressive jigging.

Once you try this jig, you'll never go back to the standard way of rigging hootchies on halibut jigs.

How To Fish Leadheads

Like many marine species, halibut are opportunistic feeders, meaning they will inhale whatever is edible. However, our experience shows that for optimum success, anglers should match the forage items for the area fished. Biological studies show that predatory species are often prey selective, meaning if crabs are the predominant item in an area, and halibut have been feeding on them, and the crabs have hit a sweet tooth, halibut will continue to search out crabs. Knowing such food items are tasty, they are not as cautious when taking a crab-colored lure as they might be when mouthing an uncommon bait. Even though this is generally an exception rather than a rule, too many times we have used fluorescent orange jigs bounced along the bottom (many crabs are orange) and outfished anglers using herring by 4 to 1.

Structure also serves a purpose in attracting and holding the major components of a food chain. Crabs attract juvenile cod and pollock, which attract halibut. Structure also creates rip currents, which dislodge and disorient baitfish from their hiding or holding areas, making them susceptible to feeding halibut.

Jig And Bait

In my underwater observations of fish, I've noticed that swarms of small fish zip around a bait. The smaller fish are more agile, maneuverable, and faster than the larger fish attracted to the feeding frenzy. Often, these larger fish hold a short distance away and are hesitant about moving in. At other times, a big fish charges in, and the baitfish scatter. Simply put, drop down a small lure, and you'll hook small fish all day. Drop down a huge lure, and the smaller fish will bite and chew at the bait/lure, not making much headway. This is the cue for big halibut to charge in and grab the larger bait. And believe me, they will. Even if they are not in the area, large halibut can sense the frenzied movements of smaller fish trying to bite away tiny mouthfuls of a large bait. While a portion of the bait may be gone before that barn-door arrives, there's generally enough leftover for the halibut to charge in and engulf the bait and jig.

Therefore, if you want to catch big halibut, fish that exceed 100, 200 or 300 pounds, increase your jig's effectiveness by adding anything from a whole herring to a two-pound belly slab of cod.

Herring Teaser

Herring is the mainstay of the commercial and sport charter fleet for one reason: it's a cheap, readily available bait, and it is effective. But you can always make a good herring better. Here's how:

Fill a hypodermic needle with herring oil or some other type of baitfish oil. Take a partially thawed herring and inject the oil into six different locations along the length of the body cavity. Although an injection into a single location is sufficient to fill the body cavity, I favor multiple injections that allow the oil to ooze out, and create a powerful scent field.

Unlike topical scents that wash off quickly, injecting scent into a herring is similar to time-released medication: it delivers the goods slowly and steadily over a long period of time. Chuck Crabaugh showed me this "injection process" years ago, and judging by the thousands of pounds of halibut he catches each year using this refinement, I realized this blue-ribbon method not only attracts halibut from long distances, but also gets them to hang on once they have mouthed the bait.

Crabaugh uses partially frozen herring because it stays on the hook longer than thawed herring, and seeps the oil at a slower

You can easily create a powerful scent field that is faster and more effective than fields created by unmodified baits. With a hypodermic needle, inject a herring with fish attractant or herring oil, filling the body cavity in several areas. The oil will slowly ooze out of the fish over a prolonged period of time, drawing in halibut from all directions.

rate. Buy the herring oil from commercial fishing dealers, or from some sporting goods stores. Buy the gallon-sized containers, and if you can't find herring oil, other baitfish oil will still work better than no oil at all.

Walking A Leadhead

Walking a leadhead is a technique used when tidal currents are too strong for the jig to stay on the bottom. The current lifts the jig, planing it in the current and out of the halibut strike zone. Many anglers stop fishing during this time because walking a jig requires finesse and attention to detail. Most jigging neophytes hang up frequently until they learn the nuances of this technique, so take extra jigheads the first few trips. There's not a better way to catch big halibut when your fatigued angling buddies have decided to take a break until the next slack tide. This means more room on the boat, and your choice of fishing locations.

Walking a leadhead should be done slowly, with the rod tip pointed down at all times. Strikes usually occur when the jig is falling or as it starts to rise.

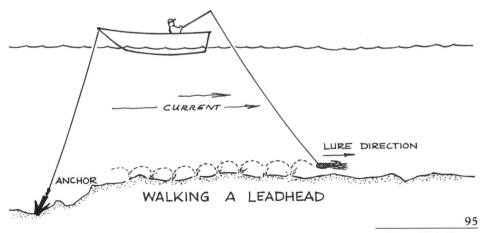

WALKING A LEADHEAD

I remember walking the jig on an outgoing tide near Seldovia. I had impaled a whole herring on my eight-ounce Sebastes jig, and was bottom bouncing it out with the current. With my finger on free-spool, I'd "tap-tap" the jig on bottom, using my rod tip. If upon lowering the rod tip, the jig didn't hit bottom, I'd free-spool some line out slowly and raise the rod tip to near vertical until I'd feel bottom, and again begin walking the jig. During this process, I'd never allow the line to go slack, as a halibut can strike at any time. When you have 80 to 100 yards of line out, plus 120 feet down, a tight line is imperative for consistent hookups.

About 100 yards out, the jig "disappeared" on a drop. It didn't hit bottom when it was supposed to, a sure indication of a take. I set the hook, and 30 minutes later, had an 89-pound halibut on the deck. No record-book halibut, but enough to convince me this technique worked, especially since everyone else was in the cabin, taking a break because the tidal currents were too strong to fish.

My graduation day with this technique came several years later, when fishing with Chuck Crabaugh of Cie Jae Ocean Charters. I used a 24-ounce jig and three-pound, 14-inch strip of cod and by walking the jig, landed two, 100-pound fish, and lost a few more because I wore out before the fish did.

This brings us to my preferred big bait rig for halibut: belly meat or fillets.

Belly Meat Jigs

The belly meat from cod or other bottomfish is a superior bait to use for big halibut. A belly strip/jig combo provides the meat a big halibut is hungry for, and exhibits a flipping, swimming action only a heavy leadhead can help provide. It has natural scent, oozes fresh oils and blood, all advantages over cut or old bait. I've used belly meat on charter boats, with anglers on either side of me fishing herring or chunk bait, and experienced consistent and regular strikes. On one trip, I was having so much fun I stopped fishing when the catcalls got too loud, and my "buddies" threatened to toss me overboard if I didn't switch locations. I sheepishly journeyed to the bow of the boat, where no one was catching fish, and proceeded to hook two more before I voluntarily stopped fishing for the day, for fear they would carry out their threats.

A leadhead with a big bait is extremely effective down to 180 feet. Deeper water requires a thorough knowledge of aggressive hook-setting techniques to compensate for the large

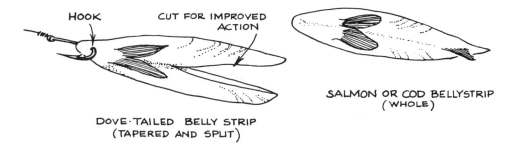

HOOK

CUT FOR IMPROVED ACTION

SALMON OR COD BELLYSTRIP
(WHOLE)

DOVE-TAILED BELLY STRIP
(TAPERED AND SPLIT)

jig, hefty bait and line stretch. To envision why it becomes increasingly difficult to set the hook properly with a rig of this size at depths of 250 or 300 feet, imagine a 14-inch pollock fillet, three inches wide. Now roll it up. It takes both hands to hold it, doesn't it? Now in the center of that, place a 24-ounce HOOKLESS jig and hootchie tail. Hang onto it. Now have a friend take your halibut rod, clip on the main line to the hookless jig, and walk back 300 feet. Squeeze the bait and jig into one jumbled ball, and hold on as tight as you can, as if you were squeezing the life out of it. Now have your friend attempt to set the hook, or try to pull the jighead out of your hand to imitate setting the hook. It doesn't budge very far, does it?

If you're inexperienced in halibut and deepwater jig fishing, you're better off fishing extreme depths with large baits on a slip-sinker rig and circle hooks, where a powerhouse hookset is not required.

For best hook-setting success in deep water, use jig and slab baits only with new technology rods, reels and line, or if using Dacron or monofilament line, restrict jigs and slab baits to shallow to medium-depth waters.

The proper way of carving a salmon or cod belly strip. For better action, dove-tail the belly strip and taper each tail with a knife.

When using large fillets or belly strips from salmon or bottomfish, you have many options on how to prepare them for a leadhead. Here are some of the most popular among halibut anglers.

Tapered

Carved

Split Tail

Fillet

Skin Strips

Always use as small a jig as possible to get the bait down to the bottom. When you feel a take, set the hook if you have a stinger hook, otherwise, you'll need to allow the halibut to ingest and chew a big bait before setting the hook. This technique works better on smaller jigheads like the eight and 10-ounce models. The fish won't be bothered by the weight or hardness of the leadhead, as halibut regularly consume hard-shelled items like crab. Because of their weight, the 24 and 32-ounce versions generally require an immediate hookset.

When using any jig, you'll eventually experience a worse-case scenario where the halibut attempts to cover the bait, a behavior that is used to incapacitate the baitfish and hide it from other halibut. From an angling standpoint, it's impossible to differentiate between a take and a halibut lying on your bait. You must set the hook, and oftentimes it is into the side of the fish. If it's a hundred-plus-pounder, expect an arm-wrenching battle that can last an hour or more!

If a fish strikes and you fail to hook the fish, allow the jig to drop back to the bottom, and dance it erratically in place. You want to convince the halibut that is circling back around that the bait is crippled. This means you twitch, jump and hop that bait all around, imitating a fish that can't maintain its equilibrium.

With your rod tip down, ready yourself for the hookset. Many anglers miss fish because they don't use the full arc of a hookset to generate seven or more foot pounds of energy to bury the barb.

Watch anglers on a halibut charter. Most hold their rods at a 45-degree angle, because this is the laziest and most comfortable way to jig for halibut. If they receive a strike with the rod tip at this or greater angle, they are only able to generate two foot-pounds or less of hook-setting force, which is barely enough to poke your finger into a tub of soft margarine. I assure you my friends, a halibut's jaw is much more resilient.

When you feel that "tap-tap", and your rod tip is already pointing down toward the fish, set the hook immediately. If your rod is horizontal or higher, lower the rod tip while reeling in slack. This is a lightning fast, fluid motion. With your rod tip now pointing toward the water, snap the rod upwards and hold it there. Let the initial surge of the fish help bury the hook. Some anglers prefer to set the hook a second time, which is oftentimes recommended when fishing deepwater with Dacron or mono lines.

After a while, you'll learn to fish your jig with your rod tip pointing down at all times, swimming the jig along bottom by using a variety of sideways and vibrating rod tip movements and quick hops that keep you 100 percent ready for that strike.

In summary: Experiment. Jigging is hard work. Rather than fish incessantly, take a break, get a drink, refresh, and resume jigging. You'll lose fish if you stay out there till your arm is numb and you're falling asleep on your feet. Pace yourself and you'll be ready when that barn-door strikes.

Basic Jigging Technique

I prefer to fish a leadhead in an irregular pattern: I use one to two-foot jumps off the bottom, followed by a few seconds to allow the lure to flutter back. Remember, halibut will invariably strike an artificial while it's settling, or before you snap it off bottom, so keep a tight line at all times. And unlike bait fishing, there is no mistaking a halibut engulfing a leadhead. This is one of the main reasons I favor this type of fishing so much. The strike can best be described as a hard "chomp". The angler's response should be a brutal hookset. And if the fish is 100 pounds or larger, it's best to have a good brace against the railing as the fish will definitely yank back.

HOT TIP

Be The First To Hook Up

When using a jig on a charter boat, rather than drop it straight below the boat, toss it out away from the boat, allowing it to free-spool to bottom. Slowly swim the jig back to the boat. A fish following the scent pattern will see your jig first, giving you first hookup, where the halibut would otherwise "run the gauntlet" of rigs below the boat.

How To Create An Effective Slab Bait For Jigs

1. Using a jig tipped with herring, catch several cod or pollock. Fillet the sides and belly into three sections. You'll want to end up with the two side fillets, and a tapered section of belly meat.

2. Trim the fillet two to three inches wide and 12 to 14 inches long. Leave the skin attached. On the skin side, insert an eighth-inch incision about an inch from the shoulder area of the fillet. This is for the jig hook. Round the front corners to streamline. If you're using a stinger hook, insert it about

10 inches from the front hook. The stinger should ride hook up. Take a knife and create a four-inch split in the tail, for added appeal. Impale the fillet skin-side down onto the jig, via the incision. Cut shallow, diagonal cuts into the skin to release fright pheromones and additional scent. Scent with herring oil if the fillets are more than several hours old.

3. Fish in a slow jigging manner during slack tide, and walk the jig in current flows.

4. Always use bait when halibut are finicky toward lures or standard jigs; in murky water, when fish feed more on smell than sight; when water temperatures are colder in deeper holes and drop-offs, and when fish are feeding with less vigor.

Here's another tip passed on to me by sportfish biologist Durand Cook: He believes the white belly skin of halibut is extremely effective when fished as a trailer or as an added attractor with bait. I've tried it, and agree. It equals the more expensive pork rind I have used in the past. Best of all, it's free. Freeze your skins after a day's fishing, and save them for future trips.

Is It Important To Match Lure Size To Local Prey?

Can't decide what size leadhead, fly, metal jig or bait to use for that trophy halibut? Oftentimes, the right lure depends on two criteria: what the halibut prefer and the availability of that prey.

For instance, halibut feeding on pollock might ignore a crab-imitating leadhead, even though two weeks prior, halibut were in the shallows gorging on crab. Pollock are the most abundant food item available at the time, and fish are concentrating on this food form at the exclusion of all others. We've all experienced this response to some extent in all species of sportfish, freshwater and salt.

Prey morphology can have a strong influence on predator preference. For instance, fish often refuse a pattern that is dressed too heavily or is a tad longer than the real thing. In other words, while some species of saltwater fish ignore unusually shaped prey, or patterns that are dressed too heavily or a tad longer than the real thing, halibut are generally not as finicky over size, movement and shape of the prey. Numerous biologists have found that prey motion is the primary factor involved in the detection of prey by predators. In one study, Protasov concluded that prey movement and size influence fish to strike, and prey color and shape are of secondary importance.

How to Catch
Trophy Halibut

Studies done by Main (1985) support these conclusions.

When fishing, remember that visibility of prey is an important factor to consider, especially in low light situations where halibut are found. Take into consideration the environment: Is it weed-filled? Clouded with plankton bloom? Glacial turbidity? What about light penetration? The amount of light reaching a jig/hootchie in 40 feet of clear saltwater is far greater than the few rays that make it down to 300 feet in the silted waters of Glacier Bay.

Realizing that colors change as depth increases, success depends on reviewing the range of depths fished, and matching the color that is best suited for that depth. Remember, action means little if the fish cannot see the fly or lure. Add scent and jig aggressively to produce underwater sounds to compensate for reduced visibility. Halibut regularly home in on the "noise" created by the lure.

Light Up Your Leadhead

When fishing deepwater shelves, at night, or on cloudy days with poor light penetration into the depths, you will enhance your success rate by fishing glow-in-the-dark leadheads. But a word of caution. Shop carefully.

Many anglers buy fluorescent hootchies, thinking they will glow in the dark. An explanation of phosphorescence, luminescence and fluorescence will help you buy and use the right colors for conditions you'll face on the open water.

Fluorescence, phosphorescence and luminescence are not interchangeable. Each describes a different set of chemical and physical properties that, when used properly, can make fish catching a possibility rather than a dream.

Fluorescent lures and flies are the mainstay of the Alaska halibut angler's arsenal. Ultraviolet light activates a fluorescent color and intensifies it, making it more visible than standard colors. Fluorescent lures or flies work best in medium to deep water jigging, in glacially silted bays and inlets and when tidal rips produce turbid conditions. However, these colors lose their visibility when the light level drops below a certain, measurable factor.

In extremely low light conditions, or at night, it's necessary to use a lure that is phosphorescent, or one that "glows in the dark" after being charged with a beam of light, either from a flashlight or car headlight. Light is emitted because the molecules in the paint, dye or plastic are put into an excited, unstable molecular state by a beam of light, and spontaneously

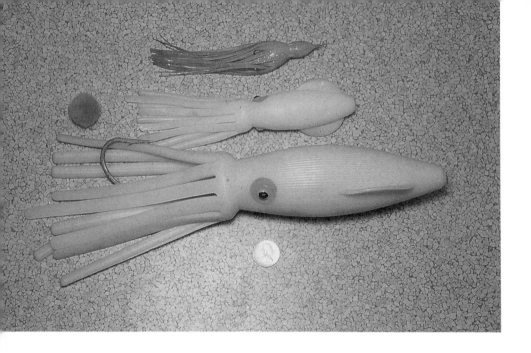

For extreme deepwater fishing, the B-2 Triple-Glow squid is a favorite among trophy halibut anglers. The lure comes either weighted or unweighted and can be trolled, jigged or drifted. A single flash from a camera strobe activates this lure for optimum visibility at extreme depths.

emit light without heat for longer than ten to the minus eight seconds.

I've found phosphorescent lures to be effective when night fishing for halibut or when jigging in deep holes or off the Continental Shelf. Halibut fishing often dies off in dark, overcast days in late afternoon or evening because fish can't see the lure. A phosphorescent fly or lure creates a suitable illusion and prompts the fish to strike. I've personally caught halibut on phosphorescent hootchies when action has died off for all other anglers using standard bait and rigs.

The term luminescent is one that incorporates both fluorescence and phosphorescence, and is a recent newcomer into the fishing lure industry. The introduction of American Cyanamid's Cyalume sticks have provided even more reason to fish deep water, and return the next morning with fish stories to tell.

Anyone who scuba dives at night knows how visible the Cyalume sticks are. In halibut fishing, I strap them onto the main body of a jig or bait with rubberbands. People think I'm crazy at first, but when I start catching big halibut, I can sell my remaining Cyalume supply at a premium.

To enhance the stick (use those the size of your index finger for best results) band it to the shank of a jig that is surrounded with a clear or translucent Crystal Hair. The hair will act as optical fibers and "hold" the glow, increasing the jig's visibility. Again, this rig works best in low-light, deep water or at night. Forget daytime applications.

How to Catch
Trophy Halibut

In closing, there are many more applications and techniques for catching halibut on jigs that would take several volumes to explain. But you have the creme de la creme of the best rigs and techniques we've found in our decades of halibut fishing. Modify and adapt them to your own waters, with your own ideas, and write us with your success stories. Jig fishermen always love to share ideas, and we may use your tip in the revised edition of this book.

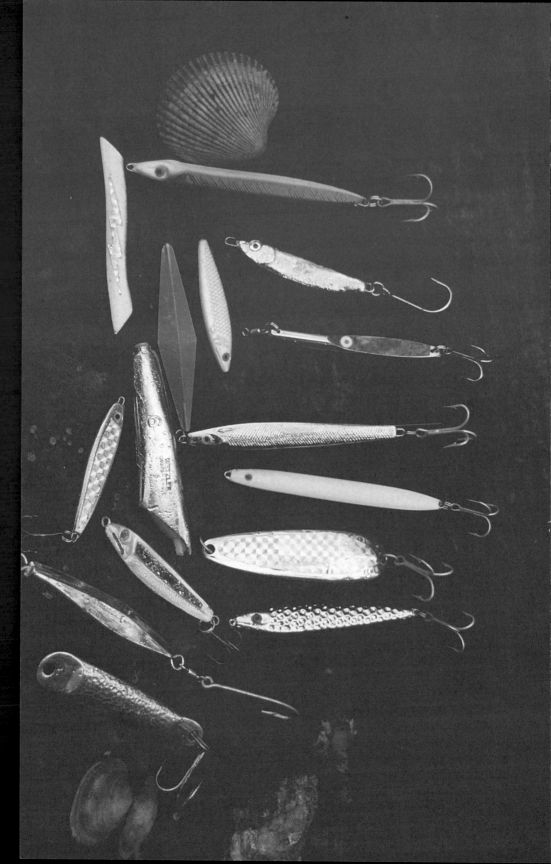

CHAPTER 7

Heavy-Metal Halibut

Many experienced halibut anglers, if forced to use only one fishing method for all situations, would choose vertical jigging with metal, slab-type jigs. Their decision would certainly be justifiable, because these metallic offerings account for more than their share of the halibut caught along the Pacific Northwest coast and its various inland waterways every year. Just as Northwest salmon anglers began to discover in the late-seventies and early eighties, a well-fished metal jig will attract a wide range of marine sport fish, including halibut of all sizes.

A metal jig catches halibut for one very simple reason: big fish eat little fish, and these flashy slabs of metal imitate the herring, candlefish, anchovies and other baitfish on which Pacific halibut and other trophy saltwater fish feed.

Some metal jigs look a lot more like real baitfish than others, at least to we humans whose intelligence is arguably greater than that of our intended piscatorial victims. Jigs such as the Crippled Herring, Point Wilson Dart and Deep Stinger owe at least some of their popularity among halibut anglers to the fact that they look almost exactly like the real thing.

Halibut, however, don't seem to be quite so choosy about the phony baitfish we bounce in front of their noses. If it's the approximate size and shape of the real thing, it's likely to be mistaken for an easy meal by a hungry halibut, which tends to make its decision to strike without even bothering to look closer for artificial eyes, prism tape or a multi-tone paint job that precisely imitates the coloration of a real herring, anchovy or candlefish. That explains why the home-made pipe jig manufactured from a foot of copper tubing will often fool halibut just as well as the $5 store-bought model that comes

These are just some of the many metal, slab-type jigs available to Northwest halibut anglers. Manufactured in a wide range of sizes from a fraction of an ounce to several pounds, there's one for almost any halibut fishing situation.

from the tackle shop looking so real that we expect to see it wiggle.

Metal jigs may take halibut under almost any circumstances, but they are perhaps most valuable to the halibut angler fishing over deep water. Some of the Northwest's best halibut fishing is found at depths of 200 to 400 feet or more, and fishing bait at those monstrous depths can be an exercise in total frustration and wasted energy. Every missed strike presents a dilemma: do you reel in and check it or not? Murphy's Law dictates that if you spend 15 minutes cranking your gear up, the bait will be just fine. If, on the other hand, you choose to let it soak, chances are good you'll be fishing with bare hooks the next hour or two.

Fishing with a jig, though, when you miss a strike at 300 feet, you simply keep on jigging, not wasting any time or effort reeling in to check the results of the missed opportunity.

Deep-water halibut fishing with bait can drive you crazy and wear you out, while fishing metal jigs at great depths will only wear you out. The difference is that the bait fisherman may spend much of the day cranking gear up and down to check his bait, while the jigger puts all his energy into fishing and playing fish.

As their names imply, pipe jigs and all the slab-type metal jigs must be jigged in order to work. The history of halibut angling includes many accounts of fish being caught on lifeless jigs that were just hanging there, but if you take the easy-chair approach to jigging, your odds of success will be greatly reduced. Most metal jigs have little or no built-in action of their own, but when moved through the water they come to life. It's the angler's job to give these hunks of metal their life-like action.

The key to successful jigging, however, is to breathe life into the jig without sending it into hyper-mode. Some anglers put too much effort into jigging for halibut, lifting and dropping the jig five or six feet at a time and effectively pulling the lure away from potential customers. Actively feeding halibut might chase a jig that far, but your average Pacific halibut isn't always so energetic or so persistent. Pull the lure away from it a time or two and it will usually lose interest.

The most productive jigging action is one that keeps the lure bouncing bottom at fairly regular intervals and never rising more than a couple of feet at a time. A two-foot "jump" off bottom is enough to draw attention from nearby halibut while giving the jig a chance to flatten out into the horizontal position and flutter downward.

JIGGING OFF SHELVES AND DEEP DROPOFFS

Jigging with short strokes and bouncing bottom regularly ensures that your lure is always "working" and is always within the halibut's strike zone.

Achieving that not-too-drastic, not-too-subtle jigging action with a metal jig isn't always an easy task, since halibut fishing conditions are not constant. For example, fishing a heavy jig in deep water with monofilament line (which isn't recommended in the first place) will require an angler to make long sweeps of the rod in order to move the jig only a few inches.

At the other extreme, an angler fishing a light jig on braided line in only 50 feet of water may move the lure great distances up and down with only moderate rod strokes. Most halibut fishing is done under circumstances that fall somewhere between these two extremes, but you should keep them in mind when adapting your jigging stroke to your day-to-day jigging situation.

Metal jigs have achieved such great popularity that an angler can find a size, style and color for virtually every halibut-fishing situation, from under an ounce to several pounds, fast-sinker to slow-sinker, black to white and every shade in-between.

The right size jig is the one that will allow you to reach bottom easily without staying there permanently. Depth, wind and current speed and line diameter are all factors in determining the right size for the job, but the best advice is to use the lightest jig that will still reach the depth you're trying to fish. If you can get by with a four-ounce jig, don't wear yourself out and increase the odds of hanging up and losing a lure by continuing to fish with an eight-ouncer. Jigging all day is hard

Halibut are almost always found on shelves adjacent to deepwater drop-offs. Work a metal jig in a fluttering, erratic manner on an outgoing or slack tide for best results.

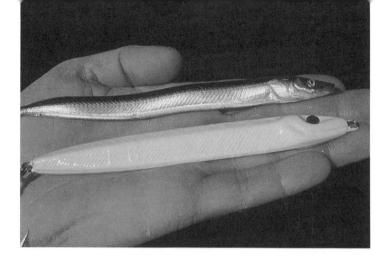

Halibut hit metal jigs for one very obvious reason: These little slabs of metal closely imitate the herring, candlefish, anchovies and other small baitfish on which halibut often feed. If this Terminator jig looks like a candlefish to us, it's easy to understand why a hungry halibut might mistake it for an easy meal.

enough work without using an extra-heavy jig when you don't need it. Save the heavier lures for some other day; there will no doubt come a time when they're needed.

One such time is when a small jig is too lightweight for the water conditions. Vertical jigging is supposed to be just that, vertical, and the flatter the line angle into the water, the less effective this technique becomes. Yo-yoing a metal jig at a 45-degree angle doesn't allow you to throw any slack in the line when you drop the rod tip, so the jig remains in pretty much the same vertical position as it's lifted and dropped through the water column. A metal jig is most enticing—and most strikes occur—when the lure is horizontal and wobbling toward bottom on a slack line, and the more vertical the line angle, the easier it is to achieve that horizontal lure position when you quickly drop the rod tip.

Therefore, when fishing strong currents or on days when the wind is moving the boat too fast, you may have to go to heavier jigs to fish effectively. The alternatives are to motor into the current or wind to keep the lines straight down, cast slightly down-current when you drop the lure to the bottom, or, if all else fails, fish bait or some other offering during those times of heavy water movement or moderate winds.

We haven't yet talked about another important factor that may determine what size metal jig to use on a given day. If halibut are feeding on a particular baitfish species, they just might not show any interest in a jig that's vastly different from the forage fish upon which they're feeding. Fly fishermen call it "matching the hatch," and there are certainly times when it applies to halibut fishing. Co-author Chris Batin talks about how to match leadheads to prey in the previous chapter. Much of the same holds true with metal jigs, with a few minor, yet important variations.

If the big flatties are gorging on candlefish atop Washington's Hein Bank, for example, and you're having no luck jigging a big, flat, five-ounce Krocodile, try a 4½-ounce Deep Stinger or a Point Wilson Dart in the candlefish style and you may be in business. If you suspect (or know) that the halibut are feeding on big herring, go with the Luhr Jensen Crippled Herring or some other jig that closely resembles that baitfish. Precise matching of the local baitfish isn't always necessary for successful halibut fishing, but you're better off carrying a wide selection and experimenting from time to time. Opening the stomach of the day's first halibut might provide a key to which jig in your tackle box is going to produce best that day.

Some metal jigs come from the package equipped with single hooks, some with trebles, but in most cases you can change hooks to suit your individual preference. Many halibut anglers feel that a large single hook holds better in a fish's jaw than a treble, especially when two or three of the treble's hook points are stuck in various parts of a halibut's mouth, providing the opportunity to use leverage and either work the hooks loose or bend them open.

A single hook is also less likely to hang on the bottom if you happen to be fishing over unusually rugged structure, and it could certainly be argued that in situations where many small halibut are being caught and released, you'll do less damage in removing a single hook than you'll do with trebles.

A single hook, on the other hand, may slip through a halibut's lips without making solid contact on the hookset, resulting in almost certain missed opportunities now and then.

Whatever the number of hook points and whatever the hook size, though, keep them needle-sharp. A big halibut has a tough, hard mouth, and you won't sink a dull hook far enough to do you any good. Carry a good hook hone on every halibut trip, and use it often.

Halibut—and most other fish—usually take a jig on the drop, as it's fluttering horizontally through the water. The angler usually doesn't feel the strike until he or she lifts the rod to begin the upward portion of the jigging motion. There is a short delay in response time when it comes to setting the hook, and it's important to act quickly to try to make up that lost time. Reel down quickly, and when you feel solid tension, come up with a hard hook-set. If you're fishing deep water or using stretchy monofilament line, reel down a second time and set the hook again. If you delay, or don't firmly set the hooks in those first couple of seconds, your odds of getting a jig-hooked halibut to the boat are greatly diminished.

Pacific halibut, like other flatfish species, don't always take baits or lures with their mouths, and the angler who fishes metal jigs regularly is likely to take notice of this little quirk sooner than other anglers. The halibut's habit of pouncing on an intended prey species and simply lying atop it is well-documented, and the constant up-and-down movement of a jig tends to produce a surprisingly high percentage of "belly-hooked" halibut. Jigs with treble hooks, as you might guess, are especially likely to stick in the underside of one of these "sitters." The resulting battle with a belly-hooked halibut is one you won't soon forget, especially if the fish is a large one.

Some of the most popular metal jigs for halibut are produced in the Pacific Northwest and are readily available throughout the region. Some favorites from this part of the country include the Crippled Herring, Deep Stinger and Krocodile, all made by Luhr Jensen & Sons of Hood River, Oregon; Point Wilson Darts in both anchovy and candlefish styles and the Metzler Mooch-A-Jig, all three of which were developed on Washington's Strait of Juan de Fuca; and the Zzinger, which is manufactured by the same British Columbia company that gave us the popular Buzz Bomb jig.

Metal jigs made in other parts of the country—and other parts of the world, for that matter—have also proven their effectiveness on Pacific halibut. The Bridgeport Diamond Jig, Vi-Ke and Slab Jig, all from Bead Tackle Company in Monroe, Connecticut, are good examples, as is the Hopkins No-EQL from Virginia and the Norwegian-made Stingsilda.

Rather than trying to list and describe all the dozens of manufactured metal jigs available to halibut anglers, let's just say there is at least one for virtually every halibut-fishing situation you may encounter, and you would be wise to familiarize yourself with the many possibilities. Some have a higher weight-to-size ratio and therefore sink very fast, making them good choices for deep-water situations. Others are thinner, lighter and livelier, making them better suited to shallow-water fishing or especially useful when the halibut are less-active and need a little extra wiggle to coax them into striking. Some brands of jigs are available in only one or two colors, others in a wide range of shades and finishes. A few are manufactured only in two or three sizes, while others are available in weights from fractions of an ounce to a couple of pounds. Get to know what's on the market and what jigs work best for your particular halibut-fishing situations.

The Poor Man's Guide To
Making Your Own Metal Jigs

While extremely effective, these metal jigs aren't cheap, so some halibut anglers choose to save money by making their own. Most common—and likely the oldest—of the home-made metal jigs is called a pipe jig, and there are times when it will catch Pacific halibut with the best of them. There are several variations on the basic theme, but the standard pipe jig is simply a length of small-diameter metal tubing or pipe filled with lead. One way to create a pipe jig is to first cut the tubing or pipe into lengths of six to 20 inches, depending on how heavy a jig you want, and insert a strand of stiff wire through the pipe so that it extends about two inches beyond both ends. Fill the pipe with molten lead, all the while keeping the strand of wire as close to the center as possible. When the lead hardens and cools, you can twist a swivel into the wire at one end and a large treble hook into the other end.

Another jig-making strategy is to fill the pipe only about half-full of lead, let it harden, then hang the already-formed wire loop in the open end before filling the top half with lead.

Putting a bend or hook in the bottom of the wire holds it in place after the rest of the lead is poured around it. After all the lead hardens and cools, drill two holes through the pipe—one near the bottom and one about half-way up—and use a cotter pin in each hole to hold a treble hook. Run the cotter pins through the pipe in opposite directions, so that there's a hook on each side of the finished product.

Depending on what you have lying around the garage or shop in the way of wire, wheel weights, copper tubing, bicycle handlebars, old metal furniture and other "parts," you might be able to manufacture a summer-long supply of three-ounce to three-pound pipe jigs for only a few dollars. Hooks, swivels and cotter pins may be the only items you'll have to buy.

What colors and finishes work best for halibut? Many veteran halibut anglers prefer white, and chrome is probably a close second. It's easy to understand why chrome works, since it reflects sunlight and tends to sparkle and shine the way we think a baitfish does, but that light-reflecting quality is only an advantage when there is some light to be reflected, and there isn't much light when you get into deep-water halibut-fishing situations. It might be good advice to recommend chrome for shallow-water fishing and white for deeper water. White "holds" its "shade" and therefore shows up better in the depths than any other color. To paraphrase Henry Ford,

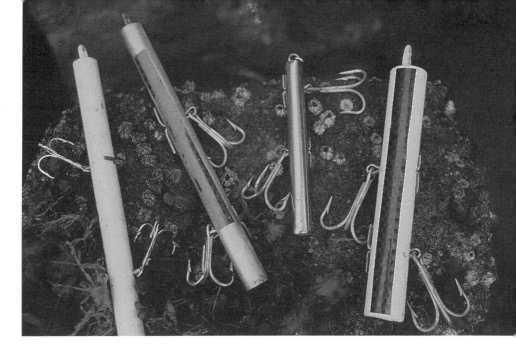

the deeper your favorite halibut spot, the better off you might be choosing a metal jig in any color at all, as long as it's white!

Some anglers tie their main line, whether monofilament or braid, directly to their metal jigs. Doing so has one definite advantage, in that it's a one-knot system. Every knot connecting lines and leaders to swivels, snaps and lures is a potential weak spot in a fishing system, so the line-directly-to-jig approach eliminates all but one potential weak link.

The system does, however, have some drawbacks. For one thing, there are times when it's actually advantageous to have a weak spot somewhere between your rod tip and your lure. Without it, bottom hang-ups can result in several hundred feet of lost line.

When that happens, you may find yourself sitting in a boat with an empty reel while your fishing buddies are busy catching halibut. If you're using expensive Spiderwire or one of the other new-age braided lines, losing a reelful is like tossing several $10 bills overboard.

Tying your jig directly to your main line also can cost you some fish, especially if you like to fish light line for halibut. Although most jig-caught fish are hooked near the outside of the mouth, a big flatty may inhale your jig completely, and when a light line comes into contact with those jagged teeth, it's over in a hurry.

That's why it's a good idea to use a stout "shock leader" when jigging for halibut. A foot or two of large-diameter monofilament or braided wire greatly reduces "chew-offs" and

Pipe jigs are easy to make, and you may have most of the materials on hand. Using tubing and pipe of several diameters and cutting it to various lengths, you can fashion pipe jigs suited to any depth you may want to fish. It's also easy to add paint or prism tape to achieve any finish you want on the final product.

gives an angler some versatility he otherwise wouldn't have. Berkley Big Game in 50- or 60-pound test is a good choice, but you can get by with any of the premium-grade monos in that approximate test range, or heavier if you prefer. Connect the leader to the main line with a quality McMahon or ball-bearing swivel, and use a strong snap at the bottom end of the leader to accommodate quick lure changes when you need to go heavier, lighter or experiment with colors and jig styles.

If you prefer braided wire to mono leaders, you'll find them available in various lengths, pre-tied with snaps and swivels, from Berkley and some other manufacturers, or you can buy the hardware and rig your own any way you want them.

Avoid The Cheapo Swivel

The in-line swivel connecting your line and leader is very important, and it should be the best you can afford. Those cheap, brass swivels selling for a few cents each don't hold up well to saltwater or to a 150-pound halibut, and you don't want to loose that fish of a lifetime to swivel failure. A quality McMahon (barrel) swivel may be adequate for use with most small metal jigs, but some of the more active styles, such as the Metzler Mooch-A-Jig, require a ball-bearing swivel to eliminate line twist; using anything less will be an exercise in twisted line and shattered nerves.

Besides providing a means of connecting line to shock leaders and reducing problems due to twisted lines, swivels give the halibut angler a convenient place to add a second lure, or "teaser," which will be discussed a little later in this chapter.

Tails, Rind And Tape Increase Lure Appeal

As long as you keep it moving, a metal jig will take halibut all by itself. On the other hand, it doesn't hurt to spice up these lures a little. A smooth-sided jig, for example, might be more effective if you add a strip of prism tape to at least one side.

It may or may not impress the fish, but your fellow anglers will certainly notice the improvement! Adding some wiggle to a metal jig, in the form of a plastic grub or strip of pork rind on the hook, can make a great deal of difference, especially if the plastic or pork is a different color than the jig and provides some contrast. Pork rind makes an especially good addition; it's so tough that it will stay on the hook through several halibut battles and still remain appealing to fish. A plastic skirt will do the same thing, whether you add it to the hook or slide it down the leader at the top end so that it drapes over the jig.

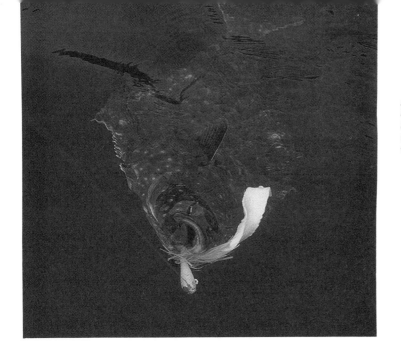

A strip of pork rind or the belly skin of a fresh-caught halibut increases the effectiveness of any leadhead or metal jig.

Sweetening The Jig: A Deep Creek Experience

Adding a touch of the "real thing" to a metal jig can also make a difference in the lure's halibut-catching effectiveness. I learned that lesson quite clearly a few years ago while fishing the depths of Alaska's Cook Inlet with Deep Creek guide Tim Berg. Thirty minutes of bouncing jigs along the bottom had drawn only one strike, and that fish got away unscathed. Berg earlier had suggested that I add a strip of herring to the jig, and when he made that suggestion a second time I agreed to give it a try. Next time I brought the jig up I picked a small herring out of the bait bucket and sliced off a two-inch fillet that included the tail.

The jig bounced bottom twice before something heavy inhaled it and headed off toward Soldotna. Unfortunately for me, another angler in the boat using much heavier line was already playing a good fish, and when our lines crossed I lost my halibut, my jig and about 100 feet of my line.

Ten minutes later, after tying on another jig and adding another herring strip, I was into another halibut, which turned out to be a 40-pound keeper. I added another herring strip to my jig and lowered it to the bottom, where it was quickly grabbed again, but I missed the fish. Out of laziness, I left the jig down and kept working it along the bottom. Twenty minutes later I hadn't had another hit, so I retrieved the lure and found the herring strip was missing. I "re-baited" the jig, hit bottom again, and within a couple of minutes rounded out my limit with a 35-pounder.

Halibut Success Secret

Why didn't I simply go to whole herring and forget about the jigs altogether? Because the people fishing straight bait weren't doing all that well, either. For whatever reason, the halibut that day wanted a meal that had both the life of a bouncing jig and the down-home flavor of a fresh herring. Either of those ingredients, by itself, held relatively little attraction.

A herring strip is only one of the many options available if you're looking to give that metal jig a touch of real smell and flavor. A thin strip of squid or octopus will do the job very well and probably stay on the jig's hook a lot better than herring. A strip of skin from a cod, pollock or another halibut is also a very durable addition to any metal jig, adding both scent and lots of enticing action to the lure. You might even try smearing some of the more durable manufactured scents to your metal jigs. Smelly Jelly, Mike's Glo Scent Gel and similar products are available in a wide range of "flavors" and will adhere to a jig and provide long-lasting scent.

Favorite Metal Jig Rig

That special something you add to your metal jig doesn't have to be attached directly to the lure. In fact, if you add it to the line some distance above the jig, it may pay off even better. Call it a teaser, a dropper lure, or whatever you want, but it can be as simple as an unweighted hook, size 5/0 or larger, tied to a short, stiff dropper leader 18 to 30 inches above the metal jig. I use four to six inches of 60-pound Berkley Big Game, and tie it directly to the in-line swivel connecting my line and leader. The short, stiff leader holds the teaser hook out, away from the swivel, to ensure against tangles that would impair the lure's effectiveness. Keeping the teaser hook away from the main line also keeps the sharp teeth of hooked halibut away from the main line, which can be very important.

Thread a three to six-inch plastic, curl-tail grub or pork rind strip of about the same size onto the bare hook and you have yourself a teaser rig. White is always a good color choice, but you might want to make the teaser lure a different color than your jig, at least until you discover what color is working best that day. If you're fishing deep water with a white jig, try blue or chartreuse, since these cooler colors hold their visibility in the depths, yet offer some color contrast to the primary lure.

Instead of a pork strip or plastic grub, some anglers use a commercially tied "shrimp fly" or even a home-tied streamer

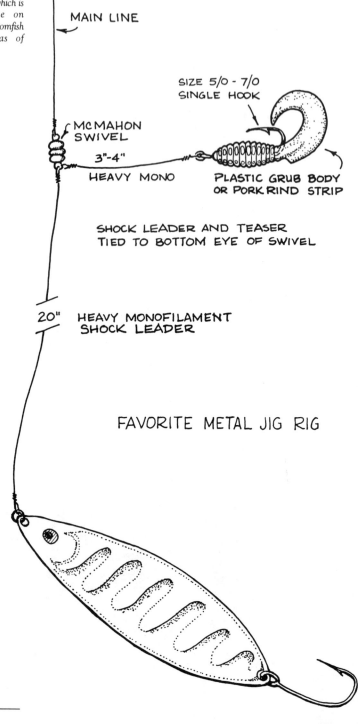

Two-lure teaser rig, which is especially effective on halibut and other bottomfish in deepwater areas of 300-plus feet.

MAIN LINE

SIZE 5/0 - 7/0
SINGLE HOOK

McMAHON
SWIVEL

3"-4"

HEAVY MONO

PLASTIC GRUB BODY
OR PORK RIND STRIP

SHOCK LEADER AND TEASER
TIED TO BOTTOM EYE OF SWIVEL

20"   HEAVY MONOFILAMENT
SHOCK LEADER

FAVORITE METAL JIG RIG

as their teaser, and the halibut don't seem to mind.

Besides offering halibut two choices, the teaser serves an even more important purpose. Wiggling and flashing about two feet above the primary lure, it helps to draw fish in from a distance. Halibut that might not see your jig bouncing along the bottom may spot your teaser rig that's up higher in the water and therefore visible at greater distances over the uneven bottom.

The teaser may also attract cod, pollock, rockfish, greenling and other smaller fish to your rig, and those smaller fish in turn may attract big halibut. If a small Pacific cod should take your teaser and become hooked, it's like placing out a big "OPEN" sign down there at the halibut diner!

At the time of this writing, teasers and other two-lure rigs are legal for halibut fishing in Oregon, Washington and Alaska, but NOT in British Columbia. Provincial regulations are very clear on the subject, stating: "It is illegal to use, on a line, gear designed to catch more than one fish at a time, except when fishing for herring."

Try a metal jig on your next trip for the big flatties. Follow the guidelines in this book, and we promise that you won't be disappointed.

CHAPTER 8

Fly Fishing For Halibut

Looking for one of fly fishing's greatest challenges? Consider the halibut.

Montana trout fishermen will tell you how difficult it can be to coax a wary brown trout from the darkness of an undercut bank to inhale a tiny dry fly tied to the end of a fragile tippet. Florida fly-casters certainly have a right to brag about their accomplishment when they manage to hook and land a high-jumping, 100-pound tarpon on a fly. Likewise, catching a big sailfish or even-bigger marlin with a fly line, fly rod and fly reel is an angling accomplishment of which any angler can be proud.

But all of these fly-fishing trophies spend a good portion of their time near enough of the water's surface that they're within reasonable range of an artificial fly. On the other hand, halibut—and especially the larger Pacific halibut—rarely come near the surface of their own free will. Oh yes, they'll do it from time to time, but it's certainly more the exception than the rule. If your goal in life is to catch a halibut on a dry fly by sight-casting to a surface-feeding fish, you may not live long enough to have even one opportunity.

That's not to say, however, that fly fishing for halibut is a total waste of time. The International Game Fish Association's annual listing of world record fish includes several impressive Pacific halibut and a few not-quite-so-impressive California halibut taken on fly tackle. It certainly can be done, but we're not going to lie and tell you that it's a piece of cake. The fact that the same few names appear in several spots among the fly-rod halibut records in the IGFA record book illustrates the fact that only a few anglers are taking halibut on a fly with any kind of consistency.

Mike Hood is proud of his 83 pound, 12-ounce halibut caught near Gore Point, Alaska. The fish is the current, IGFA world record in the flyfishing category, 16-pound tippet line-class. Photo courtesy Tony Weaver/Mike Hood.

Steve Probasco isn't a record-seeker, but he is a well-known Northwest outdoor writer and lecturer on angling subjects. He is an avid fly fisherman whose line of work and angling abilities have taken him throughout the western United States and Canada in search of freshwater and saltwater fly-fishing trophies. Although best-known for his angling exploits on the West's steelhead streams and trout lakes, Probasco also has coaxed halibut to his creations of fur and feathers, and like other halibut fly fishermen he'll tell you that there are two keys to success.

"You need calm water and you need to find fish within a reasonable distance of the surface," he states bluntly." Just having one or the other won't do it."

"Calm water" to the halibut angler means that combination of slack tide, no current and no wind that allows you to drop a bait or lure straight down and fish it as vertically as possible. It can be an important factor to any halibut angler, using any kind of tackle, but it's an absolute necessity to the fly fisherman. The bait fisherman can add a bigger sinker to keep his offering near the bottom as the wind picks up or the tide begins to move. Likewise, the jigger can go to a heavier jig for moving water. But even the heaviest of fly lines won't sink as fast as a 40-ounce sinker or a 32-ounce metal jig. The line simply catches too much water and has too much resistance, so it won't sink straight down unless conditions are perfect.

"Even when the tide is dead-slack, the slightest breeze can be enough to foul you up when you're trying to get a fly line down in 60 feet of water or more," says Probasco.

Which brings us to the second factor in halibut fly-fishing success: Finding fish within reasonably shallow water.

"I've fished as deep as 90 feet, but it wasn't much fun," he says. "If you can find halibut in 50 or 60 feet of water you're a lot better off, and 40 feet is even that much better."

Finding decent numbers of Pacific halibut in less than 60 feet of water, of course, is within the realm of possibility, especially in some areas of British Columbia and Alaska. Even anglers in Oregon and Washington can find the occasional fish at those depths if they're willing to put in the time. But you must remember that this isn't where halibut spend most of their time, so searching out shallow-water halibut haunts is likely to take up a considerable portion of the fly fisherman's time over the long haul.

Seeking out spots where abundant bait supplies draw fish from deeper water to gorge on the bounty is always a good

How to Catch
Trophy Halibut

strategy for finding halibut in shallow-enough water to reach them with a fly. I would be willing to bet that in the spring, when millions of candlefish dot the bottom of Washington's Hein Bank, there are halibut to be found in water 70 to 90 feet deep. The problem here is that there always seems to be at least some water movement, even on slack tide. What's more, the wind is almost always blowing down the east end of the Strait of Juan de Fuca, making it a tough place for fly fishing about 98 days out of 100.

There are, however, hundreds of other places, some of them more protected from the wind and tidal currents, where large numbers of candlefish, herring and other baitfish congregate in shallow water with some kind of frequency, and these are the kinds of spots the fly fisherman should concentrate much of his effort.

And what about Alaska creek and river mouths, where large numbers of pinks and other salmon often draw hungry halibut during the summer and early fall? Yes, fly fishermen should certainly investigate these spots, since they provide an opportunity to find halibut in water as shallow as 15 feet! (See the section on fishing stream mouths for halibut, page 171, and the Alaska section in this book for additional details.)

While halibut spend most of their time on the bottom, remember that they sometimes move up into the water column, either in search of food or for other reasons. When you can locate these "suspended" bottomfish, obviously, your chances of getting at them with a fly rod may increase substantially. Clouds of baitfish may draw them up, or they may follow hooked halibut toward the surface. Whatever the reason for their ascent, watching for this phenomenon on the screen of your depth sounder or noticing that other anglers are hooking fish as they drop their baits and lures through the water column could be clear signals that halibut are within easy reach of an artificial fly.

Anyone who has done much halibut fishing (or who has read other parts of this book) knows that these big bottom sweepers may be enticed into trying a wide variety of entrees, so if someone tells you that he or she has the sure-fire halibut fly, you can be assured that it's only one of many flies that will do the job. All anglers have a favorite bait or lure that they use most of the time or go to when the fishing gets tough, and fly fishermen are no different from anyone else in that regard. Don't, however, believe that using a particular fly pattern is going to ensure success when all else fails, and never assume that using the "right" fly for halibut is more important than fishing when conditions are right. You can use any size, color and style fly you want when the tide is running hard and have absolutely no chance of hooking fish.

While there are no magic halibut flies, there are certainly some guidelines to consider when you're fishing for the Northwest's biggest saltwater sport fish, a fish with an appetite to match its behemoth proportions. Even a 30-pound halibut can inhale a pink salmon or choke down a decent-size Dungeness crab, so there's no reason to pack a fly box with Fan-Wing Coachman patterns tied on size 10 hooks. Some of the sea lice and other parasites on a halibut's belly are larger than that. Offer them a mouthful—large streamers and the like—so that the fly is big enough to make it worth their effort.

Flyfisher Tony Weaver has helped pioneer flyfishing for halibut in Alaska waters. He has developed a fly tied with Fishair on a 5/0 hook, with the shank wrapped heavily with lead wire. Once the Fishair wing is tied on, he feathers a thin layer of Shoe Goop onto the wing, and when partially dry, imparts a slight bend to it. Once cured, the fly exhibits a darting, rolling action, much like a cut-plug herring. This action helps keep the fly working effectively in deeper water as the boat drifts with the current.

One of Steve Probasco's favorite halibut flies—one that's also effective for lingcod—is a creation of his own that he calls Half a Rabbit. The name comes from the fact that it takes a whole lot of rabbit fur to build one of these full-figured beauties.

First cut four or five thin strips of orange, rust-brown or white fur-on rabbit hide. Tie them in a manner where they extend about six inches beyond the bend of the hook. To these tentacle-like tail strips add some crystal hair or other kinds of tinsel to give the fly a little flash, then wind several more strips of rabbit fur around the hook to give the creature some added bulk. A pair of large, lead eyes tied at the head end completes the fly, adding a realistic touch and giving it a little more weight. Half a Rabbit is usually tied on a heavy-gauge 4/0 or 5/0 hook.

It takes a lot of nerve just to carry a box full of Probasco's favorite halibut fly patterns, but casting one is something you shouldn't ever try at home, at least not without a flack jacket.

Luckily, "casting" as we know it isn't really a priority of the halibut fly fisherman.

"It's really more of a lob than a cast," Probasco admits. The idea, after all, is to get the fly down into the depths as quickly as possible, and the more time it's in the air, the less time it

How to Catch
Trophy Halibut

has to sink.

To get the fly down where it belongs, of course, you need a fast-sinking fly line. Probasco uses a 900-grain, 12-weight fly line that he says sinks like a rock. But he admits that there is a down side to such heavy duty line.

"This is heavy artillery, and you need a concealed weapon permit to fish with it," he jokes.

Scientific Anglers offers a Deep Water Express fly line in weights from 550-grain for 12-weight rods, to 850-weight for 14-weight rods. Many anglers prefer to make their own 25 to 30-foot sinking head with 100 feet of running line. In the minor tidal fluctuations often found in southeast Alaska, Dutch Harbor, and sections of Prince William Sound, you will be able to get by with standard Sci-Anglers Uniform Sink IV and V lines, or even sink-tip lines for salmon or herring-chasing halibut in and around salmon streams. Too heavy a line in shallow water will quickly fray on rocks and barnacles. Take several lines and be prepared for all scenarios.

What you use between that big, honkin' fly and that adults-only fly line is also important. The Pacific halibut is a toothy critter that lives down there where the environment can be rough and nasty. If a 60-pounder inhales your fly clear to the back of its throat, your leader had better be tough or the fight will be a short one. To reduce the chance of "chew-offs," Probasco uses a three-foot length of 40-pound monofilament for tippet material. If you're a record-conscious angler with sights set on a tippet-class IGFA record, you're limited to a maximum of 12 inches on that heavy shock leader. You could, then, fish with an eight-pound tippet and have up to a foot of heavy mono between the end of that tippet and the fly. A shock leader may be of any strength, according to IGFA fly-fishing regulations.

If you're going to cast—or even lob—a 12-weight fly line, of course, you have to use a rod that will handle it. Probasco and other fly fishermen who fish seriously for Pacific halibut commonly use the big fly sticks—equipped with fighting butts—that are typically associated with tarpon and other big-game species. Taking on deep-water fish such as halibut with anything lighter, they agree, is asking for trouble.

According to Tony Weaver, a standard 10 to 12-weight rod is OK, but most of these rods are too soft in the mid-section and not designed for lifting barn-doors. He warns that trying to pump up a big fish from deep water could snap a standard-type salmon rod. He prefers a 13 or 15-weight Mega Rod, which is designed for big fish and has ample strength in the butt section.

As in any saltwater fishing for large fish, picking the right reel is very important. While the trout angler on a shallow stream might get by with almost anything that will hold his fly line and a 100 yards of backing, the halibut fly fisherman has to depend on his reel to work smoothly while the fish is giving and taking line. Probasco's large-capacity Charlton reel holds several hundred yards of 30-pound braided Dacron backing and has a smooth, flawless drag that will hold up to the toughest halibut's fastest run. Co-author Chris Batin prefers his saltwater Alvey 425 SWF or Scientific Angler's System reels for heavy saltwater use.

Techniques

Fishing a fly for halibut will be pretty much the same as fishing bait, with the exception that more work is required of the angler. The skipper can backtroll against the current or into the wind, allowing your line to sink to bottom. This is a must-do boat-handling technique to reach fish in 30 to 60-foot depths. Ideally, pull out that fly rod on calm days at slack tide, where you can expect minimal line drag and halibut coming up off the bottom to feed.

Another technique is to cast in the direction your boat is drifting. Strip out additional line as needed for the weighted fly to sink. Once parallel to the fly, begin your strip. The skipper may want to hold the boat in place, to allow you to slowly work the fly through the depths.

Record-Book Fish

If you're interested in the possibility of setting an IGFA fly-fishing record for halibut, you have a wide range from which to choose. In the mid to upper tippet classes, the current world-records are fish less than 100 pounds, with these records expected to be topped in the months to come. The IGFA record book also lists several fly-caught records in the California halibut division, and it certainly seems that this smaller cousin to the Pacific halibut would be a more likely target of fly fishermen. The California halibut is usually found in much shallower water, where fly anglers can get at it more readily, and where tidal currents and wind don't make it virtually impossible to reach the fish. All the fly-fishing records for California halibut listed in the recent IGFA book came from Baja's Magdalena Bay or California's San Francisco Bay, both of which offer the opportunity to find halibut in only a few feet of water. You wouldn't need a 12-weight fishing system to take halibut from these waters or from any of California's more productive halibut-fishing spots, and you could use fly tackle to reach fish pretty much wherever and whenever anglers could catch them on bait or jigs.

The fact that the record book lists only a few, smallish fly-caught Californias attests to the fact that fly fishing for these fish isn't a snap, but it's certainly possible. If you're sitting around with your fly rod in your hand, and are within driving distance of San Francisco Bay, Santa Monica, even San Diego, you might want to do a little experimenting over the sand flats with a few large streamer patterns.

CHAPTER 9

Choosing The Right Bait: An In-Depth Look At What Halibut Eat

When it's time for halibut to eat, they don't brown bag it; most head for one of the Pacific's all-you-can-eat buffets and become gluttons, while others are more selective, preferring to satiate a sweet tooth for cod or octopus. When faced with the decision of what bait or lure to use, consider the eating habits of these flatfish in the area you'll be fishing. Here are a few examples to help you understand what types and sizes of food halibut prefer:

• According to IPHC surveys, one Pacific halibut caught off the coast of Oregon, "contained all at the same time, a hake, a silver salmon and a red rockfish. Each of these weighed fully 10 pounds, and had been swallowed only a short time before the halibut was caught."

• A sport-caught halibut from near Petersburg, Alaska, weighing 370 pounds contained a freshly eaten octopus weighing 12 pounds, plus the remains of Pacific cod and sculpins.

• One large (six-foot) halibut contained one 28-inch salmon, the remains of crab, fish and octopus and the posterior section of a halibut that measured 16 inches long, 10 inches wide and approximately four-inches thick. The piece of halibut appeared to have been freshly sliced from a medium-sized fish, probably discarded by one of the fishing vessels in the vicinity.

• Halibut have BIG appetites. Mature halibut from 32 to 43 inches long were held in captivity in nine-foot circular tanks for several years. They were fed two to three six-to 10-inch Pacific herring daily plus some supplemental salmon or other fish. These fish ate little or nothing during February and March, and did not resume feeding until May. (Source: IPHC).

Favorite foods of Pacific halibut include octopus, shrimp and herring. Crab, squid, salmon, cod and other bottomfish round out the menu. Halibut tend to be opportunistic in their feeding habits, ingesting whatever forage items are predominant in an area. At times, however, they do show a tendency to search out specific prey at the exclusion of all else.

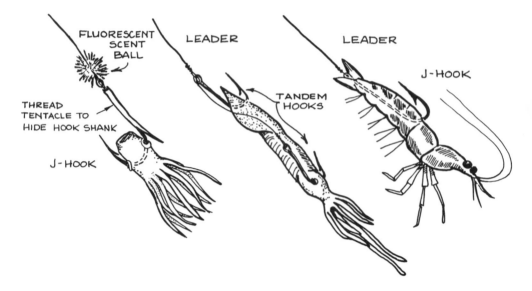

FLUORESCENT SCENT BALL

LEADER

LEADER

J-HOOK

THREAD TENTACLE TO HIDE HOOK SHANK

TANDEM HOOKS

J-HOOK

J-HOOK

Popular bait rigs.

These examples show that halibut are generally opportunistic in their feeding habits. The species does show, on occasion, some selectivity in their feeding habits, especially when halibut have encountered prevalent numbers of sandlance, Tanner crab and shrimp, feeding on these items at the exclusion of all else. By taking time to learn the preferred food items of big halibut, you'll choose the right bait or lure for the various conditions you're likely to face along the Alaska-Pacific Northwest coastline.

For over five decades, the International Pacific Halibut Commission has conducted extensive research on what halibut eat, how much, and why. Here's a synopsis of their findings.

Small halibut feed almost exclusively on small crustaceans, while larger fish prefer larger crustaceans and fish.

A major study entitled *"Pacific Halibut as Predator and Prey"* was published in 1988 by authors E. A. Best and Gilbert St-Pierre. The authors compiled stomach analyses from 2,700 juvenile halibut from the Gulf of Alaska and over 1,300 halibut caught off the coasts of British Columbia and Alaska. The findings are enlightening to any serious angler. They write:

"Novikov gave a detailed breakdown of the percent of halibut prey by species from the eastern, central and northwestern parts of the Bering Sea. He found that halibut under 12 inches long fed primarily on crustaceans, with a preference for shrimp. Larger halibut (three feet and larger) fed to a much greater degree upon fish, with yellowfin sole and walleye pollock as the dominant food items. Halibut less than two feet long in the northwest Bering Sea fed heavily on crustaceans, with hermit crab the primary species. Larger halibut utilized more fish, with walleye pollock the main prey item.

"In the Kodiak Island area, halibut less than a foot fed mainly on shrimp, and those from one to two feet depended less on shrimp and more on pollock and Pacific sandlance. Halibut over two feet utilized walleye pollock and Tanner crab.

"From the stomachs of halibut caught by otter trawls off Kodiak Island during the summer months, clams, shrimp, and hermit crab were the most prevalent food items. In a 1977 study of Cook Inlet, Tanner crab was the primary species observed in halibut stomachs."

Using This Information For Halibut Success

Wherever you fish, learn as much as you can about the predominant food items in the area. In mid May in Cook Inlet, for example, I personally have caught halibut with distended stomachs filled with crab, which are abundant in the food-rich, rocky waters of lower Cook Inlet. As a result, we do best at this time of year with red and orange jigs fished slowly along bottom structure. During the same time frame in western Cook Inlet, however, in waters near David Coray's Silver Salmon Lodge, the mud and sand flats are home to an abundance of cod. Here, as well as off the Continental Shelf, we catch most of our large fish with cod and belly strips. Rule of thumb here is to match the local forage as closely as possible. If you're experiencing no success, or are uncertain as to which forage foods are predominant in the area you are fishing, switch to a large fish bait or leadhead jig.

Empty Or Full?

Not all areas offer optimum forage concentrations, causing halibut to search for food. IPHC studies show that from 1955 to 1981, 1,253 halibut stomachs were examined, and 568, or 45 percent, contained food items. This differs with a May 1983 stomach analysis survey when the stomachs of 178 trawl-caught halibut were examined, and 143, or 80 percent contained food.

When the biomass of halibut is large, as it often is in remote or seldom fished areas, their voracious feeding patterns can have a devastating effect on local prey species. In the absence of prey, the halibut inhale bait, jigs, most anything. This can often be seen during the tidal flows experienced near Unalaska

Island, where halibut can be seen on sonar units shingled on top of each other. This concentration of fish also takes place the first few weeks of the halibut fishing opener near Alaska's Barren Islands, when the shots of .410s and .22 pistols dispatching halibut resembles a 4th of July fireworks celebration.

Some biologists suggest that in areas of high forage, well-fed fish are less likely to ingest a bait, in which case they might exhibit the same tendency as other fish in becoming species-specific and finicky. I recommend catching a fish and taking time to observe any regurgitation on the way up, at boatside or on deck. If it's shrimp, go to a jig covered with or trailing a red or orange hootchie, or go with a slip-sinker bait rig if they're dining on bottomfish.

For Large Halibut Use A Large Bait

In the stomach analysis table listed in the appendix, fishes were the predominant prey observed in the stomachs of large halibut. Octopus was found to be a preferred food item, occurring nearly twice as often as the next most frequently identified species.

In this scenario, it's possible the bottom cover (consisting of rocky structure) was suitable for octopus as well as halibut. Before clipping on a bait or lure, anglers who will fish off an anchor should bounce a lead weight on bottom to determine bottom type and structure. This also applies to anglers making repeated drifts through an area.

When I bounce a jig on bottom, and feel lots of irregularities, I'll go with a tentacled lure like the Batin Halibut Bouncer over a flip-tail or metal jig. The configuration of this jig closely matches a crab or octopus, a prevalent food in this type of area. In and around kelp beds, I'll clip on a herring rig or metal jig because baitfish prefer such cover.

Crab Jigs

In areas that exhibit a sand or mud bottom suited for crabs, stomach analyses of halibut taken from sand or mud bottoms show that crabs were favored over all else.

Don't restrict yourself to matching the crab size here. Many of the crabs I find in halibut stomachs are no larger than the palm of my hand. Terry and I recommend you start off with the lightest jig that gets to the bottom quickly. If you need to fish a 32-ounce jig, don't despair. Halibut do feed on larger crab. Alaska halibut skippers have told me they have seen halibut regurgitate crabs with carapaces up to seven inches wide.

Again, a Halibut Bouncer in the 24-ounce size inched along bottom is your best bet for imitating a crab.

In researching this chapter, I found some interesting reports from the Timbered Islet area, where the stomachs of 37 large halibut containing identifiable food were examined. Fish, especially flatfish, were most prevalent in the stomachs sampled. It is possible that small flatfish were attracted to the bait and may have been taken by larger fish, which in turn took a baited hook. Biologists say, however, that there is no clear evidence that this indeed had been the case. Over 20 percent, however, of the identifiable food items in the halibut stomachs from this area was halibut. This is yet another reason to use a large jig or bait.

If you're hooking lots of small fish, go to a larger jig or bait with fish trailer and cast away from the boat, and jig in slowly. Chances are your lure will be inhaled by a larger halibut waiting to ambush an unsuspecting feeder. It has worked for us.

Small crabs, like this one regurgitated by a 112-pound halibut, are abundant in shallow bays along the Pacific Northwest coastline. When a halibut is landed, examine it closely. A stomach that feels like it's filled with walnuts reveals a crab diet. For best results, clip on an orange crab jig, like the Halibut Bouncer mentioned in the leadhead chapter.

Salmon As Prey

While the reduction in salmon numbers returning to coastal waters in the lower Pacific Northwest may not attract the numbers of halibut as in years past, many areas of Alaska still receive huge returns of salmon. Anglers fishing major river systems during the in-migration of fish—as well as during the exodus of dead and spawned out salmon into intertidal areas—find plenty of halibut action. The huge numbers of salmon migrating into southcentral Alaska's Cook Inlet offer a prime case history study of how halibut interact with salmon migrations and current.

In July and August, coastal drainages flush out tens of thousands of dead and dying salmon. On an outgoing tide, halibut will feed in these brackish water currents. During high slack tide, halibut will swim into shallow water, chasing salmon that are attempting to in-migrate into steep, coastal streams.

Understanding Migratory Patterns Of In-migrating Salmon And How It Translates Into More Halibut

It's no secret that halibut follow in-migrating salmon to the mouth of their spawning streams, much like Dollies follow salmon into freshwater for their eggs.

The circulation patterns of Alaska's Cook Inlet are highly complex, and are the function of tides, freshwater input and surface winds. Tides range from 12 feet at the mouth of the inlet to 27 feet at Anchorage. Coriolis is evident in the overall circulation pattern of the inlet, with oceanic waters entering the Inlet on the east side, and turbid freshwater exiting the Inlet on the western side.

The mid-channel rip in Cook Inlet has been proven to be a major concentrator of salmon, and is a popular halibut fishing grounds among the 300-plus boats fishing out of the Deep Creek/Anchor Point/Homer area.

FACT: Studies show that salmon entering upper Cook Inlet do so where low salinity water is most intense, and continue their migration into the Upper Inlet along this gradient of freshwater influence.

ACTION: Establish a drift along these visible breaklines for halibut that are following migratory schools of salmon.

FACT: Other studies have shown the importance of freshwater orientation among salmon. In a large saltwater bay in Japan, biologists found that when river water from the head of the bay flowed along the south shore, chum salmon swam into the bay along that route. When river water moved along the north shore, the salmon chose that route. Fish were located within nine feet of the surface where the influence of fresh river water was greatest.

ACTION: Halibut may be holding in the current, wherever it may be flowing. If flow is minimal at slack tide, fish shallow water bays at various depths as fish move off the bottom to feed on salmon migrating below the surface.

FACT: In Cook Inlet, evaluation of the surface current suggests that surface waters move north out of Kachemak Bay along Anchor Point, and are then diverted westward. Ninilchik is an area where diversion of surface waters westward and mixing of Upper Inlet waters is strong.

ACTION: Fish the scum lines or tidal rips frequently found in these areas. While turbulence is high, and often makes a tangled mess of bait rigs, go with a 24-ounce jig and bait off bottom, and hold on. You'll catch BIG fish!

FACT: Biologists have noted a southward entry into the Kenai River system by sockeye salmon ever since the 1920s. They have observed large numbers of sockeye salmon moving south along Salamatof Beach, against the flooding tide, to enter the Kenai River. The overall circulation pattern of the inlet suggests Kenai River water is mixed with inlet water and moves northward along Salamatof Beach. Attraction water of the Kenai River heads north with diversion to the west and exit via the mid-channel rip. This is due to the existence of a large eddy which develops on the north side of the east forelands.

ACTION: Factors that control migratory pathways of salmon also affect the feeding habits of halibut. Because halibut are an ambush species, they will swim into and hold in intersecting currents to ambush in-migrating salmon, or wait off coastal areas and drop-offs to feed on spawned-out salmon. In this case, a slip-sinker rig with a salmon belly or salmon head is an effective bait.

Stomach analyses show that cod, like this one caught by angler Ken Lomax, is a primary food sought by halibut. Find cod and you'll find halibut nearby.

More Stomach Analysis Surveys
Fish/Crabs Top Bait For Halibut

A report on stomach analyses of Pacific halibut provides some interesting prey-predator information of interest to anglers.

The survey was conducted in two fairly confined areas in both the mid-shelf region of the Gulf of Alaska and around the Pribilof Islands. Halibut caught here had the tendency to consume mostly larger nektonic and benthic prey. Pagurid and Tanner crabs were the most important invertebrate represented. Fishes were dominant on a weight basis, however, contributing over 75 percent of the biomass consumed. Walleye pollock made up about one-half of this total and was followed in importance by yellowfin sole, Pacific herring, Pacific sand lance, and Pacific cod. Overall, a relatively diverse prey spectrum was utilized by Pacific halibut.

In 1915, William Thompson examined halibut stomachs from northern British Columbia and Alaska and listed 17 species of fish observed, roughly in order of importance. Halibut was listed as number 11 with the comment "principally viscera," which would indicate they were feeding on the refuse of the dressing process aboard the halibut vessels fishing in the area. In other surveys, Halibut from off Vancouver Island had "stomachs full of crabs"; they were feeding heavily on Pacific sand lance in Hecate Strait, and Pacific cod off Kodiak Island.

He also reported that fresh octopus, salmon and viviparous perch were considered good bait.

Off Amchitka Island, Alaska, lithodid crabs, golden king crab and red king crab were found in halibut stomachs in the shallow waters. In deeper offshore area, an equal number of halibut had eaten no crabs.

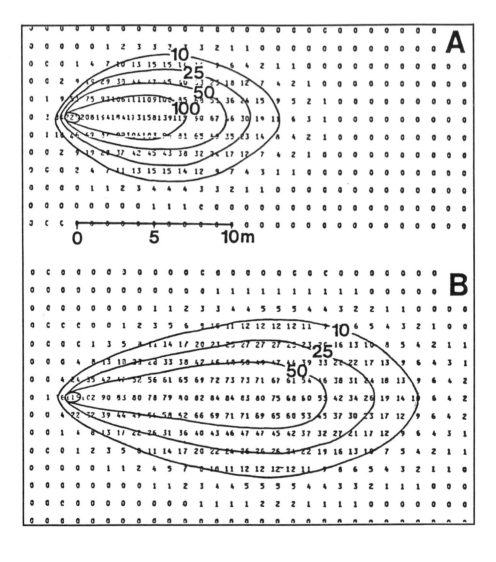

CHAPTER 10

Understanding And Creating
Drift Scent Patterns For Halibut

Research conducted by NOAA biologist Olsen (1983) has shown that in most fish, distant location of food is by olfactory stimuli. In other words, the smell from bait used by sport anglers fishing for halibut is distributed by currents and their associated turbulence. What this boils down to is that an anglers' success is enhanced or diminished by the speed and direction of the current.

Biologists have studied the distribution of smell in currents with numerical methods of advection as used in Hydrodynamical Numerical (HN) models, or computerized plotting.

As most anglers know, the smell of a bait decreases the longer it is in the water. This is known as leaching. The interaction between the leaching rate and tidal currents will result in complex smell distribution patterns, otherwise known as smell or scent fields, which attract the fish to the bait.

Anglers can alter the size and extent of the "scent field" by varying the height of the bait above the bottom, proper anchoring in the current, and monitoring optimum soak times before changing baits.

The primary purpose of using bait—whether it is for halibut or scent on a fly—is to attract fish into the area where they'll see the bait and take it or a nearby lure. According to Olsen, the bait "has to emit stimuli which are attractive to the target fish, at levels of intensity sufficient to induce the fish to search out the source of smell. The bait also has to remain intact, (i.e. stay on the hook) and continue to emit stimuli for a period long enough to permit the attracted fish to find the bait."

Distribution of smell from a bait in a current speed of 0.2 cm/sec or 1 inch/13 sec; A—after one hour soaking B—after two hours soaking. Chart courtesy NOAA

Vision can be of great importance, but only in close quarters. According to Kleerekoper, 1969, attraction beyond a few inches is nearly always based on olfactory stimuli. In certain species of fish with less developed olfactory organs, chance foraging also will be of significance in their feeding behavior (Pipping 1926, 1927). Both co-author Terry Rudnick and I believe that a flasher or flashing attractor, when used with a bait, is most effective in attracting halibut or other fish to the bait.

Since fish are able to detect substances at minute levels of concentration, it's important to believe that any fish in a nearby area will always detect the bait. However, there are numerous factors that control the distribution of the stimuli. These include time of day, season, previous diet, physiological state of the fish, water temperature, food and feeding conditions and water clarity.

According to biologists, the bait smell must exhibit a "level of intensity" of a certain threshold before the fish reacts by starting to search for the bait. This reaction threshold may be modified by the duration of stimulation. In the accompanying chart, this level of intensity is 10, the minimum amount required.

According to studies, bait such as herring and squid contain water soluble proteins that have been found to be attractive olfactory stimulants. These are rather quickly dissolved and dissipated in the water. Some experiments indicate emission rates of as much as 40 percent of the total contents of soluble proteins being dissolved within an hour at normal ambient sea water temperature (Solemdal and Tilseth 1978). It is no surprise these are the baits of choice among veteran halibut anglers.

The bait stimuli is not emitted at a constant intensity for that hour. Rather, it is done at a fast pace that takes a matter of minutes and starts at a slowly decomposing rate. Studies indicate that emission of a bait is most likely ended before the bait has reached bottom. Thus, in our opinion it is important to change bait every 15 minutes.

Underwater TV observations of fishing gear show that bottom currents are weak but variable, both in velocity and direction, even when there is a clear main direction of water transport. The scent will remain near the bottom, and vertical distribution is probably caused by near-bottom turbulence. In other words, in slack water, the smell isn't going much of anywhere. It's imperative to jig the bait aggressively to distribute as much of the stimuli as possible in all layers of the water column.

How to Catch
Trophy Halibut

The scent does lose its intensity the longer it is in the water and the farther out it spreads in the current. In such cases, fish attracted by the bait at a distance would swim into decreasing stimuli intensities whichever direction they are heading. "While high intensity gradients and distinct chemical trails provide sufficient information for localization, the gradients in the stimuli farfield of a bait are normally so weak that other non-chemical cues are required (for the fish to find the bait.)" (Kleerekoper, 1975).

"Knowledge and understanding of the mechanisms in food localization of fish are as yet rather incomplete, but it is believed that fish are able to sense the direction of water movement and locate the source by swimming upstream when aroused by smell stimuli. (Atema 1980)."

This is why a large bait, fished with or in a moderate current, is usually the method of choice in attracting fish to the area.

There are numerous factors that attract fish to a bait. Some of the most important are fish density, area of attraction, and variability of attraction rate within the area. According to biologists, the total number of fish attracted to the bait, when plotted against soak time, will, therefore, form a sigmoid curve, ascending slowly during the early part of the soak, then at a gradually steeper rate which falls off again as the rate of attraction decreases.

They believe the time required for the stimuli to be dispersed below the attraction level plus that required for the most distant attracted fish to get to the bait is the maximum soak time required to attract fish. Unless fish from outside move into the stimuli area, any further soak time will be non-productive, even if the bait is still emitting stimuli.

The molecular diffusion of a bait smell in the water is very slow by itself. Therefore, it's necessary that current and bottom turbulence (eddy diffusion) carry the scent.

We believe this explains the fantastic catches of large halibut among boat operators who fish the outer islands, which typically exhibit rotary currents.

Biologists made computer-generated models that indicate smell distribution patterns in various current strengths. In many parts of Alaska, tidal currents dominate. Whether they are diurnal or semi-diurnal, the change and direction of speeds is usually ellipse-like. In water shallower than 100 feet, wave action can reach the bottom and affect the molecular diffusion of baits.

At current speed of .07 inch per second, the initial strength

Adding bait to a leadhead jig increases the lure's effectiveness by creating a scent field. Change baits often for best success.

of smell emission after one and two hours of time varies. After two hours, the nominal field strength of 10 has reached 66 feet from the bait, and the width is about 106 feet. With a speed of .23 inch per second, the length of the 10 field is about 288 feet after one hour and its width about 18 feet. After two hours, the maximum width of the 10 field remains about the same, but the length is about 129 feet from the bait, with lower concentrations in between the bait and this higher concentration area. This is caused by the rapid decrease of smell emission with time. In higher currents, such as half an inch per second and higher, the smell field gets longer and wider, but its concentrations lower. In rotary currents, the smell field becomes C-shaped.

When fishing on a party boat, the smell fields will overlap. It's possible that close spacing of the baits, within six feet, will attract fish better by creating a stronger smell field.

Creating a strong scent field is imperative if you want to attract big halibut to your bait or lure. Use Halibut Call, scent injections into bait and other oils and methods as described in this book's various chapters, and you're virtually guaranteed to catch more fish.

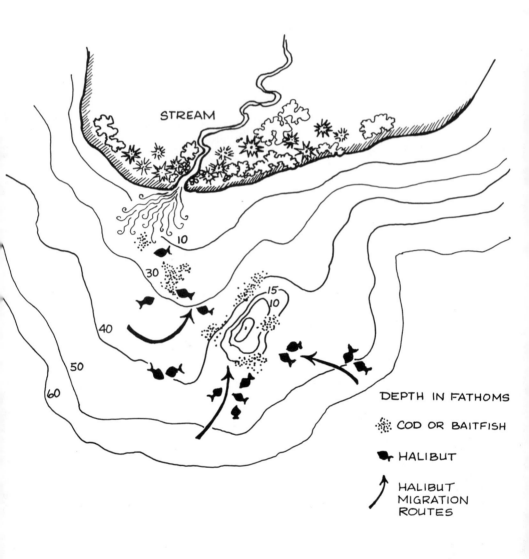

STREAM

10

30

15
10

40

50

60

DEPTH IN FATHOMS

COD OR BAITFISH

HALIBUT

HALIBUT
MIGRATION
ROUTES

A hydrographic map is imperative to locate not only geological structures that hold halibut, but bottom types and areas that also hold baitfish. An experienced angler will be able to look at a map and determine current flows, backeddies, tidal rips and other halibut-attracting structure, from which he can create his own maps for use by himself or others. This map shows a dropoff near a salmon stream and an adjacent underwater mound, where baitfish such as cod and sculpins find safety in the kelp and rocks. These scavengers dart out and feed on the drifting salmon carcasses. Big halibut migrate in from deepwater holding areas on an incoming tide and feed on whatever they can catch.

CHAPTER 11

A Halibut Success Equation
Time of Year + Structure + Food = Fish

No matter when or where you are fishing for halibut, always remember the above equation. If you're able to fill in the blanks, you'll enjoy greater success than others who are fishing blind or without the right equipment.

Time Of Year: Halibut can be found at any depth throughout the year. Generally speaking, they are deeper in the winter and shallower in the spring and summer. Study the migration patterns mentioned earlier in the life history section of this book, and talk to your local fish and game offices for specific info on your particular area. Have an answer? Good. Now you're ready to hit the water.

Structure And Food: Locate the food concentrations at each depth or structure point, and you'll find fish. There may be 1000 halibut feeding on sandlance and crab in 90 feet of water in May, and a mile away, another 1000 fish gorging on cod and herring on mud bottom in 340 feet. Both are good areas to fish. The tide brings in new baitfish and halibut to the same structure each day. Keep detailed records of your successes...and failures. Eventually you'll see a trend emerge that you can follow year after year with astonishing results.

If you don't know where to fish, first look to a map for structure that attracts bait. Learn the habits of cod, crab, pollock, herring, salmon and other baitfish species and rather than seeing a map with numbers on it, you'll see a living web of life, and how halibut interact with it.

Fat lingcod are also found in areas favored by halibut. Look for them in rocky areas or on the edge of kelp beds. Doug Olander photo.

Let's take Alaska's Cook Inlet halibut fishery as an example. Look for prevalent structure in the area you'll be fishing and depths that will allow you to effectively hook halibut. I've found the best depths for halibut vary from 40 feet to 40 fathoms over sandy and rock bottoms, tidal-induced depressions, shelves and major channels, such as those emptying upper Cook Inlet into Shelikof Strait. Such structure is prevalent off the shores of Deep Creek and Anchor Point, and remain hot for trophies through the summer, with occasional lulls in the action when the halibut temporarily move into deeper water or to wherever the food concentrations exist. Tidal rips, reefs and channels at the Cook Inlet entrance seem to produce the most lunkers during the entire season. The reason is obvious: Halibut use these structure points and routes as "off ramps" into Cook Inlet for a quick meal before returning to the nearby Continental Shelf, which is the major highway for numbers of big halibut.

Finding and fishing these migration and holding routes is generally hit and miss unless you're equipped with a sonar recorder and hydrographic map. Charter operators equipped with a global positioning system (GPS), a navigation aid that can put them within a few yards of any charted or previously recorded hotspot, have a definite advantage. This is why many anglers without similarly equipped cruisers patronize the charter operators. The skippers have usually spent months finding fish-holding structure.

However, I've found that by scouting with a graph recorder and handheld GPS and marking my halibut hookups on a large hydrographic map, it's possible to locate and hook big halibut from a small boat on a regular basis. You can purchase a handheld GPS unit, like the Magellan that I use, for less than $300. My GPS is waterproof, has enough memory to hold all my halibut hotspots and their names, and fits in my tacklebox or pocket for easy transportation. If you are serious about halibut fishing, you must invest in a map, sonar and GPS unit, a simple, yet effective success system. At the very least, invest in a GPS system and map and you'll be on the road to success. Now apply this formula to wherever you fish. You will not only catch larger halibut, but also learn lots about natural history, baitfish habits and migrations, and underwater geography and structure.

Time of Year + Structure + Food = Fish. Yes, the equation may be simple, but it yields big results. Fill in the variables, and see for yourself!

CHAPTER 12

The Most Common Halibut Fishing Scenarios You'll Encounter, And Proven Techniques For Success

As an angler in search of trophy halibut, a variety of structures and scenarios await you on the water. Terry and I have listed common and not-so-common situations you're likely to encounter, and valuable advice on how to fish each one for optimum success.

Catching Halibut From Shore

An improbably high number of halibut (as well as other bottomfish) are reportedly taken from shore. Given the lack of roadside accessibility to halibut habitat, these fish are probably either flounders, or are halibut taken from boats fishing near shore, and this situation essentially represents a combination of the previous two. Alaska Department of Fish and Game reported shoreline harvest represents 0.9 percent, a very small portion of the annual halibut harvest.

If you don't own a boat, or the water is extremely rough, you can possibly catch halibut from shore if you're fishing near a drop-off, ledge or similar habitat. I've caught chicken halibut on fly tackle while fishing for esturine silver salmon. Nothing more than a few pounds, but nevertheless, halibut.

Tackle shops occasionally buzz with a tale of an angler actually hooking a huge flatfish from shore. One lucky angler managed to wrestle a "slab," 400-pound-plus halibut into the surf near Deep Creek; another hooked into a big halibut from the Homer Spit and was about to lose all his line to the rampaging fish when a boater picked up the angler, ran down, and subsequently landed the flatfish.

Abrupt drop-offs located near steep salmon spawning streams—like those found in many southeast Alaska or British Columbia waters— are ideal locations from which to catch halibut from shore. Fish these areas on an incoming tide.

If you happen to be fishing in the right place at the right time, you may hook a halibut from shore. But don't expect lots of action. If you insist on trying, fish the many points and rocky outcroppings in Prince William Sound, southeast Alaska, and British Columbia. Position yourself where a stream or river spews dead and dying salmon into saltwater, and always, always fish with patience, the key to success.

Shallow-Water Jigging

"Phenomenal" is the only word that adequately describes the halibut-fishing action on that sunny August afternoon. Hordes of fish had moved in from the depths of southeast Alaska's Chatham Strait, into water as shallow as 25 feet, and to say they were cooperative would be a drastic understatement. It would be far more accurate to say they had a death wish, and I had the good fortune to be among the five anglers on hand for the festivities. We were fishing with Chuck Chandler of Baja Alaskan Experiences, and each member of the group was fishing a jig of some kind, and what the jig looked like didn't seem to make much difference. When it became obvious that every drop of a metal jig resulted in an automatic hook-up, a couple of us switched to leadheads, just to see if we could find a lure the halibut WOULDN'T take, but every offering brought the same quick, positive response. We even switched to lighter—and then even lighter—tackle, so that we could fish smaller and smaller jigs. The lighter lines and softer rods made it a little harder to stick the hooks, so we lost more fish than we brought to the boat, but the action remained fast and furious.

The halibut, ranging in size from tiny five-pounders to as large as 50 pounds, stayed on the bite until we simply grew too tired to play and release any more of them. I wouldn't even venture a guess as to how many fish the five of us hooked, but I did take notes, at least for most of the day, on how many I brought to the boat myself. I quit counting about a half-hour before we stopped fishing, after hitting the magic number of 50! Since I spent nearly as much time shooting photos as I spent fishing, I can only assume that the four other anglers onboard Chandler's 40-foot "Striker" caught even more fish than I did. It was fast-action halibut fishing at its finest.

If there's such a thing as "easy" fishing for Pacific halibut, it's to be found when you locate good numbers of fish in shallow water. The definition of "shallow," of course, depends on who you happen to ask, but for the sake of this conversation let's

call it any depth of about 150 feet or less. Jigging with either metal, slab-type jigs or with leadheads can be very effective for halibut found at such depths.

A Winning Combination: Shallow Water And Light Tackle

Part of the beauty of shallow-water jigging is that it allows the use of light tackle. Locate halibut in 75, 100, even 150 feet of water and you can get down to them with light jigs, and those light jigs can be fished easily with light lines, light-action rods and small, comfortable reels. If you aspire to add your name to the IGFA's line-class world record list, or if you simply want to catch an impressive halibut on sport tackle, shallow-water jigging offers you a very good opportunity to accomplish your goal. Fishing depths of 250 or 300 feet might require the use of jigs weighing eight, 12, even 16 ounces or more, but fish 100 feet deep at a time when the current is light and you might be able to reach bottom with a two or three-ouncer. You can handle such lures with tackle normally associated with freshwater bass, walleye or even steelhead fishing.

You can even get by fishing monofilament at these depths, as opposed to the low-stretch braided Dacron or new-technology lines that are required for fishing deeper halibut waters. The 30 to 40-percent stretch that eliminates monofilament as a good line for deep-water fishing is much less a problem when you're fishing only 100 feet down, because you can still feel the bottom and still get enough power in the hook-set to fish effectively. The added shock-absorbing quality of a stretchy monofilament may even be an advantage when you hook a brute of a halibut on a short line. A braided line is still going to give you better sensitivity and hook-setting power, but in shallow water at least you have the option of fishing mono if you want to.

Dance The Jig

The basic strategy of jigging in shallow water is much the same as deep-water jigging, in that the whole point is to convince a halibut that your lure is an easy meal. To do that, you bounce it along the bottom and work it up and down through the lower end of the water column as though it were a living thing, a tasty, bite-sized creature that might make a great main course for a hungry halibut. You watch your depth sounder for any sudden changes in bottom topography and you stay in close contact with the bottom by paying out and

How to Catch
Trophy Halibut

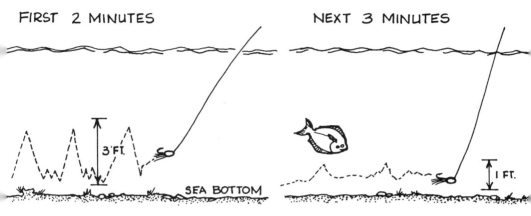

FIRST 2 MINUTES

3 FT.

SEA BOTTOM

NEXT 3 MINUTES

I FT.

retrieving line as needed. You don't want the jig dragging along bottom all the time, but neither do you want it suspended in open water several yards above the bottom.

Bouncing your lure in the sand and gravel every few seconds not only ensures that you're fishing down where you want to be, but also helps to kick up a little cloud of sediment and create a soft but audible "thud" that might draw fish in for a closer look. Like other species, halibut hear and feel what's going on in the water around them, so the sound of a bouncing jig and the vibration it creates moving up and down through the water may be as important in attracting fish as the visual signal the lure presents.

While the main goal of putting a life-like jig in front of a halibut's nose is the same for deep-water and shallow-water jigging, the shallow-water angler is able to achieve that goal with a lot less effort. If you're used to jigging in over 200 feet of water and move into the shallows to try your luck, the biggest mistake you're likely to make is that of over-working your jig. It takes a pretty energetic jigging motion to breathe life into a 16-ounce leadhead that's being fished in 250 feet of water, but if you use that same jigging motion in working a three-ounce jig at 90 feet, you may jerk the lure away from many more fish than you manage to hook. The shallow-water jigging stroke should be a subtle lift-and-drop that moves the lure a foot or two, not several yards at a time.

When you first drop down a jig, use an aggressive jigging motion to visually attract fish to the lure. After several minutes, or when you feel a tap, slow to a minimal jigging motion, twitching and fluttering the lure as much as possible. Try to imitate a fish in its death throes, which telegraphs an easy meal to any approaching halibut.

Different Strokes For Different Jigs

Not only are shorter jigging strokes more effective in shallow water, but slower jig movement may also be better. By keeping the jig close to the bottom and moving it slowly, you give halibut plenty of time to catch up with and take your lure.

As a general rule, you can fish a leadhead and plastic grub or leadhead and pork rind eel more slowly and with less jigging motion than a metal jig. That built-in action of the plastic or pork body wiggling in the water is often enough to trigger halibut strikes without any added lift-and-drop motion, so in some shallow-water fishing situations you may not have to work the leadhead at all.

Shallow-water jigging with a leadhead doesn't mean sticking the rod in a holder and forgetting it until you hear the reel scream. You can't follow the bottom contours effectively without using the rod and reel, nor can you make an effective hook-set unless the rod is in your hands. Shallow-water jigging isn't particularly complicated, but it does require your participation and attention, so keep the rod in your hands and be ready to react when a barn door inhales your jig.

Be a High Seas Drifter

Drifting with the current or the wind is one of the best ways to fish a proven halibut area or to prospect for potentially productive halibut-fishing spots. Staying on the move provides the opportunity to take your bait or lure to fish wherever they might lie, and when that bait or lure is bouncing and drifting along the bottom more or less naturally, any halibut you encounter may be just a little more eager to take it.

Halibut often feed actively during those periods of tidal flow at the beginning and/or the end of an ebb or flood, so drifting "downstream" with a light to moderate current flow is an excellent way to find and catch fish. Not only do you cover a lot of territory, but you are taking your offering to fish that are looking into the current and on the prowl for an easy meal. Even actively feeding halibut may choose to lie low and let the current bring food their way, including the "food" you offer when you're drifting with that current.

What many halibut anglers consider a perfect drift is one that takes them "downhill," from shallow water to deeper water. Halibut often lie in wait just over the edge of a reef, gravel slope or any other underwater high spot, waiting for the current to wash baitfish and other feed to them. By starting high and working your way down the slope, you're taking your bait down that path where halibut are likely to be looking for it.

Another advantage in drifting downhill is that it results in fewer hang-ups and less lost tackle. Working uphill, especially over a hard, grabby bottom and against the bottom contours, is a tough and frustrating proposition.

And, when you think about it, it's much easier to free-spool your reel and pay out line as you drift deeper and deeper than it is to continually retrieve line in an effort to take up the slack as you drift uphill into shallow water.

Tips For Controlling And Maintaining The Proper Drift Pattern

Don't think for a minute, however, that all drifting for halibut is a matter of working downhill from shallow to deep water. Many fishing situations may call for a drift that keeps you parallel to bottom contours, maintaining a more or less constant depth as you fish the edge of a break line, a tidal rip or even the top of an underwater plateau. If halibut are concentrated at a particular depth, you're obviously better off maintaining a drift at that depth than you are running uphill, drifting back down the slope and hitting fish only as you pass through that "magic" depth line.

We've already talked about drifting with the current, and it's a kind of drift that's more or less predictable and easy to plan around, but there's a second kind of drift that isn't so easy to predict, and that's a wind drift. The wind on any given day, quite frankly, may not take you in exactly the direction you want to go, and that can make fishing miserable. It may also change direction and speed quickly. Murphy's Law dictates that such changes in wind direction or speed will occur just about the time you figure out the perfect drift for a spot you've been trying to fish all morning! If you're trying to fish a downhill slope and the wind is blowing you uphill, you're obviously going to have problems. Or, the wind may be blowing the same direction the current is flowing, which may speed your drift to a velocity that could make it impossible to fish effectively.

The key to accomplishing a good drift that will take you where you want to go lies in playing all the variables that may determine your course. You should also remember that you don't have to be totally at the mercy of the elements. There are certainly things you can do to help control the speed and direction of your drift.

For starters, use a motor to help maintain the proper drift speed and direction. Backing into the tide or the wind as it

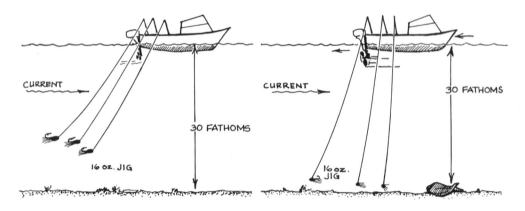

DRIFTING WITH CURRENT

CURRENT

30 FATHOMS

16 oz. JIG

BACKTROLLING AGAINST CURRENT

CURRENT

30 FATHOMS

16 oz. JIG

Drifting with the current will result in excess belly in your line, which will contribute to missed strikes. Have the skipper backtroll into the current. This will minimize line drag and allow you to fish your bait or jigs vertically for a better hookset and enhanced lure control.

carries you along allows you to make a slower drift and gives you a chance to work back and forth across the current as you go, covering the bottom much more thoroughly and effectively. Some boaters use their "big motors" to accomplish this, but many veteran Northwest anglers learned long ago that a smaller, "kicker" motor does it even better.

Although it isn't as much help in controlling direction, some kind of sea anchor will certainly help to slow your drift, and many halibut anglers use them. The most common sea anchor in many halibut-fishing areas is pretty low-tech, consisting of a plastic five-gallon pail tied to a few feet of strong line.

If you have the luxury of fishing around other boats, you may not have to pay much attention in order to make a good drift over the halibut-holding spots; simply get in line behind a boat that seems to be finding success and there's a chance that you'll do the same. Most of the time, though, it's a safer bet to be your own navigator, using chart, depth sounder, landmarks, GPS or loran, even marker buoys, to be sure you're starting and ending your drifts where you want to.

The direction or speed of your drift can change subtly if you don't use all those tools of the trade. Out on wide-open water you can lose the drift completely and never find it again if you let your mind wander too long. Lock in the coordinates on your loran or GPS as needed. Pay attention in lining up landmarks to know where you should be as you make your drift. Keep a close eye on the depth sounder to be sure you're staying on track, or set out a marker to identify your starting spot so that you may come back to it easily at the end of a productive drift. Doing any or all of these things will pay big dividends in the way of covering the water you want to fish and in making better halibut catches.

How to Catch
Trophy Halibut

As for specific angling techniques that work in this situation, drifting can be the perfect venue for dragging a whole herring through the depths. A properly rigged herring comes to life in the moving-water conditions of a good drift, and if boat/water movement is adequate, you may not even have to work your rod and reel to fish the bait effectively.

Don't get lazy, though, and assume that you can always drift fish bait effectively with the rod in a holder.

You may have to keep working the baitfish when the boat is moving slowly to ensure proper action, especially if the halibut refuse to take a dead-drifting bait.

When, on the other hand, boat movement is on the fast side, you'll have to man the rod to be sure of staying in close enough contact with the bottom, as the bait will want to work up into the water column on a fast drift.

While drifting with bait you're continually presenting a potential meal to new customers as you move along, while leaving a scent trail that may draw passers-by in for a closer look. Herring will usually do the job just fine, but don't be afraid to experiment with other bait rigs in this situation.

Smaller baits are especially effective here, since halibut may be called upon to make their decision and take the offering quickly as it sweeps by them. In other words, that large salmon head or whole cod that works well for barn doors when you're fishing at anchor may be too big for drift-fishing, so you're better off using easy-to-eat "snacks" such as squid, strips of halibut skin, tomcod, cod strips, small pieces of octopus and other bite-sized baits (For details, see the Bait Rigs chapter).

Jigging with metal or leadhead jigs may also be effective on the drift, but only if you move slowly enough to keep the jig pretty much straight down. Covering lots of productive water on a slow drift is great for the jigger, but when you gain speed and that jig gets well off behind the boat, jigging becomes much less effective. Switching to heavier jigs or casting ahead and drifting toward your lure as it sinks may help, but when boat speed becomes too fast you're better off setting your jigging rod aside and picking up a bait-fishing outfit.

Fishing Over Smooth Bottom

Unlike such rock-loving marine fish as ling cod and many of the various rockfish species, the halibut is a fish that tends to be found where the ocean bottom is relatively smooth and gentle. Some of the Northwest's most productive halibut-fishing grounds, in fact, feature bottoms of cobble, gravel, sand, even

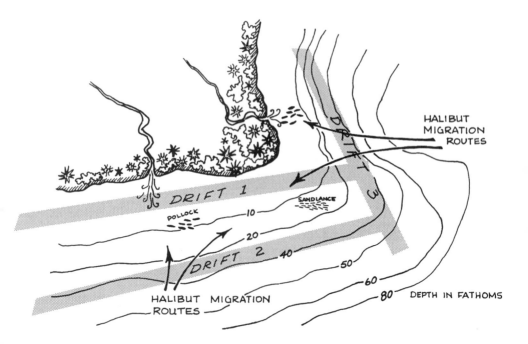

HALIBUT
MIGRATION
ROUTES

DRIFT 1

POLLOCK

SANDLANCE

DRIFT 2

DRIFT 3

10
20
40
50
60
80

HALIBUT MIGRATION
ROUTES

DEPTH IN FATHOMS

Anglers in search of trophy halibut never fish blindly. They establish drifts based on wind or current direction, always floating over the best halibut-holding structure the area has to offer. A sonar unit will provide ample details about available bait and bottom type and composition. As the illustration shows, always try to drift along contours rather than against them.

mud, or combinations of the four. Such areas can be fished rather easily and painlessly, but they do offer their own particular challenges. Let's look at the advantages and disadvantages of smooth-bottom halibut fishing, as well as some angling techniques that produce good catches from those areas.

Ocean bottoms of sand, gravel and small rock often attract a wide range of smaller fish, the little creatures on which bigger fish such as halibut like to feed. Washington's Hein Bank, for example, features lots of sand and gravel bottom where sandlance (needlefish) congregate by the millions. Those needlefish, in turn, attract hungry halibut throughout the late-winter and spring, providing good fishing opportunities. Walleye pollock and various cod species, as well as herring, may also be found over smooth bottom, and all of these are likely to attract halibut in good numbers.

Smooth-bottom areas are easy to fish, in that you can scrape bottom without losing too much valuable tackle. Sinkers, jigs and other gear have a tough time getting a foot-hold in sand, gravel and golf ball-sized rocks, so you may be able to get away with bouncing a bait or lure along the bottom all day and never get snagged. These "softer" bottoms also tend to be more gradual, so that you may fish long periods without ever having to pay out or retrieve line because of changes in depth.

These smoother, flatter, less dramatic bottoms offer yet another advantage to the halibut angler, that of increased bait or lure visibility. A flat ocean bottom with few changes in

How to Catch
Trophy Halibut

contour allows a bottom-dwelling halibut to spot a potential meal a long ways away, so your bait or lure has a better chance of being noticed and being attacked by a hungry barn door.

Smooth bottoms aren't necessarily the promised land for all halibut anglers. Fish may be scattered over vast areas, so that it takes a great deal of prospecting between strikes. On the other hand, small changes in bottom structure, composition, depth or bait concentrations may draw large numbers of halibut into small areas, and fishing action may be boom or bust depending on whether or not you locate these hot spots.

There are two keys to fishing smooth-bottom areas for halibut. If the fish are scattered, one here and one there over large areas, or if they are concentrated but you don't know exactly where, your best bet is to stay on the move until you find action. Every place you locate fish—especially if there are indications of good bait concentrations or noticeable bottom variations—stop and spend some time there. If a spot produces only one fish, keep working on the assumption that fish are scattered. Any spot that produces more than one strike, however, should be fished slowly and carefully.

If, on the other hand, you have reason to believe the fish are concentrated in specific spots and you have some ideas (or inside information) about where these spots are, fish these known or suspected hot spots and don't waste a lot of time prospecting. A small hump jutting a few feet above the surrounding area, a subtle breakline at the edge of an underwater plateau, or a small patch of gravel surrounded by acres of sand are the kinds of places that attract halibut or halibut feed, and sometimes it's just a matter of fishing these spots until the bite starts.

These areas where halibut concentrate may be several acres or only a few square feet in size, and locating them may depend on precise work with loran or GPS equipment. Your ability to acquire "hot" numbers from other anglers and to pinpoint those locations with your own equipment may determine whether you find red-hot or ice-cold halibut fishing.

What fishing methods, then, are best-suited to smooth-bottom halibut fishing? Ask any angler who needs to cover lots of ground in his search for fish and he'll tell you that trolling is the best way to do it, and trolling is certainly an option for the angler in search of halibut over smooth bottoms. Trolling for Pacific halibut may be one of the sport's best-kept secrets, and in areas where the bottom structure—or lack of it—allows, it can be a productive option. In other chapters of this book we establish the fact that the often sedentary halibut, when actively feeding, may demonstrate both the willingness and the ability to chase down a fairly fast-moving bait or lure, so there's no reason to overlook this angling method that's often reserved for such well-known speedsters as the coho salmon.

Dick Johnson, the late owner of Kingston Tackle Specialties in Kingston, Washington, and an avid halibut angler, did a great deal of trolling for his fish, and he was constantly experimenting and refining his tackle and technique.

One of his standard rigs, which he trolled on a downrigger, consisted of a large, plastic squid behind a big flasher. While trolling with artificials such as the plastic squid may seem an unusual halibut-fishing method to some, Johnson got results when other halibut anglers failed. He used squid baits manufactured by his company that ranged from as small as six or seven inches to as large as 16 inches.

Trollers working the gently sloping bottom of the mouth of the Twin Rivers in Washington's Strait of Juan de Fuca tend to go more with natural bait than artificials, with some using whole herring and others opting for fresh or frozen squid. In either case, the offering is fished behind a large dodger, usually chrome but sometimes white, chartreuse, blue or combinations of these colors.

The key to trolling for halibut over smooth bottom, whether with bait or artificials, is to keep the offering four to six feet off bottom, so that it's within striking range of hungry fish but far enough up in the water column that it's visible from several yards away. Keeping your bait or lure at that level requires paying close attention to your depth sounder and downrigger ball, but over smooth, fairly level ocean bottoms that shouldn't be too difficult.

If conditions are right, both jigging and mooching with bait will also take halibut from smooth-bottom fishing areas. If you're prospecting for fish you'll need some wind or tidal flow to move you along, but if you have the location coordinates for a hot spot where fish are concentrated, you're better off using these methods on the ebb or flood, when water movement is at a minimum. Or, if water depth allows, you may want to anchor and fish these spots where halibut are concentrated.

Fishing Over Rocky Bottoms

The old adage about there being an exception to every rule is as true in halibut fishing as in anything else, and just about the time you come to the conclusion that these trophy flatfish

How to Catch
Trophy Halibut

are ALWAYS found on relatively easy-to-fish sand, gravel or small-rock bottom, you'll find yourself catching them at the edge of a rocky drop-off or among the jagged, tackle-grabbing rock pinnacles that lingcod love to call home. Fishing for halibut on and around such extreme bottom contours is difficult, but it can also be rewarding, so be ready to give it your best shot should the situation arise.

The key to rough-bottom halibut fishing is to keep your line angle vertical, or as close to it as possible. If your bait or lure is straight below the rod tip, you reduce the odds of hanging a hook or the sinker on the grabby bottom, and the more the line flattens, the greater the risk of hang-ups, lost tackle and wasted fishing time.

Fishing a vertical line also allows some "accuracy" in where you put your bait or lure, which can be very important when fishing areas with hard, rocky bottoms. Halibut found around rocks often congregate in certain areas rather than scattering throughout the rocky structure the way lingcod and some of the larger rockfish species tend to do. One particular rocky slope, a certain boulder patch or a small bed of cobble surrounded by jagged pinnacles may be the one spot that holds halibut, and the most precise way to fish such a specific piece of underwater real estate is to get directly over it and fish straight down. Bouncing your bait or lure directly beneath the boat ensures that you're fishing within the area covered by the cone of your depth sounder signal, so that you can tell exactly what's going on down there.

Having your line straight down also reduces the odds of losing hooked fish to the snaggy surroundings as you try to coax them toward the surface. If you can bring them straight up toward the boat, there's less possibility they'll find their way into a hiding spot or scrape your line across abrasive rocks.

Unless you know the particular spot like your own living room and can keep your offering just above all the jagged, tackle-grabbing rocks, you don't want to troll over rocky halibut spots, nor do you want to drift over them at high speed on a strong wind or heavy current flow. Both will result in frequent hang-ups and miserable days on the water.

Fishing rocky-bottom halibut spots on the deadest of tides is one way to keep your line straight down, reduce hang-ups and fish these areas most effectively. It stands to reason that if your boat is holding its position in dead water you can hang a bait or lure straight down from the rod tip.

Another way to reduce line angle is to motor into the current or the wind to hold your position. Whether "backing in" with your kicker motor or running into it with your main motor, it's a good way to hold your position over a productive rock pile to keep line angle at a minimum.

Anchoring is another way to stay put over a halibut-holding hard spot, but it's not the easiest task in the world, especially if the water is a couple-hundred feet deep or more. Positioning your boat over the place you want to fish, of course, means dropping the anchor some distance up-current and calculating things pretty closely, but if you do it right it will hold you directly above the hot spot so that you can fish straight down.

You might also want to use heavier sinkers and heavier lures to keep your line vertical when fishing rocky halibut areas. Lighter terminal tackle will "drift away" from your position faster and hang up more often.

While we're on the subject of terminal tackle, you might consider equipping your metal jigs and leadheads and bait rigs with single hooks rather than trebles when fishing extremely rocky bottoms for halibut. A large siwash or two will do the job just fine when it comes to piercing the jaw of a big barn door, but will reduce the risk of sticking a point in a boulder that won't budge.

The trade-off in this strategy, however, is that the stronger single hook is less likely to straighten and give if you do hang it on a rock, so a solid hang-up is more likely to result in a lost lure.

Remember, too, that hook damage is more likely when fishing over hard bottom, so it's more important than ever to keep a hook file or hone on hand and to use it regularly.

Fishing The Continental Shelf

So, you're one of those people who is always looking to expand his horizons and boldly go where no other man has gone before. And you don't mind working hard for your fish, even if some days that translates to all work and no fish. You're the kind of angler who's willing to put in lots of time and effort in your search for the mother lode of halibut. If you meet all those criteria, and if you own or have access to a boat adequate for fishing the wide-open Pacific, you may be ready to challenge those lightly fished halibut grounds where the end of the known world meets the great abyss. It's truly fishing on the edge, the edge of the Continental Shelf, and it's what some might call hard-core halibut fishing.

We got a taste of this doomsday halibut fishing for the first

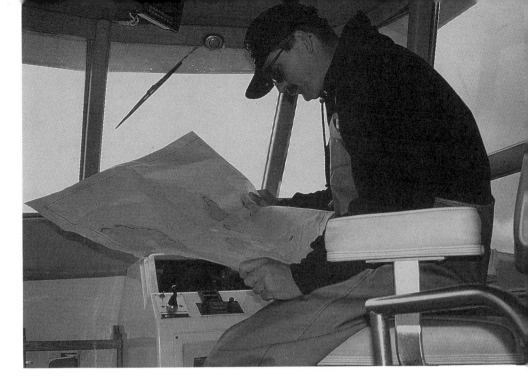

time back in the late-eighties, when Westport, Washington, charter skipper Phil Westrick extended an invitation to join him aboard his brand-new charter boat "Ultimate" for a two-day bottomfish trip that would take us to several of his favorite halibut and lingcod spots and give us a chance to explore some new possibilities as well. One of those "possibilities" was an area at the edge of the shelf where others had reported previous halibut catches.

Darryl Dossett of Dutch Harbor examines a hydrographic map to determine where the best fishing will be for the current, weather and tidal conditions. Dossett fishes the Aleutian Islands bordering the Continental Shelf for halibut that range from 80 to 400 pounds.

Most of us were using some kind of combination rig consisting of two baits, two artificials or one of each, and the sinkers or jigs that took them down weighed 40 ounces or more. On our first drift we free-spooled over 700 feet of line off the reels to reach bottom. We were in for a long morning!

The experience was enough to illustrate that fishing at the edge of the Continental Shelf isn't for the weak-bodied or the weak-willed. Although we managed to coax only three or four small halibut that morning, all but one came up as a double-header, with a large yelloweye rockfish, boccaccio or sablefish dangling from another of the rig's hooks. Each of these doubles felt like a monster barn-door, at least for the first three or four hundred feet, and we caught enough other big bottomfish to give everyone plenty of sore muscles. Had we located several big halibut down there, some of us may have died in action before it was all over!

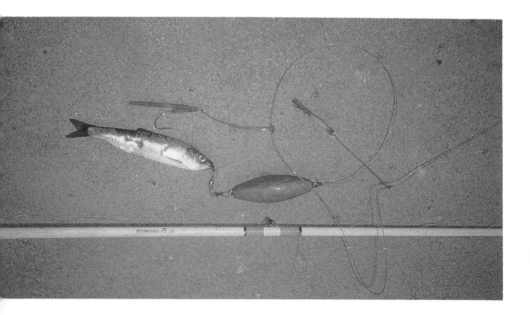

A popular slab bait and shrimp fly rig for the Continental Shelf. If the bait is stolen the fly will still catch fish, an important consideration when an angler has to crank up 400 or more feet of line to check the bait.

Commercial halibut fishermen have known about and explored the waters at the edge of the shelf for decades, and some of their secrets have leaked to charter operators and private-boat anglers.

Other potentially productive offshore halibut grounds have gone lightly fished or totally unfished. These deep-water areas offer a wealth of angling opportunity, but just knowing about them is only part of the equation; fishing them effectively is quite another matter.

Working the edge of the Continental Shelf means fishing deep, often in water 100 fathoms (600 feet) or deeper, so don't even bother taking the ultralight tackle along. Reels must be big enough to hold several hundred yards of line and rods must have enough backbone to handle sinkers and jigs weighing as much as three or four pounds. Use monofilament line out there only if you want to work your tail off and be totally frustrated; the super lines of braided Spectra or the traditional braided Dacron lines are the only sensible things to use at these extreme depths.

As for terminal tackle, there are several ways you can go. Fishing bait requires the use of a wire spreader or some other means of getting the offering down as quickly as possible without tangling it in the main line. While a large herring is one of the Northwest's most commonly used halibut baits, it's one of the worst for this kind of deep-water fishing, because it's relatively soft and likely to be stripped off the hook on a missed strike. Reeling up 700 feet of line and 48 ounces of sinker is a lot of work and costs a lot of fishing time in order to check your bait every time you miss a strike. Using nothing but herring on your hook may put you in that position.

Instead, if you prefer fishing bait, go with something a lot tougher, such as squid, octopus, halibut skin or a belly strip from a cod or some other bottomfish. Or, if you can get them, use whole Pacific cod, tomcod, pollock or other fish that are small enough to make a good meal for a hungry halibut. Remember, though, the bigger the bait, the harder it is to reel up from the depths.

If, however, herring is the only bait available, you're not out of luck if you know how to rig and fish any of several bait/lure combinations that are well-suited to this kind of deep-water halibut fishing. The first involves use of the time-proven wire spreader, but instead of using the traditional cannon ball for a weight on the short arm of the spreader, use a large leadhead jig with a plastic curl-tail or large pork rind strip on its hook. By replacing the sinker with a jig, you now have both a bait and a lure working for you down there in the depths, so if your bait is stolen you can keep on fishing with the artificial.

Yet another way to fish a bait/lure combination for deep-water halibut is to simply add a herring, anchovy, squid, belly strip or strip of halibut skin to the hook of a leadhead or metal jig. The bait increases the lure's effectiveness, but if it's lost you don't have to replace it until you bring up your lure for some other reason.

Rob Waddell, long-time skipper out of Newport Tradewinds Charters in Newport, Oregon, showed me yet another effective rig that employed both bait and artificials. His set-up, long a favorite with other deep-water halibut anglers along the Oregon coast, consisted of a commercially manufactured "Shrimp Fly" above the sinker and a whole herring on a large, single hook below the sinker. The Shrimp Fly is nothing more than two brightly colored streamer flies made of tough nylon fibers, tied about 18 inches apart on a stout leader. Waddell looped a large torpedo sinker (which has a brass eye at each end) to the end of the leader. Using a snap-swivel, he attached the herring-baited hook to eye at the back-end of the sinker. As the sinker was bounced along the bottom, the streamer fly danced a foot or two above it and the herring dragged immediately behind. When a herring was stripped off the hook, the angler kept on jigging the fly as though nothing had happened. Typically,

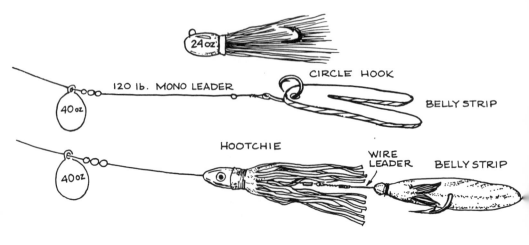

24 oz

120 lb. MONO LEADER

CIRCLE HOOK

BELLY STRIP

40 oz

HOOTCHIE

WIRE LEADER

BELLY STRIP

40 oz

Popular rigs for fishing the Continental Shelf.

he says, about half the halibut caught on this rig are hooked on the fly, the other half on the herring.

While a bait/lure combination can be productive, anglers should check the regulations before using it. The three-hook Newport rig just described, for example, is illegal in Washington, where two is the maximum number of baits and/or lures attached to a single line. In British Columbia, only one bait and/or lure may be fished at a time.

Some anglers may prefer fishing artificials and simply forget about the bait. Remember there is little light at the bottom of the ocean in 600 to 800 feet of water, so you have to assume that a halibut is going to have trouble seeing a conventional lure down there. Offering them something luminescent might help, and you have a wide choice of glow-in-the-dark goodies now available, whether you like plastic jig bodies or metal jigs. Many deep-water halibut anglers who favor artificials won't use anything but a luminescent lure.

Luckily, halibut use other senses besides sight to locate potential meals. Even if you don't use bait with your rig, you might add a little scent of some kind so that roving halibut can use their noses to help find your offering. Some of the commercially manufactured jelly-type scents work well with both metal jigs and soft plastics, or you can add a herring tail or small strip of fish skin to a hook and accomplish the same thing.

Be constantly aware of the great distance between your rod tip and your bait or lure when fishing the edge of the shelf.

Jigging is especially hard work at these great depths, because you have to use lots of the lift to move the lure only a foot or two. Even though lines made of Spectra or other braids stretch only one or three percent, that equals six to 18 feet of stretch when you have 600 feet of line out, and you need to compensate for that stretch when you're jigging.

The same rule applies to your hook-set when fishing extreme depths. A casual, half-hearted set won't do, so plant your feet and come back hard on every strike, reel down, and come back hard a second time.

Since fishing the edge of the shelf means fishing some distance offshore, a loran or GPS is a must, not only for finding proven locations that others tell you about, but for recording and staying on productive places you may find for yourself. There's no such thing as lining up that tall tree on the beach with the red barn on the hillside or any such foolishness when you're several miles offshore, so you have to depend on electronic equipment to do the job for you. Without it, it's a mighty big ocean out there, and it all looks much the same.

Finding Halibut:
The Early Angler Gets The Fish

When you're fishing heavily fished areas like some of the spots out of Homer or Deep Creek, where a 360-degree look reveals no less than 70 or more boats, it's important to be the first on the scene. Big halibut do move around. Talk to any halibut skipper, and they all have their secretly guarded loran or GPS coordinates of underwater topography because those areas attract fish on a regular basis. Many locations are well known, especially those off the Continental Shelf, Aleutian Trench, or similar deepwater holding areas.

Think of the halibut grounds as a beach at low tide. Each day brings new types of marine life and objects that wash up on shore, so does underwater structure in these areas attract new stocks of halibut each day. Get there first, and you have a better chance of catching that big fish. And if you don't believe me, ask yourself, why do all these boats race out to the fishing grounds each day?

Fish The Drop-Offs

If you begin thinking like a halibut, you'll readily locate areas where the lunkers lurk. As we've mentioned many times, a halibut is an ambush predator. The more uneven the bottom contour, the better the bigger halibut like it. They like to hide

The Pacific Northwest coastline, especially those areas in and around present or previous intertidal glacier activity, is carved with steep walls and jutting shelves which attract and hold big halibut, crab and baitfish. Fish these shelves along their length, or bounce a jig from shallow water to deep on an outgoing tide.

on the shelves immediately offshore and near islands. Find areas with abrupt depths changes and you'll also find halibut that use the deepwater area to digest their meal, and later cruise the shallows, especially if there are concentration points for forage. Some of my best halibut fishing has been along the rock cliffs of Kodiak Island and Prince William Sound, where the boat was a mere 10 to 20 feet from a vertical rock wall. Baitfish swimming along the wall were virtually trapped and confused when the halibut darted up from the bottom.

Glacial Saltwater

In many areas of southeast and southcentral Alaska, the bays are a milky green from suspended silt from nearby glacial run-off. The silt reduces visibility, and halibut found in these areas usually require a bait to be fished closer to the bottom than in clearwater areas. In some bays, especially where there is active currents or freshwater inlets to purge glacial silt from an area, the surface layer is turbid, but 10, 15 or 20 feet down, the water is crystal clear. The same applies to an area where there is little mixing going on, such as a windless bay where definite glacial water/saltwater breaklines can be seen.

How to Catch
Trophy Halibut

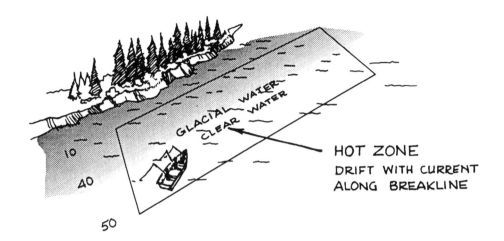

HOT ZONE
DRIFT WITH CURRENT
ALONG BREAKLINE

Find the area with the most visibility or structure. Consider areas with current such as a freshwater river emptying into a glacial bay. Also consider the underwater moraines, eskers and other geological formations created by the glaciers. These structures are halibut hotspots. I've found halibut concentrated on or near underwater glacial structure in Whittier, Sitka, Cook Inlet, Valdez, Glacier Bay National Park, and Petersburg. Once found, record these hotspots with a sonar unit and GPS.

Glacial bays often exhibit sandy or rocky bottoms. Under cover of the turbid glacial water, big halibut will move into bays and bury themselves in the sand in or near the clear water/glacial water breakline. From there they have a perfect opportunity to ambush unsuspecting cod and pollock. You'll find these glacial water/clear water breaklines throughout southeast Alaska, the western side of Cook Inlet, and in many waters of Prince William Sound and British Columbia.

Anchoring

When conditions permit, anchoring is one of the best ways to effectively fish an area for the following reasons:

1) You don't snag bottom as often as you do on a drift.

2) A much stronger scent field is created by fishing baits in one location. Because big halibut are ambush species, they won't chase a bait over long distances.

3) Anchoring allows you to effectively "walk the jig", even when the tide is running full-bore.

4) If fish have just finished feeding, anchoring will allow you to remain in an area and provide enough visual or olfactory stimuli to entice fish to strike just one more time.

5) Anchoring allows you to fish pin-point structure or bait concentrations by stationing the boat directly over a hot spot.

6) You learn the bottom cover better than drifting because you'll catch a variety of species in one spot. Anchoring allows

smaller baitfish to swarm in and create a feeding frenzy that draws in large halibut. The down side of this is that the Irish Lords and cod can get so numerous that you'll need to pull anchor and find another location. Also, anchoring doesn't allow you to cover the water as much as drifting. You might want to drift until you find fish, then anchor and fish the area. I always recommend this procedure when fishing a new area.

Before anchoring, review a hydrographic map and determine bottom contour and type. Also determine current and wind direction. Because the right amount of anchor should be three times the depth of the water you are in, a quick calculation will tell you that to fish the edge of a sandy flat in 100 feet of water, you need 300 feet of anchor line.

Once anchored, employ one of several techniques: vertical jigging, bait fishing, walking the jig or downrigger fishing, all of which have been discussed in various chapters.

A good technique while anchored is to cast your jig or bait away from the boat, using slightly lighter tackle than the elephant clubs you normally fish with. Bruce Mallory taught me the fine art of light tackle jigging many years ago. Mallory, one of Homer's legendary halibut anglers, had a knack for catching big halibut on his salmon rig of 20-pound test, level-wind spool and rigged herring. After anchoring the boat, he'd toss out the bait on a three-ounce sinker. He'd fish it about six feet above the bottom, out of reach of bottom feeders (which prefer not to leave the sanctuary of bottom cover) yet in sight of halibut.

I was convinced when I saw him bring in 60 and 80-pound fish when the 120-pound rigs would catch chickens. He'd never touch the rod. It would stay in the rod holder, bouncing lightly in the waves, the limber tip of the salmon rod giving the herring a nice, rolling, jigging motion. When the rod doubled over, he'd always have a halibut.

Next time around, using my own salmon gear, I managed to bring to boat a 125-pounder on 20-pound line.

The thrills and excitement of such a fish on light line was a combination of the right rig and of course, being anchored during slack tide.

You can duplicate this success also.

If you haven't already done so, it's imperative that you read the chapter on scent fields, a key component to drawing in fish once anchored.

Once you have a fish on while anchored, use caution. The fish can surge and wrap around the anchor line. On one trip to outer Cook Inlet, the skipper backed over the anchor line on a heavy, outgoing tide. The boat jolted violently on its side, and the 14 of us on the charter boat nearly tipped over into the raging currents of the inlet. Fortunately for all, the skipper was able to lower someone down and cut the anchor rope, righting the boat.

Never, never anchor in heavy current if you have a combination of waves and heavy current, a combination which could swamp the boat. Always have a knife ready to cut the anchor rope should you snag on a rock, if a bore tide hits, or other potentially dangerous scenarios.

Also consider dropping anchor in backwater eddies near islands, on or near major drop-offs, on a shelf that drops off into deep water, or at the mouth of salmon rivers or streams. When the tide is running full-bore, it's imperative to anchor in order to fish an area effectively.

Fishing Near Rivers And Streams

One of the best times to find halibut along the Pacific coast is when salmon begin migrating into inshore areas in midsummer to late fall.

After spawning, salmon lose their stamina. The current carries them out to sea, where they swim feebly along the surface or near bottom; easy prey for halibut. At times, the biomass of halibut in such areas is unbelievable. In August and September, this juncture of salmon and flatfish is even more pronounced, as halibut are following silvers into the spawning bays. Fresh silvers are migrating upriver, while spawned-out pinks, reds, kings and chums are washing out to sea; a virtual smorgasbord. Salmon belly strips fished on a leadhead, or salmon head and halibut skin teaser fished on a jig are especially effective at this time.

Big halibut lie right on bottom in the main drift corridor of a bay, much like a trout stations itself in a feeding corridor in a stream. It doesn't take long to determine if fish are shallow or deep. If the current is extremely strong, the fish will hold right on the brackish water breakline on the sides. These bottoms are usually silty/cobbled/sandy/muddy, and provide an excellent spot for a halibut to lie in ambush of salmon.

Sometimes the mouth of a river or stream will course over a massive tidal flat, making it impossible for the halibut to get close to the salmon spawning grounds. As a result, few salmon are flushed out of the system. Nevertheless, halibut will be attracted by the scent of salmon in the water. Find

171

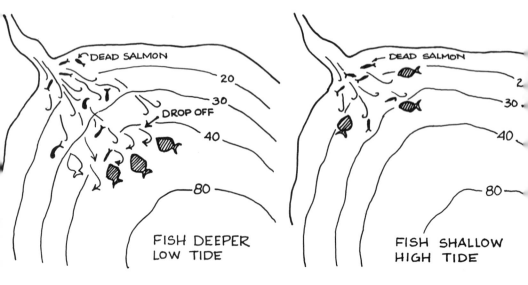

FISH DEEPER
LOW TIDE

FISH SHALLOW
HIGH TIDE

When salmon are in coastal streams, the rule of thumb for flyfishers and light-tackle halibut anglers is to fish deep at low tide, and shallow at high tide.

halibut in the deepwater portions of the bay or near the esturine delta. Look closely, and you'll find a small channel or currentline. This is where you want to fish on an anchor or establish a drift pattern.

In southeast Alaska, many salmon streams are steep and short. They empty into saltwater and drop off immediately. Salmon can only migrate up these steep streams during peak high tide. They'll mill around the freshwater runoff cascading down the rocky shoreline, oftentimes numbering in the thousands. Basically, these fish are suspended over deep water as they hold in the current. This is a prime area for halibut to move into and feed. You'll often see a swirl and boil of fish as a halibut swims in to grab a pink or chum salmon. When you find one of these gems, fish it! You won't be sorry.

Points And Islands

Points of land are common along the Alaska and Pacific Northwest coast. They are ideal food and fish magnets.

A tidal current impacting an island shoreline creates backeddies that attract feeding shrimp, baitfish and larger fish. Such areas are ideal for halibut, especially with deepwater holding structure, channels or depressions nearby. Islands often form numerous backeddies, as they are an oasis for all parts of the food chain, especially if they are adjacent to deep water. These backeddies are what make islands such a great place

How to Catch
Trophy Halibut

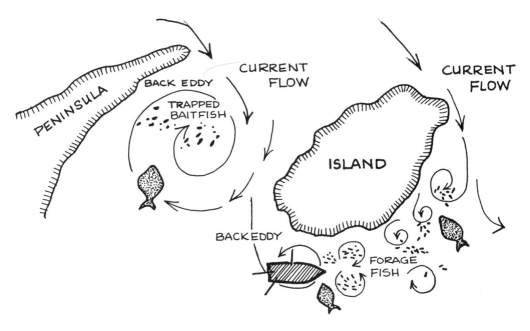

to fish. While fishing can be good on all sides of an island, the back side and sides of the island not exposed to tidal currents are worth fishing first. If there are shelves on the drop-off, you have the best of both worlds.

Tidal Or Scum Lines

These are readily identified by a wavering line of debris and current types created by shifting tides, tidal bores or backeddies. On one side is a turbulent or moving current, the other is a calm, quiet haven for shrimp and forage fish...and big halibut. During slack tide, halibut can be caught from bottom to surface. I've seen a halibut holding near a scum line chase a jig all the way to the surface before grabbing it.

Underwater Points

Backeddies not only take place horizontally around islands, but also in a vertical form known as vertical eddies. This is especially common in southeast Alaska's glacier country.

A prime example is the terminal moraine near LeConte Glacier near Petersburg. A terminal moraine is a deposit of gravel, sand and rock that may stretch for hundreds of yards or more and which are usually adjacent to deepwater areas. During tidal flows, backeddies form near the edge and over and behind abrupt changes in bottom topography such as house-sized boulders. Sometimes you can identify the vertical

If deepwater areas are too difficult to fish during full tidal flows, try fishing protected water. Tidal currents impact rocky points, spits and islands and create backeddies, which trap shrimp, crab and baitfish. Halibut move into these backeddies to feed.

173

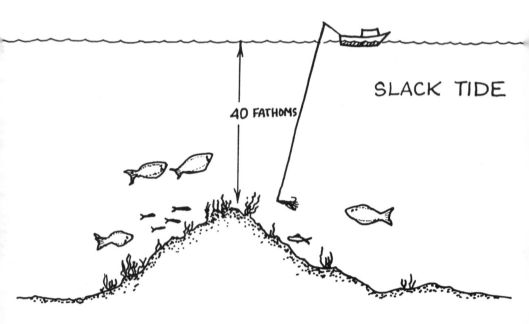

SLACK TIDE

40 FATHOMS

Underwater mounds or pinnacles regularly produce big halibut. Consider these structures as underwater oases, covered with baitfish, vegetation, shelves and halibut. During slack tide, halibut will move up from the surrounding depths to feed on the free-swimming baitfish near the pinnacle.

Opposite page: Charterboat fishing can be shoulder-to-shoulder or limited to a few anglers per boat. Choose one that best suits your personality and needs.

and horizontal backeddies by the roily or boiling surface water; an upwelling in severe cases. Others are miles wide, such as those found near the Barren Islands near Seldovia, and the smaller islands near Kodiak, and the backeddies off the many points of Prince of Wales Island.

Anchor or establish a drift along the length of the underwater moraine, or anchor in shallow, with the boat in deeper water. Bounce a jig down the drop-off. Use a large jig because such areas are also home to a variety of rockfish, lings and other species.

Fishing Near Processing Boats/Canneries

In some areas where you find canneries in operation, discharge of bait attracts all types of feeding fish, sharks and big halibut that follow the boats around, waiting for scraps. If you see sea birds and gulls working, there's bait in the water and halibut beneath. If you're lucky enough to find one of these opportunities knocking, motor up and drop down a bait or jig, and hold on!

How to Catch
Trophy Halibut

CHAPTER 13

Harpooning, Gaffing and Landing

Anyone who has ever watched at least two of those television fishing shows out of the southern part of the country has seen an angler—usually some guy named Junior, with lots of belly hanging out over the front of his belt and at least some of his butt hanging out over the other side—lift his fishing rod high into the air and hoist a writhing bass out of the water and into the boat in a smooth, single motion. Halibut anglers with even the slightest knowledge about their quarry should know better than to try that move; do it once and it could quickly become the worst day you'll ever have on the water!

There are, however, several safe, effective and efficient ways to deal with a halibut at boatside. The "right" strategy for any particular fish depends on its size, the size of the boat from which you're fishing, whether or not you're planning to keep the fish, how much help you have to do the job and what equipment you have with you.

You might be able to get away with a little trick that a friend and fellow outdoor writer has used, although we don't recommend this strategy. He says that you can actually soothe a halibut into quick submission by dragging it into the boat belly-up and rubbing its underside while you remove the hook. We've actually seen him do this with some fair-sized halibut that he planned to release, and it worked every time. In fact, the folks at the International Pacific Halibut Commission— who are often called upon to handle large numbers of smaller halibut during research projects—say that holding the fish belly-up does seem to have a calming effect. Try the belly-rub method if you want, but we'll stick to more time-proven, less subtle techniques for controlling this muscular, unpredictable fish.

Washington Department of Fish and Wildlife information

Boating a 175-pound or larger halibut can be a hefty chore for skipper and angler alike. During the gaffing, the angler should stand away from the guard rail, yet ready to continue the battle should the skipper miss and the fish races for bottom cover.

177

Shot placement on this
200-pounder could have
been better, but the load of
bird shot from a .410 at a
distance of perhaps three
inches did the job, and the
fish stopped without a
wiggle. A halibut's brain is
to the right, directly behind
the anterior eye.

officer Tony Floor loves to tell the story about an incident that
occurred on Washington's Hein Bank back in the mid-eighties.
During a good mid-morning chinook salmon bite, an angler
in a nearby boat hooked up with something that was obviously
much larger than the six to 12-pound salmon that were keeping
other anglers busy. Some time into the battle, Floor and his
party drifted by within ear-shot, and the chain of events went
something like this:

"'Scuse me, but could y'all maybe tell us what kinda fish
we got on here? It's big and flat, with a speckled brown back."

"Sounds like a halibut; way to go."

"Uhhh, are they any good?"

"Yeah, they're great eating. Better net it and get it in the
boat."

(After some frenzied conversation aboard the nearby boat
and a lot of splashing by an angry halibut alongside it), "'Scuse
me again, but y'all got a net?"

"Yeah, sure," said Floor, holding up his salmon net by the
handle.

As they pulled closer to hand-off the landing net, Floor and
his group got a closer look at the fish that was causing all the
excitement.

"You're not going to get that fish in this net," he said. "You'd
better gaff it."

(A little more frenzied conversation aboard the other boat,
then...) "'Scuse me, but y'all got a gaff?"

By this time Floor's friend Dave Nelson had motored up in
his boat to get a closer look, and when he realized the dilemma
of the obvious out-of-towners, offered to come aboard and lend
a hand. They gladly accepted, so Nelson grabbed two or three
pieces of halibut-persuader equipment and jumped into the fray.

The angler soon brought the barn-door fish to the surface
again, and without warning, Nelson drew a .38 from beneath
his coat, popped the big flatty between the eyes, quickly grabbed
his gaff and sunk it into the fish's shoulder, then heaved the
behemoth over the gunwale and into the boat. Most of the
other folks went running for cover, but it was all over before
they could find safe hiding places.

"I don't know where they came from," says Floor, "but they
went back home with a heck of a good story to tell about
monster fish and guys who shoot 'em with handguns."

The moral of the story, of course, is to have the right
equipment and to be prepared for success whenever you head
for the halibut grounds. "Be prepared" isn't just the Boy Scout

How to Catch
Trophy Halibut

credo; it's good advice for any angler who wants to boat most of the halibut he hooks, and to do it with minimal risk to life and limb.

At the other end of the spectrum from the southern folks in Tony Floor's Hein Bank halibut story is Chuck Chandler, a veteran halibut angler out of Juneau and owner of Baja Alaskan Experiences, a floating fishing camp in Southeast Alaska's Chatham Strait. When co-author Terry Rudnick hooked his first-ever halibut of over 200 pounds, he had the good fortune to be fishing with Chuck Chandler, and Chandler's decisive action and thorough knowledge of what to do when a big halibut comes to the top allowed him to control and dispatch the big flatty in a matter of seconds.

Chandler's technique was simple but effective. He was standing by with his .410 "Snake Charmer" as the halibut was coaxed to the top, and he placed a load of No. 6 shot behind its eyes at point-blank range the instant the huge head touched the surface. The halibut thrashed only a couple of times at the shot, and the second it stopped, Chandler sank a shark hook (which he was holding in his left hand the whole time) into the fish's lower jaw. The shark hook was attached to a stout line about 10 feet long, and deckhand Jeff Gregory held the other end of the line.

Chandler quickly exchanged the shotgun for another handy piece of halibut-handling hardware. It was a two-foot length cut from the butt section of a broken fishing rod, with the end of a long piece of half-inch nylon line threaded through it. The line emerged from the small end of this "probe" and had an overhand knot in it to keep it there. Chandler shoved the rod under the halibut's gill cover and out through its mouth, then brought it back and ran it through a loop tied into the opposite end of the half-inch line. Snugging the line up so that the big halibut's head was nearly out of the water, he tied off the line to one of the boat's cleats.

The next step was to throw a half-hitch around the base of the fish's tail with another sturdy line and tie it off to another cleat. When the halibut was secured, head and tail—which was maybe a minute after it first hit the surface—Chandler used a heavy-bladed, razor-sharp knife to cut through a couple of its gill arches and start a gusher of blood that poured out of the fish for several minutes.

Yes, this particular halibut cooperated fully throughout the entire process, but even if it had been a really crazy customer it probably wouldn't have mattered. Chuck and Jeff knew

How to Catch
Trophy Halibut

exactly what to do and did it quickly to get full control over the fish.

That's what you want to do when you bring a husky halibut to the top.

Granted, you don't necessarily need a firearm, a shark hook or a special tool for running a rope through the fish's gills on every halibut trip. Depending on your strength, experience and the size of your boat, you might feel comfortable handling even 60-pound halibut with little more than a gaff. The problem is, even in Oregon and Washington where 90 percent of the halibut will weigh in at under 30 pounds, you never know when that next one will be the trophy of a lifetime. Fish of 100, 150, even 200 pounds or more might turn up anywhere throughout the Pacific halibut's range, and you want to be ready if it happens to be your day to hook such a monster.

Mind Over Halibut

Mental preparedness is very important to success when it comes to dealing with husky halibut. Whatever equipment and technique you use, the important thing is to have a plan and to act quickly when you bring a big halibut to the surface. Anglers not involved in playing the fish should reel in their lines, get things in order for dealing with the lunker and be ready when the fish makes its appearance.

Landing a big, strong halibut requires strategy, alternate battle plans and a whole lot of teamwork, so you have to start thinking—and talking—about what you're going to do long before it's time to do it.

What's Your Stance On Halibut Fishing?

Hooking a halibut is considered by many to be the "easy" part. Getting them to the boat, however, is when the real work begins. The proper stance has a large bearing on not only your success in placing that fish in the cooler, but also the amount of energy you have left to continue fishing.

Pacific Northwest outdoor writer and halibut fishing expert John Beath regularly gives seminars on the proper ways to catch and fight big halibut. He offers this advice:

"Fighting halibut can be fun and strenuous, even hard work, but it should never be a back-breaking activity. Your stance on halibut fishing, or more importantly, how you physically fight the fish, can make the difference between a comfortable outing or a trip to the doctor's office at day's end.

"How do you 'stand up' against halibut? Here are a few tips:

Avoid leaning back while fighting the fish (left). Use your arms, fighting belt and legs to work the rod and ultimately the fish. Keep your stance straight and you'll win most battles (right). John Beath photos.

Rod Length

"Use a short rod, usually six to eight inches longer than your height, to even the odds. A longer rod increases the leverage that undoubtedly will gouge your mid-section unnecessarily and causes you to bend your back from the increased leverage.

"A long rod butt is nice, but only if the angler doesn't have to reach too far for the reel handle. The reel handle and the rod butt provide a pivot point to turn the tables on the fish when pumping it to the surface."

Drag

"As soon as pressure is applied at or above the reel, the angler turns the rod into an effective lever against the fish. But the amount of energy expended by the halibut directly relates to the reel's drag. Too much drag equals too much energy applied to the rod, line and reel, and ultimately your mid-section. Not enough drag equals a run-away fish. Try to adjust the drag to allow the fish to run when needed, without doubling the rod and you over like a wishbone."

Your Midsection

"Fighting belts save mid-sections while providing another pivot point to use against hard-fighting fish or heavy lures/weights that need to return to the surface."

Your Stance

"Without the proper stance, you probably won't want to catch a second "barn door" halibut or a "chicken" for that matter. A proper stance means staying upright, with feet pointed forward and directly under your shoulders, all the while keeping your center of gravity vertical with knees slightly bent to engage the leverage of both legs. Don't give in to the desire to arch your back into the rod or lean back; this just applies unnecessary pressure your spine—not the fish."

The Whole Body

"Use your arms, fighting belt and legs to work the rod and ultimately the fish. Keep your stance straight and you'll win most battles."

Gaff Hooks

If the fish is under, say, 50 pounds and you know how to use a gaff, that's a good way to go.

The most common gaff in halibut country is one of those short-handled, straight-pointed jobs that looks like a fish club with a spike sticking out of it. That style gaff has put an end to the careers of many Northwest halibut, but it has also cost lots of anglers their hard-earned fish. The problem with this club-style gaff is that it sticks best when applied with a sharp, downward swing. Unfortunately, when you hit a halibut with a gaff, you want it coming upward, so smacking it with a downward motion tends to give it a boost in the opposite direction from where you want it to go. Sometimes they'll jerk the gaff from an angler's hand and keep going.

If you try to stick the straight-point gaff into the underside of a halibut with an upward motion, the point often misses its mark completely, and your hooked fish suddenly becomes not only angrier, but maybe just a little wiser about your intentions.

Another serious problem with the straight gaff is that halibut tend to come "un-gaffed" quite readily. Without a bend in the hook, big fish are impaled on nothing more than a sharp spear, and they often writhe, twist and flop free, even before you can get them into the boat.

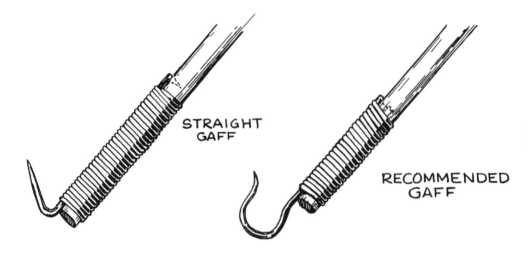

STRAIGHT
GAFF

RECOMMENDED
GAFF

A gaff with a round hook and a bent-back shank such as the 5/0 Mustad 2286TD is superior to the straight spike gaff commonly used for salmon and other bottomfish.

A sturdy, round-hooked gaff is a better tool for tackling halibut. Many a home-made or flimsy gaff has been straightened or broken to pieces by angry halibut, so buy a quality gaff. AFTCO Manufacturing Company of Irvine, California makes a complete line of 'hooks' that are tough enough to do the job. The Model 354-H bought by co-author Terry Rudnick in 1986 has helped boat dozens of fish in the 20- to 50-pound range and is still doing the job today. It sells for about $25 retail and is worth every dime.

There are various points of view on the best place to gaff a halibut. Wherever you choose to plant it, be sure of your aim. Flailing away with a gaff hook in hopes of sticking it somewhere will result in lost fish, some of them swimming away to die of the injuries you cause.

Some veteran halibut anglers prefer to stick halibut in the head, usually between an inch or two behind the eyes. One advantage to gaffing halibut in the head is that, if done correctly, it results in a solid "stick," with the hook piercing the fish's skull, where it's likely to stay hooked. Another plus is that a good head-shot with the gaff may hit the halibut's brain and go a long way toward killing it or at least stunning it long enough for you to get control.

A bad head-shot with a gaff, however, is probably worse than a bad shot anywhere else in the fish's body. If you're off an inch or two you might sever the leader or knock the hooks out of the fish's mouth. Stick a halibut poorly in or around the head and you might rip a gill arch, puncture the tongue, rip off a jaw or pop out the fish's eye, only to lose it, in which case your prize may limp to the bottom to suffer a slow death.

You're much better off sticking the gaff into the halibut's shoulder, the meaty part of the body immediately behind and above the gill cover. The flesh here is solid and will hold the hook firmly, yet if the fish should twist off, it's less likely to die of its injuries. What's more, gaffing a halibut a little farther back in the body gives it less leverage in fighting you and your gaff than it has when stuck in the head.

If one gaff is good, two can be even better. Big, strong fish such as halibut can be controlled better if you sink gaffs into them fore and aft, and having two gaffs in the boat also ensures that you will have a back-up in case one gets broken or dropped overboard.

Whether you carry one, two or more gaffs on your boat, keep them sharp, clean and within easy reach. To be safe, keep the point covered when the gaff isn't in use. A short piece of tight-fitting rubber or plastic tubing makes a good gaff sheath.

Shark Hooks And Flying Gaffs

Chuck Chandler's shark hook, mentioned earlier in this chapter, is somewhat of a variation on the gaff hook theme. The main difference is that, instead of a long handle, the shark hook has attached to it a length of strong line. The strategy for its use is to stick the hook into the halibut, usually in the lower jaw, then hang on to the line to control the fish at boatside. The line has much more "give" than a gaff handle, so the fish has less leverage to work against than it would with a gaff.

A shark hook attached to a rope with one end anchored to a boat cleat is an effective tool for subduing small to medium-size halibut. Ensure the cleat is securely fastened to the boat. These gaffs are inadequate on 300-pound-plus fish that have not been shot first. After the shot is made and the fish subdued, quickly insert one or more gaffs to anchor the fish.

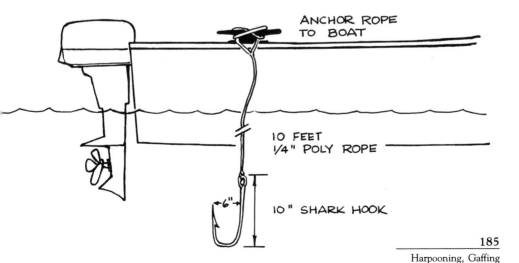

ANCHOR ROPE TO BOAT

10 FEET 1/4" POLY ROPE

←6"→

10" SHARK HOOK

The flying gaff offers the best of both the solid-handled gaff and the shark hook. The head of the flying gaff has a cupped base, which fits over the end of the gaff handle, and there's a stout line attached to the head. When the gaff's point is stuck into a fish, the head comes off the handle, so that only the line connects the fish to the person doing the gaffing. As in the case of the shark hook, the line to the flying head has more give and isn't as likely to allow the halibut to twist off or rip loose from the gaff.

Harpoons

Harpoons have grown in popularity as interest in halibut fishing has increased and anglers have searched for better ways to deal with these big, strong,

The harpoon, with its detachable head that's connected to the boat or to a large buoy, has in recent years become the standard piece of equipment for handling big halibut. This brass, arrowhead type is still popular with some halibut anglers, but others prefer a long, thin, "spike" type head, usually made of stainless steel.

unpredictable bottomfish. Harpoons used for halibut have a flying head with a strong line attached to it and rigged so that the head slides off the handle after it is plunged into the target. The principle is the same as with the flying gaff, mentioned previously.

Two styles of harpoon head are popular among halibut fishermen. One is the flat, brass type, which resembles the shape of an arrowhead. The other, usually made of stainless steel, is longer, narrower and round, looking somewhat like a short, thick, ball-point pen. The line attaches to both styles of head about in the middle, so that after it's plunged through the fish and tension is applied, it "opens up," turning 90 degrees so that it lays across the exit hole. A line—most often braided stainless steel—is attached to the harpoon head. The head and steel leader is run through the halibut's body. The tag end of the steel leader is usually connected to a strong nylon line, which runs to the boat, so that a harpooned fish is pretty much tethered unless the line breaks.

The key to using a harpoon is to plunge it into the halibut with enough force to run it all the way through the fish's body. To hold properly, the flat side of the harpoon head should pull against the fish's side. If the head penetrates only part-way,

How to Catch
Trophy Halibut

it's likely to pull out when the halibut makes a strong surge against the line.

In past years, many halibut anglers either secured their harpoon lines by tying them off to the boat, or held them in gloved hands and tried to out-muscle their quarry. Both methods resulted in the loss of some big halibut. When a strong 150 or 200-pounder tethered by a harpoon line decides to go the other way, something may have to give. Often it's the harpoon line itself, but sometimes its the boat cleat, and occasionally it's the wrist, elbow or shoulder of the poor slob holding the line.

Thankfully, somebody came up with a better way, and it's becoming standard operating procedure for dealing with hefty halibut. Attaching the harpoon line to a large buoy lets the halibut wear itself out with much less chance of a broken harpoon line, broken boat or broken human body parts. A big fish may take the buoy under and keep it down for as long as several minutes, but man's ingenuity almost always wins out, and when the big, orange ball bobs to the surface, it usually means the toughest part of the battle is over.

While many anglers favor using a harpoon for halibut, they have a broad range of opinions on exactly where to stick a big fish when it's brought to the side of the boat. Some go for the head, which offers both advantages and disadvantages. One advantage is that a well-placed harpoon through the noggin may also kill or stun the fish. Just as with a gaff, though, a bad job with a head shot may knock the fish off the hook or break the leader, and it may also cause a mortal injury to the fish without securing it.

Some harpoon advocates prefer to stick a halibut through the stomach, for a couple of reasons. First, they say, a harpoon head through the belly of a fish doesn't ruin any valuable fillets. Secondly, the halibut's stomach is softer and easier to penetrate with the harpoon head. That same softness, however, may allow a surging halibut to tear itself free of the harpoon line, escaping to die on the ocean bottom.

Rod Kelly, who operates Alaskan Sports, a Sitka-based charter operation, likes to run his harpoon through the front portion of the gill cover, near the back edge of the head. He says such placement not only holds big fish, but serves another purpose as well. A newly harpooned fish will usually lunge forward and downward, he says, and the wire harpoon line will cut through several gill arches on the entrance side of the hole, causing a rapid loss of blood that helps to tame the fish very quickly.

Probably the "safest" place to harpoon a halibut, though, is through the shoulder area, about one-third of the way down its body from the tip of its nose. If the harpoon head enters above the fish's lateral line, you're penetrating heavy muscle, bones and tough skin, which will hold a harpoon no matter what the halibut does. If you hit as low as the lateral line itself, you may even sever the spine, helping to immobilize the fish. Keep in mind, however, that this is the thickest, toughest part of the halibut's body, maybe a foot through or more on trophy fish, so you have to ram that spear home with everything you have or you won't get the harpoon head all the way through the body.

Shooting Halibut

Firearms are often used to dispatch big halibut, especially in Alaska, where the practice is perfectly legal and where truly large fish are quite common. When done right, it's an effective way of dealing with big, unruly fish; when done wrong it results in lost trophies that swim away to die on the ocean bottom.

The idea, of course, is to kill the fish quickly, so that it can be handled safely at boatside, and that old saying about making the first shot count definitely applies here. The secret to success is in being ready when the halibut comes to the top, and placing the shot where it will stop the fish instantly.

Too many anglers shoot halibut without first thinking about it, apparently assuming that if they hit a fish anywhere in the front half of the body it will die on the spot. That's why we hear stories about "really tough" barn doors that had to be shot three, four, five times before they could be subdued. An angler who shoots a halibut four or five times probably doesn't know what he's doing; the fish finally bleeds to death and he's damn lucky to salvage it at all.

Too many halibut are shot in the gills, stomach, lips, eyes, even the middle of the body, by anglers who aren't sure what it's all about. A bad head-shot is a good way to knock a halibut off the hook, while a body shot is an almost sure way to send the fish rocketing back toward the bottom. Either way, there's a good chance it will escape, mortally wounded.

The best place to shoot a halibut is in the brain, no easy task when you consider the size of the fish's think box compared to its overall body size, and it's easy to miss even if you work hard at hitting it. Don't make the mistake of thinking, as many anglers do, that the brain fills up the halibut's entire skull. That's true with humans but not with fish.

Stan Malcom, who operates Magic Man Charters out of Petersburg, Alaska, is a master at making his shots count once he makes the decision to use firepower on a halibut. Although .410 shotguns using either slugs or bird shot and .30 caliber handguns are the most commonly used firearms for halibut-busting, Malcom does it with a .22 pistol, and he almost never needs more than one shot.

The handgun allows him to get up close and personal, so that the muzzle is only an inch or two away and exactly where he wants it pointed when he pulls the trigger. His target is a spot one to two inches behind the halibut's anterior (top) eye, and when the tiny .22 slug hits its mark, the fish usually doesn't even wiggle.

When you do shoot a halibut, even if you make a clean-kill shot, be ready to secure the fish quickly. The dead or dying fish may turn toward bottom and begin to sink, head-first, and you may not be able to stop it with the rod and reel. Take it from someone who's been there, a dead 150 or 200-pound halibut is nearly impossible to crank up from the depths with standard fishing tackle. Don't make the mistake of shooting and then standing around waiting for the halibut to make the next move. Act quickly to get a shark hook in its lip or a heavy line around its tail and get it secured. Some anglers even shoot big fish and then stick a harpoon through them so that they have a buoy line connected to the creature.

Make your decision whether or not to use a gun before the fish reaches the surface, so that you're ready to shoot when the fish comes to the top and flattens out, as they usually do.

A buoy attached to a harpoon head is an excellent way to subdue trophy halibut. Anglers who use this method on 300 to 400-pound fish have said the float can stay down for five to 15 minutes before popping back to the surface.

Harpooning, Gaffing

If you decide that it's a "shooter" after it comes into sight, the fish may have time to make other plans before you can spring into action.

Keep in mind also that in the area you're fishing it may not be legal to shoot a halibut. The regulations in British Columbia, for example, are very clear: DON'T DO IT! Washington regulations also ban the use of firearms for dispatching fish, and fisheries enforcement agents say they'll cite anglers who shoot halibut, yet the practice is quite common. We're not saying to go ahead and do it anyway, but we are saying we don't know of a single instance where a Washington halibut angler has ever been ticketed for shooting a barn-door fish. In Oregon waters, halibut-shooting also occurs, but the regulations are a little grey there. While shooting is listed as an illegal method of harvesting fish in the Beaver State, so are netting and gaffing, but both are commonly used to land fish.

As if a halibut angler doesn't have enough to worry about when he brings a monster flatty to the boat, he should also consider whether the fish might be a potential record-breaker before he decides how to subdue it. The International Game Fish Association (IGFA) bans the use of guns or harpoons on any fish to be considered for all-tackle or line-class world record status (See "Is It A Record?" chapter for more information).

Bleeding Halibut Is Important

Okay, so you have finally gained control of that halibut at boatside, have it secured with a stout line or two, and you think it's dead. What do you do now?

First, never assume a halibut is dead until it's cut and wrapped! You're better off always thinking the fish has some life left, because then you'll be more careful about dealing with it.

Next, while the fish is still in the water, cut a couple of gill arches or stick a sharp knife into the soft tissue immediately behind and near the bottom of the gill cover to sever the aorta.

If you make the proper cut and the fish has any life left at all, the water should instantly turn red with blood.

Bleeding the fish serves two very important purposes. In the short term, it helps to take the wind out of its sails and speeds the dying process. Over the long term, a fish that's properly bled will taste a whole lot better on the dinner table, especially if it's kept in the freezer for some time before you eat it. The edibility factor, by the way, applies to any fish you plan to eat, not just halibut.

Alan Veys, owner of Pybus Point Resort on Southeast Alaska's Admiralty Island, and Stan Malcom of Magic Man Charters in Petersburg both go a step further when it comes to bleeding halibut. They make a cut not only in a gill arch or two, but also across the base of the tail, so that the fish is opened up at both ends and therefore bleeds much more freely.

Do You Boat It Or Not?

Now comes the decision on whether or not to boat the fish. As a general rule, it's usually best to leave really large fish outside the boat, but they must be well-secured. Two lines, one around the base of the tail and one through the mouth and gill cover, then tied off in different directions to "stretch out" the critter, will immobilize it and ensure against the kind of break-off that may occur with a single line at one end or the other.

If you decide to bring a big one aboard, it's best to do so after it's had plenty of time to bleed out and settle down. "Green" fish just up from the bottom are the most lively and the most dangerous, so don't bring one into the boat unless you are absolutely sure that you're ready to deal with it effectively. Even a 30-pounder can wreck havoc if allowed to dance all over the deck, so have a sturdy club in hand and be ready to use it—about a half-dozen times right behind the eyes should do it—if you decide to go that route.

If your boat is equipped with a large fish box, get any halibut you boat into it as quickly as possible, preferably in one motion directly from the water. Then slam the lid shut and sit on it

It looks as though the ball game may be over for this halibut in the 80-pound range, as it starts over the gunwale at the business end of a hay-hook type gaff. A couple of good head-shakes and the fish squirms off the gaff's straight point. It remained hooked for a few seconds, then pulled free from the leadhead jig that had been stuck in its jaw for nearly a half-hour. An inadequate gaff and sloppy fish handling costs another angler his prize.

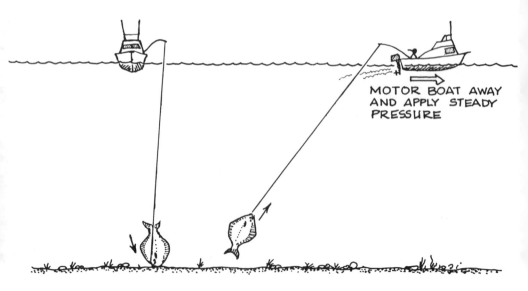

MOTOR BOAT AWAY
AND APPLY STEADY
PRESSURE

To budge bottom-hugging, barn-door halibut, motor boat away from the fish while applying pressure and you'll start the fish planing to the surface.

until the fish calms down. If it's a big fish, piling atop the box for several minutes might not be a bad idea.

If you decide to bring halibut aboard and don't have a fish box big enough to hold them, you might want to "bow" them or "U" them, which means slipping a loop around the base of the tail and sliding the other end of the line through a gill cover and out the mouth, then cinching the line as tight as you can get it to bring the head and tail together. Having several pre-tied pieces of 3/8-inch cord with a loop in one end and a two-foot length of broom handle tied to the other makes the job much easier and safer. You don't want to try sliding that line through those gill covers with your bare hands unless you have extra blood and couple of fingers you don't need.

One of the trickiest and potentially most dangerous situations in halibut fishing is dealing with really big halibut in really small boats, and those circumstances crop up every year, especially in Alaska waters. What anglers in that situation sometimes forget is that no fish is worth dying for, so don't gamble or leave anything to chance. The dangers include capsizing or swamping the boat, as well as the broken bones and other physical abuse you're likely to suffer when you find yourself going one-on-one in a very confined area with 200 pounds of slimy muscle.

Sticking a harpoon into the fish and letting a big, buoyant buoy do its job is probably the best course of action if you find yourself in the small boat/big halibut predicament. While the fish struggles against the buoy, you have time to ready another line or two, which you may be able to use to tie off the brute's head and tail to opposite ends of the boat.

How to Catch
Trophy Halibut

If you're fishing near shore, you might use the buoy line or add a second line to tow a big fish into the shallows and onto the beach. This tactic can be a little tricky and can get you wet, but it has helped many small-boat anglers secure some very large halibut. If you're going to wrestle with a halibut as big as or bigger than you, you're certainly better off doing it on a gravel beach than within the confines of 14-foot skiff.

A word of caution, though, is in order whenever we talk about towing a big halibut with a small boat. Several things can happen when you start leading a big fish around like a dog on a leash, and many of them are bad. You might start out as the tow-er and suddenly find yourself becoming the towed, heading for places you don't really want to go, such as the bottom of the ocean! For that reason, depending on the size of the fish and the buoyancy of the skiff, you may want to hold the tow line instead of tying it off to the boat. You also have to keep the fish from taking the line into the propeller, which can lead to any number of problems, the least serious of which is losing your hard-earned halibut.

The bottom line is to use common sense, have a game plan, act quickly and don't take any unnecessary chances when it comes to controlling and securing any big halibut. Having the right equipment on board and knowing how to use it at the moment of truth is also a must. In a nutshell, prepare for success and you'll be successful.

Co-author Chris Batin hooked this 100-pounder while fishing for rockfish from a 12-foot skiff in Prince William Sound. The boat was not equipped with a gun, gaff or net. Angling partner Mark Wade helped the author plane the fish 120 yards to shore, where Batin quickly jumped out of the boat and beached the fish. The hook ripped free and the halibut flopped back into the water. The author wrestled an arm into the upper gill of the fish. He grabbed a rock and ended the battle with a quick blow to the fish's head. Adela Batin photos.

CHAPTER 14

Is It A Record?

While the old saying, "A trophy is in the eye of the beholder," may apply to any fish caught that has special significance to the angler, the same does not apply to fish considered for the record books.

Each year, many trophy halibut are disqualified from record consideration due to anglers not being familiar with record-book regulations. It isn't necessary to catch a 300 to 400-pound "barn-door" halibut to make the record books. Various line-class categories, men and women's categories, annual contests (largest fish caught each year) and flyfishing categories entice anglers to catch 50 to 70-pound-plus fish and make the record books. These categories were created by various agencies to provide additional opportunities for anglers to experience the thrill and recognition of catching a record-book fish.

The coveted all-tackle, world-and line-class records are issued and maintained by the International Game Fish Association (IGFA). The IGFA is internationally known and respected as the central-processing center for world-record catch data. The association also represents a variety of angling interests, maintains a 10,000-book library of angling literature, operates museums, supervises angling clubs and tournaments and distributes information to government officials. Every angler should be a member of IGFA. But more on this later.

If you desire to be a world-record holder for halibut, first join IGFA and obtain a copy of their book, *World Record Game Fishes*, updated and published each year. Each species is broken down into various categories, giving you an idea of the records you have the best chance of breaking.

John Lucking and Ken Stuckey with a 439-pound halibut that missed breaking the Alaska state record by two pounds. Because the fish was harpooned, it was ineligible for consideration as the all-tackle, IGFA world-record Pacific halibut. Photo by Greg Obeso.

For instance, a 54-pound fish currently holds the IGFA men's six-pound-line-class record, while a 350-pound fish holds the men's 130-pound-line-class record.

In the women's category, the six-pound line category is currently vacant, and a 131-pound fish holds the 16-pound-line-class record. The California halibut categories—in both men's and women's ranks—also provide good opportunities to break existing records.

The current, all-tackle record for halibut recognized by IGFA is a 395-pound fish taken from Unalaska Bay, Alaska in 1995 by Mike Golat.

"Only 395 pounds?" you may ask. "I read about 400-pound fish being caught and landed each year in the sporting press and newspapers."

You are correct. Many of the landing techniques universally accepted for landing large halibut (such as shooting, harpooning, marker buoys attached to harpoon heads) are illegal under IGFA rules and when used disqualify the catch.

Shooting a sport-caught halibut is perhaps the single largest reason fish are disqualified. Shooting a fish—either with a .410, .22 or .38—is a popular practice among charter operators, not only for show, but also for safety reasons. Landing a 100 to 300-pound halibut can be dangerous, especially with other anglers standing on deck. Unless the skippers and deckhands are told about your desire to land the fish under IGFA guidelines, they will attempt to subdue the fish as quickly as possible, with whatever means available to them.

Read The Fine Print First

If you're a hard-core record-seeker, you've spent countless hours on the water trying to land that qualifying fish. You know the regs inside and out. You've invested hundreds of dollars in specialized rods, reels, tackle and charters. This section isn't for you. It's for the reader who is unfamiliar with record-book rules and regulations.

It is extremely important you read this section NOW, and not skip to another chapter. Here's why: Once you're on the water and hook a fish that nearly drags you overboard, your first and foremost concern is to land the fish. There is neither time to read regs, nor interpret them. If you know the requirements for world-record qualification, you rig accordingly and direct the landing of that fish. Simple.

Unfortunately, most anglers disregard this advice. They learn of the following regulations at the scales. The skipper reveals that their fish beat the current record by 30 pounds, but it is disqualified because it was harpooned and/or shot. Many times I've seen the resulting, disappointed look on a potential record-holder's face. Vow never to have this happen to you. The thrill of catching a world-record fish is perhaps a once-in-a-lifetime occurrence. The pleasure is doubled when you and your fish are recognized via a world-record certificate.

Yet be careful not to mix or confuse the various regulations. For instance, under the State of Alaska trophy fish program, shooting and harpooning a trophy halibut is legal.

There is a list of do's and don'ts provided by IGFA and they fall into three categories: preparation, the catch, and follow-up.

To enter a catch in a line class, your line must test out at a breaking strength less than that figure.

Since IGFA records are set up in specific line classes (except all-tackle records) you should fish 2, 4, 8, 12, 16, 20, 30, 50, 80, or 130-pound-test line. You should try to ensure the line will break at or less than the rated breaking strength on the package. The break-strength of many lines are understated on the package, so what you think is 8-pound-test line actually breaks at, say 10 or 11 pounds, or more. You may enter a fish caught on that line for the 8-pound class record, only to find that the line was much stronger than the package said it was, and your catch qualified for the 12-pound class. Records are disallowed when the angler's line overtests.

There are several items that should accompany you on every excursion to waters that might produce a record fish. You should pack a flexible tape measure at least 15 feet long, a camera, a length of heavy cord, a six-inch square of stiff cardboard to wind the line to submit to IGFA, and several plastic bags.

Be sure the reels are spooled with fresh line, that rod guides and reel seats are in good repair, and that drags are smooth. Use hand scales to check the drag.

Check your terminal tackle. Be sure the swivels and swivel clips are Sampo ball-bearing types rather than barrel swivels which won't turn freely under load. Check all knots and crimped sleeves, as well as wire and monofilament leaders. Retie knots and re-do crimps with a crimping tool.

Are all hooks honed sharp enough, and is every bit of tackle between angler and fish matched to the possibility of a record-size catch?

No one may touch the rod, reel, double line or standing line from the moment of the strike to the landing. Once you bring the fish to the boat, a crew member may grab the leader—but only the leader and not the double line. You're on your own from the strike to the wiring.

It is your responsibility to see that the fish is weighed on a certified scale, and you must measure the fork length and girth of the fish.

Clear photos are required by IGFA to confirm your identification of the species. The IGFA Rule Book spells out in detail all procedures to apply for a world record.

Inform The Skipper and Deckhand of Your Intentions

Whether you desire to have your name in the IGFA record book, receive a trophy halibut certificate from the State of Alaska, or perhaps qualify for a state angling record in the lower 48, make a point to follow through on this bit of advice if you decide to charter: inform your skipper and deckhand of your requirements prior to fishing. Take along a copy of this book and IGFA's World Record Game Fishes so they can read for themselves the requirements for a world-record catch.

As the International Gamefish Association's senior representative for Alaska, I see many halibut skippers over the course of a summer. Most are not as well versed as they should be with IGFA regs. Ultimately, it is your responsibility to know what is allowed and disallowed should you want to pursue an IGFA world or line-class record.

Again, I emphasize preparing the boat and crew ahead of time so no mistakes are made in handling or landing your record-book fish. Many fish are disqualified each year because the deckhand grabs the mainline rather than the leader.

While you're at it, check out the gaffs and tackle. Don't expect that $175 for a day charter will guarantee you the same quality equipment you use on your boat. It's best to bring your own gear, and have the deckhands use it to land your fish only. Do this while in port so you'll have time to replace illegal gear or tackle.

IGFA has allowed us to reprint the following rules and regulations to familiarize you with a few of their requirements for world-record catches. For a complete copy of the regulations, official forms and membership information, write or call:

IGFA
Dept. BH
1301 East Atlantic Blvd.
Pompano Beach, FL 33060
(305) 941-3474

How to Catch
Trophy Halibut

IGFA Regulations—An Overview

The following angling rules have been formulated by the International Game Fish Association to promote ethical and sporting angling practices, to establish uniform regulations for the compilation of world game fish records, and to provide basic angling guidelines for use in fishing tournaments and any other group angling activities.

The word "angling" is defined as catching or attempting to catch fish with a rod, reel, line, and hook as outlined in the international angling rules. There are some aspects of angling that cannot be controlled through rulemaking, however. Angling regulations cannot ensure an outstanding performance from each fish, and world records cannot indicate the amount of difficulty in catching the fish. Captures in which the fish has not fought or has not had a chance to fight do not reflect credit on the fisherman, and only the angler can properly evaluate the degree of achievement in establishing the record.

Only fish caught in accordance with IGFA international angling rules, and within the intent of these rules, will be considered for world records.

Following are the rules for halibut fishing and a separate set of rules for fly fishing.

Equipment Regulations

A. Line

1. Monofilament, multifilament, and lead core multifilament lines may be used.

2. Wire lines are prohibited.

B. Line Backing

1. Backing not attached to the fishing line is permissible with no restrictions as to size or material.

2. If the fishing line is attached to the backing, the catch shall be classified under the heavier of the two lines. The backing may not exceed the 130 pound (60 kg) line class and must be of a type of line approved for use in these angling rules.

C. Double Line

The use of a double line is not required. If one is used, it must meet the following specifications:

1. A double line must consist of the actual line used to catch the fish.

2. Double lines are measured from the start of the knot, braid, roll or splice making the double to the farthest end of the knot,

splice, snap, swivel or other device used for securing the trace, leader, lure or hook to the double line.

Saltwater species: In all line classes up to and including 20 pound (10 kg), the double line shall be limited to 15 feet (4.57 meters). The combined length of the double line and leader shall not exceed 20 feet (6.1 meters).

The double line on all classes of tackle over 20 pound (10 kg) shall be limited to 30 feet (9.14 meters). The combined length of the double line and leader shall not exceed 40 feet (12.19 meters).

D. Leader

The use of a leader is not required. If one is used, it must meet the following specifications:

1. The length of the leader is the overall length including any lure, hook arrangement or other device. The leader must be connected to the line with a snap, knot, splice, swivel or other device. Holding devices are prohibited. There are no regulations regarding the material or strength of the leader.

Saltwater species: In all line classes up to and including 20 pound (10 kg), the leader shall be limited to 15 feet (4.57 meters). The combined length of the double line and leader shall not exceed 20 feet (6.1 meters).

The leader on all classes of tackle over 20 pound (10 kg) shall be limited to 30 feet (9.14 meters). The combined length of the double line and leader shall be limited to 40 feet (12.19 meters).

E. Rod

1. Rods must comply with sporting ethics and customs. Considerable latitude is allowed in the choice of a rod, but rods giving the angler an unfair advantage will be disqualified. This rule is intended to eliminate the use of unconventional rods.

2. The rod tip must be a minimum of 40 inches (101.6 cm) in length. The rod butt cannot exceed 27 inches (68.58 cm) in length. These measurements must be made from a point directly beneath the center of the reel. A curved butt is measured in a straight line. (The above measurements do not apply to surf casting rods.)

F. Reel

1. Reels must comply with sporting ethics and customs.
2. Power driven reels of any kind are prohibited. This includes

motor, hydraulic, or electrically driven reels, and any device which gives the angler an unfair advantage.

3. Ratchet handle reels are prohibited.

4. Reels designed to be cranked with both hands at the same time are prohibited.

G. Hooks For Bait Fishing

1. For live or dead bait fishing no more than two single hooks may be used. Both must be firmly imbedded in or securely attached to the bait. The eyes of the hooks must be no less than a hook's length (the length of the largest hook used) apart and no more than 18 inches (45.72 cm) apart. The only exception is that the point of one hook may be passed through the eye of the other hook.

2. The use of a dangling or swinging hook is prohibited. Double or treble hooks are prohibited.

3. A two-hook rig for bottom fishing is acceptable if it consists of two single hooks on separate leaders or drops. Both hooks must be imbedded in the respective baits and separated sufficiently so that a fish caught on one hook cannot be foul-hooked by the other.

4. All record applications made for fish caught on two-hook tackle must be accompanied by a photograph or sketch of the hook arrangement.

H. Hooks And Lures

1. When using an artificial lure with a skirt or trailing material, no more than two single hooks may be attached to the line, leader, or trace. The hooks need not be attached separately. The eyes of the hooks must be no less than an overall hook's length (the overall length of the largest hook used) apart and no more than 12 inches (30.48 cm) apart. The only exception is that the point of one hook may be passed through the eye of the other hook. The trailing hook may not extend more than a hook's length beyond the skirt of the lure. A photograph or sketch showing the hook arrangement must accompany a record application.

2. Gang hooks are permitted when attached to plugs and other artificial lures that are specifically designed for this use. Gang hooks must be free swinging and shall be limited to a maximum of three hooks (either single, double, or treble, or a combination of any three). Baits may not be used with gang hooks. A photograph or sketch of the plug or lure must be submitted with record applications.

I. Other Equipment

1. *Fighting chairs* may not have any mechanically propelled devices which aid the angler in fighting a fish.

2. *Gimbals* must be free swinging, which includes gimbals that swing in a vertical plane only. Any gimbal that allows the angler to reduce strain or to rest while fighting the fish is prohibited.

3. *Gaffs and nets* used to boat or land a fish must not exceed 8 feet (2.44 meters) in overall length. In using a flying or detachable gaff the rope may not exceed 30 feet (9.14 meters). The gaff rope must be measured from the point where it is secured to the detachable head to the other end. Only the effective length will be considered. If a fixed head gaff is used, the same limitations shall apply and the gaff rope shall be measured from the same location on the gaff hook. Only a single hook is permitted on any gaff. Harpoon or lance attachments are prohibited. Tail ropes are limited to 30 feet (9.14 meters). When fishing from a bridge, pier, or other high platform or structure, this length limitation does not apply).

4. *Floats* are prohibited with the exception of any small flotation device attached to the line or leader for the sole purpose of regulating the depth of the bait. The flotation device must not in any way hamper the fighting ability of the fish.

5. *Entangling devices*, either with or without a hook, are prohibited and may not be used for any purpose including baiting, hooking, fighting, or landing the fish.

6. *Outriggers, downriggers, and kites* are permitted to be used provided that the actual fishing line is attached to the snap or other release device, either directly or with some other material. The leader or double line may not be connected to the release mechanism either directly or with the use of a connecting device.

7. A *safety line* may be attached to the rod provided that it does not in any way assist the angler in fighting the fish.

Angling Regulations

1. From the time that a fish strikes or takes a bait or lure, the angler must hook, fight, and land or boat the fish without the aid of any other person, except as provided in these regulations.

2. If a rod holder is used and a fish strikes or takes the bait or lure, the angler must remove the rod from the holder as quickly as possible. The intent of this rule is that the angler shall strike and hook the fish with the rod in hand.

How to Catch
Trophy Halibut

3. In the event of a multiple strike on separate lines being fished by a single angler, only the first fish fought by the angler will be considered for a world record.

4. If a double line is used, the intent of the regulations is that the fish will be fought on the single line most of the time that it takes to land the fish.

5. A harness may be attached to the reel or rod, but not to the fighting chair. The harness may be replaced or adjusted by a person other than the angler.

6. Use of a rod belt or waist gimbal is permitted.

7. When angling from a boat, once the leader is brought within the grasp of the mate, or the end of the leader is wound to the rod tip, more than one person is permitted to hold the leader.

8. One or more gaffers may be used in addition to persons holding the leader. The gaff handle must be in hand when the fish is gaffed.

9. The angling and equipment regulations shall apply until the fish is weighed.

Any of the following will disqualify a catch:

1. Failure to comply with equipment or angling regulations.

2. The act of persons other than the angler in touching any part of the rod, reel, or line (including the double line) either bodily or with any device, from the time a fish strikes or takes the bait or lure, until the fish is either landed or released, or in giving any aid other than that allowed in the rules and regulations. If an obstacle to the passage of the line through the rod guides has to be removed from the line, then the obstacle shall be held and cut free. The line may not be held or touched by anyone other than the angler during this process.

3. Resting the rod in a rod holder, on the gunwale of the boat, or any other object while playing the fish.

4. Handlining or using a handline or rope attached in any manner to the angler's line or leader for the purpose of holding or lifting the fish.

5. Shooting, harpooning, or lancing any fish (including sharks and halibuts) at any stage of the catch.

6. Chumming with or using as bait the flesh, blood, skin, or any part of mammals other than hair or pork rind used in lures designed for trolling or casting.

7. Using a boat or device to beach or drive a fish into shallow water in order to deprive the fish of its normal ability to swim.

8. Changing the rod or reel while the fish is being played.

9. Splicing, removing, or adding to the line while the fish is being played.

10. Intentionally foul-hooking a fish.

11. Catching a fish in a manner that the double line never leaves the rod tip.

12. Using a size or kind of bait that is illegal to possess.

13. Attaching the angler's line or leader to part of a boat or other object for the purpose of holding or lifting the fish.

14. If a fish escapes before gaffing or netting and is recaptured by any method other than as outlined in the angling rules.

15. When a rod breaks (while the fish is being played) in a manner that reduces the length of the tip below minimum dimensions or severely impairs its angling characteristics.

16. Mutilation to the fish, prior to landing or boating the catch, caused by sharks, other fish, mammals, propellers, or other objects that remove or penetrate the flesh. (Injuries caused by leader or line, scratches, old healed scars or regeneration deformities are not disqualifying injuries.) Any mutilation on the fish must be shown in a photograph and fully explained in a separate report accompanying the record application.

17. When a fish is hooked or entangled on more than one line.

Rules For Fly Fishing

Equipment Regulations

A. Line

Any type of fly line and backing may be used. The breaking strength of the fly line and backing are not restricted.

B. Leader

Leaders must conform to generally accepted fly fishing customs.

A leader includes a class tippet and, optionally, a shock tippet. A butt or taper section between the fly line and the class tippet shall also be considered part of the leader and there are no limits on its length, material, or strength.

A class tippet must be made of nonmetallic material and either attached directly to the fly or to the shock tippet if one is used. The class tippet must be at least 15 inches (38.10 cm) long (measured inside connecting knots). With respect to knotless, tapered leaders, the terminal 15 inches (38.10 cm) will also determine tippet class. There is no maximum length limitation.

A shock tippet, not to exceed 12 inches (30.48 cm) in length, may be added to the class tippet and tied to the lure. It can be made of any type of material, and there is no limit on its breaking strength.

The shock tippet is measured from the eye of the hook to the single strand of class tippet and includes any knots used to connect the shock tippet to the class tippet. In the case of a tandem hook fly, the shock tippet shall be measured from the eye of the leading hook.

C. Rod

Regardless of material used or number of sections, rods must conform to generally accepted fly fishing customs and practices. A rod shall not measure less than 6 feet (1.82 meters) in overall length. Any rod that gives the angler an unsporting advantage will be disqualified. Extension butts are limited to 6 inches (15.24 cm).

D. Reel

The reel must be designed expressly for fly fishing. There are no restrictions on gear ratio or type of drag employed except where the angler would gain an unfair advantage. Electric or electronically operated reels are prohibited.

E. Hooks

A conventional fly may be dressed on a single or double hook or two single hooks in tandem. The second hook in any tandem fly must not extend beyond the wing material. The eyes of the hooks shall be no farther than 6 inches (15.24 cm) apart. Treble hooks are prohibited.

F. Lures

The lure must be a recognized type of artificial fly, which includes streamer, bucktail, tube fly, wet fly, dry fly, nymph, popper and bug. Only one fly is allowed. The use of any other type of lure or natural or preserved bait, either singularly or attached to the fly, is expressly prohibited. Scent of any kind may not be added to the fly. Scented material may not be used to create the fly. The fact that a lure can be cast with a fly rod is not evidence in itself that it fits the definition of a fly. The use of any lure designed to entangle or foul-hook a fish is prohibited.

G. Gaffs & Nets

Gaffs and nets used to boat or land a fish must not exceed

8 feet (2.44 meters) in overall length. (When fishing from a bridge, pier or other high structure, this length limitation does not apply.) The use of a flying gaff is not permitted. Only a single hook is permitted on any gaff. Harpoon or lance attachments are prohibited. A rope or any extension cannot be attached to the gaff.

World Record Requirements

Game fish catches can only be considered for world record status if they are caught according to IGFA's International Angling Rules. An application fee of $10 U.S. for IGFA members and $25 U.S. for nonmembers is required for each claim. All materials submitted become the property of IGFA.

State Of Alaska Trophy Fish Program

Rules and an entry form for participating in the State of Alaska Trophy Fish Program can be found in the Alaska sport-fishing regulations.

All entries must meet minimum weight qualifications and must be weighed on a currently certified scale. A copy listing state-certified scales can be obtained by contacting the Chamber of Commerce in the area you are fishing.

Halibut entries may also qualify by meeting a minimum length requirement of 84 inches. The fish must be measured in the presence of a trophy fish official (list available through ADF&G offices). Keep in mind, however, while a measured-only halibut may win you an honorary certificate, the fish must also be weighed on a certified scale in order for it to qualify for either a state or annual record. Play it safe. If you have a potential annual or world record, have it weighed.

According to Jon Lyman with ADF&G, over the last two years, 75 percent or more of all the trophy certificates issued for halibut have been for fish caught from Cook Inlet, with Seward, Kodiak Island and southeast Alaska contributing the bulk of the remaining entries. Currently, only 13, 24 and 12 trophy fish awards for halibut have been issued (or are being prepared to be issued) the last three years. While this indicates that record-book fish are available in the Cook Inlet area, it does not mean that large numbers of fish are unavailable elsewhere in the state. Many factors influence the issue or non-issue of a trophy catch application: many are tourists and desire the award; many Alaska residents don't want to publicize their local fishing grounds; non-availability of a certified scale or trophy fish official; time of day, travel schedule and other factors.

In contrast, look at the IGFA record book and you'll find entries equally distributed from Kodiak to southeast Alaska. In short: don't allow the figures to mislead you as to where you can find large halibut. Big fish can be caught all along the state's coastline, from the Bering Sea to Ketchikan.

For information about state trophy-fish programs, contact:

Alaska Department of Fish and Game
Division of Sportfish
P. O. Box 25526
Juneau, AK 99802-5526

Washington Department of Fish and Wildlife
600 Capitol Way North
Olympia WA 98501-1091
(360) 902-2200

Oregon Department of Fish and Wildlife
P. O. Box 59
Portland OR 97207
(503) 229-5400

California Department of Fish and Game
1416 Ninth Street
Sacramento CA 95814
(916) 445-3531

CHAPTER 15

Keep 'em Cool And Clean

The cook deserves only part of the credit whenever that halibut entree turns out sweet, moist and delicious. If the fillets you bring home are to live up to the halibut's reputation as one of the best-eating fish anywhere, the preparation begins out on the water, the moment the fish is subdued. A successful halibut-fishing trip might produce hundreds of pounds of prime fillets, but sloppy care of your catch can turn that top-notch table fare into so much cat food. If you're going to catch 'em, you owe it to yourself and to the halibut resource to take proper care of your fish right from the start. It's really quite easy.

The subject of bleeding halibut in order to kill them was described in a previous chapter, but it merits further mention here as well, because it's one of the most important things you can do to help ensure quality table fare. As a charter skipper whose identity we can't even remember told us many years ago, "If you're going to bother killing a halibut, you'd damn well better bleed it." Much of the strong, "fishy" smell and taste found in fish is the result of blood that remains in the carcass after the fish is dead, and the halibut is certainly no exception. If your halibut is to taste its best, bleed it before it dies. A fillet from a well-bled halibut will look clean and white when it's packaged, smell fresh when it's unwrapped, and taste sweet and mild when it reaches the dinner table.

Differences in quality between bled and unbled halibut are especially noticeable after freezing for prolonged periods. The flesh from a halibut that hasn't been bled seems to develop a stronger and stronger taste the longer it's in the freezer, even if it's well-wrapped and otherwise cared for properly.

Co-author Chris Batin with a 90-pound halibut he caught while fishing 340 feet of water with an Alvey Deep Sea snapper reel and Sabre rod. The fish was bled and iced, which resulted in excellent eating fillets.

Many halibut anglers prefer to bleed their fish outside the boat, and that's not a bad idea. It certainly eliminates some of the mess on the boat's deck, and it probably allows the fish to bleed out a little more thoroughly.

Some anglers believe that leaving halibut in the water rather than boating them is also beneficial in another very important way, especially on warm, sunny days. Yes, the waters of the chilly Pacific tend to be much cooler than the deck of a fishing boat on a calm July day, and keeping fish cool is always a very good idea. Remember, though, that the surface water is much warmer than the depths from which you just cranked that fish, and prolonged exposure to this warm water may not be all that good for the quality of your catch. It's easy to understand why a halibut that bakes in the sun all day won't provide the same firm, quality fillets you'll get if you keep the fish cool from the time it's caught until the time it's packaged and frozen.

If you choose not to keep your halibut tethered outside your boat, do your best to keep fish shaded and cooled down with liberal dousings of water. Having several burlap sacks on hand is a good idea, because they can be dampened and draped over your catch to keep it cool and shaded.

A large fish box or cooler will also protect halibut from the drying and warming effects of the sun, especially if you're really prepared and throw a couple blocks or bags of ice in it at the start of the day. If the box has a drain, keep it open and use plenty of water every now and then to wash out excess blood and slime. If there isn't a drain, you might want to bleed the fish before putting it in the box, or at least mop the mess out to keep fish from slopping around in the slimy goo all day.

Some conscientious halibut anglers go so far as to gill and gut their fish before tossing them into the fish box, and that extra effort certainly doesn't hurt, especially if it's certain that fish won't be filleted for a long time. Fish spoilage usually begins in the gills and innards, so removing them can slow the process considerably.

Of course, if you really want the best halibut dinners possible, you'll bleed your fish, get them on a bed of clean, crushed ice immediately and fillet them as soon as possible, never allowing the flesh to warm much above freezing throughout the entire process. Halibut treated with that kind of tender, loving care provide fillets that will make you a hero, maybe even a legend!

The University of Alaska Sea Grant Program published a booklet for commercial halibut fishermen entitled, *"Care of Halibut Aboard the Fishing Vessel"* by Donald Kramer and

Brian Paust. We have found much of the advice also pertains to sport-caught halibut, especially on charter boats where the hurried conditions to make the most of a bite, the competition, and "let it go until later" attitude also affects the quality of fish destined for dinner tables. The marine advisory bulletin reiterates some of the above points, as well as elaborating on methods of halibut care, and we intentionally repeat several pointers.

This section is for the many charter boat deckhands we've observed over the years who have violated two or more of these guidelines. If you see your fish baking in the sun, shot full of holes, or improperly cared for, speak up and demand proper care of your halibut. You'll be the one eating this fish, while the deckhand will be sunning himself somewhere in Mexico or Hawaii. Most anglers haven't the foggiest notion of how to care for halibut, and after their fish are caught, have allowed such transgressions to take place unchallenged. Read on and never again plead ignorance!

The following advice from "Care of Halibut Aboard the Fishing Vessel" is reprinted here with permission:

Stun and bleed halibut as soon as they are brought onboard. They are very active fish; allowing them to struggle on deck before killing can result in several problems including physical damage to the muscle which later shows up as bruising. For this reason, large halibut should not be allowed to flop on deck or on a layer of previously killed fish. Take special care when stunning a fish positioned on top of other halibut to be sure that all stunning blows are accurately directed. In addition, allowing excessive exhausting of halibut may impair quality and lead to a condition called "chalkiness."

The stunning blows should be accurately placed, as blows to the body cause as much physical damage and bruising as if the fish had been left to flop around on the deck.

As mentioned previously, bleed halibut immediately after they are stunned. If fish are bled just after stunning, most of the removable blood will drain out in five to ten minutes. Less blood will drain when fish are not bled until after they are dead. When halibut are not properly bled, fish color will be poorer.

When practical, halibut should be dressed 20 to 30 minutes after bleeding.

At all times when fish are on deck, efforts should be made to keep the fish temperature from increasing. Control of temperature is the most important means the fisherman has of protecting quality. Both bacterial spoilage and deterioration due to enzymatic action will proceed much more rapidly at high temperature. If considerable time is expected to elapse before the fish are dressed, they should be kept wet and iced. If it is not practical to use ice, a number of other materials can be used to cover the fish to provide evaporative heat removal. Clean burlap sacks saturated with water are good, and, if nothing else is available, wet seaweed fronds can be used. Protect halibut from sun and weather with an awning, ice, clean wet burlap or canvas whenever there is a delay in getting the fish dressed and into cold storage.

Some halibut fishermen "cool" their halibut by holding them alongside their boats. The actual result of this practice is to cause a "warming" of the fish. Delays in getting halibut up out of the surface water will result in a rise in flesh temperature as the water at the bottom where the halibut are caught is about 10 to 15 degrees colder than the water at the surface. The recommendation given for holding tuna at the surface in sea water to cool is the opposite of what should be recommended for halibut. Tuna are pelagic fish, meaning that they live closer to the sea surface, in warmer water. In addition, the body temperature of a tuna can be considerably higher than that of its environment (as much as 10 to 15 degrees F). As a result, holding tuna in sea water can result in cooling.

Halibut, however, are demersal (bottom-dwelling) fish which live in water much colder than at the surface. Immersion of halibut in sea water at the side of the boat is not a practical means of keeping the fish cool. Most serious increases in fish flesh temperatures will be due to delays in cooling or dressing the fish, which will also be faster for smaller fish.

Bleeding Methods

A halibut is seldom instantaneously killed by the stunning club since the heart continues to beat after the stunning. Bleeding is absolutely necessary for the production of quality fish. It can be quickly accomplished by either opening the gill cavity and slashing one or more of the gill arches, or by severing the narrow band of tissue known as the isthmus that connects the halibut head to its lower body. Both cuts cause rapid arterial bleeding, which is completed in five to ten minutes.

A third bleeding cut involves making an incision at the lower part of the body just forward of the tail fin, upwards to the spine. The cut severs a major artery located just below the spine. Some buyers consider the tail cut a blemish and potential source of bacterial contamination.

Halibut which are well fed and in a good nutritional state appear to have better storage characteristics. This is possibly due to a higher amount of glycogen in well-fed fish which is converted to lactic acid during storage. This results in lower muscle pH (higher acidity) and lower rates of bacterial growth. It must be recognized that this will make the fish more susceptible to development of the condition referred to as "chalky" halibut.

Take a few minutes to properly care for your halibut, and you'll have fine eating for months to follow.

CHAPTER 16

Filleting Made Easy

Okay, so you've just caught yourself a 50-pound halibut—an absolutely gorgeous example of prime table fare—and you look around to realize that you aren't at a fly-in fishing lodge and aren't on a charter day-trip. There's a fresh halibut to be filleted and you're the only one around to do it! No problem. The job isn't as difficult as it might at first seem. Compared to some fish, halibut are pretty easy to fillet. It's just a matter of making a few cuts in the right places and taking the time to slice that sweet, white fillet off the skeleton.

The most important tool for the job is a good knife, and your pocket knife won't—please pardon the pun—cut it. You'll need a fillet knife with a fairly flexible blade at least eight inches in length. For large halibut, a 10-inch blade or longer will do the job even better. The knife, of course, should be kept razor-sharp at all times.

A cleaning glove is also a good idea, whatever kind of fish you may be filleting. The good ones are made of fine-weave wire, coated with plastic or nylon, so they protect your hand from fish spines, teeth, bones and errant fillet knives. The coarse fabric also helps hold slimy halibut and halibut parts. Some people wear one of these gloves on each hand, but most go with only one, and it's worn on the opposite hand from the one you use to wield the knife.

To do a good job of filleting, start with the fish on a table, stump or some other flat surface that's about waist-high. Working at ground level is tough on your back, neck, shoulders and knees, and you'll do a lousy job on the fish if you're in a hurry to get done and straighten up. To keep halibut from slipping away, many people lay a strip of indoor/outdoor carpet,

Veteran Homer halibut skipper Bruce Mallory begins an afternoon of work filleting halibut for his clients. Mallory often kept several sharpeners and razor-sharp knives nearby to speed up the chore.

burlap or some other coarse material down on the top of the cleaning table. Another option is to hammer a long nail or two up through a sheet of plywood, so that the fish may be thrust down, impaled and held in place while you're working on it.

Starting with the halibut dark-side-up, first remove the succulent cheek that lies between the eyes and the gill cover. It's easy to feel the edge of this round patch of soft flesh, and all you have to do is insert the knife point into the skin at that edge and make a circular cut all the way around it. Inserting the knife blade at an inward angle will make the job easier, since the cheek lies in a shallow cup in the halibut's skull, and you don't want to fight the bone as you carve the cheek away from it.

You can, if you wish, remove the entire cheek, skin and all, then slice the flesh away from the skin after the whole thing has been removed. Some people, though, leave an inch or two of skin attached to the head as they near the end of the circular cut to remove the cheek. By leaving it attached, they can fold the cheek "open" and slice it off the skin with the skin flap remaining on the carcass. This leave-the-skin-attached method is demonstrated below in Figure 1.

FIGURE 1

After turning the fish over to fillet the white side, you can first remove that cheek in the same way as you removed the first.

Now you're ready to fillet the halibut. Start by making a semi-circle cut behind the pectoral fin (Figure 2). The cut should extend all the way across the dark side of the fish, from the ventral fin to the anterior edge ahead of the dorsal fin. Don't

FIGURE 2

cut too deeply on the ventral (belly) end of this incision or you'll slice the stomach open and make the job a little messier than it has to be.

Next, make a deep cut the full length of the lateral line, which extends from your first cut all the way to the upper edge of the tail (Figure 3).

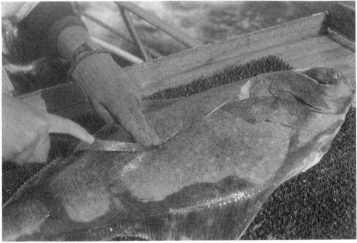

FIGURE 3

Note that the lateral line makes a gradual arc around the body cavity for about the first one-quarter of its length, then runs straight down the middle of the fish, diving the body into two pretty much symmetrical halves.

FIGURE 4

Separate the upper fillet from the skeleton (Figure 4), starting at the center cut and working toward the outer edge. Keep the knife blade as flat as possible against the ridge of bones, with the edge of the blade slicing the firm fillet away from the skeleton in one uniform, continuous piece. The cut should end on the top (dark) side of the dorsal fin, so that the fin remains on the carcass when this first fillet is removed. If you are going to skin the fillets, you may want to leave them attached at the tail, so that the carcass may be used as a "handle" to pull against as you slide the knife blade between the fillet and the skin that's being sliced away from it. If you prefer, though, the fillet may be removed from the carcass with the skin still on it.

Now remove the second fillet the same way as the first, starting at the center and working toward the outer edge. (Figure 5). Note how the thumb is being used to keep the fillet pulled away from the bones as the cut is being made. Be careful at the head end so that you don't gouge the stomach.

FIGURE 5

How to Catch
Trophy Halibut

FIGURE 6

You may leave the belly flesh attached to this fillet (Figure 6), or cut up and around the stomach to leave the belly flesh attached to the carcass (Figure 7).

FIGURE 7

Then it's simply a matter of turning the halibut over, removing the cheek from the white side (Figure 8), and repeating the entire process (Figure 9).

As for removing the skin from halibut fillets, it's an easy job. Simply lay each fillet on a flat, smooth, solid surface, skin-down, then insert your knife edge at one corner, where the flesh meets the skin. Keep the blade horizontal, flat against the inner side of the skin, with the cutting edge away from

Photo opposite page: A deck or tabletop makes filleting big halibut quick and easy.

FIGURE 8

you. Slowly pull the skin toward you, so that the knife stays in one place and the fillet does all the moving. If you keep the knife blade flat and pressed down firmly, the hide should melt away from the fillet as it's pulled in your direction. You know you're turning the blade downward if you cut through the skin. Likewise, if the blade is turned up it will slice through the fillet rather than separating it from the skin.

FIGURE 9

Skinning a halibut fillet is somewhat more difficult if your knife blade isn't long enough to span the entire width of the fillet. In this situation you may have to carefully slice the skin away from one side of the fillet, turn it around and finish the job by repeating the process from the other end. Turning the fillet from one end to the other allows you to keep the knife facing away from you as you pull the skin across it.

CHAPTER 17

Getting Home With The Bounty

When you take a moment to consider the fact that two or three halibut might provide *several hundred pounds* of prime, boneless fillets, it becomes readily apparent that planning and preparing for the trip home with your catch is an important part of scheduling any halibut-fishing trip. Depending on where you fish, how you get there and how successful you are, bringing home the bounty in the best possible condition might require a great deal of effort on your part.

The more someone else does, of course, the less you have to worry about doing, and most fishing lodges include filleting, wrapping and boxing your catch in the price they charge for the trip. In some cases, they will even ship the boxes to your home, or at least to the airport nearest your home. This no-brainer approach to getting home with your halibut makes the whole thing easier, but you pay for the luxury one way or another. And there are still some things for you to plan for and to do.

Many halibut anglers, on the other hand, like to do it all themselves, including packaging the fillets and caring for them all the way to the home freezer.

Either way, there are important things to consider when it comes to getting home with all that freshly caught halibut, so let's walk through the entire process of caring for and transporting it from the fillet table to the dinner table.

For starters, package your halibut in meal-size portions. If you have a family of four and you bring home five-pound packages of fish, you'll have to invite half the neighborhood over for dinner every time you open one, and you may not like your neighbors that well! Determine how much fish you'll need

When it comes to prime table fare, it's hard to beat freshly caught halibut, but some effort is required if those hard-earned fillets are to reach their destination in the best possible condition. Most fishing camps and lodges include fish cleaning, wrapping and freezing of the catch in the price of their trips, but don't take anything for granted. Ask plenty of questions beforehand about what they provide and what they don't.

for a typical meal and limit your packages to that size. You (or the lodge employee packaging your halibut) may soon discover that it takes longer to process a big catch this way, but it will be worth it when you get home.

Some lodges get a little sloppy in this regard, especially if they have lots of customers with lots of fish, but if you tell them you want your halibut packaged in two-person portions, don't let them get away with handing you packages the size of a large tackle box. You're more likely to waste prime halibut fillets if you have to thaw out a five-pound package every time you want a meal for a small family.

Air-tight packaging is extremely important in preserving the quality of halibut or any other fish, so most lodges have gone to vacuum-packaging systems. Vacuum-sealing is the easiest and best way to keep damaging air off your prime halibut fillets, which helps to eliminate freezer-burn and ensures that fresh-caught flavor even after several months in the deep-freeze. The more fish you bring home, the longer some of it is likely to spend on ice, and the more important a process such as vacuum packaging becomes. If you fish out of a lodge that doesn't vacuum-seal your catch, you might consider investing in a small vacuum-packaging machine and re-packaging the frozen halibut after you return home. Many vacuum machines work better on frozen fish than on fresh, so even some halibut that was vacuum-packed at a lodge might require re-packaging with that home vacuum machine.

Some of those home machines, by the way, are small and portable enough to take with you when you go fishing. As long as there's electricity available at that do-it-yourself halibut destination or at a lodge that doesn't have vacuum-packaging equipment, you can give your fish the best possible protection by taking along your own vacuum-packer and packaging material.

It's possible to do a good job of packaging halibut without a vacuum-sealer, but it takes more care and effort. Those zipper-seal-type freezer bags are popular with many anglers, and if you take the time to squeeze the air out as you close them, they're fairly effective at protecting delicate halibut fillets. Another way to use them is to add a cup of water to each bag before sealing it. The water replaces air in the bag, thereby protecting the flesh from freezer burn. That water, however, adds weight and bulk to each package, and if you're dealing with several dozen packages, it makes a lot of difference. But use caution here: Water may protect the fish from freezer burn

How to Catch
Trophy Halibut

in the long run, yet the fish may spoil in the short term. Never drop a box of halibut into your chest freezer, expecting it to freeze overnight. The fish in the middle of the box, soaking in water, can take days to freeze, and may spoil in the process. By placing a few packages on an even and single layer in your freezer, you ensure they freeze quickly.

When compared to vacuum sealing, however, water is a poor substitute. It's better to spray the fish with water, allowing an ice glaze to form, then package it. Sure it takes time, but the extra effort is worth it.

Some anglers and a few lodges still package their halibut the "old fashioned" way, simply wrapping it with cellophane, and it can be a moderately effective way to protect fillets if done right. As with other packaging methods, it's best to press out as much air as possible as you wrap the meat, and be as liberal as needed with the wrapping material to be sure the fillets are completely covered.

Once packaged, halibut fillets that aren't going to be eaten right away should be frozen as quickly and as thoroughly as possible. Many lodges and fishing resorts that cater to halibut anglers feature large, walk-in freezers that are capable of flash-freezing hundreds of pounds of fillets in a few hours. Such quick freezing protects against spoilage and, as they say in the commercials, "locks in the freshness" of those halibut fillets you worked so hard to collect. Those rock-hard bricks of frozen halibut also hold up well for the trip home, even if home is a long day's flight away.

If proper freezing of your catch is up to you rather than some lodge employee, spread the packages out as best you can to ensure that they freeze as quickly as possible. If you stack them in big pile or box them up before putting them in the freezer, the packages in the middle will be insulated by those on the outside, thus taking substantially longer to freeze and as mentioned above, may spoil.

Most fishing resorts and many anglers use manufactured shipping boxes for getting frozen halibut home. These boxes, the majority of which are made of waxed cardboard, are available in several sizes up to a capacity of 70 pounds. Unless a hole is punched in them, which is fairly easy to do, they're relatively leak-proof and very strong. The cardboard material itself, however, doesn't provide much insulation, so the boxes are sometimes lined with thin strips of foam to help keep the contents cold. Some styles, in fact, include foam liners.

The majority of lodges and some other fishing operations

provide shipping boxes for their customers, while the do-it-yourself angler may have to provide his own. They're available for sale in most popular salmon and halibut fishing areas, and the price may vary a great deal depending on whether you buy them from, say, a charter office or from a supermarket. They may be re-used as long as they're in good condition, so if you make lots of trips to places where you must provide your own, you might save $15 or $20 a trip by packing the boxes back and forth. The problem is that they take up a lot of room whether empty or full, and getting the empties to your destination may be a monumental hassle, especially if you're flying. The solution to this problem, however, will be revealed when you read a few more paragraphs.

When using shipping boxes to transport your halibut, fill each box as full as possible. This helps keep the contents frozen as well as reducing the chance of boxes collapsing and being damaged in transit. Using a smaller box tends to work out much better than leaving a large box only half-full. When filled, each box should be wrapped at both ends with duct tape or strapping tape to keep the lid securely in place and to help strengthen the box against damage. Your name, address and phone number should be written in large letters on each box with a wide-tip felt marker.

Large coolers offer an alternative to cardboard shipping boxes, but if you're thinking about buying those cheap, foam coolers for shipping halibut, we advise against it. They don't hold up well to the rigors of air travel, and you may arrive home to find your fish coming off the luggage conveyer one thawed-out package at a time rather than in a single box. If you're in the situation of needing to buy a container for getting your halibut home, either spend the extra bucks for a durable cooler or buy shipping boxes.

Another alternative is to bring your cooler or coolers from home. Like the re-used shipping boxes, they take up a lot of space on your trip to the fishing grounds, so here's a suggestion: use them as luggage and put all your clothes and equipment inside them as though they were suitcases. Be sure to include a soft, nylon duffel bag or two so that you have luggage to hold your clothes and gear on the return trip, when the coolers are—we hope—full of fish. If you're one of those folks who saves the shipping boxes from previous trips, you can do exactly the same thing, using it as luggage on the way to your destination as a fish box for the trip home.

Like a shipping box, the cooler containing your halibut

should be taped securely and have your name, address and phone number clearly visible before it takes to the skies on any commercial airline. Many of the carriers that service the halibut-fishing areas of Alaska and British Columbia have lots of practice when it comes to shipping fish, and they are often more than happy to help you do it right. They don't want your halibut spilling into the cargo hold of their planes any more than you do, so they may even provide the tape!

While airlines are usually more than happy to haul your fish home for you, there may be an additional charge if you hit it big and your bounty fills several boxes and/or coolers. Whether or not you have to pay extra baggage charges may depend on how full the plane is, the length of the flight, how many extra boxes you have, or even the mood of the attendant when you check in for your flight.

If the trip home involves days of driving rather than a few hours in the air, keeping your catch frozen becomes a much more difficult task. A cooler alone won't do it, not even if you keep it closed and wrap it in thick layers of blankets. If dry ice is available, though, you can keep fish frozen in a cooler by adding a couple of small blocks every 20 to 30 hours. Be sure to put dry ice at the top of the cooler, though, and not in the bottom.

If you don't use dry ice and the drive home involves over-night hotel or motel stops, make an effort to locate a freezer to store your fish, even if it means paying a few dollars more.

The key to getting home with halibut fillets in the best possible shape is to plan ahead, be prepared for success when it happens, and be willing to extend a little extra effort to protect those hard-earned delicacies.

Best Recipes
of Alaska's
Fishing Lodges
Adela Batin

CHAPTER 18

Halibut Recipes And Cooking Tips

For many anglers, catching halibut is only half as much fun as eating it. The white, flaky meat is excellent baked, poached, boiled or grilled, and as a main ingredient in salads or spreads. When steamed it is scrumptiously known as "poor man's lobster" and is dipped in melted butter until nothing but empty plates remain.

Some of the best halibut recipes come from the chefs working at Alaska's fishing lodges. These culinary experts prepare fresh halibut for guests in scrumptious fashion.

An excellent source for halibut and other fish recipes is the 320-page book, *"Best Recipes of Alaska's Fishing Lodges,"* by Adela Batin. On the following pages, Adela has provided several recipes and fish-cooking tips from her award-winning cookbook.

For your personal copy of **Best Recipes of Alaska's Fishing Lodges**, send $24.95 plus $4 shipping to Alaska Angler Publications, P.O. Box 83550, Dept HB, Fairbanks, Alaska 99708 (907) 455-8000.

How To Cook Halibut

Fish is a very delicate meat and should be treated that way in handling and cooking. The most effective way to maintain color, flavor and moisture in halibut is to either poach or bake it. Halibut in the 50-pound range are best, with the large 100 to 400-pound fish not as tasty or tender as the smaller fish.

Poaching Halibut

When poaching fish, use a court bouillon made by boiling carrots, onions, celery and herbs in the poaching water. Some favorite herbs for fish are dill, basil, bay leaves and thyme. When

Best Recipes of Alaska's Fishing Lodges contains 200 best recipes from 16 of the author's favorite fishing lodges.

poaching halibut, place the fish in a sieve or perforated pan before submerging. This makes it easier to retrieve the fish from the water. It is important to not overcook the fish. *Bring* the water to a boil. *Submerge* the fish—an 8 to 10-ounce portion about 1 to 1½ inches thick—and *reduce* heat. *Steep* the fish uncovered for 5 to 6 minutes before checking with a fork. You should be able to separate the muscle fibers without breaking up the portions. Remember, fish will continue to cook after it is removed from the water so it is better to undercook than overcook. Always use fresh ingredients and again, *don't over-cook.* All the spices and sauces in the world won't cover up overcooked halibut, which is dry and leathery in texture.

Baking Halibut

Coat bottom of cookie sheet with butter. *Roll* fillets in butter, *season* to taste with herbs and spices. *Pour* enough white wine around the fish to create steam while fish is baking. *Place* fish in 500-degree oven for 8 to 10 minutes. When baking halibut, the key is to *use high heat.* Whether baking steaks or fillets, it's important to keep moisture in the fish. *Use* white wine and drawn butter under the fish to keep it moist and add flavor. Drawn butter works well because it has a higher burning point than whole butter, and a more distinctive flavor. When cooked, the fish should be firm but not dry. Muscle fibers should separate easily with a fork, and the meat should have a translucent appearance. It is best to undercook the fish a bit, since the residual heat will continue to cook the fish after it is removed from the oven.

Smoked Halibut

1 cup soy sauce	2 teaspoons black pepper
½ cup brown sugar	2 cups water
3 cloves garlic, crushed	3 pounds halibut
½ cup salt	

In a large glass or plastic bowl, *mix* soy sauce, brown sugar, garlic, salt, pepper and water until well-dissolved. *Cut* halibut into slabs not to exceed one-inch thick. *Place* halibut in sauce. *Refrigerate* 1½ to 2 hours, *stirring* occasionally. *Remove* halibut from refrigerator and *pat* dry. *Let stand* uncovered at room temperature for 45 minutes, or until a tacky glaze forms on fish. Meanwhile, *heat* smoker and *have* chips burning. *Smoke* halibut for 6 to 8 hours, or until done.

Half-Moon Halibut

Half-Moon Bay is located on the north shore of Kvichak Bay, northwest of Naknek in the Bristol Bay region. This dish is named not only for the bay, but for the cut of halibut. When cross-cut steaks are cut from halibut, they look like a moon with the bone in the center. When a smaller portion is desired, the full moon steak is cut in half, which is the traditional half-moon steak.

3 eggs
½ cup canned milk
½ teaspoon dried dillweed
1 teaspoon garlic powder
1 teaspoon minced garlic
½ teaspoon seafood seasoning
¾ cup flour
1 cup finely crushed saltine crackers
3 pounds fresh halibut fillets or half moon steaks,
    cut into smaller equal size pieces
olive oil

Preheat oven to 300 degrees. In a bowl, *beat* eggs and canned milk together; *stir* in dillweed, garlic powder, minced garlic and seafood seasoning. On a plate *mix* flour and crackers together. *Dip* pieces of halibut in milk/egg mixture and *roll* in flour/cracker mixture. *Fry* both sides of halibut in olive oil until golden brown. *Don't overcook! Stack* fish pieces in baking pan and *bake* in 300 degree oven for 15 minutes. Serves 6—8.

Icy Strait BBQ Halibut

Barn-door-size halibut of 100 to 200 pounds will yield anywhere from 60 to 140 pounds of boneless, white fillets that more and more people are preferring over steak. This is enough halibut for a block party barbecue when you return home. If you use the recipe be certain you've saved a few fillets for yourself, because there won't be any leftovers.

5 lbs. of halibut fillets
2 sticks of butter
2 onions, sliced
2 tomatoes, diced
2 tbsp pressed garlic
1 lemon
5 tbsp. fine white wine

3 tbsp. grated Parmesan
    cheese
1 cup fresh mushrooms
2 tbsp. butter
dash of garlic powder
1 tbsp. white wine

Cut the fillets into serving portions and *place* on a piece of heavy duty foil large enough to fold it over the top and seal so that the juices from the fish can steam the fillet while cooking. *Slice* the butter. *Place* butter slices, along with the sliced onion, tomatoes and garlic, on top of the fillets. *Squeeze* the juice of the lemon over the top. *Sprinkle* with the wine and Parmesan cheese. *Seal* the foil over the fish and *place* in your preheated BBQ grill. *Add* a few green sticks of alder to the hot coals just before putting the fish on. *Let* the fish *simmer* over the coals for about 10 to 12 minutes, then *open* the seal on the foil to allow a touch of the unique alder-smoke flavor to seep into the fillet. *Cool* with the foil open for another 8 to 10 minutes

This is the most critical time, because the cook must test the fillet to make sure it is perfect for those who have gathered to savor the moment. The key is to not overcook...*let* the fish cook just until it loses its shiny translucence and is white throughout.

While the fish is cooking on the grill, *prepare* the fresh mushrooms, *sauteing* them in two tablespoons butter. *Add* a dash of garlic powder and a tablespoon of wine. *Top* fish with the lightly sauteed mushrooms. *Have* the rest of the meal preparation completed, because you need to *serve* this immediately, hot and steaming.

20-Fathom Halibut

For many anglers, the only way to prepare deep-water halibut is deep fried in beer batter. Expect your guests to go overboard when it comes to second and third requests for more halibut.

Serve these crispy golden nuggets alongside baked potato wedges and fresh corn-on-the-cob.

2   cups all-purpose flour
1½   teaspoons salt
½   teaspoon lemon pepper
¼   teaspoon garlic powder
1   tablespoon paprika
1   tablespoon parsley flakes
2   tablespoons butter, melted
1   12-ounce bottle of beer
4   eggs, separated
3   pounds fresh halibut, cut into 2-inch squares
     grease or cooking oil for frying fish

Sift together flour, salt, lemon pepper, garlic powder and paprika. *Stir* in parsley, butter, beer and egg yolks. *Let* stand 1½ hours at room temperature. *Whip* egg whites until stiff. *Fold* stiff egg whites into the batter. *Heat* grease or cooking oil in a deep fryer. The grease needs to be maintained at 300 to 325 degrees. *Flour* individual pieces of fish and *dip* into the batter. This will help the batter stick to the fish while frying. *Drop* the pieces into hot grease and *fry* a few at a time for approximately 4 to 5 minutes or until golden brown and the pieces float to the surface. *Drain* fried fish on paper towels. Serves 6.

A-Ward's Alaskan Halibut Supreme

(The following recipe is from Robert, Sandra and Alie Ward of A-Ward Charters in Anchor Point. Bob claims this is one of his all-time favorites.)

Butcher one live whole Dungeness crab, *break* out of shell and *remove* viscera, *cook* legs and body meat 10 to 15 minutes in boiling water, *let* cool and *remove* meat.

Combine above crab meat with one cup each of two of the following: sour cream, plain yogurt or mayonnaise, creating a paste-like mixture. *Add* one tablespoon lemon juice, one tablespoon lemon pepper, a dash of parsley flakes and a dash of dill seed. *Add* a half cup of chopped mushrooms to the paste.

Prepare a two to three pound halibut roast (1 to 1½-inch thick) by *placing* it in a baking dish and *cutting* deep slices with the grain, ¾-inch apart throughout the roast. *Stuff* the paste mixture into the slices and *paste* the roast all over with the remaining mixture. *Grate* 1½ cups cheddar cheese over the entire fish as desired. *Cover* fish for baking.

Bake in oven at approximately 375 degrees for 15 to 20 minutes. Serves 6 (or two Alaskans).

CHAPTER 19

Alaska Halibut Hotspots

Alaska offers North America's best trophy halibut fishing. Size and numbers of fish, uncrowded waters in most regions, and availability of experienced charter boat skippers make Alaska the "Number One" choice for any angler serious about enjoying the creme de la creme of Pacific halibut fishing.

Also to be credited are the Gulf of Alaska and Bering Sea; food-rich environments especially suited for the halibut's lifestyle. And each year, anglers from various seaports from Ketchikan to Dutch Harbor make the news with their 250 to 400-pound-plus catches.

You, too, can partake in the fun of catching these "barn-door" flatties by knowing where and when to plan your trip. While it is beyond the scope of this book to cover all of Alaska's shoreline, listed are the gateway cities that cater to halibut anglers, either with a few boats or an entire fleet. These gateways have a sportfishing infrastructure in place (charter boats, guides, accommodations, transportation), to help you experience the best halibut fishing possible, either on your own or with a guide.

Planning Your Trip

Planning a halibut fishing trip is half the fun of halibut fishing. Even for Alaska residents, the drive to the halibut grounds requires from a few minutes to 11 hours, depending on where one plans to fish.

In years past, anglers from the Lower 48 wouldn't consider spending a few extra days fishing for halibut. Nowdays, if you haven't planned at least a two-day side trip fishing for halibut, you're not playing with a full deck of fish. Formulating the

Skipper Dale Anderson and a little fishing buddy with a 212-pound halibut caught near Juneau, Alaska. The fish regurgitated octopus and fish immediately after this photo was taken. Anderson's client broke a rod while landing the fish.

plans for a trip often results in more questions than answers. Which areas offer the best chances for success? With hundreds of charter operators from which to choose, who provides the most knowledgeable skippers and deckhands? Who has the best gear? These are questions asked each year by resident and non-resident anglers.

Here is some advice on choosing a charter operator:

Don't Be Deceived By Numbers.

• Many areas boast of catching more and larger halibut because of the sheer number of boats they have and businesses that are able to cater to the masses. Some promote an occasional huge catch in their ads and brochures, whereas the uninformed angler believes this is what takes place every day. Shame on the angler. Remember, halibut fishing can be poor in the best of areas, and good in the worst of areas. Caveat Emptor! "Let the Buyer Beware!"

• Choose a charter operator who has many years of experience in the area you plan to fish. Avoid newcomer skippers. Local knowledge is critical for success. You want more than somone who follows the other boats out to the best fishing grounds. Choose a skipper who flows with the fishery each day, who lives and breathes it. Find this man or woman, and you are on your way to success.

• Consider planning your trip to coincide with many of the halibut derbies that take place in nearly all of Alaska's gateway cities. The halibut derbies award anywhere from $100 to $31,000 for all categories of fish. Numerous day prizes are offered. Contact the local Chamber of Commerce for derby information and exact dates.

In planning your trip, first start with the area of the state you will be visiting or would like to fish. Then choose a city or a gateway from which to base your activities. I'll start with southcentral Alaska, the easiest for most anglers to access via the road system.

Southcentral Alaska

According to Dave Nelson, sportfish biologist for the Alaska Department of Fish and Game in Soldotna, halibut movements in the southcentral Alaska area are seasonal in nature. The fish move into the shallow-water areas to feed on the abundant marine life. In mid-July, the fish move out into deeper water, and in August, another minor migration takes place into the shallow water areas. Nelson speculates that halibut feed on the salmon carcasses that are being washed out to sea from the many salmon rivers emptying into Cook Inlet.

According to ADF&G catch surveys, the Kenai Peninsula offers numerous areas to catch halibut, especially in the Anchor River, Deep Creek and Whiskey Gulch area, as well as Lower Cook Inlet and outer Gulf Coast regions.

A day trip out of any of the cities from Soldotna to Seldovia offers a quick and easy way to catch halibut. The day trip is ideal if you're short on time, part of a tour group with only a few hours to spare, or just want to sample the thrill of that head-shaking surge a big halibut can provide at the end of a line.

Currently, there are about 275 charter boat operators out of Ninilchik and Deep Creek because many Kenai River guides have listened to their clients and jumped on the halibut fishing bandwagon. Many offer halibut fishing excursions out of Deep Creek because of its close proximity to Soldotna/Kenai. Kenai guides claim that they can fish their clients, and get them back to Soldotna-area accommodations faster. Others choose to take their clients to the Homer area, saying the fishing is better for larger fish. Halibut fishing, nevertheless, in each area is good for numbers of fish. Fishing the outer islands generally means a larger-size fish, on average. Of course, fishing 300 feet of water is work, you'll pay more for the trip, and spend more hours traveling to and from the Gulf of Alaska and Shelikof Strait islands.

Simply put, you can catch big halibut in either location, depending on the time of year and the charter operator you choose. The secret to success here is choosing the right operator and the right trip.

A 1985 study conducted of the Homer halibut charter fishing industry by Douglas Coughenower with University of Alaska Sea Grant Program reveals a few insights about the charter halibut business in this area.

How did customers select a charter company? Thirty-eight percent said they based their choice on someone's recommendation, 14 percent on past success with the operator, 18 percent on good reputation, 9 percent knew the skipper, 4 percent said they had only one choice available for charter, 2 percent on newspaper advertising and 1 percent reserved their trip at an outdoor show. About 13 percent were other reasons such as yellow pages, overflow from another company or brochure.

Southcentral Alaska & Kodiak

The survey also provided information in other areas. For instance, 66 percent of the respondents would not have come to Homer if there were no charter fishing available.

When asked, "What did you like most about your trip?" the answers were consistent. Coughenower writes: "By far the most positive (38 percent) thing people noticed about their Homer charter experience was the captain, crew and staff of the charter company. Words such as friendly, courteous, professional, helpful and service were used consistently. Customers appreciated good staff even more than good fishing. Under good fishing, catching the big one was mentioned often as what people liked most."

The response to, "What did you like least about your fishing trip?" Rainy, cold weather and rough seas drew 33 percent of the comments, seasickness was mentioned 12 percent of the time, and poor fishing had 20 percent of the comments. Under the poor fishing category, customers mentioned things such as no fish, didn't get the limit, and no big fish or fish too small. The long boat ride to the fishing area and back drew 7 percent response, and is related to another complaint of too little fishing time (2 percent). Some of the least-liked aspects of the charter that operators can control are: cost (5 percent), unprofessional crew (3 percent) and tangled lines (2 percent).

If you're from the Lower 48, choosing the right operator can be particularly frustrating and exasperating, especially if you've had a bad experience with a charter operator. In 1994, I remember receiving a letter from a Mrs. Baum, who wrote me about her frustrations with a well-known halibut charter company. I quote from her letter:

"Because we depend on charters for fishing, what do you suggest and who do you suggest and why? I would like to know something about various charters for halibut. We are at their mercy because we know nothing of their success ratio or their expertise and knowledge. Our halibut charter sold us out to another company and then lied to us. That day was our biggest disappointment. We see pictures of 200-pound halibut in everyone's window and we caught 20-pound fish. We got sold to (halibut charter number 2), that was the worst! We had paid for a boat from (charter number 1) in early spring, as there was 21 of us and we wanted to book early, and had spoken to them on the phone a couple of times, but they never told us they would take our money and sell us to another company. All the while they continued to make us believe we were with them. It was a rotten day. We had used (charter number 1) before and wanted them again."

Here's what you can expect to avoid the problems experienced by Baum, who is now an Alaska Angler® subscriber and who receives regular updates on the best charter operators for salmon, trout and halibut.

1) The average size halibut is in the 20 to 30-pound range. Catching a 200-pounder is as much a matter of luck as it is skill of your charter crew and deckhand. There are areas better than others if you're looking for trophy fish. Decide on whether action or numbers is important. But for the number of halibut caught each day, 200-pounders are few and far between.

2) Do your homework. If you're treated like a number on the phone, chances are you'll be treated like a number on the boat. Talk to the skipper you'll be fishing with, not an office receptionist. Ask questions. Ask for a guarantee that you'll be fishing on a specific boat with a specific skipper. If they refuse, take your business elsewhere. If the business doesn't have the courtesy to install at least an answering machine during the winter booking months (many disconnect their phone lines), look elsewhere.

3) A Cook Inlet day trip for halibut is a fabulous experience when you book with the right charter operator. The area offers the scenery, wildlife and fish. If you have limited time and/or budget, consider a day trip from any of the ports on the lower Kenai Peninsula.

Deep Creek—Anchor Point

The Deep Creek Wayside is located on the Kenai Peninsula, about two miles south of Ninilchik, directly adjacent to Alaska Highway 1. The area offers a good halibut fishery for those short on time or searching for a budget trip.

For the do-it-yourself angler with a car-topper or small boat, there are numerous areas close to shore where you can fish for halibut. In fact, each year halibut from "chickens" (five to 10-pounders) to 400-pounders are caught within sight of shore.

Before you load that boat atop the car, a few words of caution. Cook Inlet weather can turn from clear to stormy in a matter of minutes. If you launch and land on the beach, be sure you know the dangers of each, and know how to pilot your boat on open water.

Many local anglers consider Homer sportfish biologist Nick Dudiak to be one of the most knowledgeable halibut experts in the area. "My boss says I spend too much time out on the water," he said, a trait indicitive of any true sportfishing researcher.

"Out in the middle of the inlet, off Stariski Creek, is a popular area for halibut," Dudiak said. "The Deep Creek Wayside or Whiskey Gulch is where most anglers launch their craft at high tide, either from the sandy beach or via boat ramp. At high tide, you can also launch from the mouth of the Ninilchik River."

Anglers can also launch at the Anchor River. If you have a large boat, it helps if you have a 4WD and are familiar with the tidal fluctuations for that day.

"There is plenty of structure off the Anchor Point area and Stariski Tower area," Dudiak said. "Anglers should look for rock ledges and trenches, drop-offs, and underwater pinnacles. It's important to fish variations of structure, not only in bottom topography, but also composition."

Halibut guru Pete Hardy recommends looking for halibut in areas with mud/sandy bottoms, as well as the cobble and rocky areas. Anglers should look for channels that attract halibut migrating in from deeper waters. Drifting is the most preferred method of fishing, but carry an anchor should you find that hotspot. Some of the best fishing for the angler with a small boat is three to five miles out from either Deep Creek, Happy Valley or Twin Falls.

I've found the best depth for halibut varies from 10 to 20 fathoms over sandy bottoms, tidal-induced depressions, and major channels emptying upper Cook Inlet into Lower Cook Inlet. Finding and fishing these areas is generally hit and miss unless you're equipped with a sonar recorder, GPS and hydrographic map.

To find fish in the Cook Inlet area, all one has to do is listen to a citizen's band radio and find out where the action is best. Charter boat skippers talk to each other throughout the day. Over a period of time, you can learn where the best action is taking place. Of course, many have code names for their locations, so don't expect to find many of them on the map. And if the action is hot, give skippers the courtesy of fishing the area that day without competition from you or anyone else. But do make a mental note of the area for another time.

Guide Brian Lowe says the new tractor service has transformed the Deep Creek area into the most popular halibut fishery on the Kenai Peninsula.

"We can launch up to 30-foot boats, which make for more comfortable and safer fishing," he said.

Lowe says that he prefers to fish early in May and June when halibut are in 30 to 120 feet of water. He says that for clients who are looking for barn door halibut, he'll travel out as far as 20 miles from shore. But the best action, he says, is in shallow water.

"I try to talk them out of pursuing barn doors," he says. "They're not as good eating as the smaller fish. The average size halibut we catch in shallow water is 20 to 30 pounds. On an average day, an angler can expect to catch and release from 10 to 20 fish."

Lowe uses a slip-sinker rig mentioned in this book, baited with either an entire small herring or half of a larger herring. He says the smaller herring rig also catches king and silver salmon.

He finds that anchoring rather than drifting is best because clients don't get hung on bottom as often. He's an advocate of circle hooks, but uses J hooks when using the lighter-weight salmon rods.

Always fish high slack for the best action, but don't ignore low slack as a close second.

You can find halibut in rocky areas, but most like to bury themselves in the Cook Inlet silt. Far to the south of Deep Creek, look for halibut on the perimeter of kelp beds.

Homer Long-Range Trip

While local anglers and charters hammer the halibut in nearby coastal waters, many boats will head out to the larger islands off the tip of the Kenai Peninsula. Some of the most popular islands include Elizabeth, Chugach, Pearl, Flat and Barren.

The long ride out is often worth the extra one to three hours it may take. Although lately, there has been lots of interest in traveling to the outer islands, and fishing pressure is increasing.

While large fish are caught close to Homer, your chances of success for consistently larger fish are a tad better if you charter a boat to Lower Cook Inlet. When booking a trip, specifically request a "long range" trip. Prices on these longer trips over standard day rates are usually $50 or more per person. Exact price depends on length of trip and operator. Since the boats have to navigate Alaska's notorious Lower Cook Inlet and Shelikof Strait, this type of trip is best left to skilled seamen or charter skippers.

One option offered by several Seldovia operators eliminates the lengthy boat ride to and from the Barren Island halibut grounds. From Homer you'll fly to Dogfish Bay, where

you'll stay in comfortable accommodations. According to David Cloninger of Seldovia Fishing Adventures, getting to the halibut fishing grounds from Seldovia is easy. You'll travel 15 to 30 minutes to the deepwater halibut holes, fish and then return to base camp. You can fish for halibut all day, or enjoy salmon fishing in a nearby stream during evening hours. Prices vary for the flight to Seldovia, fishing and accommodations, so check around first before booking.

Skipper Chuck Crabaugh is directing crew members who are preparing the ship's hold to receive the 1,000 pounds of sport-caught halibut that shingle the deck of his boat.

If you have the time and budget, consider an extended or overnight trip aboard a 50 to 70-foot boat, two personally favorite choices. Here's why I like them:

• Longer Fishing Times: An extended or overnight trip allows you to spend more time in productive areas, fish more tides, and have a shot at larger fish.

• The Continental Shelf is a migratory route for halibut. While big fish can be found in the offshore areas of Deep Creek and Anchor Point, there are more big fish along the shelf because of the deepwater shelter and schools of cod and other bottom-fish trophy halibut prefer.

These are the facts, despite what some close-to-port operators would have you believe. While you can catch an occasional large fish in close, you will catch more and larger fish, on average, the farther out you travel. This may change in the years to come, as the current restructuring of the commercial halibut fishery has spread out the commercial season over the year and implemented individual quotas. No more free-for-all, catch-all-you-can openers. Many commercial fishermen are now avoiding the summer season, which is expected to provide more and larger fish for sport anglers in areas closer to shore.

I really enjoy overnight trips for halibut. To reach one of Homer's premier halibut fisheries requires an overnight trip to the edge of the Continental Shelf at the mouth of Cook Inlet, where it empties into the Gulf of Alaska. Roark Brown of Homer Ocean Charters says that for what you'd spend for two days of separate charters and accommodations, you can enjoy two days and one night of fishing the area's best halibut waters, possibly have better fishing, and cut travel time in half when compared with two separate day trips to the same area.

The three-hour journey to the halibut grounds offers outstanding photographic opportunities. Killer whales, porpoises, myriad seabirds and otters along with alpine glaciers, spruce-covered mountainsides and waterfalls form a panoramic backdrop for the fishing that takes place offshore.

I experienced several overnight trips with Skipper Chuck Crabaugh of Cie Jae Ocean Charters. The last one was as memorable as the first.

After the three-hour boat ride to "Magic Mountain," Crabaugh searched the sonar image for the right bottom topography. "This is it," he said. "Drop 'em overboard."

Within ten minutes we were into halibut. First a 54-pounder then a 30-pounder, followed by a 94-pounder. The frenzy continued. When the angler to my right set the hook, the fish retaliated by nearly pulling him overboard.

"Hold on," Crabaugh smiled, grabbing the angler's jacket. The angler grimaced and the pool-cue-like rod bent into a soft right angle, the 80-pound Dacron line humming with tension.

Neither side was able to budge the other for what seemed like an eternity. Then the hook tore loose. Halibut fishing has its share of disappointing moments, but they are short-lived.

There was no slow-down in the action. I jigged my bait and immediately felt a thump. Big halibut don't peck at a bait. They often engulf it with enough force that you can feel it 300 feet down. I was excited, but remembered to put some slack in the line. Another thump, and the line tightened. I set the hook and the rod throbbed as the fish fought to stay on bottom. For 10 minutes there was no take, only give. Then I gained ground, only to lose it again as the fish surged to the ocean floor.

Thirty-five arm-aching minutes later, a seemingly huge form materialized beneath the boat. The deck crew scrambled, while Crabaugh grabbed his .410 shotgun. Deck hand Ken Avery buried the gaff behind the fish's head, and the shotgun blast boomed across the expanse of ocean. The surface exploded in a cataclysm of spray as the fish erupted out of the water.

Minutes later, my arms hung like wet, limp dishtowels as Ken and Chuck struggled to lift my 98-pound fish over the transom. I was proud of the fish, even though it was an average catch for this area.

I had caught my limit, and watched as other anglers enjoyed the non-stop fishing action. In two drifts we hooked into several 80-pound and one 140-pound halibut. It wasn't long before all 10 of us had our limit of two fish in the hold, and we headed for the protective confines of a nearby bay for the evening. The back of the boat was shingled with nearly 1,000 pounds of halibut.

Once the fish were placed on ice in the hold and the deck cleared of tackle, the crew barbecued halibut and New York steaks, served up baked potatoes, fresh salads and appetizers. Talk turned to fishing, interspersed with quiet moments of contemplation as everyone took their turn to visually drink in the scenery of mountain goats in alpine pastures, cascading waterfalls, or smell the invigorating tang of ocean air.

Private berths soon called everyone to sleep. The next morning, we ate a full breakfast and were fishing by 8 a.m. No one could envision the fishing being any better, but it was. Humpback whales porpoised continuously around us, their huge forms shooting up geysers of spray. Anglers were shouting exclamatory remarks, hoops, hollers and a few profanities. For an hour, it sounded like a feud taking place, with gunshots going off every few minutes. Halibut were gaffed and grunted over the transom, one after another. At lunch, we took turns eating freshly-made lasagna, or guzzling a soda to quench a fish-fighting thirst. Anglers started to take longer and longer rests. By mid-afternoon, the hold was filled with our two-day limit of 40 fish. It was time to head in.

The journey back was a long one for the crew, who set about cleaning the boat and the halibut. Crabaugh smiled and said, "When you consider the market price of halibut is about $4 a pound, this is one fishing trip where an angler can have a great experience and come out ahead with lots of great-eating fish."

Homer Day Charter

I've been fishing the Homer halibut scene since the early 1970s, and have seen many good skippers come and go. Bruce Mallory and Frank Kempl started when less than a dozen charter boats existed. Now, the long range and day charter fleet has grown to over 100 boats, and has its share of top-notch skippers such as the Thompsons, Bob Ward and Rick Swenson. A few other skippers you need to avoid at all costs. I've found that service and people skills can vary greatly in the halibut day charter industry. If in doubt, call the Alaska Angler® Information Service listed in the back of this book for an update on day charters our subscribers have found to be top-notch.

Several years ago, I remember reading of a Homer skipper who guided six anglers to a one-day catch of 1,095 pounds.

Every person on board caught a fish over 100 pounds. One angler hooked two over 100. The largest was 150 pounds, followed by 145, 140, 130, 125, 115 and 110-pounders. The remaining fish weighed in at 40 to 60 pounds.

After the sixth fish, the skipper started to worry about running out of shotshells. To prevent damage to anglers, boat and tackle, it's common for most skippers to grab a .410 and shoot all fish over 50 pounds prior to bringing them onboard.

When planning a Homer halibut day charter, you would be wise to plan early. Weekends book quickly, as do holidays. You'll also need to make advance reservations up to a year in advance for long-range trips, the current trend in trophy halibut sport-fishing. For best success, fish during those weeks with minimal tidal fluctuation. Refer to a tide chart book for exact times.

Western Cook Inlet—Fly-in for Halibut

David Coray of Silver Salmon Creek Lodge on the western shore of Cook Inlet offers a new twist on halibut fishing that not only eliminates the long boat rides to the halibut fishing grounds, but also adds a touch of class to the experience.

"Halibut fishing is phenomenal in just 30 to 65 feet of water, just off the shore in front of the lodge," he says. "With two guests staying five days in mid-June, the three of us caught 148 halibut, the largest being 110 pounds with an average of 25 pounds. With other boats going farther and farther out, rough sea conditions, and the average size of halibut diminishing somewhat in certain areas, I hope to attract more fly-in anglers for halibut. With one plane mostly full (four to five fishermen) the cost of the flight plus charter (with lunch provided) would be close to many of the Homer charter costs of $150 to $200 per person. In late May and June, this halibut venture could also be combined with saltwater king salmon fishing." Coray also fishes the flats near Tuxedni Bay, where huge schools of cod migrate into the glacial flats in early spring and summer.

Seward

Seward is a coastal Alaska city where nothing is done in a small way. The 720-square-mile Harding Ice Field directly behind the city attracts arctic explorers from across North America. The annual footrace up 3,022-foot Mount Marathon is one of the most strenuous and rugged mountain-climbing races in the world. And of course, the lucrative Seward Silver Salmon Derby is one of the largest single sporting events in the state. Yet for many, the single most exciting challenge is a bout with the heavyweight champ of the North, the Pacific halibut. And Seward is gearing up to be one of Alaska's favorite halibut sportfishing seaports.

In our 21 years of reviewing Alaska fishing operators and destinations, we've found that big halibut and fast action are also found near cities that anglers generally don't read about in the major outdoor magazines, cities such as Dutch Harbor, Petersburg, Sitka, Yakutat and Seward. If you're serious about a quality halibut fishing trip, and want to drive there from Anchorage, you owe it to yourself to seriously consider the small coastal city of Seward.

Now Seward has offered good halibut fishing in years past, but only recently have anglers discovered its true potential. Near the outer islands, expect not only to catch halibut on jigs or bait in 60 to 300 feet of water, but also good catches of salmon and bottomfish. Seward offers advantages you'd be foolish to ignore. Consider the facts:

Seward is a scenic, 120-mile drive from Anchorage. You can fish Seward in a day, and return to Homer, Soldotna or

The crew of Saltwater Safari's LEGEND with a portion of their record, one-day catch of 3,000 pounds of halibut.

Anchorage that same evening. Boats fish wherever the weather will permit, and as far out as the halibut flats near Montague Island.

Some of the best halibut fishing out of Seward is in and around Rugged Island, and at the mouth of Resurrection Bay. I've caught halibut off points within the bay, but most of the charter efforts are concentrated around the Chiswell Islands, Granite Cape, Aialik Cape, Cape Resurrection, Outer Island areas, Bear Glacier, Johnstone Bay and Montague Island.

Weather is a major deterrent in accessing these waters. Inside Resurrection Bay offers fair halibut fishing, but don't expect the same action you'll experience in and around the outer islands. If inclement weather keeps you in port, try casting for salmon off Lowell Point or Dollies near the falls outside of town.

Stephen Babinec and Bob Candopoulos of Saltwater Safari Company know what it takes to catch slab-sided halibut. Over the years, they have thrust a sleepy Seward halibut fishery into the limelight with record-breaking catches of large halibut.

They fish a variety of structure, depending on where the often-inclement Gulf of Alaska weather allows them to fish. "We'll fish off pinnacles and sloping shorelines to the flats off Montague Island," Candopoulos said. "We prefer finding and fishing for halibut near baitfish or salmon concentrations during the peak of their perspective runs. Big halibut are always near such concentrations."

The crew uses artificial lures when water conditions allow, because lures provide more action during the heat of a bite. "If halibut strip a bait, you may not know it for a few minutes," Babinec said. "In effect, the end of your line has nothing that appeals to those huge fish swimming around near bottom. A grub-tailed jig is always working, and offers the best chance of catching a barn door at any time, but especially during short bursts of feeding activity."

Valdez, Eastern Prince William Sound

Numerous opportunities exist for the do-it-yourself halibut angler out of Eastern Prince William Sound. Some of the most popular are the remote land camps and houseboats located in remote, protected bays of the Sound. While the halibut fishing generally isn't fast and furious near shoreline (although it can be), anglers do catch enough of the big flatties in shallow-water areas, especially in mid to late August when dead and dying salmon start washing out to sea. This phenomenon draws in big halibut from deepwater holding areas. I remember catching a 100-pounder within 100 yards of a small bay filled with salmon. Small boats and 9.9-horse kickers provide the optimum vehicle for poking around the nooks and crannies of the Sound that the charter boat operators don't hit. For those with larger boats, try fishing off Hinchinbrook Island in depths from 40 to 120 feet of water.

John Goodhand of Goodhand Charters in Valdez regularly fishes the outer edges of Valdez Arm, 30 to 40 miles from Valdez Harbor. Most fish will average between 20 and 50 pounds.

"We have our favorite areas that regularly produce halibut for us," he said. "We just keep hitting different areas until we find the fish we want."

Some good areas to fish for halibut include southern reaches of Galena and Jack bays, moving into these areas in July and August when the salmon begin running into the bay and drop-off areas near Bligh Reef. ADF&G harvest surveys show that most halibut are caught in Valdez Bay, Orca Inlet, Esther and Montague islands. Look for halibut on the outside edges of Montague and Hinchinbrook Islands.

Goodhand says the Valdez halibut fleet consists of specially designed boats, which are among the fastest on the coast. "These boats reach 25 to 30 knots at cruise, and can reach the halibut grounds faster than other six-passenger boats."

The Valdez fleet concentrates its efforts primarily along the southwest tips of Montague and Hinchinbrook islands.

The islands bottleneck the food coming out of the sound, and halibut will concentrate in these areas to feed, especially when the tides change. Then there is the water emptying an abundance of feed from the Copper River drainage and delta. With these two currents converging in and around the islands, anglers can expect good fishing for large halibut. Goodhand says his average catch rate is 1.8 fish per customer.

For the do-it-yourself halibut angler, it pays to schedule your first halibut trip with an established professional before trying a long-range halibut trip on your own.

"It takes lots of time to learn how to fish Valdez-area waters for halibut," Goodhand says. "We don't have lots of sandy and mud bottoms like they have in Cook Inlet. Anglers need to know where to find and how to fish underwater pinnacles, rockpiles, mounds and deepwater drop-offs. Out by the islands, shallow-water areas require anglers to use heavy weights, especially with the very fast currents found at the entrance to the Sound."

One of Goodhand's favorite rigs for extreme tidal current

is a standard three-way-swivel or slip-sinker rig. He places a 2/0 flasher about 18 inches above the sinker. To the flasher he'll attach a 12-inch leader baited with a piece of octopus or herring and colored plastic skirt. This rig also works extremely well early in the season off the Continental Shelf in about 220 feet of water.

Another popular Valdez-area rig is a two-hook set-up of heavy mono leader with fluorescent tubing slipped over the hooks for added visibility and to prevent tangling. One hook is placed near the weight, while the other is attached 18 inches higher on the mainline. Skippers claim that double the bait releases twice as much scent into the water, which attracts more fish. Most of the halibut will hit the lower bait, which is why this should be one that is tough and resilient to bait thieves. A piece of cod, herring or other bait is placed on the higher hook. Goodhand recommends jigs for anglers who have the skill and expertise necessary to fish them effectively. He warns that the big leadheads can be difficult to replace in mid-season in the Valdez area, so bring a good supply.

Like many other charter operators, Goodhand is offering two-day trips to access remote halibut waters.

"Anglers can fish all night if they want," he says. "Even if the weather turns bad, there are ample coves and areas in Prince William Sound that offer protection from the storm and good halibut fishing. Another plus of the overnight trip is we hit areas seldom fished by the commercial halibut fleet. This area is well into the Gulf of Alaska, beyond the entrance into Prince William Sound."

Individuals with their own boats can catch halibut within Valdez Arm. Skipper Skip Blandford says an occasional halibut is caught close to town. "I remember two fishermen who each hooked a 100-plus pounder from right inside the port," he said. "Catching them in the port area, however, is quite rare."

According to Goodhand, the fishing out of Valdez is as good as any other coastal city. "When compared to the larger halibut fisheries, we produce excellent results for 15 full-time charter boats," he said. "Plus we have glaciers, whales, and all the other sights offered by the other seaports, plus a few they don't have, like Columbia Glacier."

Goodhand says there are no signs of soiled beaches or environmental damage from the Exxon Valdez oil spill. "Nature has cleaned it up pretty good," he said.

Valdez-area halibut fishing can be slow or fast, depending on when the commercial halibut boats fish and weather

conditions. Fishing right after the commercial fishermen finish their haul will leave you searching long and hard to find fish. But by traveling farther out and fishing deeper water, you can strike it rich. Right after a halibut opener, a boatload of sport fishermen traveled out to 40 fathoms, and caught 14 halibut in 1½ hours, with two fish over 100 pounds.

Goodhand says most Valdez skippers stress catch and release for the larger halibut. "For instance, one of our clients may be a person who has driven up from the Lower 48 in a motorhome. They may have room for 40 pounds of fillets, but not 150 pounds, so we tell them the advantages of releasing the larger fish. We have a tailer on board for those anglers wishing to pursue an IGFA record."

One last tip: Try not to handle the halibut you intend to release. The slime is the fish's immune system, and oftentimes it is easier to cut the line and let the hook rust out than landing a halibut on deck and wrestling out a hook with pliers. Keep the fish in the water as you unhook it, or if necessary, cut the line, and we'll all have more halibut in the years to come.

David Coray of Silver Salmon Creek Lodge on the western shore of Cook Inlet gaffs this halibut for angler Ken Lomax.

Detailed Halibut Fishing Information on Southcentral Alaska

No matter what we write, we always have disgruntled charter boat operators who feel threatened by recommendations made by the sporting press of areas other than the ones they fish. This primarily takes place in the competition-heavy southcentral Alaska halibut fishery. Co-author Terry Rudnick and I felt it imperative to reveal the actual health and direction of the halibut fishery in this region. We wanted facts and figures to help the consumer decide how and where to fish, and precautions to keep in mind.

In searching for impartial information on the health of this fishery, we obtained the report, *Recreational Halibut Fishery in Southcentral Alaska with Harvest Composition*, by ADF&G biologist Scott C. Meyer. He has assembled detailed scientific information on popular fishing areas, problem areas, and more. Portions of Meyer's report and findings are reprinted below.

Introduction

Pacific halibut, *Hippoglossus stenolepis*, is the primary bottomfish targeted by the saltwater recreational fishery in southcentral Alaska (International Pacific Halibut Commission Regulatory Area 3A). Area 3A harvests in recent years have made up 70 percent (in number) of the Alaska statewide recreational halibut harvest and 60 percent (in weight) of the recreational halibut harvest of the entire North American west coast. Recreational harvest in Area 3A grew from 18,000 fish in 1977 to a current 190,000 fish. Area 3A anglers release 31 to 46 percent of the fish they catch. Sport harvest estimates are based on a postal survey of resident and nonresident households; estimates had a relative precision of 3.5 percent. Since 1977, the Cook Inlet fishery has accounted for 72 to 83 percent of the harvest in Area 3A. Growth in the Central Cook Inlet fishery has offset declines in the Lower Cook Inlet harvest since 1990. Age, size, and sex composition of the sport harvest were estimated at Kodiak, Homer, Seward, and Valdez. Ages ranged from 3 to 20 years, but 90 percent of the harvest was 5 to 14 years old (n equals 2,835). The 1987 year class was strong at most ports. Most harvested fish were between 28 and 52 inches.

Mean lengths and weights were lowest at Seward (14.6 pound net) and highest at Homer (24.9 pound net). Halibut harvested by chartered anglers were larger than fish taken by unguided anglers at Homer, Seward, and Valdez. Mean length at age of harvested halibut was not significantly higher across all ages for any one port. Females made up 55 percent of the harvest at Seward and 80 to 87 percent at other ports. Estimates of age, size, and sex composition were consistent with past years. Most of the Kodiak fleet fished within 12.4 miles of port, while fleets at other ports ranged up to 60 miles in search of halibut. Charter boats generally fished farther from port than private boats. Bait accounted for 67 to 98 percent of the effort and 70 to 99 percent of the harvest at the four ports.

Recreational Fishery Background

Importance Of The Halibut Fishery

Participation in recreational marine fisheries in southcentral Alaska has grown steadily over the last decade due to growth in the state's population and increased tourism. More anglers have also turned to marine fisheries as competition and restrictions on freshwater fishing opportunities increase. Recreational effort for all marine fin fishes increased from about 200,000 angler-days in 1980 to over 453,000 angler-days in the area from Cape St. Elias westward through Bristol Bay.

Cook Inlet fisheries accounted for about half of the effort during this period. In total, southcentral Alaska fisheries have accounted for about half of the statewide marine recreational fishing effort since 1980.

Pacific halibut is a primary target of anglers in southcentral Alaska. The International Pacific Halibut Commission (IPHC) manages halibut stocks throughout the North Pacific and has divided the coast into 11 major regulatory areas. IPHC regulatory Area 3A encompasses most of southcentral Alaska and a small portion of southeast Alaska, extending from Cape Spencer westward to Cape Trinity on the southern end of Kodiak Island. Recreational halibut harvest in Area 3A has grown from about 18,000 fish in 1977 to over 190,000 fish. Cook Inlet fisheries have traditionally dominated the Area 3A harvest, but most of the modest increase in the Area 3A harvest since 1990 has been due to growth in other fisheries. Anglers also release a large portion of their catch. An on-site creel survey estimated that 37 percent of halibut caught by the Valdez fleet were released. Area 3A anglers also released an estimated 31 to 46 percent of the halibut they caught, or 86,000 to 153,000 fish per year. Halibut made up 45 percent (in number) of the Area 3A finfish harvest in the 1990s compared with 33 percent in 1987.

The Area 3A recreational fishery is important on a statewide as well as well as coast-wide basis. Recent Area 3A sport harvests made up about 70 percent (in number) of the total Alaskan recreational halibut harvest. On a larger scale, the recent sport harvest in Area 3A made up about 60 percent by weight) of the entire recreational halibut harvest on the North American west coast.

The recreational halibut fishery is vital to the economy of southcentral Alaska. For example, sport anglers spent $18.6 million to catch 85,200 halibut in Cook Inlet fisheries in 1986.

They also indicated a willingness to pay an additional $25.2 million to ensure continued availability of halibut fishing opportunities. Most port communities sponsor halibut derbies to attract anglers, and proceeds from derbies are often donated to support a wide variety of community projects and organizations. Although there are no recent estimates of the economic value of the recreational fishery, it has undoubtedly increased concomitantly with effort and harvest.

The charter boat industry is an important economic component of the recreational fishery. For example, the Homer halibut charter boat industry generated $9.1 million in gross income for the Homer economy as well as an equivalent of 64 full-time, year-round jobs in 1985. Fifty-eight percent of the chartered anglers in Homer were Alaska residents in 1985. Two-thirds of chartered anglers surveyed said they would not have come to Homer if charter services had not been available.

Fishery Descriptions

Regulatory Area 3A is composed of many regional and local fisheries that are conducted in more or less separate geographic areas and possess distinctive patterns of harvest and use. The vast majority of harvest is taken in four major fisheries: Cook Inlet, Kodiak, the North Gulf Coast, and Prince William Sound. A local fishery based in Yakutat harvests an insignificant number of fish.

Cook Inlet

The Cook Inlet fishery is the largest recreational halibut fishery in North America and has grown rapidly. Since 1977, the Cook Inlet fishery has accounted for 72 to 83 percent (in number) of the Area 3A recreational harvest. The 1992 Cook Inlet harvest made up about 73 percent (by weight) of the Area 3A harvest and 44 percent (by weight) of the entire North American sport harvest of halibut. Estimated harvest increased from 13,500 fish in 1977 to a current 143,000-plus fish.

The Cook Inlet halibut fishery can be conveniently divided into two areas: (1) Central Cook Inlet (CCI), consisting of waters south of the West Foreland and north of the latitude of Anchor Point; and (2) Lower Cook Inlet (LCI), consisting of waters south of Anchor Point and north of a line from Cape Douglas to Gore Point. Major access points in CCI include boat ramps and beach launch sites at Deep Creek, Ninilchik and Anchor Point. Boats that launch in CCI generally fish the eastern half of Cook Inlet north of Anchor Point.

Halibut are rarely caught north of the mouth of Kenai River. The primary access point for the LCI fishery is Homer, with a few boats also launching at Seldovia and other communities on the south side of Kachemak Bay. Boats based out of Homer fish primarily south of Anchor Point but may range south of the Barren Islands and as far east as Port Dick.

Recent growth in the CCI fishery has offset declines in the LCI fishery. Harvest in CCI has increased every year since 1987, while LCI harvest has been stable or decreasing since 1988. Most of the increase in CCI has been due to a rapidly expanding charter fleet, particularly at Deep Creek. Until recently the Deep Creek fishery had been dominated by unguided anglers. Harvest by chartered anglers increased from 3 percent in 1986 to over 41 percent currently in CCI. In contrast, the proportion of harvest taken by chartered anglers has remained relatively stable at 50 to 68 percent in LCI. The number of bottomfish charter boats active at any level is estimated at 120 to 130 in LCI and 220 to 250 in CCI. This includes boats that spend only a portion of the day targeting halibut, as well as boats operated on a "full-time" (120 days or more per year) and "part-time" (less than 120 days per year) basis.

The recent decrease in harvest in LCI is probably more attributable to redistribution of fishing effort than a decrease in halibut abundance. The Deep Creek and Anchor Point fisheries are capturing the business of anglers that formerly fished at Homer. In addition, Kenai River guides are reportedly moving to Deep Creek to circumvent restrictions on the Kenai River chinook salmon fishery. The CCI saltwater fishery offer opportunities to harvest halibut as well as chinook salmon, is a shorter drive from Anchorage than Homer, and is a shorter and often smoother boat ride to the fishing grounds. Use of tractors to launch boats has reduced congestion at boat ramps and allowed launching of larger boats on any tide.

Kodiak

Halibut are harvested from numerous locations surrounding Kodiak and Afognak Islands, but the vast majority of harvest is taken in Chiniak Bay and other waters close to the port of Kodiak. Most boats based in Kodiak fish north of Cape Chiniak and only occasionally venture farther west than Whale Island and as far north as the north side of Marmot Bay. The most heavily fished waters are in the vicinity of Buoy 4, Spruce Cape, Woody Island, and Long Island, all less than 12 miles from port.

Although Kodiak is the hub of a thriving commercial longline fishery for halibut, the sport fishery is of much lower magnitude. Harvest in the Kodiak area, including waters surrounding Kodiak, Afognak, and the Barren Islands, grew from about 1,000 fish in 1977 to 12,100 fish in 1991, then decreased slightly in 1992 to 10,900 fish. The Kodiak harvest makes up only 6 percent (in number) and 8 percent (by weight) of the Area 3A total harvest. Approximately 30 boats are fully licensed to participate in the halibut charter fishery, but only about 12 to 15 are consistently active in the fishery. In addition, an estimated 18 to 20 lodges provide bottomfish services in Kodiak area waters. Most effort and harvest in the Kodiak area, however, is by unguided anglers. A noteworthy portion of the unguided effort for halibut is by anglers utilizing a small fleet of 17-foot boats leased by the U.S. Coast Guard. Growth of the Kodiak fishery will probably continue to be constrained by geographic isolation and the high cost of transportation from the mainland.

North Gulf Coast

Although Seward is practically the only access point for this fishery, effort is spread over an extremely large geographic area. Boats occasionally fish as far west as Nuka Bay and as far east as Cape Cleare, a maximum distance of 66 miles from Seward. Most of the halibut effort and harvest, however, are distributed outside of Resurrection Bay between the Chiswell Islands and Cape Puget. A net redistribution of effort outward from Seward has occurred in the last 20 years.

Harvest in the North Gulf Coast fishery rose from 1,700 fish in 1977 to over 18,600 fish today. Most of the growth has occurred since 1985. Harvest reached a low in 1989, presumably because of diversion of anglers and vessels to the Exxon Valdez oil spill clean-up in Prince William Sound. Harvest, particularly by chartered anglers, has increased steadily since 1989. Seward currently supports a bottomfish charter fleet of 40 to 50 boats, including 15 boats at the Seward Military Recreation Camp, and about one-half of the halibut harvest has been taken by chartered anglers in recent years. Although the Seward harbor is overcrowded and has a long waiting list for slips, some growth of the fishery is likely. Seward is only a two-hour drive from Anchorage, and the City of Seward is currently planning construction of an additional launching ramp.

Prince William Sound

Halibut harvest in Prince William Sound grew from 1,250 fish in 1977 to 17,900 fish in 1992. The majority of the Prince William Sound recreational halibut harvest is taken from boats based in Valdez. Valdez currently supports an active civilian charter fleet of about 30 boats, with about half that number consistently active. Although Whittier is close to Anchorage and supports high recreational boating use, most boaters do not fish for halibut and the harvest is a small percentage of the total for the sound. There are only four charter fishing vessels. Likewise, Cordova supports a large and active commercial fleet, but there is relatively less interest in recreational halibut fishing and only two charter vessels. Planned construction of a road connecting Cordova with the Alaska Highway system would probably result in some growth of the recreational fleet and increased harvest.

Valdez-based boats generally fish a north-south corridor between Valdez Arm and Hinchinbrook Entrance, on the eastern side of the sound. Popular sites include Bligh Reef, Knowles Head, Hinchinbrook Entrance, and Seal Rocks. Few private boats from Valdez fish sites south of Knowles Head, but most charter boats are equipped to handle rougher water and often fish the Hinchinbrook Entrance area, 60 to 72 miles from Valdez. Although Whittier-based boats concentrate bottomfishing effort in the northwestern corner of Prince William Sound, in Passage Canal, Blackstone Bay, and in waters near Esther and Perry Islands, they have reportedly fished the southwestern corner of Prince William Sound, 66 miles from port.

Halibut harvested by sport anglers are generally smaller and younger than fish taken in the commercial fishery. Most of the age and size differences between sport and commercial harvests are due to the fact that the sport fishery is not constrained by the 32-inch minimum size limit applied to the commercial setline fishery. Fish under 32 inches made up about 30 percent of the Kodiak, Homer, and Valdez sport harvests,

Southcentral Alaska

Map courtesy USGS

19. Seward	25. Valdez Arm
20. Resurrection Bay	26. Bligh Island
21. Day Harbor	27. Port Fidalgo
22. Aialik Cape	28. Cordova
23. Cape Cleare	29. Hinchinbrook Entrance
24. Valdez	

19 20 21 22 23 24 25 26 27 28 29

and 53 percent of the Seward harvest in 1992. Most of the recreational harvest is 24 to 54 inches long, while commercial setline harvest is all over 32 inches. About 90 percent of the recreational harvest in recent years was 5 to 12 years old, with the modal age at 8 to 10 years. By comparison, roughly 90 percent of the commercial harvest in recent years was 9 to 16 years old, with modal ages of 10 to 12.

There are significant geographic differences in size, age, and sex composition of the sport harvest even within Area 3A. One of the largest differences is that males make up roughly 40 percent of the Seward harvest, compared with 15 to 20 percent at other ports. As a result, fish landed at Seward are considerably smaller than fish taken at other ports (however isolated catches of big fish have set per day and per boat catch records—ed.) Differences among ports in age composition are not as dramatic or apparent. There was some evidence in 1992 that the mean length at age was lower for males and females landed at Seward, and this question was investigated using 1993 data. Reasons for regional differences are not understood, but some of these differences must be accounted for when estimating the recreational harvest biomass for Area 3A.

Changes in size and age composition of the recreational harvest appear to reflect changes in the stock to a limited extent. For example, even though the sport fishery is selective for certain ages and sizes, relatively strong and weak year classes correlate and track over time. Because halibut recruit to the sport fishery at a younger age, sport harvest age data provide clues to upcoming year-class strength.

The relationship between harvest and stock composition is influenced by seasonal changes in fish availability, changes in the fishery patterns, and improvements in technology. Each year the size composition of halibut harvested from Cook Inlet varies within the season, with more large fish taken in July and fewer large fish taken toward the beginning and end of the season. This pattern is consistent with tagging data that suggest summer time on-shore migrations of adult halibut. Halibut harvested in May 1992 at Seward were unusually large relative to other months. This was because most of the fish taken in May were caught by anglers on civilian charter boats, and fish taken by this group were significantly larger than fish taken by other types of anglers. In general, there are often significant differences in the sizes and catch rates of various user groups that may be a function of fishing expertise, onboard equipment, and boat size. The catch rate of chartered anglers;

for example, was five times that of unguided anglers at Valdez in 1988. If effort, fishing methods, and waters fished are relatively constant over time, then observed trends in harvest composition probably represent real changes in the halibut stock itself. It is therefore important to continue to monitor the percentage of harvest by each user group, size composition by user group, and the geographic distribution of effort and harvest at each port.

Length and Weight

A total of 3,577 fish was measured from all ports. Estimated mean lengths by port ranged from 32.9 inches at Seward to 39 inches at Homer. Mean net weight was lowest at Seward (14.6 lb) and highest at Homer (24.9 lb). Corresponding average round weights ranged from 19.5 pounds at Seward to 33.1 pounds at Homer. The Homer estimates of mean length and weight were stratified to account for seasonal changes.

Most fish measured were between 27.3 and 50.7 inches. Fish landed at Seward had the lowest proportion of large fish in the harvest of all ports. For example, 10 percent of sampled fish were over 42.9 inches at Seward, compared with 25 percent at other ports. Homer was the port with the lowest proportion of smaller fish in the harvest.

Differences in length composition among all months were significant at all ports. At Kodiak, however, most of the difference resulted from a high proportion of large fish taken in September. Differences among May, June, July, and August were not significant. Length composition changed over the season at Homer following the same pattern observed in recent years. Fish were generally smaller early and late in the season, and largest in July. Monthly differences at Seward were caused by a lack of large fish in June and lack of small fish in September. There was no pronounced trend to account for differences among months at Valdez.

Length composition varied among user groups as well, and these differences were significant at all ports. Fish harvested by chartered anglers were larger on average than fish taken by private (unguided) anglers at Homer, Seward, and Valdez. In contrast, fish taken by unguided anglers using U.S. Coast Guard morale boats at Kodiak were slightly larger than fish taken by other private or chartered anglers. Chartered anglers at Homer harvested more large fish and fewer small fish than private anglers. Surprisingly, roughly equal proportions of halibut over 39 inches were taken by private and civilian-chartered (as opposed to military-chartered) anglers at Seward, but private anglers were more likely to harvest fish under 35 inches. Military-chartered anglers at Seward harvested very few halibut over 39 inches. Private anglers at Valdez appeared more likely to harvest halibut under 39 inches than chartered anglers, but conclusions are weakened by the small number of fish that could be positively identified as private-caught. Length composition of halibut taken by military and civilian charter boats at Valdez were similar.

Sex Composition

As in past years, females dominated the recreational harvest at all ports, but to a lesser extent at Seward. Females made up 87 percent of the harvest at Kodiak, 84 percent at Valdez, 80 percent at Homer, but only 55 percent at Seward. Excluding Seward, differences in sex ratio among the remaining ports were still significant.

There were no significant differences in sex ratio among months at Homer or Seward. Differences among months were significant at Kodiak and Valdez. At Kodiak, the proportion of females in the harvest was lowest in July and highest in September. In contrast, females made up a generally higher proportion of the Valdez harvest early in the year, and a much lower proportion later in September. Even though differences were significant among months at Kodiak and Valdez, stratification of overall estimates of sex composition was not necessary. Weighted and unweighted estimates differed by 1.2 percent at Kodiak and less than 1 percent at Valdez.

Geographic Distribution of Effort and Harvest

Recreational effort and harvest for halibut were spread over large geographic areas at all ports but Kodiak. Most of the effort and halibut harvest by Kodiak anglers occurred in Chiniak Bay. A total of 1,349 angler-days and 1,215 harvested halibut were observed through an interview sample representing 429 boat trips. Eighty-three percent of bottomfishing effort and 85 percent of the halibut harvest was in stat area 525733. The most popular areas fished included Buoy 4, Woody Island, and Long Island.

The Homer interview sample included 213 boat-trips representing 1,310 angler-days and an observed harvest of 2,123 halibut. Effort and harvest by Homer boats was spread from the west side of Cook Inlet to Gore Point and south to the Barren Islands. Harvest was concentrated, however, in three stat areas. Stat area 525902 west of Point Adam accounted for 23 percent of effort and 31 percent of harvest. Stat area 525931, west of Anchor Point accounted for 14 percent of effort and 17 percent of harvest. Finally, stat area 515905 southwest of Elizabeth and Perl Islands accounted for 19 percent of the effort and 23 percent of the harvest. In general, charter boats ranged farther from port than private boats.

Interviews with the civilian fleet in Seward included 311 boat-trips representing 1,411 angler-days and a harvest of 1,223 halibut. Effort and harvest by interviewed anglers were spread over an 84-mile-long arc from Black Bay west of Seward to Cape Cleare. The bulk of effort and harvest was spread from the Chiswell Islands and Cape Aialik (stat area 495932) eastward through lower Resurrection Bay and Day Harbor (stat area 495938) to Johnstone Bay (stat areas 485933 and 485935). Private and charter boats took advantage of relatively calm seas, spending 22 percent of effort and taking 28 percent of the harvest more than 37 miles from Seward in the Johnstone Bay area (stat area 485935).

The military fleet reported a total effort for the season of 7,292 angler-days on 822 boat-trips, and a total harvest of 6,487 halibut. Military charter boats generally did not range as far as civilian boats. Military-chartered anglers expended 56 percent of their effort and took 55 percent of their harvest in the Chiswell Islands/Cape Aialik area (stat area 495932). The Johnstone Bay area was also popular with military boats, accounting for 21 percent of their effort and 34 percent of their halibut harvest.

Finally, the Valdez interview sample represented 1,627 angler-days on 346 boat-trips, and an observed harvest of 1,717 halibut. Effort and harvest by the Valdez fleet were spread throughout Prince William Sound.

Most of the effort and harvest were in a north-south corridor running from Valdez Arm to Hinchinbrook Entrance. Stat area 466033, including Bligh Island and Port Fidalgo, was the most heavily fished area with 16 percent of the effort but only 6 percent of the halibut harvest. Surprisingly, 27 percent of the effort and 41 percent of the harvest was in six stat areas outside of Hinchinbrook Entrance, more than 62 miles from Valdez. Most boats fishing these outside areas were charter boats.

User Group, Target Species, and Gear Type Composition

User Group Composition

The percentage of effort and halibut harvest attributable to each user group varied by port. In general, chartered anglers were more effective at catching halibut; their proportion of the harvest always exceeded their proportion of the effort. For example, chartered anglers at Kodiak only made up 24 percent of the effort (in angler-days) but took 33 percent of the harvest (in number of fish). In addition to being more effective, chartered anglers also took the majority of harvest at all other ports. Chartered anglers accounted for 77 percent of the effort and 88 percent of the harvest at Homer. Within the civilian fleet at Seward, guided anglers made up only 46 percent of the effort but took 56 percent of the harvest. Finally, chartered anglers (civilian and military) at Valdez made up 69 percent of the effort and took 85 percent of the harvest.

The military charter fleet at Seward was composed of two groups: (1) anglers fishing from four large boats (43 to 50 feet), and (2) anglers fishing from eleven small boats (27 feet). Catch rates of the two groups were roughly equivalent. For example, chartered anglers on large boats made up 57 percent of the effort and 55 percent of the harvest.

Target Species Composition

Halibut were the primary bottomfish species of interest at all ports. The percentage of angler-days targeted exclusively on halibut ranged from 67 percent at Seward to just under 100 percent at Homer. Anglers at Kodiak and Seward spent a considerable portion of their effort targeting other species in combination with halibut (18 percent and 25 percent, respectively). The percentage of angler-days spent targeting bottomfish other than halibut was highest at Seward (8 percent).

As expected, anglers targeting halibut exclusively accounted for the majority of the halibut harvest. All of the Homer harvest was by anglers targeting halibut only, compared with 99 percent at Valdez, 80 percent at Kodiak, and 77 percent at Seward. About one-fifth of the Kodiak and Seward halibut harvest was by anglers targeting halibut in combination with other bottomfish.

It was impossible to determine the proportion of effort by Seward Military Recreation Camp anglers that was targeted exclusively on halibut. Military charter boat operators recorded target species data as "bottomfish," "salmon," or "both." All of the harvest, and nearly all of the effort (99.7 percent) fell in the "bottomfish" category. Although camp personnel have indicated in past years that lingcod are a primary target (particularly for small boats), this may be changing somewhat due to recent institution of time and area closures and reduced bag limits in the lingcod fishery.

Gear Type Composition

Many angler responses did not fit gear type categories used in angler interviews. Anglers employed a wide variety of gear types, and often used several per day or several in conjunction (e.g. baited jig). Gear type categories were therefore simplified to (1) bait only, (2) bait plus other gear types, and (3) other gear types. Bait was clearly the preferred terminal gear type. An estimated 67 percent to 98 percent of the total effort and 70 percent to 99 percent of the harvest was accounted for by anglers using bait exclusively. In addition, bait accounted for an unknown portion of the effort and harvest in the "bait plus other" category.

The Seward Military Recreation Camp recorded gear use as either (1) jig and bait in combination or (2) troll gear. Gear categories for the recreation camp were originally established to evaluate the lingcod fishery. Troll gear accounted for 39 percent of the recreation camp effort, but much of this effort was probably targeted on lingcod or rockfish. Surprisingly, 27 percent of the recreation camp halibut harvest was reportedly taken with troll gear.

Management and Allocation Issues

The State of Alaska does not have management authority over halibut fisheries in state or federal waters. Instead, the halibut resource is managed for optimal sustained yield by the IPHC under the Halibut Convention of 1953 and its 1979 Protocol. The IPHC annually estimates halibut abundance using catch-at-age data and establishes the total allowable harvest under a constant-exploitation-rate strategy. Estimated biomass of the exploitable stock in Area 3A peaked in 1988 at 172 million pounds and is expected to decline at a rate of 5 to 10 percent per year for several more years. Recruitment and stock biomass are believed to be cyclical; if this holds true then recruitment is expected to remain low for several years.

Continued growth of the sport fishery in Area 3A necessitates the inclusion of accurate sport harvest data in annual stock assessments by the IPHC. Historically, only commercial removals were used to estimate exploitable biomass because other removals such as sport harvest were considered ineligible. The IPHC has recently attempted to account for all sources of removal including sport, subsistence, bycatch, and wastage. Incorporation of sport harvest in the 1991 stock assessment led to a 10 percent to 15 percent increase in overall harvest and a 10 percent increase in estimated biomass over recent years.

Allocation of the allowable halibut harvest among user groups in U.S. waters is the responsibility of the North Pacific Fisheries Management Council (NPFMC), under the Magnuson Fisheries Conservation and Management Act of 1976. The sport fishery in Alaska has not been managed under a harvest quota and has in effect been allocated all the fish it can harvest. The recreational fishery accounted for 3.9 million pounds or 10 percent (by weight) of the total halibut removals in Area 3A in 1992. Other removals (in millions pounds) included: 26.8 commercial harvest (72 percent), 5.0 bycatch mortality other fisheries (13 percent), 1.0 waste (3 percent), and 0.5 personal use (2 percent). Waste is defined as mortality of sublegal size halibut and fish killed by lost or abandoned setline gear. Directed commercial harvest, bycatch in other commercial fisheries, and waste accounted for 88 percent of all removals.

The Alaska Longline Fishermen's Association (ALFA) submitted a proposal to the NPFMC in May 1993 to establish a harvest quota for the sport charter industry in Alaska. The proposal was intended to address what ALFA perceived to be "rapid, uncontrolled growth of the guided sport halibut charter industry" in Alaska. ALFA believes that continued growth of the sport fishery, particularly the guided component, is inevitable. Given that the halibut resource is fully utilized, ALFA believes that without restriction this growth will cause reallocation of halibut away from the directed longline fishery. This reallocation would result in economic and social costs to the traditional longline fishery. The objective of their proposal is to minimize such impacts. The NPFMC is currently studying this issue. There is precedence for establishing a halibut allocation to the sport fishery. The sport fishery in IPHC Regulatory Area 2A (coastal waters of Washington, Oregon, and California) has been allocated an annual harvest quota consisting of a fixed percentage of the total allowable harvest. Unlike the ALFA proposal, the Area 2A harvest quota applies to the overall sport fishery, both guided and unguided.

Responsible decisions regarding allocation of the resource should incorporate the best available information on the status and effects of the sport fishery. Even though the Alaska Department of Fish and Game lacks management authority for halibut, it is committed to obtaining and providing the IPHC and NPFMC with the information needed for wise management and fair allocation.

Effects of a Bag-Limit Reduction

Overall, institution of a one-fish daily bag limit would be expected to reduce halibut harvest by about 26 percent at Kodiak, 45 percent at Homer, 32 percent in the civilian fishery at Seward, 28 percent in the military charter fishery at Seward, and 35 percent at Valdez. These estimated reductions assume that angler effort would remain constant. The number of halibut harvested could increase if, for example, effort increased as a result of more half-day trips by charter vessels. Biomass of the sport harvest could also rise if anglers responded to a bag limit decrease by preferentially keeping larger fish.

Impacts of a bag limit reduction would be greater for chartered anglers than unguided anglers. Thirty-three percent of the harvest by chartered anglers at Kodiak consisted of second fish in the creel, compared with 22 percent to 24 percent by unguided anglers on private boats and U.S. Coast Guard morale boats. At Homer, 47 percent of the harvest by chartered anglers was composed of second fish, compared with 34 percent by private boat anglers. Civilian charter and private anglers at Seward would probably be affected similarly; 33 percent of the charter harvest and 31 percent of the private harvest were second fish. The harvest by chartered anglers on Seward Military Recreation Camp boats would be affected the least. Depending on boat size, 27 percent to 29 percent of their harvest was made up of second fish, but they tend to target other bottomfish in addition to halibut. Finally, civilian and military charter anglers at Valdez took 38 percent and 31 percent of their harvest as second fish, compared with only 23 percent by unguided anglers.

Discussion

Estimates of age, size, and sex composition of the recreational harvest were generally consistent with past years. Modal age groups tracked with 1991 and 1992 data for the most part. The 1982 year class (age 11) appeared relatively weak at most ports as it did in 1991 and 1992. As in past years, harvested fish

How to Catch
Trophy Halibut

were smaller at Seward than at other ports, and the Seward harvest again had the highest proportion of males.

There were, however, some notable deviations from past data. Halibut harvested at Kodiak in 1993 were considerably smaller and younger than fish taken in 1992. Ages 5 to 7 appeared strong relative to recent years and made up a significant portion of the harvest. The study design was altered in 1993 to include sampling of harvest by Coast Guard morale boats. This change, however, probably did not cause the observed reduction in size and age composition because halibut taken on these boats were larger on average than fish taken by other user groups. The strong showing of the 1987 year class at Kodiak and Valdez correlates with observation of this strong year class in eastern Bering Sea trawl surveys.

In contrast, fish taken at Homer were generally older and larger than in past years, and the 1987 year class did not appear particularly strong. At least two explanations are possible. First, a large percentage of the Homer harvest was by chartered anglers, and landings by chartered anglers include few small halibut. This apparent selectivity for larger fish may be due in part to encouragement by charter crews to release small fish, and also in part to cleaning of small halibut at sea. Some charter operators clean small fish at sea to expedite meat handling and return to port with the largest fish for weighing and photographs. If a significant portion of the harvest was in fact small fish cleaned at sea, then length, weight, and age parameters for Homer were overestimated. Even though most of the harvest of fish under 27.3 inches (ages 5 to 7) was by unguided anglers, the 1987 year class should still appear strong relative to adjacent age classes. The eventual appearance of this year class in the Cook Inlet harvest may provide information on recruitment mechanisms in this fishery.

Surprising results were obtained with respect to the sizes of fish caught by various user groups. Private (unguided) anglers at Seward caught more large halibut in 1993 than in 1992, probably because of improved boating conditions. The Gulf of Alaska was relatively calm, particularly in July, and private boats fished farther from Seward than in past years. Most military charter boats at Seward continued to fish the lower Resurrection Bay and Chiswell Islands area, and the length composition of their harvest was similar to last year but smaller than that of private anglers. At Kodiak, unguided U.S. Coast Guard personnel generally caught larger halibut than other anglers, but fewer of them kept two fish per day. This is

surprising because Coast Guard "morale boats" are restricted to only the near-shore portion of Chiniak Bay.

Interview data from Homer show that 88 percent of the harvest was by chartered anglers, compared with postal survey estimates of 50 percent to 68 percent for the Lower Cook Inlet fishery during the period 1986 to 1992. This difference is probably due to the fact that port sampling was conducted only within the Homer harbor during the summer months, while the postal survey includes harvest from all boats accessing the fishery at all points during all times of year. In another comparison, interview data indicate that 63 percent of the Seward harvest was taken by chartered anglers, assuming that military charter boats accounted for 16 percent of the Seward harvest as they did in 1992. This is slightly higher than the postal survey estimates of 36 percent to 55 percent for 1986 to 1992. This is understandable given the recent modest growth in the Seward charter fleet. Finally, chartered anglers at Valdez took an estimated 69 percent of the harvest in 1993. This estimate too is understandably higher than the only previous estimate of 58 percent in 1988, given that the charter fleet has grown. Charter operators are under financial pressure to produce halibut, while private boat anglers often spend a good portion of their angling day boating, sightseeing, or targeting other species.

The target species and gear composition estimates obtained were previously not available for any Area 3A fisheries. The most important conclusions from these data are that (1) halibut are the primary bottomfish targeted at all ports, (2) bait is the primary terminal tackle used, and (3) compared with other ports, more anglers at Seward target bottomfish other than halibut and use gear types other than bait.

This 140-pound halibut, taken aboard a Saltwater Safari charter out of Seward, is typical of many big halibut caught in the shallow water areas of Montague Island.

Acknowledgements

Numerous Department of Fish and Game personnel contributed to this study and report. Catherine Coon, Alan Heckart, William Romberg, and Michael Parish collected biological and interview data, validated results through personal observations, and assisted the public on a daily basis. Paul Cyr aged all halibut otoliths and assisted with figures. William Romberg assisted with data reduction and preparation of tables and figures. James Hasbrouck assisted with operational planning, and Pat Hansen analyzed the mean length-at-age data and provided valuable biometric guidance and interpretation. Paul Suchanek and Doug McBride provided editorial insight and Margaret Leonard whipped the report into publishable form. Finally Doug Vincent-Lang provided overall project guidance, supervision, and perspective.

Other individuals were instrumental in the study. Calvin Blood of the IPHC once again shared his wealth of knowledge of halibut aging. Jack Dyer and staff of the Seward Military Recreation Camp generously provided daily harvest records and sampling facilities. Commander Troth and other U.S. Coast Guard personnel allowed on-base sampling of recreational harvest at Kodiak. Harbormasters throughout the region provided valuable advice for planning and sampling. Most importantly, this project would have been impossible without the cooperation of the angling public. The vast majority of anglers and charter boat operators were generous with information and facilities, courteous, and genuinely concerned for the halibut resource.

Kodiak Island

Kodiak Island is one of the best halibut fisheries in Alaska. If you're traveling from mainland Alaska, Kodiak does take a bit more time and expense to reach, but the scenery and fishing opportunities are worth the effort. This section elaborates on the Kodiak information presented above in the ADF&G survey.

For many years, the International Pacific Halibut Commission listed Kodiak as the commercial fishing world's "Halibut Capital of the World." A review of the bottom topography of the shelves, ledges and other structure that surrounds Kodiak will give the angler an idea as to why this area is an "island oasis" for halibut.

Kodiak offers its own oceanography, and the smart halibut angler would be wise to study these factors before planning an extended trophy fishing trip.

Very little information is known about the actual circulation over the Gulf of Alaska Continental Shelf. This is what scientists do know, and what trophy halibut anglers fishing Kodiak waters can put to use:

Kodiak inshore and shelf waters are influenced primarily by tides, seasonally variable fluvial run-off (as those described in the Cook Inlet oceanography section), and wind.

The distribution of bottom water shows an apparent intrusion of oceanic (colder) waters just west of Kodiak, along the topographic depressions leading into Shelikof Strait. According to AEIDC data, normal sea waters may intrude far onto the shelf at times during summer and fall. It has been suggested

How to Catch
Trophy Halibut

that the distribution of fish on the shelf may be closely related to these intrusions and to the ponded oceanic waters that may be left behind when the halocline recedes (Plakhotnik, 1964).

Bottom type consists of variable sediment types. Coarse materials are being deposited near headlands, and reefs. The underwater plateaus are generally covered with a thin veneer of pebbles, gravel and sand. Finer sands and muds are generally found in the deepwater bays and fjords around Kodiak, while encrusted pebble gravels, rock fragments and boulders are found in the banks and shoals. Many areas offer no bottom cover whatsoever, with hard rock bottom predominating.

Three bottom types exist in Kodiak area waters: areas, plateau surfaces, and narrow, shallow sections of the continental shelf. According to AEIDC, nearshore areas comprise the narrow, shallow parts of the shelf adjacent to the coastline, such as those found in deep inlets and fjords found in Chignik Bay and Northwest Kodiak Island. These areas generally range from three to 4.8 miles wide and 90 to 150 feet deep. They include many reefs and skerries (stacks).

Anglers frequently fish the main part of the shelf, which is characterized by large expanses of plateau-like surfaces with depths ranging from 240 to 360 feet and gentle slopes. This is typical of bottom structure found in the southwest and southeast portion of Kodiak Island. Of special interest to halibut anglers are the many isolated banks and shoals that abruptly rise to near the surface, or above. The islands, skerries and reefs with flats, gouges and holding areas not only attract forage fish, but large numbers of halibut.

In the Unimak Island area, the bottom is rugged, dissected topography, with shelfs from 45 to 60 feet, dropping to 390 feet.

In my years of fishing Kodiak waters, I've found the water near Buoys 3 and 4 in Chiniak Bay are good. Cod here group up during large tidal fluctuations, which attracts halibut into the shallow-water areas such as Williams Reef. Also try Marmot Bay, Woody and Long islands, Cape Chiniak, Ugak Bay, Uyak Bay, Alitak Bay and Point, and Whale Pass.

Kodiak is home to an excellent number of salmon streams, and halibut fishing in or near these streams can be fish-after-fish during August and September. While good fishing can be had around the island's perimeter, I've had the best success (weather permitting) in the southern and western islands, as well as Afognak. Try the drop-offs near Shuyak Island, Shuyak Strait, as well as Ban Island, Perenosa Bay, and Foul Bay. The problem here is there is so much good water to fish, and not enough time in the summer to try 'em all. If possible, charter a boat for a week and hit the seldom fished areas to the north and west, and you won't be disappointed.

Many anglers choose to pursue halibut from Silver Salmon Lodge or one of the other quality, land-based camps located on Kodiak and Afognak islands. Saltwater and freshwater salmon fishing, rockfish and ling cod round out the offerings. Guide Peter Guttchen says anglers should choose a lodge located in or near a protected cove, which will allow you to fish rather than twiddle your thumbs during stormy weather.

Kevin Adkins of Lion's Den Lodge on Kodiak is in the heart of some of the island's best halibut fishing. "We only travel 10 minutes from the lodge to catch big halibut," he says. "We have a range of water and conditions from 60 feet to 400 feet deep. In the deeper water, I look for a sharp edge that has a ledge jutting out. Halibut swarm to such a ledge, especially during an outgoing tide, to prevent themselves from being flushed out into deeper water. I'm sure they also find it an ideal location to ambush baitfish. A favorite area that has this type of structure is in Whale Pass. Look for a flat spot about half way down the drop-off.

Another excellent type of structure in the Kodiak area is a narrow pass or gorge, with shallow water on each side.

"The type I prefer is 30 feet in the shallows, dropping down to 70 feet at the bottom of the pass," Adkins says. "Depending on the tide, I'll fish the leeward side. The bait is channeled down this 'trough' and halibut are waiting in good numbers."

Adkins fishes a variety of gear and equipment.

"In July, select bays in the Kodiak area are packed with herring. The halibut follow the herring, and swim off the bottom and feed on them, right under the surface.

"When I first saw this happen, I thought the boiling and feeding frenzy was caused by sharks, because these fins would knife right under the surface of the water," Adkins says. "As it turned out, they were halibut. Halibut can't feed under the surface while swimming flat, so they turn upright, which juts their body and fin out of the water. We caught them on spinners at first, within 15 feet of the boat, before I tied up this goat hair fly. For the flyfisher, it's spectacular fishing without the deepwater dredging with heavy lines."

Adkins also fishes bait rigs and twister-tail jigs.

When fishing Kodiak, choose those tides with minimal fluctuation. With larger tides, the feed is widely dispersed. Low tide keeps feed concentrated in select areas, which concentrates halibut. Also, smaller tides allow the angler to fish deeper water, fish vertically, and remain stationary for a longer period of time.

Schedule your Kodiak halibut fishing anytime from May through October. In years of large salmon returns, expect halibut fishing to remain good until late October, otherwise it starts to wind down in mid September.

While halibut fishing is good around the island, numbers of larger fish are caught on the east side of the island, bordering the continental shelf. Disadvantage here is unprotected waters, which can keep anglers in port for days. Adkins combats this by having anglers drive to Anton Larsen Bay, where he fishes them in protected waters.

ALASKA PENINSULA

The Gulf of Alaska has long been a popular area for commercial halibut fishermen. Only recently have sport anglers penetrated this area for the sole purpose of fishing for halibut. Many lodges are now offering halibut fishing as a primary species, where in years past it was a secondary species or incidental catch.

Dutch Harbor/Unalaska

For years, I've been skeptical of the occasional halibut stories that have filtered out of Dutch Harbor, located on the tip of the Alaska Peninsula in the mixing grounds of the Bering Sea and the Gulf of Alaska. But when regular reports of 300 and 400-pound fish began crossing my desk, I decided to check it out myself. What I found is some of the best Pacific halibut fishing in North America.

Consider the facts:
• The area receives little if any sportfishing pressure. Geographical conditions make it an ideal halibut feeding area.
• Tidal fluctuations are minimal.
• Because the area borders the deepest waters of the Gulf of Alaska and Bering Sea, deepwater holding sanctuaries favored by trophy halibut are just minutes away.
• While the average halibut catch statewide is 30 pounds, the average catch among several skippers at Dutch is 80 pounds!

"You can't catch record-sized fish in many places anymore," says J. Richard Pace, president of Uni-Sea, Inc. "For gigantic halibut, salmon and adventure, it's hard to beat Dutch Harbor."

While Dutch Harbor is home to one of the largest commercial fishing fleets in the North America, it harbors only

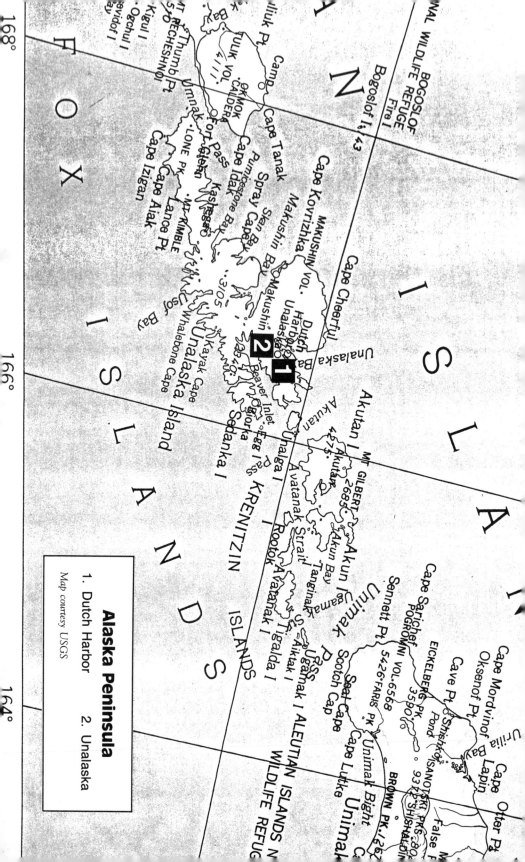

Alaska Peninsula

1. Dutch Harbor   2. Unalaska

Map courtesy USGS

a handful of sportfishing boats. Locals name two men who pioneered the area's halibut sportfishery: Darryl Dossett and John Lucking.

Dossett said he and Lucking didn't know each other in the beginning, but they would often see each other zipping out to halibut grounds, each in his 18-foot skiff.

"We'd wave to each other, and after a while, I realized he was just as crazy as I was for tackling this water and size of fish in such a small boat," Dossett said. "Eventually we started sharing notes about the areas and hotspots. What we found was incredible.

"Halibut down there shingle the bottom like tiles on a roof," he said. "I'll see them stacked up off the bottom in some areas. There is no waiting in this halibut fishery. You drop down your lure, jig it a few times, and you have a 50 to 80-pound or larger fish on. It's unbelievable until you see it with your own eyes."

One of Dossett's favorite fishing spots is a rip tide between two islands where the Gulf of Alaska and Bering Sea meet.

"The water boils from the tidal flux and can get pretty hairy at times," he said, "but the bait and fish get caught in the current, which draws in big halibut from nearby areas."

Lucking is becoming a legend in the area for consistently finding and catching barn-door halibut.

Jane Schroeder of Grand Aleutian Adventures said a halibut that missed the state record by a pound was caught by Lucking and Ken Stuckey during the last day of their 1995 season (for details, see Halibut Lore chapter).

Because the best halibut grounds are within a half hour to an hour from port, anglers stay at the Grand Aleutian Hotel and journey out each day to the halibut grounds. Inclement weather can keep anglers in port, where halibut fishing for 80 to 100-pound fish is possible, as I experienced one blustery day with a 120-pounder. Add spectacular scenery, salmon fishing, World War II ruins, and miles of remote wilderness (and no bears) and it's easy to see why I believe Unalaska is destined to become the "TROPHY halibut capital of the world." I strongly recommend a journey to this area and fishery, NOW, while you still can enjoy its many wonders. It's a bit expensive to reach, but worth every penny. Unalaska is located in the middle of the North Pacific, where sportfishing is an unknown word to these fish! Try Unalaska if your heart is searching for adventure. You won't be disappointed.

In other areas along the Alaska Peninsula coastline, anglers can experience good to excellent halibut fishing. Halibut migrate freely along the Alaska Peninsula coastline. Catches averaged higher in weight per hour trawled during exploratory fishing in waters less than 270 feet deep. The most productive depths were from 175 to 420 feet in the vicinity of Chirikof Island. Off the northeast corner of Kodiak Island, excellent catches are regularly taken in 150 to 390 feet of water. While fishing from the various salmon camps along the Alaska Peninsula, I oftentimes was able to take out a skiff and catch halibut in the tiny, calm bays less than 100 feet deep. Wilderness saltwater beaches, volcanoes and glaciers in the background, and fish-after fish action makes for a fishing adventure that is seldom matched anywhere in the world. And you'll only find it on the Alaska Peninsula.

SOUTHEAST ALASKA

Much of the bottomfish effort in southeast Alaska is for halibut. In sampled fisheries, biologists estimate that 33,795 halibut were harvested out of 45,482 halibut that were hooked. Most of the halibut effort takes place near the larger cities of Juneau, Ketchikan and Sitka, with Petersburg, Wrangell, Haines and Yakutat offering equally good fishing in select areas. Estimated average round weight of halibut ranged 24.4 pounds from Ketchikan waters to 37.9 pounds from Sitka waters. About 1,051,500 pounds of Pacific halibut were taken in the sampled fishery, with about 46 percent of this harvest taken in Sitka-area waters.

Yakutat

While several operators offer good, overnight halibut adventures out of many Alaska ports, Chuck and Roberta Crabaugh typify the "best of the best," those operators who offer outstanding personalized service for veterans as well as beginning halibut fishermen. Crabaugh is a former commercial halibut fisherman who has earned a reputation as being one of Alaska's top sportfishing halibut guides.

Your day trip or overnight halibut adventure is based aboard the 53-foot Shenandoah, a comfortable vessel well-suited for Alaska waters. Recently, Crabaugh moved his charter operation from Homer to Yakutat.

"I felt the heavy fishing pressure in southcentral Alaska was not providing the number or quality of fish our clients have come to expect in years past," he said. "Southcentral still offers a good halibut fishing experience, but I felt it was time to move on. I grew tired of the long travel times to and from the halibut

Southeast Alaska

1. Yakutat Bay
2. Yakutat
3. Icy Point
4. Cross Sound
5. Elfin Cove
6. Icy Strait
7. Funter
8. Lynn Canal
9. Berners Bay
10. Juneau

Map courtesy USGS

grounds. Here in Yakutat, it's a half-hour out and we are into larger fish than I caught when traveling three hours one way to the outer islands of Cook Inlet."

But Crabaugh doesn't promote keeping the larger fish.

"The smaller ones are best for eating," he said. "Anglers and charter operators have to do all we can to release the larger fish, the spawners, so we'll have halibut in the years to come. If somone books with me and wants to go for a large fish, I'll do my best to find him one. But I'll also do my best to convince him to release it and keep the smaller fish for the freezer. We don't want to deplete our stocks here like they are elsewhere."

Yakutat's halibut fleet consists of fewer than a dozen boats, with most fishing the waters of Yakutat Bay.

Crabaugh says he catches and releases lots of fish over 100 pounds, but attributes that to the 250-foot and greater depths he fishes. The trend among Yakutat charters is to fish 70 to 100 feet of water, where action is fast and furious, but fewer numbers of large fish.

Monte Bay, and across the mouth of Yakutat Bay, are popular fishing areas. Anglers have better success in the clear waters to the west, as the glacially silted runoff from Yakutat Bay empties out the east side. Halibut can be caught, however, in the turbid east-side waters.

For bait, Crabaugh uses standard herring rigs mentioned in this book, and salmon heads obtained from the local fish cannery.

"I can use less weight here because of the 14-foot tides," he says. "From 20 ounces to two pounds is generally enough."

Halibut anglers fishing Yakutat waters will find a variety of underwater structure. You'll find everything from cliffs to pinnacles to sand. Pinnacles are good locations that attract big halibut, as are rocky bottoms that drop off fast. Underwater hills or humps are a favorite for halibut, and plentiful in the region. With a depth finder, you can usually see halibut swimming above these humps, searching for cod and shrimp. The halibut average about 75 pounds, and Crabaugh's records show that one out of every eight fish is over 100 pounds. Charters in the area run eight hours, with up to one-hour travel each way. You can catch your halibut and still have time to fish the nearby rivers in the evening. Crabaugh and many area charters do not offer overnight trips as they are able to reach good fishing on day charters and nothing would be gained via an overnighter.

How to Catch
Trophy Halibut

Juneau

The Juneau area is well-known for its halibut fishing. Most of the fishing effort takes place in an area from Doty Cove to Berners Bay and west to Point Retreat, followed by waters in the Angoon area. Stephens Passage, Admiralty Island waters and Funter Bay provide fair catches of halibut. Point Retreat offers some of the best fishing in the southern Lynn Canal area. Concentrate your efforts in water 180 feet or less.

To the south, expect good fishing at the drop-off adjacent to Kadashan Bay in Tenakee Inlet and the northern tip of Basket Bay. Fish deepwater structure at the mouth of Pavlof Harbor in spring and summer. The flats of Gambier and Pybus bays receive thousands of pink salmon each year, which attract small to large halibut. You'll find halibut in the bays, or waiting on the underwater mounds and deepwater holes near the many islands in these waters. Use caution when navigating this area, as a large number of underwater reefs and rocks are right under the surface. Also try Wood Spit and Cape Fanshaw and western Whitney Island to the south. Near Juneau, try Grand Island, the entrance to Taku Harbor and Midway Island. Harbor Island in Holkham Bay is good during slack and incoming tides.

Long-time Juneau resident Dale Anderson of Admiralty Tours spends his summer investigating the halibut hotspots in the Juneau area. He fishes Icy Straits and Icy Point, Chatham Strait, Frederick Sound and Funter Bay.

"Some favorite areas of the day charter halibut fleet include the shelves around Lincoln Island, and Point Couverdon and Rocky Island," he said. "Sisters Island in Icy Straight is also good, as well as Spasski Island."

The charter fleet also fishes along the northern Admiralty Island coast, from Young Bay to Point Arden; Scull, Horse, Colt, Grand and Aaron islands; the Saginaw Channel between Barlow Cove and Shelter Island; inside Auke Bay and Gastineau Channel; and the outer edge of the Breadline. In northern Lynn Canal, the charter boats hit St. James and William Henry bays; Benjamin Island and Vanderbilt Reef; Poundstone Rock and Sherman Rock.

Anderson says halibut fishing is on the upswing in the Juneau area. He believes halibut run in a seven-year cycle.

"The size and number of fish bottomed out about two years ago, and the local fishery is now in an upswing. We're not catching as many 150-pounders as before, but lots of 100-pounders," he said.

Much of the saltwater charter boat fishing activity in this

region is from non-residents. "They disembark from the cruise or tour ships for a day and want to target salmon," he says. "Salmon have been promoted as "the Alaska species" to catch. They provide more action than halibut and are easily caught around Douglas. But for those who want to pursue halibut, fishing can be excellent."

When searching for halibut, Anderson looks for either schools of herring or salmon.

Fishing techniques vary depending on the stage of salmon migration. He fishes for halibut in shallow water, when fresh-in salmon are concentrated at stream mouths. Several weeks later, he switches to deeper water when spawned out salmon are being washed out to sea.

Anderson says many anglers can increase their catch of halibut by identifying the important correlation between bottom structure and tidal influence. As a diver, Anderson has seen this phenomenon first hand.

"There are many underwater plateaus along the southeast Alaska coastline, ranging from broad expanses several miles long to just a small mound. If the tide is ebbing, the feed will be pulled off the top of the plateau into deeper water. Find a cliff, and you've found a real hotspot. The water rolls like a breaker in reverse, capturing fish and debris in its vortex. This current rolls off the plateau and into the depths. Concentrations of big halibut wait to feed along these cliff edges. Don't waste your time fishing the top of the plateau. The fish are not there, because the food has been washed away. On other hand, if the tide is flooding, those same currents are working up the cliff. These upwelling currents roll over the top of the ledge, keeping feed on top of the plateau."

Anderson says you don't have to identify massive structures to catch halibut, as long as they exhibit the above characteristics.

"There is this tiny bight I fish regularly, and I always have success there," he says. "It stays flat for a long time at the mouth of the bay, then rises up sharply to another flat. The tide swirls into the bay and keeps food there. Fish it on an ebb tide, and you won't have much action. On a flood tide, however, hang on to your rod. The area is, at most, 100 square yards, but it is one of my most consistent halibut producers."

"When salmon are staging at creek mouths, halibut will swim into 60 to 70 feet of water and pursue these schools of fish, or wait for the dead and dying ones to drift down into the depths. Because of the rapid drop-offs exhibited at the mouths

How to Catch
Trophy Halibut

of most small salmon streams in southeast Alaska, I often fish my clients within casting distance of shore, or closer."

As for specialized rigs, Anderson builds and uses a three-way swivel that consists of two ball-bearing Sampos connected via a split ring, to which he connects a clip. He connects a 12 to 16-ounce ball weight to the clip, which he can quickly remove when the angler has the fish near the surface.

"By using a six-foot, 80 to 100-pound mono leader, I can disconnect the weight while the fish is still several feet below the surface," he says. "This keeps anyone from getting smacked with a wildly swinging weight while I attempt to either dispatch or release the halibut. If I'm using big-fish bait, such as salmon heads or pieces, I'll attach a steel leader with large 10/0 hooks."

Anderson finds this set-up helps reduce breakoffs, especially at boatside.

Wrangell and Petersburg

Remote, quiet and fjord-like in nature, the waters near Wrangell and Petersburg offer fair to good fishing for halibut. Charter boat skippers regularly fish the northern tier of Biorka Island as well as the waters of Sitka Sound.

The sound has lots of flat, sand-silt bottom areas which attract halibut. Some of the best fishing takes place in holding structure from Krestof Point, down along the eastern side of Kruzof Island to St. Lazaria Island, and selected spots of sandy flats and rocky stretches between the latter and Vitskari Rocks. Frederick Sound and Blind Slough, Wrangell Narrows, the mouth of Thomas Bay and waters surrounding Petersburg are also fished. Vank and Zarembo islands are popular fisheries among the lodge and day charter fleet.

Also try the mouth of Starrigavin Bay north of Katlian Bay. Olga Strait where it meets the mouth of Nakwasina Sound is another top location. The mouth of the bays offer the best fishing when the spawned-out salmon begin drifting back out to saltwater.

The Stikine is a major salmon river near Wrangell, which attracts large numbers of halibut from the outer waters of Sumner or Stikine Strait. While virtually no fishing is conducted in or near the mud flats, good fishing is available a short boat ride in the Bradfield Canal and Zimovia Strait. Wrangell receives relatively minor halibut fishing pressure from residents and non-residents alike, due to the massive amounts of halibut water and relatively few anglers who fish it each year.

Southeast Alaska

Map courtesy USGS

In or near Sumner Strait, try McArthur Reef or Kah Sheets Bay to the left of Lung Island. At the river delta mouth of the Stikine, best fishing can be had on either side of Rynda, Wilson or Kadin islands, especially during the salmon in-migration in July and August. Many of the charter boats hit the waters within a three-mile radius of Tide Island, located between Zarembo Island and Prince of Wales Island. If the area is crowded, head south and fish the many holes around Blashke Island. Occasionally, anglers pick up big halibut drifting along the northeastern shoreline of Woronkofski Island.

While virtually no fishing is conducted in or near the mud flats, good fishing is available a short boat ride into the Bradfield Canal or Zimovia Strait. Anglers do well off the drop-off at the mouth of LeConte Bay, where baitfish and salmon are trapped by the tidal currents. This area is hit hard by commercial halibut fishermen, so success rates may vary. If LeConte Bay isn't producing, head north and try around the Sukoi Isles, Icy Cove and Wood Point, as well as the southeast tip of Point Vandeput. The northern Kupreanof Island coastline stretching from Portage Island to Pinta Rocks is a proven producer of halibut. If you've traveled this far from Wrangell, also try Turnabout Island.

Many of the local, smaller operators are concerned about the increase in halibut fishing pressure in the Wrangell area.

Ken Wyrick of Alaska Star Charters says he used to fish Snow Pass, and be the only boat there. "Now you see at least 12 to 15 boats, with most of these concentrating on halibut," he said.

Wyrick said many of the hotspots that regularly produced lots of halibut don't produce as many fish nowdays. Wrangell operators have said that although they still catch lots of halibut, fish are becoming harder to find, and as a result, fishing methods have changed.

Drifting over 120 feet or deeper water is now the method of choice among halibut guides, especially in heavily fished areas near Wrangell and Petersburg. Drifting allows a boat of anglers to cover more water, and hopefully find schools of halibut. This method requires finding stretches of smooth bottoms. Pinnacles, ledges and rocky areas are taboo, especially for novice halibut anglers.

Anglers are also switching to Spiderwire to fish deeper water during heavy current flows, waters that only the best anglers could properly fish in years past.

Wyrick has noticed that halibut have become shy of exposed

hooks in bait, especially in areas hit hard by the big lodges. He attributes this to the intense fishing pressure some areas receive.

According to Wyrick, a few operators in southeast Alaska cater to the angler who tries to pay for his trip by catching as many fish as possible. Wyrick runs five-day charters, and encourages the release of large fish.

"A pair of anglers I talked to who fished at one of these lodges said they took home over 800 pounds of halibut fillets," he said. "With a catch-and-keep philosophy like this, there won't be any halibut fishing left," he said.

It's easy to see how certain area halibut stocks could be suffering from overfishing. Most boats in the area can carry up to six fishermen. An operation open during June, July and August will fish six people a day for roughly 540 anglers. Let's cut this number to 376, owing to bad weather days, down time and no bookings. This is the number of people one boat fishes. Multiply this times 34 boats, and nearly 13,000 anglers are hitting a select area. Multiply this number by two fish a day, (include 5 to 10 percent mortality for improperly released and lost fish) and it's easy to see how some areas can be quickly fished out.

These figures are meant to illustrate the intense fishing pressure that can occur not just in this area, but anywhere. If boats don't disperse their efforts, everyone suffers.

One pilot I talked to in the early 1990s said that in one summer, he flew over 1,200 fish boxes from one lodge to the Ketchikan airport. Each box weighed from 40 to 70 pounds, he said, and were all sport-caught fish.

As far as I know, this massive harvest of fish is continuing, and only now are smaller charter operators trying to combat this catch-and-kill-everything-you-can philosophy. The authors wish them luck.

Despite the problems in some waters, the area offers excellent scenery and good fishing for halibut. Choose a reputable guide in this area, limit your catch, and you should enjoy a fun-filled Alaska fishing adventure.

Sitka

Perhaps the largest area for halibut take is Sitka Sound, especially the Vitskari Island area, followed by Silver Bay and Salisbury Sound. Crescent Bay, outside the Sheldon Jackson Hatchery area is also good for halibut, as is Starrigavan Bay, Biorka Island, Tenakee Inlet, Hoonah area, Chatham Strait,

Cross Sound, Elfin Cove and Kruzof Island waters. Try St. Lazaria Island; from Inner Point to the entrance to Hayward Strait; Lisianski Point and Katlian Bay are old favorites of the charter fleet. Neva Point is worth a fish or two and Nakwasina Sound offers good fishing at its innermost end. During the salmon run and at its end, the head of Fish Bay is an excellent place to fish.

Sitka Sound doesn't offer the fast and furious halibut action as it has experienced in years past. Reports indicate the area has been hit hard by extensive commercial and sportfishing pressure. Efforts are under way to place the Sound off limits to commercial fishing, which should up the sport-catch of halibut.

Bruce Parker is a veteran guide in the Sitka area, operating the 60-foot yacht Nepenthe on four-day charters to remote areas.

"While fishing isn't as good as it once was in the Sound, there is still excellent fishing for big halibut farther out. Our clients catch and release halibut all day, and keep a few 50 to 80-pound fish toward the end of their trip."

Parker likes to concentrate on the many flat benches located to the west of Sitka.

"Halibut move onto these benches to feed," he says. "We also concentrate on the large flats that stretch for miles to the west. I prefer to anchor in these locations. I'll have several clients use bait, to help draw in the fish. Several others use white jigs, and it seems the jigs always hook the first fish, due to their action. The two work hand-in-hand."

He is extremely fond of a mooching rig, with a three to six-ounce keel sinker and herring rigged with a double hook.

Parker said the Sitka fishery is not as crowded as other fisheries, and that a four-day, live-aboard boat is the way to go to effectively fish this area.

"There's no spending hours running back and forth each day," he says. "On an extended trip, anglers can get meals and fishing cheaper than going with day charters and staying in town. They can expect lots of great scenery, whales, ling cod to 60 pounds and yelloweye rockfish."

Ketchikan

In the Ketchikan area, much of the effort as shown in ADF&G harvest questionnaires takes place in Clarence Strait, followed by Behm Canals, Revilla Channels and Tongass Narrows. Yes Bay and Bell Island area are also popular fishing areas, as is Cape Chacon, about 35 miles to the southwest.

Point Alva and Dall Head have lots of bottom structure that is extremely attractive to big halibut. Start out in 40 to 60 feet of water in remote islands two to three hours from Ketchikan, down to the drop-offs in 200 to 300 feet. Other operators often hit the Grant Island area and 20-Fathom Bank. Other favorites include the northern flats of Skin Island, Point Alava and Alava Bay, rocky outcroppings in the Behm Canal, especially the entrance to the Behm Narrows and northern tip of Betton Island; and the flats off Kah Shakes Point. The southern flats of Foggy Bay produce good numbers of halibut. Charter operators favor the bays and narrows of Smeaton Island.

When fishing in the main channel, watch for floatplanes that are landing or taking off throughout the day. Also follow the marker buoys, especially at low tide as the area to the south of Ketchikan has extensive mud flats. The markers line the deepwater channels. Follow these to where they drop off into deeper water, and you'll find good halibut fishing, especially on an outgoing tide.

Prince of Wales

Perhaps the hotspot in this region is the west side of Prince of Wales Island, where over half of the total island harvest—over 17,600 fish—are taken. This is followed by the east side waters of Prince of Wales Island, Waterfall Bay, Thorne Bay and Cape Chacon, in that order. Clarence Strait offers some good halibut fishing in a nearby group of islands called The Triplets in front of Coffman Cove as well as Lake Bay. Anglers looking for hot action will investigate Bucareli Bay, Noyes Island, and the west-side bays of Dall Island. Also try the northern end of Suemez island, and the entrance to Ulloa Channel. Don't pass by the northeastern flats of San Juan Bautista Island, Roller Bay and adjacent coastline of Noyes Island; Warm Chuck Inlet and Gas Rock on Heceta Island; the pinnacles and underwater mounds on the western side of the Maurelle Islands; and the west-side bays of Dall Island. The outer edges and bays of Baker Island also produce trophy fish. Unless you have your own boat, investigating these remote fisheries can be expensive.

An affordable way is to charter a boat to fish the outside islands. Harold Haynes of Chasina Bay Charters in Ketchikan offers custom-tailored, inexpensve packages for anglers looking for trophy halibut, and who have several days to hit the outside waters of the area.

Anglers looking for inexpensive, do-it-yourself halibut fishing should investigate Deer Creek Cottage, based in Thorne Bay. A group of four anglers can rent a 19-foot boat, deluxe accommodations, vehicle and more for $125 per person per day.

Guided fishing on the open water requires a larger boat and experienced guide. Boardwalk Wilderness Lodge in Thorne Bay offers excellent halibut fishing guides and hotspots, and seldom fished areas for ling cod, halibut and rockfish.

The one truth about fishing for halibut off Prince of Wales Island is that you'll find halibut, at one time or another, in just about any cove. There is a story about a minister who walked down to the water's edge at low tide, only to find a 140-pound halibut stranded in a tidal pool. Believing the fish was placed there for his use by a Divine power, the minister harvested the fish and fed family and friends.

While fishing is not always this easy in PWI waters, do look for halibut as they move into the many inland passages and bays, especially during high tide. Al Ferrari of Boardwalk Wilderness Lodge likes to find flat areas near kelp beds, and establish drifts with the tide while fishing herring or jigs directly over bottom. Al will execute several drifts, and move on if there is no action. "Too many anglers will keep fishing an area, waiting for the halibut to "bite," he says. "If halibut are in an area, they'll hit soon after you drop down that herring or jig."

According to Kim Betzina of Alaskan Escapes out of Port Baker, Northwest PWI, his clients regularly catch big halibut from the company's small rental boats in the protected waters and bays of the island.

"Last summer we had some guests catch 100-pound-plus halibut in shallow-water bays," he said. "A 156-pounder was caught off our boat dock. When cruising the shoreline, I've seen halibut in less than six feet of water."

Betzina believes it's easier to hook a nice halibut in shallow water bays than deeper water.

"As a commercial fisherman, I'm frequently catching more halibut in the 60-foot depth than deeper water. Halibut will typically move into the creek mouths to feed in the backwash, or wait to ambush salmon that are migrating by. Also, the shallow water is home to lots of rockfish and Dungeness crab, a favorite halibut food. This is obvious by the number of crab I find in halibut stomachs. I've caught several 70-pound-plus halibut, each having three or more humpies in its stomach."

Betzina believes halibut will be found at most any depth. "I've seen them at the 60-foot depth, suspended over 600 feet of water," he says. "They're feeding on salmon or herring located just beneath the surface. I've seen this, not just at slack tide, but during full tidal flows."

Many anglers fish for halibut in deepwater holes, but I find these fish are generally dormant, and not easy to catch. Aside from using the standard choked or plug-cut herring, Betzina likes to use Buzz-Bombs for halibut, especially when salmon are running or there are lots of rockfish. Otherwise the salmon, cod and rockfish will eat all your bait in no time.

Other Prince of Wales Island hotspots include the drop-offs and sand flats near the islands at the head of Karta Bay; the flats at the entrance to Vallenar Bay and northern Betton Island; the outer drop-offs of Point Baker near Twin island, and the entrance to Port Protection. Always make time to fish the entrance of Tebenkof Bay, one of the better trophy halibut hotspots in this area, and the depths of Swaine Point.

Glacier Bay

Halibut fishing is good throughout most of Glacier Bay. Most fishing effort takes place in Icy Straits, Glacier Bay proper, and the waters near Gustavus, with a few taken in the Excursion Inlet region. Because of the area's massive and steep-walled fjords, halibut fishing is often extremely good in waters less than 100 yards offshore, often near a clearwater inlet or cascading waterfall. If possible, charters often venture out to Elfin Cove and the waters to the west of the Fairweather Range, one of the most scenic and favorite big halibut fisheries in this region. The area offers excellent charter operators, from small, one-boat operations to the professionally run Glacier Bay Lodge, which offers full accommodations, salmon fishing, and ample halibut fishing opportunities. Excellent bed and breakfasts in the area, roadside fishing, and culture. An unheralded halibut hotspot worth considering. Specific hotspots include The Sisters Island and Reef, Spasski Island and Bay, and Pulizzi Island.

Pleasant Island and the deepwater areas to the west of Port Adolphus are proven producers, as is the eastern and southern waters of Lemesurier island, South Inian Island, George and Three Hill Island. These areas receive some fishing pressure from nearby lodges.

Denny Corbin of Starbuck Charters in Pelican says one of his favorite halibut hotspots is Cross Sound in front of Yacobi Island. He uses circle hooks and spreader bars. He'll fish nearby rivers for salmon, and use the scraps as bait. He says his clients catch halibut in the 50 to 70-pound range from these waters.

He also likes Dundas Bay. "It's glacier water, with lots of sand, which attracts large halibut," he says. "Even with the turbid water, halibut fishing is excellent."

Another favorite is a large sand spit that juts out and creates Port Adolphus.

In August, salmon are being flushed out of the rivers, and the halibut move in to feed in the 30 to 60 feet of water near the rivermouths.

Corbin likes fishing on the outer edge of the Continental Shelf.

"We have lots of halibut movement through this area," he said as he pointed to a map. "The fish concentrate around pinnacles, rocky bottoms and potholes of sand in between islands and reefs. You can tell these fish are always on the move because they have red bellies, from scraping them along the rocky bottom. Stationary halibut tend to have white bellies."

CHAPTER 20

British Columbia Halibut Hotspots

A halibut angler need only glance at any map or chart of the British Columbia coastline to get some idea of the limitless halibut fishing opportunities available in this vast province. From the wide-open waters of the Dixon Entrance at the British Columbia-Alaska border, to Race Rocks in the middle of the Strait of Juan de Fuca, this westernmost Canadian province offers more than enough halibut haunts to keep any angler busy for an entire lifetime.

Cities, roads and ports have been built near some of British Columbia's more productive halibut grounds, while fishing lodges and charter operations have sprung up near a few others. Some of the province's halibut hot spots, though, are truly in the middle of nowhere, dozens of miles from the nearest outpost of regular human activity. Because much of the B.C. coast is so lightly developed and sparsely inhabited, it's a safe bet that some of the province's halibut hotspots have yet to be seriously explored.

If we had the luxury here of writing a book that was several hundred pages longer, we could make a serious run at covering British Columbia's extensive halibut grounds in great detail. A 600-page book, however, would cost you a lot more money, and even if you had the information, you would have trouble getting to and fishing some of the places we would write about because they are so desolate and so far from a major transportation hub. Instead, this chapter on British Columbia halibut hotspots will cover those places where halibut sport fisheries have been at least somewhat developed, where there are at least some facilities available to visiting anglers, and where the likelihood of catching halibut is more than just a possibility.

Sportfishing magazine editor Doug Olander used two-pound monofilament to subdue this 20-pound Langara Island halibut. Plenty of shallow-water fishing areas and large numbers of smaller fish make the north end of the Queen Charlottes a good place to fish light tackle. Remember, though, that you might find yourself going toe-to-fin with a 200-pounder on woefully undersized tackle!

PRINCE RUPERT/NORTH COAST

The waters of Chatham Sound provide near-perfect halibut-fishing conditions. The islands to the west and southwest protect it from the westerlies that come booming down the Dixon Entrance from the open Pacific and the southerlies that often whistle up Hecate Strait, making it possible for even small-boat anglers to fish throughout most of the spring and summer. The water here is relatively shallow, and much of the bottom is cobble, gravel and sand. Major commercial herring and shrimp fisheries here over the past several decades testify to the wealth of feed available to halibut and other game fish species. It's a haven for halibut, and anglers out of Prince Rupert have it all right at their front door.

What's more, changes in the management of commercial halibut fisheries that once focused heavy fishing pressure on Chatham Sound, but now spread the harvest out both geographically and seasonally, have resulted in somewhat of a halibut population explosion in the 1990s, making this an even better bet for anglers in search of top-notch halibut action.

Captain Hugh Charbonneau, who charters his 52-foot "M.V. Seatex" out of Prince Rupert all summer for fishing and cruising, says the beauty of Chatham Sound is that there's always somewhere to fish in protected and productive waters, no matter what the weather and water conditions.

The waters around the north end of the sound offer a number of excellent halibut fishing areas, including Portland Inlet, which joins the northeast corner of Chatham Sound about 15 miles north of Prince Rupert. Fed by the Nass River, the inlet is a haven for both salmon and halibut anglers, and its deep waters produce good summertime halibut fishing. Tidal flow here can be quite heavy, so it's best fished during periods of moderate tides or within an hour on either side of the slack tide. One particularly productive halibut spot, according to Charbonneau, is at the entrance to Work Channel, near the southwest corner of Portland Inlet. There are also halibut to be found well up in the waters of Work Channel, the deep, narrow ribbon of salt water that separates the Tsimpsean Peninsula from the British Columbia mainland.

Across the north end of Chatham Sound from Portland Inlet lies the north side of Dundas Island, another very productive halibut spot. The place is a natural, with the food-rich waters of Chatham Sound meeting the open expanses of the Dixon Entrance right here. "New" halibut are continually finding their way in from the open Pacific, and when they arrive at

How to Catch
Trophy Halibut

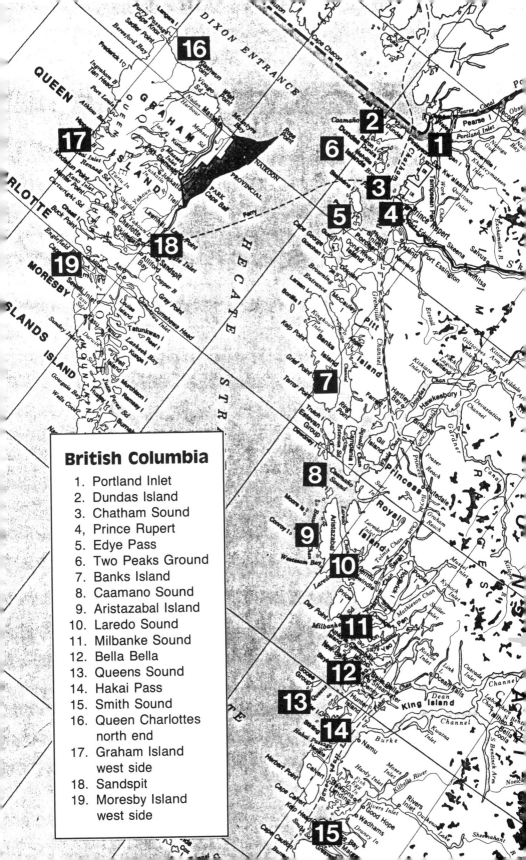

British Columbia

1. Portland Inlet
2. Dundas Island
3. Chatham Sound
4. Prince Rupert
5. Edye Pass
6. Two Peaks Ground
7. Banks Island
8. Caamano Sound
9. Aristazabal Island
10. Laredo Sound
11. Milbanke Sound
12. Bella Bella
13. Queens Sound
14. Hakai Pass
15. Smith Sound
16. Queen Charlottes
    north end
17. Graham Island
    west side
18. Sandspit
19. Moresby Island
    west side

Dundas there's little reason for them to travel any farther. The bottom throughout much of this area is relatively smooth and easy to fish, and there are productive spots to work no matter which way the wind is blowing. The halibut grounds around the north end and northeast corner of Dundas give up not only lots of halibut, but fair numbers of large fish topping 100 pounds as well.

Moving southward through Chatham Sound, you'll also find productive halibut fishing among the many small islands along the east side of Dunira and Melville islands. A little farther south, the vast flats around the east end of Brown Passage and the Lucy Islands can also be good, according to Charbonneau.

The world-famous Skeena River flows into the southern end of Chatham Sound, several miles south of Prince Rupert, and when the pink salmon runs enter the Skeena in late-July and August, the halibut follow. Marcus Passage, located between Smith and Kennedy islands near the river mouth, is a good place to fish for big flatties in August, according to Charbonneau.

The halibut fishing within Chatham Sound is good enough to keep any angler busy and happy, but the adventurous types who simply can't stand staying within the "confines" of protected water might want to venture westward into Hecate Strait. Here you can find enough lightly fished halibut hot spots to keep you more than satisfied. The entrance to Edye Passage, on the west side of Prescott Island, for example, is located just outside the south end of Chatham Sound, and has been known to treat halibut anglers quite well. Some big flatties are caught here by salmon anglers trolling the sand flats at the west end of the passage. The waters of Bell Passage, at the north end of Stephens Island, and the west end of Hudson Bay Passage can be similarly productive and often draw anglers targeting specifically on halibut.

Depending on the weather and the seaworthiness of your boat, you may even venture out to the Two Peaks Ground, a large hump near the north end of Hecate Strait, about 15 miles west of Melville Island, discovered by commercial halibut fishermen before the turn of the century and still productive today.

Many smaller, less well-known halibut areas also dot Hecate Strait, one of the wildest, woolliest and most lightly fished marine waterways in all of British Columbia. Numerous banks, seamounts and other underwater halibut havens are scattered along the west side of Banks and Aristazabal islands and the

How to Catch
Trophy Halibut

entrance to Caamano Sound along B.C.'s rugged north coast, for example, but they receive little or no pressure from anglers. Some of these areas hold huge halibut, but only the occasional cruiser or adventurous angler from one of the remote, fly-in fishing lodges scattered along the coast ever gets a crack at them. Even these halibut anglers, though, concentrate most of their efforts on safer, more protected fishing spots tucked away behind the coastal islands closer to the mainland.

The situation is much the same all the way down the coast to the north end of Queen Charlotte Strait. Major fishing lodges in Bella Bella and the Hakai Pass area, along with a few others scattered here and there along the coast, offer anglers a shot at good halibut fishing, but their range is so limited that their efforts hardly scratch the surface of the vast halibut-fishing opportunities available between the northeast corner of the Queen Charlottes' Graham Island and the northern tip of Vancouver Island. Places such as Laredo Sound, Milbanke Sound, Queens Sound and Smith Sound have untold halibut populations that are only lightly fished.

The Hakai Pass fishery provides a good example of why halibut fishing in these areas is good and will, barring some kind of biological catastrophe, remain good through the coming years. Hakai has long been recognized as one of British Columbia's top saltwater fishing spots, and several fishing lodges have developed there over the past decade or two. Even with three or four lodges, though, no more than a few hundred anglers fish Hakai each year, and their season is less than five months long. What's more, the vast majority of those anglers come to Hakai to catch salmon, which are generally easier to get at and require less effort to catch. As a result, some good summertime halibut fishing to be found around the South Pointer Islands and other areas along the northwestern corner of Calvert Island generates only moderate interest and the sport halibut harvest remains low year after year. There is, quite simply, a great deal of potential here for anyone who wants to get serious about halibut fishing on those days when the wind and water conditions allow adequate freedom to explore the possibilities.

Likewise, the waters just outside Rivers Inlet—perhaps British Columbia's most famous salmon-fishing spot—also offer good opportunities for halibut anglers, but the big barn doors get relatively little fishing pressure. Just a little farther south, Smith Sound is another fairly productive halibut area.

QUEEN CHARLOTTE ISLANDS

If there's such a thing as a last frontier for saltwater anglers along the west coast of North America, it has to be the Queen Charlotte Islands. This island group several dozen miles off the northern B.C. coast is rugged, beautiful and lightly inhabited, and it offers fishing the likes of which are found few others places in the world. Its "discovery" as an angling mecca came only recently—in the mid-1980s—and most of those early arrivals came to test the extraordinary fishing for thick-bodied chinook and high-flying coho salmon. What they soon found is that this island fishing paradise is also home to some of the Northwest's best halibut fishing.

Most of the initial angling effort was focused at the extreme northern end of the Charlottes, on and around Langara Island, which is substantially closer to the southern border of Alaska than to any part of the British Columbia mainland. Just as vast schools of chinook, coho and pink salmon funnel past Langara on their way into the Dixon Entrance and on toward some of the most productive salmon streams in North America, halibut congregate to take advantage of the abundant baitfish, crustaceans and other tasty tidbits that fill these rich waters.

Anglers who visit the several resorts on and around Langara Island, at the extreme north end of the Charlottes, have little trouble finding places to catch halibut. The island's Cohoe Point is perhaps the best-known halibut spot, and it seems to be loaded with flatties throughout the summer. Most of them, however, are smaller fish of under 25 pounds, and if you want a big one you may have to play with dozens of those little guys before finding one to keep. The Cohoe Point area is a great place to practice your light-tackle halibut technique.

The Lighthouse and tiny Lacy Island, both well-known landmarks to anglers around Langara, also produce their share of halibut, and may in fact be better bets for those in search of larger fish.

Although lightly publicized and lightly fished for halibut, other areas to the east of Langara also offer some productive halibut fishing. The waters from Klashwun Point to Wiah Point, including Virago Sound and the entrance to Naden Harbor, have large numbers of halibut throughout the summer. Farther east, the Rose Spit area at the extreme northeast corner of Graham Island has been giving up good catches of halibut since the early days of the commercial fishery more than a century ago.

How to Catch
Trophy Halibut

The wild west side of the Charlottes holds even more promise for halibut anglers than the north end of the islands, but the area's remoteness has kept recreational halibut fisheries here from doing little more than scratching the surface. One thing is for sure, however: the area has big halibut and it has lots of halibut.

I fished the waters around Hippa Island, about half-way up the west side of Graham Island, with the folks from the Charlotte Explorer floating lodge in 1993, and found more than adequate numbers of flatties ranging from 25 pounds to 175 pounds, with lots of halibut in that 40 to 70-pound range that many anglers consider the perfect size for fighting and for eating.

The "Charlotte Explorer" operation features a 195-foot mothership at anchor in a sheltered bay, and anglers fish two or three to a boat from custom-built, aluminum, center-console 18-footers that carry both salmon and halibut tackle. Equipment includes both a gaff and a harpoon rigged with a large buoy for dealing with barn-door fish. During my visit, the harpoons saw plenty of action.

The time of year was late-July and the first two days of August, and halibut were scattered all over the gently-sloping bottom from just outside the kelp at the north end of Hippa Island to well out into the Pacific.

The halibut were cooperating for almost everyone that trip, and we found them equally responsive to Crippled Herring, Krocodiles, Darts and other metal jigs as they were to whole

Anglers from the Charlotte Explorer fishing lodge boat a husky halibut from near Hippa Island, west side of the Queen Charlottes. The area is often described as the last frontier of Northwest saltwater angling, and halibut fishing can be excellent.

herring bounced along the bottom. It's accurate to say that jigs worked better up in the shallower water around the end of Hippa, where we hooked halibut as shallow as 60 feet down and as deep as 100 feet. Farther out, where a northward drift with the tide and wind carried us down a gentle slope from about 150 feet to 280 feet, bait seemed to work just a little better, although jigs were also effective. Typically, a drift of half to three-quarters of a mile produced two or three hook-ups per boat, and on at least a couple of occasions two anglers in the same boat were playing fish over 100 pounds at the same time. The top double of the trip, hooked almost simultaneously and landed within seconds of each other, weighed in at 101 and 174 pounds.

Now that's halibut action!

The food-rich waters of the open Pacific grow halibut to monstrous proportions, and the light fishing pressure on the west side of the Charlottes allows plenty of fish to grow to barn-door size. Hence, this a place where trophy-class fish are well within the realm of possibility. Just ask Seattle angler Cary Granger, who in 1994 boated a whopping 331-pounder near Kindakun Point, not far from the south end of Graham Island's coast. Granger was fishing out of the Oak Bay Marine Group's mothership "Salmon Seeker" when he hooked the fish in over 300 feet of water.

Moresby Island, the southern of the two largest islands in the Charlottes, also has plenty to offer halibut anglers. But, just like Graham Island to the immediate north, halibut-fishing pressure along much of Morseby's length is quite light. Both the Pacific Ocean side to the west and Hecate Strait to the east offer good halibut fishing, and one of the area's newest fishing resorts, South Moresby Lodge, offers its guests the opportunity to fish either side of the island. That would be a great way for visiting anglers to sample some of British Columbia's best halibut fishing in two different waterways.

Unless you happen to be a local living in Sandspit, Queen Charlotte City or one of the islands' other towns, the floating and land-based fishing lodges offer your best opportunity to sample the great halibut fishing off the Queen Charlotte Islands. Fly-in trips to the "Charlotte Explorer," "Salmon Seeker," Langara Fishing Lodge and other fish camps in the islands are the easiest and most efficient way for most of us to fish this remote halibut hot spot.

The die-hard do-it-yourself type who can't stand the idea of fishing in someone else's boat has other options for fishing the

Charlottes, but they require a lot more time. You can, if your boat is large enough, cruise to the Charlottes, or you can trailer a boat across from Prince Rupert with B.C. Ferries. The ferry run from Prince Rupert to Skidegate is about 100 miles.

Queen Charlotte Strait/Vancouver Island

Luckily for most of us, some of British Columbia's productive halibut fishing is within much easier range of most Northwest population centers. Halibut fishermen with a dependable vehicle and a trailerable boat of moderate size can reach many good halibut spots around Vancouver Island and Queen Charlotte Strait, while the owners of larger craft can cruise to these same places. If you're not a boat owner or choose not to waste valuable fishing time pulling your boat around or running it long distances, most of these same halibut-fishing spots have fishing lodges or resorts nearby and are within a relatively short plane ride of Vancouver or Seattle. Simply hop a plane and fish with a guide or rent a skiff when you get there. Float-plane services out of Vancouver and Seattle offer lots of regularly scheduled and charter trips that will take you to virtually any British Columbia coastal fishing camp or lodge.

Queen Charlotte Strait, with its numerous adjoining waterways and hundreds of islands, is a mecca for anglers and cruisers alike, a place where you could fish for halibut in a different spot every day from spring to fall without covering all the possibilities. Many boaters with time on their hands do just that, arriving in the area as early as May and staying until the weather begins to turn in September or early October.

Access to Queen Charlotte Strait by land is via Telegraph Cove, Alder Bay, Port McNeill or Port Hardy, and you might find respectable halibut fishing close enough to any of the four for decent, day-trip action.

Port Hardy offers perhaps the best potential, since it's within 10 to 15 miles of three very good halibut fishing spots. Taylor Bank sits pretty much in the middle of the Strait about 10 miles northeast of town, Farquahar Bank is about 12 miles to the north, and Pine Island is about 15 miles northwest. Several banks at the east end of Gordon Channel are also within running range of Port Hardy and offer good spring and summer halibut action. Any number of lesser-known spots also have the potential for giving up a barn door from time to time, and the Port Hardy fishery produces a few fish in excess of 200 pounds every year. Both private boats and several charters operate out of Hardy Bay each day during the season.

British Columbia

20. Pine Island
21. Farquahar Bank
22. Taylor Bank
23. Port Hardy
24. Port McNeill
25. Telegraph Cove
26. Gilford Island
27. Cape Scott
28. Quatsino Sound
29. Brooks Bay
30. Checleset Bay
31. Nootka Sound
32. Clayoquot Sound
33. Tofino
34. Ucluelet
35. Barkley Sound
36. Bamfield
37. Port San Juan
38. Beechey Head/
    Pedder Bay
39. Race Rocks
40. Victoria

Anglers fishing out of Telegraph Cove may find halibut in any number of spots around Blackfish Sound and Cormorant Channel, but one place certainly worth investigating is Stubbs Island, noted for producing some of the area's largest barn doors in recent years. In 1993 a halibut of nearly 260 pounds was caught there by an angler fishing out of Double Bay Resort, which is located on the north side of nearby Hanson Island.

To the east, the waters of Knight Inlet, Tribune Channel and Kingcome Inlet also offer a good deal of halibut-fishing potential, not to mention some of British Columbia's most magnificent scenery. The west end of Cramer Passage and the Fox Group of Islands, both near the west end of Gilford Island, provide good halibut catches from spring through summer, according to Bob Richter at Echo Bay Resort. Farther south, Slope Point, located near the southwest corner of Gilford, is another good bet. The hundreds of submerged humps and small islands between the west end of Fife Sound and the west end of Knight Inlet also provide good halibut fishing, according to Richter. Many of those underwater humps are sand and gravel, while others are pretty much solid rock, he says. Halibut anglers should concentrate on the "softer" humps and leave the rocky ones to lingcod and rockfish anglers. Anglers staying at Echo Bay who don't want to travel any distance for their halibut might try the shelf just north of the entrance to the bay. It's within a few hundred yards of the docks and gives up several good-sized fish each season.

The rugged and remote northern half of Vancouver Island's west side offers a lot of halibut-fishing potential for the adventurous saltwater angler, but the area's distance off the beaten path and relative lack of facilities for visiting fishermen keeps angling pressure to a minimum. A few cruisers make their way up the coast from Tofino and points south, while others round Cape Scott to the north and investigate the possibilities in such places as Quatsino Sound, Brooks Bay, Checleset Bay and Kyoquot Sound. Some anglers with trailerable boats enter the area via Winter Harbor, Holberg, Coal Harbour and Port Alice, all of which are accessible by water to Quatsino Sound. The entrances to these and smaller coastal inlets all hold fair to good numbers of chicken-size halibut throughout the summer, and there's always the chance of finding a big one here.

Farther down the island, the Nootka Sound area is accessible by road from the town of Gold River, and many of the anglers who come here primarily to fish for salmon are quick to discover that there are plenty of small halibut to be found throughout the summer. Most are caught off the large flat at the entrance to Nootka Sound, in 100 to 150 feet of water. Anglers who arrive earlier, from late-April to early June, might get a crack at one or two of the really big halibut that congregate in fairly good numbers in and around Nootka Sound in the spring.

Halibut fishing draws a good deal more interest from anglers around Clayoquot Sound and Barkley Sound. Fishing out of Tofino, Ucluelet and in some cases Bamfield, they concentrate much of their effort on what many call South Bank, the underwater hump that more or less parallels this stretch of the Vancouver Island coast about five miles offshore. While there are halibut on this bank throughout the season, the best combination of good fishing and good weather occurs from mid-June to mid-July, according to Mike Hicks, who operates Tyee Lodge in Bamfield, at the southeast corner of Barkley Sound.

Hicks loves to take his clients halibut fishing, but he isn't crazy about catching dogfish, which are also abundant on some parts of South Bank, so he fishes almost exclusively with metal jigs, especially a white pipe jig of his own design that's adorned with a plastic squid over the lure's lone treble hook. It's deadly, he says, bounced along bottom in about 200 feet of water over his favorite halibut spots. Chicken-size halibut of 15 to 30 pounds make up most of the catch from this area, but there are enough fish of 40 to 70 pounds to keep you guessing, and every now and then someone hooks and lands one in the triple-figure range.

Until the early 1990s, anglers out of Bamfield, as well as Port Renfrew to the south, would often run to Swiftsure Bank, the same Swiftsure that has long been so popular with Washington anglers. The Canadian side of the bank, however, was closed to halibut fishing in 1993, so anglers out of Renfrew, Sooke, Victoria and other points along the south end of Vancouver Island had to concentrate their halibut fishing efforts elsewhere. Luckily, there are other productive spots along the British Columbia side of the Strait of Juan de Fuca.

The waters around the entrance to Port San Juan often give up halibut, according to Victoria outdoor writer and long-time Vancouver Island angler Ernie Fedoruk. Farther down the Strait, he says, anglers also find some respectable flatties off Beechey Head and Pedder Bay, located a few miles apart between Sooke and Victoria.

And then there are Race Rocks, the shallow humps that jut toward the surface of the Strait about 12 miles southwest of

How to Catch
Trophy Halibut

Victoria. One of the more well-known halibut spots on the Canadian side of the Strait, the Race Rocks area gives up good numbers of halibut from late-winter until fall. Some of the best action often starts in March, when large numbers of halibut follow herring and other abundant baitfish up into the shallows, according to Fedoruk. Fresh, whole herring, jigged the evening before or early on the day of the fishing trip, is the favored bait, and it's usually fished on a wire spreader at depths of 75 to 125 feet, he says. Metal jigs in chrome and white also account for fair numbers of Race Rocks halibut, most of which range from 30 to 130 pounds. The area has, however, given up at least one fish over 200 pounds, a 212-pounder caught back in the 1980s, according to Fedoruk.

Anglers not wanting to run a dozen miles into the Strait of Juan de Fuca might find halibut a lot closer to Victoria, Fedoruk says. William Head, on the west side of the Victoria Harbor, is protected from stiff westerlies and gives up fair numbers of spring and summer halibut. Even closer to Victoria is Constance Bank, just outside Trial Island to the south of the city. A little to the north and east is Oak Bay, where spots known locally as The Gap and The Flats both produce a few flatties during March and April.

Although the waters of Haro Strait and the Strait of Georgia have for many years been considered a waste of time among serious halibut anglers, Fedoruk says there's some evidence of increased halibut populations there recently. A small halibut fishery, for example, has developed the past few years around Sidney, near the southeast corner of Vancouver Island, while halibut catches seem to be getting more and more common in other areas of the Gulf Island and the south end of the Strait of Georgia.

CHAPTER 21

Washington Halibut Hotspots

Halibut fishing has caught on in a big way with Washington anglers since the early 1980s. Although the big flatfish had always been available in the Evergreen State, declining salmon-fishing opportunity combined with an impressive upturn in halibut populations around that time gave a large number of saltwater anglers incentive to go halibut fishing, and many were surprised by their success. Places such as Neah Bay, Sekiu and Port Angeles became almost as well-known for their halibut as for their traditional salmon fisheries. Charter operations specifically targeting halibut sprang up along the coast and Strait of Juan de Fuca for the first time ever, and thousands of private-boat anglers also geared up for halibut action.

Sport-catch figures provide a graphic illustration of the growth of Washington's halibut fishery over the past two decades. The statewide total halibut catch for Evergreen State anglers in 1978 was only 6,700 pounds, but by 1982 that figure had jumped to 40,000 pounds, and it leaped to 100,000 pounds by 1984 with the "discovery" of the vast halibut populations on Swiftsure Bank near the entrance to the Strait of Juan de Fuca. Washington anglers caught an amazing 550,000 pounds of halibut in 1987, which seemed to represent the population peak in the Northwest, and they made that impressive catch in spite of a statewide 32-inch minimum size limit. The catch dropped off from 1988 through 1991 and ranged from 101,000 to 165,000 pounds during the first half of this decade.

Julie Euken, a veteran charter boat deckhand at the ripe old age of 16, shows off a Swiftsure halibut that's probably a few pounds larger than average for this favorite Washington halibut spot. This fish was caught aboard the charter boat "Blue Chip," owned and operated by Julie's dad, Ed Euken, who pioneered the Swiftsure halibut fishery in the early 1980s.

305

SWIFTSURE BANK

I braced my knees against the railing of the charter boat "Blue Chip" and strained against the heavy rod in an attempt to gain back some of the 350 feet of 80-pound Dacron line that separated me from something big and strong, and I realized that eight of the other 10 anglers on board were locked in similar combat. Everywhere I turned there was someone sweating, straining or swearing, and no one appeared to be gaining line much faster than I was. No doubt about it, we were smack in the middle of a "bite" of monstrous proportions.

The action had started about 7 a.m., tapered off and died by 7:30, then came on with a vengeance shortly after 9. It was over by 11, not because the fish quit biting, but because we had limited on halibut and had enough lingcod and big rockfish to keep us busy filleting for hours. Our largest fish was a 65-pound halibut, and we had several others over 40 pounds.

Such was my introduction to Swiftsure Bank, Washington's most productive and most popular halibut spot.

Swiftsure is a large underwater plateau, or bank, that sprawls across the U.S.-Canadian border about 20 miles north of Neah Bay, Washington. The waters around it are hundreds of feet deep, but some spots on the Canadian side of Swiftsure are under 300 feet, and there are spots on the American side as shallow as 400 feet. The bank's shallow waters draw candlefish, herring and other baitfish like a magnet from the surrounding depths, and halibut find the abundant forage much to their liking.

This sprawling bank has produced tens of thousands of halibut for Washington anglers since its halibut-producing capabilities were discovered in the mid-eighties. While season lengths and catch have varied widely due to harvest-quota distribution and related sport-fishing restrictions, Swiftsure has produced as many as 183,000 pounds of halibut to anglers in a single season. Given an average cleaned weight of about 14 pounds, that's nearly 13,000 sport-caught halibut in one summer, far and away the hottest halibut action to be found anywhere south of the Canadian border.

Catching halibut at Swiftsure, though, isn't a simple matter of heading in the general direction, dropping a line over the side and hauling up fish. Like any other fishing spot, Swiftsure has its hot spots, its not-so-hot spots and its places that might seem to an angler nothing more than biological deserts. Some of the hot spots are fairly large—and therefore well-known and heavily fished—while others are so small that they can't

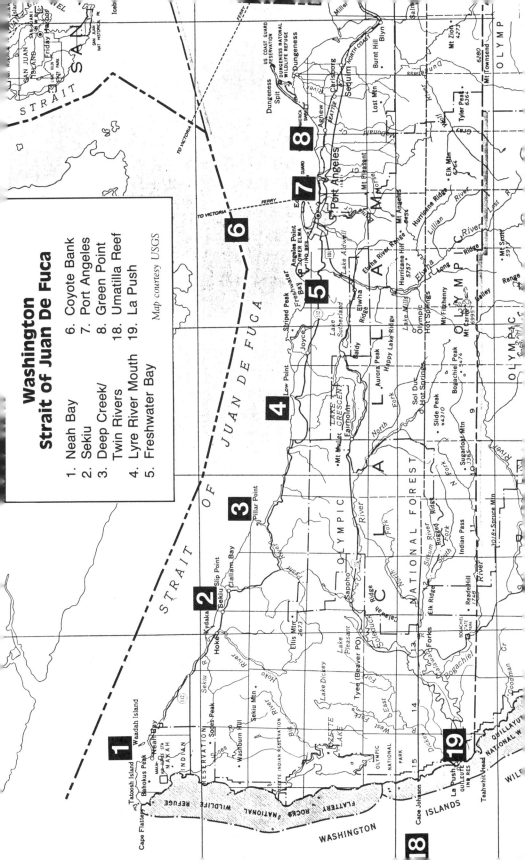

Washington
Strait of Juan De Fuca

1. Neah Bay
2. Sekiu
3. Deep Creek/
   Twin Rivers
4. Lyre River Mouth
5. Freshwater Bay

6. Coyote Bank
7. Port Angeles
8. Green Point
18. Umatilla Reef
19. La Push

Map courtesy USGS

be located without accurate electronics and are nearly impossible to fish if there's any wind or tidal movement at all.

The sport-fishing opportunities for halibut at Swiftsure Bank first became apparent in 1983, and the area's popularity has grown steadily since. That first year or two, Ed Euken, owner and skipper of the "Blue Chip," was the only one making regular trips to Swiftsure, but as word of his success got out, other charters started making the hour-long run from Neah Bay to the productive reef. These days, especially during weekends, you may find nearly a dozen charters and dozens of smaller, private boats on the bank during the spring-time halibut season.

An average Swiftsure halibut is a fish in the 15 to 25-pound range, with enough 30 to 70-pounders thrown in to keep it interesting. As is the case almost anywhere throughout the Pacific halibut's range, though, you never know when you might encounter a barn door. Swiftsure produces halibut over 100 pounds each year, and occasionally gives up fish of 200 pounds or better. It produced a 240-pounder in 1984, and in 1989 gave up the 288-pounder that still stands as the Washington State record.

Because of Swiftsure's depth and an almost always present wind or water drift, sinkers and jigs of 20 to 36 ounces are commonly used here, and so are the 50 to 80-pound braided lines, 4/0 to 6/0 reels and stout rods commonly associated with deep-water halibut angling. If you happen to hit it right and find yourself fishing slack water, you might get by with moderate-sized tackle and lure or sinker weights as light as eight or 10 ounces, but such opportunities are rare.

Whole herring and squid are the most commonly used baits at Swiftsure, and they should be fished on a spreader to avoid the hassle of tangling the bait around the line. Many anglers here use leadheads rather than cannon ball sinkers to take their spreader rigs to the bottom, so that they have an effective lure at the end of their line even if the bait is stolen.

Metal jigs account for a good number of the halibut caught here, but many of the commercially manufactured jigs are too small for Swiftsure's deep waters. Good choices might include Luhr Jensen's 16 or 20-ounce Crippled Herring, the 16 or 32-ounce Tony Accetta Yo Ho Diamond Jig, Bead Tackle's Bridgeport Diamond Jig in the 16 or 32-ounce sizes and Bead's 16 or 24-ounce Vi-Ke jig. The do-it-yourselfer can take Swiftsure halibut on 16 to 36-ounce pipe jigs.

Although relatively few anglers do it, the Washington side

of Swiftsure is a good place to add a teaser lure above your jig or spreader (assuming you don't use a leadhead for a spreader weight, which brings you up to your two bait/lure maximum). The bottom here is varied and uneven, so having that pork rind strip or plastic grub body waving around a couple of feet above your primary lure will be helpful in attracting fish to your offering. (See chapter 12 for details on tying and fishing a teaser rig.)

Charter fishing is the safest and best way to fish Swiftsure Bank, at least as far as most anglers are concerned. Some venture the 20 miles out into the open sea in relatively small boats, but it can be a long—even dangerous—trip back if the weather kicks up. If you insist on fishing the bank in your own boat, follow a charter out and back, stay in radio contact with other boats in the area, be sure all your safety equipment is up to snuff, and be on your toes. Swiftsure is a long way from the nearest port, and not a place where you want things to go wrong.

OTHER OFFSHORE AREAS

Swiftsure Bank is certainly the most well-known halibut spot for anglers running out of Neah Bay, but it's not the only one. Charter captains and some private-boat anglers have, during times of season closures and slow fishing at Swiftsure, gone prospecting for other offshore halibut haunts, and some of their hunts have paid off.

The Blue Dot, for example, has provided some fairly good halibut action in recent years for anglers willing to run some 30 miles, one-way, to find their fish. So named because it shows as a small blue spot on area charts, it has given up fair numbers of halibut since the early nineties. If you fish it, figure on working your bait or lure in water a little over 300 feet. Other, much smaller humps within a few miles of the Blue Dot may be even more productive, but those who know their locations are pretty tight-lipped.

About eight miles beyond the Blue Dot is a spot the commercial fishermen call "72-Squared," because both sets of loran coordinates describing its location end with the number 72. It's a little deeper than Blue Dot, and if you fish it you may be dragging over 400 feet of line around to reach bottom.

Around the corner to the southwest of Neah Bay lie a number of offshore humps, shelves and plateaus that are home to large numbers of halibut, some of them true barn doors of 100 pounds or more. Captain Phil Anderson, long-time charter skipper out of Neah Bay and Westport, tells of some places (the exact location of which he doesn't divulge) where 60-pound halibut are common, 80-pounders may be caught regularly and fish over 100 pounds are very much a possibility. They're within running distance of both Neah Bay and the coastal port of LaPush, but it's a fairly long trip from either place, Anderson says.

There's little question that other productive halibut beds around the northwest corner of the Evergreen State are yet to be found and explored, so if the big flatties aren't cooperating on any of the tried-and-true spots we've already mentioned, get out your charts, watch your depthsounder and do some looking.

STRAIT OF JUAN DE FUCA

Neah Bay

Although most of the halibut charter fleet from this far corner of the Lower 48 makes the long run to Swiftsure Bank, the Blue Dot and other offshore spots, small-boat anglers find fair to good halibut fishing much closer to port. You might find a halibut almost anywhere around Neah Bay, but several specific fishing spots within a half-hour run of the boat harbor have, over the years, come to be known as the better bets. I asked Al Seda, long-time owner of Big Salmon Fishing Resort, to tell me about some of them, and he gladly obliged.

Koitlah Point, whose more commonly used but certainly less poetic name is The Garbage Dump, can be a halibut producer if you hit it at the right time, and the right time is often within a day either way of the neap, when daily tidal exchange is at a minimum. More consistent fishing may be found straight out from the point, in 40 to 45 fathoms of water, according to Seda.

Even closer to port than The Garbage Dump is Waadah Island, and anglers sometimes find productive halibut fishing around its outer (northwest) edge, but again, you're more likely to find halibut straight out from the island, over the gradual bottom in about 35 fathoms of water.

An area outside the well-known whistler buoy in 40 to 45 fathoms is another known halibut spot that can be quite productive, and there are also spots just inside and just outside Tatoosh Island that give up decent catches from time to time.

A spot that produces well each spring is just off the mouth of Bowman Creek, to the east of Neah Bay, according to Seda. Anglers fishing the first slack tides of May scored well on fish

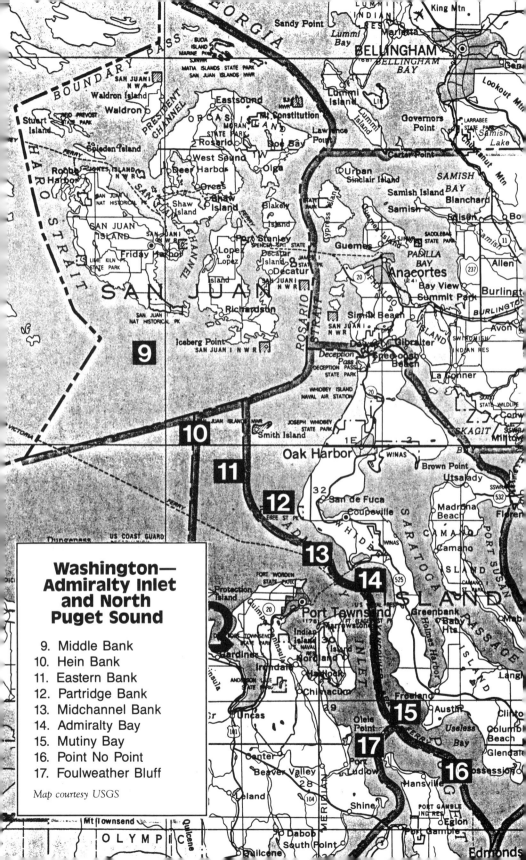

Washington—
Admiralty Inlet and North Puget Sound

9. Middle Bank
10. Hein Bank
11. Eastern Bank
12. Partridge Bank
13. Midchannel Bank
14. Admiralty Bay
15. Mutiny Bay
16. Point No Point
17. Foulweather Bluff

Map courtesy USGS

in only 60 to 80 feet of water, which is shallow-water action at its finest for anyone south of the Canadian border.

If you're planning to fish Neah Bay's inshore waters, you may want to time your trip for May or June, when the largest numbers of halibut move in to feed in and around the entrance to the Strait of Juan de Fuca. As for daily timing, the incoming tide almost always produces best.

Sekiu

Long a world-famous salmon-fishing spot, Sekiu also produces its share of halibut, including some trophy-class barn doors. Perhaps the best-known halibut area is off the mouth of the Hoko River, a few miles west of town. Anglers here start their drift in about 240 feet of water straight out from the river mouth and try to drift the outer edge of that 40-fathom shelf.

This area has produced lots of halibut over 100 pounds and even a few that topped the 200-pound mark. Some anglers slowly troll dodger-and-herring or flasher-and-herring combinations off the Hoko, others drift with whole herring on spreader rigs, while still others take halibut on Krocodiles, Mooch-A-Jigs, Darts and homemade pipe jigs.

Another place to look for halibut around the Sekiu area is the 120- to 200-foot depths off Eagle Bay, and anglers occasionally take good fish straight out from Clallam Bay in 90 to 175 feet of water. Farther west, anglers fishing the gradual bottom off the mouth of the Sekiu River make decent catches, including an occasional fish of 100 pounds or larger. The best fishing here is on a mile-long gravel hump that rises up from the depths straight out to the north of the river mouth.

Deep Creek/Twin Rivers

Two of the Strait of Juan de Fuca's top springtime halibut-fishing spots are located a few miles apart, just east of Pillar Point, one of the Strait's more well-known landmarks.

Deep Creek, which flows into the Strait about a mile from Pillar Point, and the Twin Rivers about four miles farther east, have deposited thousands of tons of sand and gravel to form gently sloping bottom contours where good numbers of halibut congregate to feed on herring, candlefish and smelt off the stream mouths.

The fishing area off the Twin Rivers is larger than that off Deep Creek, and tends to provide better fishing. It has also produced some of the larger fish, including a 235-pounder a few years ago. Although halibut are caught in this area from water as shallow as 50 feet, the best catches come from the outer edge of the 30-fathom (180 feet) line, where the bottom begins to break away a little more sharply.

Trolling whole herring behind large, chrome dodgers is popular here, but drifting a herring or squid can also be effective. More energetic anglers sometimes find success with four, six or eight-ounce Metzler Mooch-A-Jigs, four to seven-ounce Crippled Herring in white or chrome, or chrome Krocodiles in the five and seven-ounce sizes.

Lyre River/Freshwater Bay

The waters around the mouth of the Lyre River were providing some of Washington's most consistent halibut action before the Northwest halibut boom of the early to mid-eighties. As other halibut hot spots sprouted in the Strait, northern Puget Sound and along the coast, however, fewer and fewer anglers took advantage of the fishery off the Lyre and nearby Whisky Creek. In fact, the fishing here is as productive as ever, and it's an area where you have a realistic chance of setting the hooks into a halibut of 100 pounds or better.

Like the Hoko River and Twin Rivers to the west, the Lyre has deposited deep layers of sand and gravel in the Strait of Juan de Fuca, which draw baitfish that in turn draw hungry halibut. Trolling or drifting a large herring accounts for most of the fish here, and those fish tend to be scattered throughout a wide range of depths.

Whisky Creek, to the east of the Lyre, offers similar fishing on a smaller scale. If the larger halibut grounds of the Lyre don't produce, give this one a shot.

Farther east is Freshwater Bay, which can be fairly productive at times but isn't known for its consistent halibut action. Halibut catches are scattered throughout this area, so you may have to do some prospecting.

The best advice might be to start at the 25- or 30-fathom line off the mouth of Salt Creek (on an incoming tide) or off Angeles Point (when the tide is ebbing) and work that contour until you find action. A boat ramp for trailerable craft under about 18 feet is available in this shallow bay, but there are no other facilities in the immediate area.

Port Angeles

The most consistently productive halibut-fishing spot around "P.A." is Green Point, about six miles east of town.

While occasionally giving up a barn door, the gently sloping sand and gravel bottom here is more likely to give up chicken-size halibut in the 10- to 30-pound class. Many of them are caught by salmon anglers mooching herring or working metal jigs as they drift parallel to the beach in 90 to 150 feet of water, but some anglers target the big flatties by trolling or fishing bait on spreader rigs a little deeper. Gordon Matthews, long-time Port Angeles tackle shop owner and halibut enthusiast, often recommended drifting east-to-west on the out-going tide, staying as close to 28 fathoms (168 feet) as possible.

A couple of offshore humps also offer some respectable halibut fishing for P.A.-area anglers. A rough outcropping known simply as "The Rock Pile" lies directly north of the tip of Ediz Hook, and it produces some of the area's largest barn doors. Many hooked fish, unfortunately, find their way back into the rocks and cut the line to regain their freedom. This can be tough fishing, but worthwhile for bait anglers or jiggers who fish the slack tide or on days when tidal exchange is minimal.

Coyote Bank is a little more conducive to easy fishing, but it's also farther out to the north. In fact, it straddles the U.S./Canada border, so Washington anglers must be careful to stay on the south side unless they also hold a B.C. marine fishing license. Fortunately, the halibut fishing is a little better on the smoother southern side of the bank, so it can be fished effectively with trolling, jigging or spreader gear.

Other spots around Port Angeles also produce halibut, although not as regularly as Green Point and the offshore high spots. Halibut are taken from time to time along the outside of Ediz Hook, the long spit that protects the Port Angeles Harbor. I took a respectable 28-pounder here one July morning a few years ago while I ws jigging for king salmon, and as I boated my fish I looked up to see a salmon angler in a nearby boat landing one of almost identical size. The "Humps" a couple of miles to the west, long a favorite with wintertime chinook salmon anglers, also produce some hefty halibut at times.

Hein Bank

The spring months see millions of candlefish congregating in the sand and gravel of Hein Bank, an underwater plateau that rises up to within about 25 feet of the surface near the east end of the Strait of Juan de Fuca. Those candlefish draw hungry halibut and salmon, making Hein Bank a popular destination of those Washington anglers whose boats are large enough and well-enough equipped to handle these open waters. The west side and south end of the bank offer some of the best halibut-fishing prospects, although you may find one almost anywhere here. Jigging with such candlefish-imitating metal jigs as Point Wilson's Candlefish Dart or Luhr Jensen's Deep Stinger produces good numbers of Hein Bank halibut, many of which come from about 25 fathoms (150 feet) of water.

Other Banks

Several other humps around the east end of the Strait are also halibut-fishing possibilities. Expansive Middle Bank, for example, is best-known for its late-winter chinook and springtime lingcod fishing, but the relatively smooth southern two-thirds of the bank provide decent halibut action, especially for smaller fish to about 20 pounds. Some bigger halibut are sometimes caught along the deeper drop-offs around the northeast corner of the bank. Middle Bank lies northwest of Hein Bank, a short distance south of San Juan Island. Eastern Bank, which lies southeast of Hein, can be good at times during the early spring, usually when large numbers of candlefish and other baitfish turn up to help ring the halibut dinner bell. Partridge Bank is even farther to the southeast, near the entrance to Puget Sound, and offers limited halibut action, mostly near the southwestern corner of the bank in at least 25 fathoms of water. Farther south, within easy range of Port Townsend, lies Mid-Channel Bank, where halibut catches are mixed in with the chinook salmon that are abundant there.

ADMIRALTY INLET AND NORTH PUGET SOUND

Although halibut fishing in the entrance to Puget Sound and the northern reaches of the Sound itself is a hit-and-miss proposition at best, the area does provide enough sporadic action to merit at least an honorable mention here. At times, in fact, the fishing can be downright hot, although seldom for more than a few days at a time when bait is abundant and conditions are right.

Both Admiralty Bay and Mutiny Bay, on the west side of Whidbey Island, give up halibut to serious anglers willing to put in some time trolling dodger-and-bait rigs or fishing whole herring along the bottom on the slow drift. The outer edges of both bays, in 80 feet of water or more, provide the best possibilities. Farther south, Useless Bay provides some fair halibut fishing for both trollers and jiggers every now and then.

Washington Coast

Map courtesy USGS

How to Catch
Trophy Halibut

This area, though, is sometimes clogged with spiny dogfish, and when that happens, any attempts to fish with bait in Useless Bay become, well, useless. At the extreme south end of Whidbey Island, expansive Possession Bar provides some hit-and-miss halibut action, but nothing you can depend on.

West of Possession, across Admiralty Inlet, lies the north end of the Kitsap Peninsula, and at its northeastern corner, Point No Point. Although best known for its salmon fishing and past glories as a good place to catch a limit of wintertime Pacific cod, No Point occasionally produces some husky halibut, and would probably be a fairly consistent producer throughout the spring season if more anglers worked at it a little harder. The area most likely to produce is the sand and gravel bottom to the north, northeast and east of the point. Jigging, bottom-bouncing with spreader rigs, and slow trolling all will work here. Look for the moderate edge where the bottom breaks away from 100 to 200 feet, and try to time your trip to coincide with periods of low to moderate tidal flow.

To the northwest of Point No Point, at the extreme tip of the Kitsap Peninsula, is Foulweather Bluff and the entrance to Hood Canal, another spot to prospect for halibut when weather and water conditions allow. Although somewhat of a secret, the area was a favorite of the late Dick Johnson of Kingston Tackle fame, who often advised anglers to fish in about 250 to 300 of feet of water there. He, of course, suggested trolling with downriggers and a few of his effective flasher rigs adorned with his plastic squid or other Kingston gear, but jigging with large Krocodiles, Crippled Herring, pipe jigs or leadheads with plastic grub bodies will also work. If you feel up to it, you can also fish this fairly deep-water halibut spot with whole herring, squid or other baits on a wire spreader.

WASHINGTON COAST

A one-fish daily limit and restrictions on the season length that have resulted in as few as two days of fishing all summer have kept angler interest and participation in halibut fishing to a minimum along the Washington coast in recent years. As a result, exploration of and advancements in the halibut-fishing opportunities have been limited. There are, however, places worth visiting when the season is open, whether your choice is to fish in the relative comfort of a roomy charter boat or to take on the Pacific in your own craft.

One of the most productive spots for halibut along the entire Washington coast is Umatilla Reef, a large underwater plateau

Washington anglers can catch big halibut, like this 215-pounder, if they fish the deeper waters of the Continental Shelf.

several miles northwest of LaPush. Part of the reason it's so productive is that it's so far from what most of us would call civilization. LaPush is within running distance for a decent-size boat, but LaPush is many miles off the beaten path and more than a half-day's drive from Seattle. Some adventurous anglers run to Umatilla from Neah Bay, but your boat had better be big enough to make the run and carry plenty of fuel to get you there and back. Some charters out of Westport also visit this productive halibut spot, usually on two-day trips that offer the chance to fish for halibut, lingcod and rockfish at various stops along the way.

Parts of Umatilla Reef are as shallow as 150 feet, making it well-suited to comfortable fishing once you get there. Jigging, trolling and fishing bait all work here. Big halibut are a possibility, but a bulk of the catch consists of smaller fish in the 12- to 25-pound range.

Between Umatilla Reef and LaPush is the famous LaPush Rock Pile, where many a bottomfish legend has been spawned over the decades. While best-known for its lunker lingcod, this rocky hump a few miles off the coast also plays host to some halibut, and occasionally someone sticks the hooks into a barn door that heads for parts unknown and doesn't stop until the reel is empty and the angler is beaten and humiliated.

The edge of the Continental Shelf also offers productive halibut-fishing opportunities for Washington anglers, but this deep-water fishery gets only limited attention. It's tough fishing in several hundred feet of water, and, although the payoffs can be great, most anglers simply don't want to work quite that hard for their halibut fillets.

Depending on seasons and restrictions, it's possible to go out and catch halibut from both Westport and Ilwaco, but be sure to call ahead before planning a halibut trip to either. Quotas, restrictions and short seasons may interfere with your plans.

Before they head off for any of the aforementioned halibut hot spots, anglers in Washington need to remember that they must have in their possession a personal-use license, which is required for all saltwater fishing. In addition, anglers fishing for halibut in the Strait of Juan de Fuca and Puget Sound (management areas 5 through 13), must also have an annual halibut catch-record card. Both the personal-use license and halibut card are available from tackle shops, marinas, charter offices and other license vendors in those fishing areas.

How to Catch
Trophy Halibut

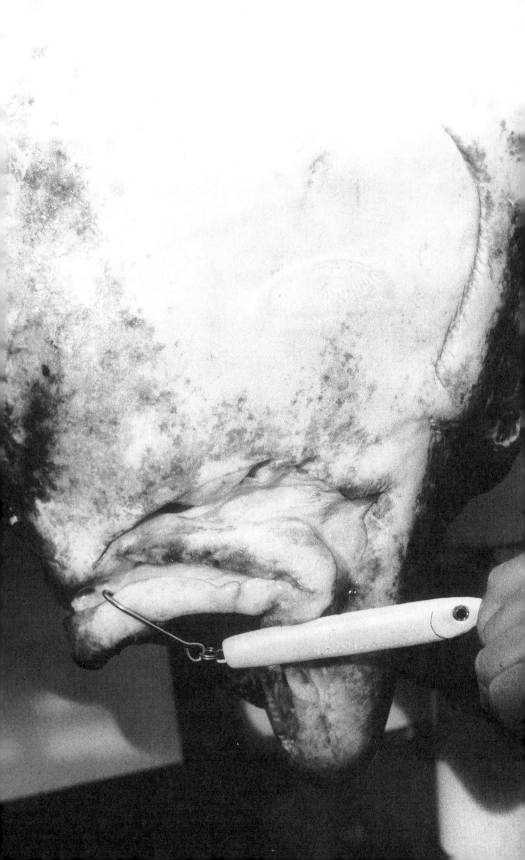

CHAPTER 22

Oregon Halibut Hotspots

Halibut mania hit the Beaver State in the mid-eighties and is running as strong as ever.

Oregon's sport halibut catch jumped from virtually nothing to an estimated 35,000 pounds (dressed weight) in 1986, according to Jerry Butler of the Oregon Department of Fish and Wildlife. The next year, with both charter and private-boat activity increasing dramatically, that catch more than doubled to over 78,000 pounds. Two years later the catch skyrocketed to more than 135,000 pounds of sport-caught halibut, then dropped back off to remain at its current figure of between 54,000 and 94,000 pounds per year.

Newport

Newport is the center of Oregon's halibut-fishing activity, and for many years held a virtual monopoly on the state's sport halibut catch, producing more than 90 percent of the harvest most years. And it's easy to understand Newport's popularity among halibut anglers. The town snuggles up against the north shore of Yaquina Bay, one of the Oregon coast's best-protected harbors. Long jetties at the north and south entrances to the bay provide further protection, and the bar at the end of the jetties is probably the safest and easiest to cross of any on the Northwest coast. That's why Newport is home to the largest fleet of charters and private boats on the Oregon coast.

Yaquina Bay and Newport also happen to be situated in a spot where offshore structure provides an expansive ridge of prime halibut habitat, places where the experts say some halibut almost certainly spend the entire year, and where others congregate in the spring to take advantage of large schools of

Bill Cork shows off a pair of 25-pound halibut that were kept for dinner. Note the slash across the tail of one fish, a sure sign that it has been thoroughly bled, helping to ensure top-quality table fare.

baitfish and other abundant food sources. Inshore from these vast, deep-water halibut magnates are other, less dramatic humps, gravel piles and gradual rock drop-offs that attract halibut from mid-spring through the summer, and where small-boat anglers can make a short run from Yaquina Bay and have a realistic chance of hooking halibut in 30 to 40 fathoms of water or less.

Since the charter fleet—which numbers up to about 20 boats on any given weekend during the season—accounts for upwards of 70 percent of the Newport halibut catch, let's take a good look at where and how it fishes.

Much of the charter-fishing activity takes place on Stonewall Bank, an expansive reef running north and south, beginning about a dozen miles southwest of Newport. Some spots on Stonewall are as shallow as 30 fathoms, but much of the fishing effort takes place in about 50 fathoms (300 feet) of water. Most anglers use braided line, either Dacron or the new-technology lines, in 40 to 80-pound test. Depending on wind speed and water movement, it will take 12 to 32-ounce sinkers or jigs to reach bottom, but in a "typical" situation 16 ounces gets the job done.

Bait/lure combinations are standard on most charter trips, and the rig often consists of a torpedo sinker with a brightly colored streamer fly tied off a dropper leader above the sinker and a long-shanked, size 8/0 hook connected by a snap-swivel to the bottom of the sinker. A whole herring is threaded onto the hook.

Rob Waddell, charter skipper out of Newport Tradewinds Charter Service, sometimes uses an entirely different rig on Stonewall Bank, especially if the halibut seem to be in a finicky mood. He uses a large swivel to attach a three-foot leader to the line, and the sinker goes at the bottom of the leader. Before adding the sinker, though, he threads the leader through the eye of a snap-swivel, which can run freely up and down the leader from the top swivel to the sinker. A short, stiff leader connects a pair of tandem-tied hooks to the snap-swivel, and he fishes a whole herring on the hooks. The only problem with this rig is that if the herring is stripped off, you're fishing with bare hooks. One option would be to add another short, stiff leader to the in-line swivel and fish a plastic grub or pork rind strip on an unweighted hook.

Some anglers, especially those who fish the bank from their own boats, use a simple spreader rig with a whole herring or other bait on the leader. The problem with using only a herring

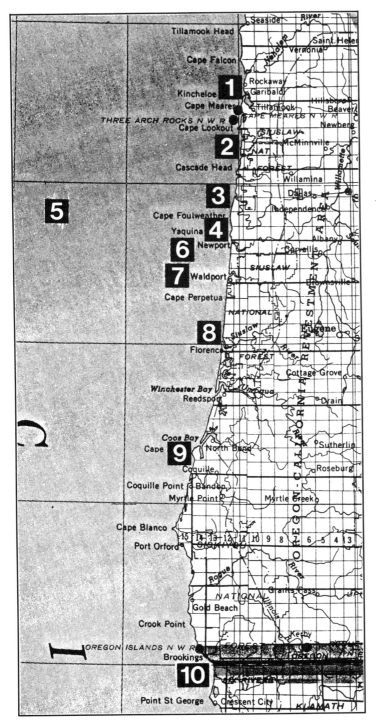

Oregon

1. Garibaldi
2. Cape Kiwanda
3. Depoe Bay
4. Newport
5. Nelson Island
6. Stonewall Bank
7. Heceta Bank
8. Florence
9. Charleston
10. Brookings

Oregon Hotspots

at the end of your line in this relatively deep water, however, is that if you miss a strike, you have a major decision to make: do you retrieve the heavy rig to check the bait or assume it's okay and leave it down there? Either way, you'll probably guess wrong.

Jerry Butler, who heads the marine finfish program for the Oregon Department of Fish and Wildlife, offers another option for Oregon's deep-water halibut anglers. He says one of his fishing companions uses a standard wire spreader rig, but instead of a herring or other natural bait on the hook, he use a large, plastic squid, and catches at least as many halibut on the offering as any of the local bait-dunkers catch. The advantage of the artificial, of course, is that it stays on the hook well and holds up even if the angler misses a strike.

Heceta Bank is a southern extension of Stonewall, and, although it's a longer run from Newport, there are times when it's producing well enough to make the trip worthwhile. Fishing strategies and techniques are pretty much the same as those used at Stonewall. It may take nearly an hour more to run to Heceta from Newport, though, and the trip home may take even longer if the afternoon northwesterly wind kicks up, as it often does throughout the spring and summer.

A third offshore halibut producer is Nelson Island, which is a large seamount rising up from the ocean bottom a little north and about 28 miles out from Newport. The first time I fished this spot I concluded that whoever came up with the name for the place must have had a little trouble with the meaning of the term "island," because the shallowest spots we fished on this particular island were about 450 feet beneath the surface! At times we found ourselves fishing in more than 600 feet of water. Just retrieving our rigs at the end of a drift was tough work, and bringing a fish to the top was just a shade short of grueling. And, since we came up only a fish or two shy of two-fish limits all the way around, most of us had plenty of opportunity to give our arms, shoulders and backs a good workout.

The same fly-and-herring rigs employed by many Stonewall Bank charter anglers also work at Nelson Island, but of course it takes a much heavier sinker to take the combo to the bottom. A 24-ouncer may do the job on a good day, but throw in a little current and a 10-knot wind and you're using 48-ounce sinkers in no time. That's when the fishing really gets tough. Needless to say, fishing with monofilament is an exercise in futility here.

Newport's inshore halibut fishery is pretty much left to the small-boat anglers. Although they seldom enjoy hot fishing, there are usually enough halibut in the 30-fathom depths by early June to make things interesting. The only problem some years is that hot, early-season fishing offshore may result in the sport halibut quota being achieved before that June fishery can even develop, leaving inshore anglers little opportunity to try their luck. When fishing is possible, working the outer edge of the 30-fathom line can be productive, especially for anglers fishing spreader-and-herring rigs or bouncing metal jigs along the bottom.

Oregon's "New" Halibut Fisheries

Newport's position as Oregon's halibut capital went unchallenged until 1993, when charter operators out of Garibaldi, at the north end of Tillamook Bay, went prospecting for halibut beds and found them off the mouth of the Nehalem River, seven or eight miles to the north. Within a year that fishery took off, and in 1994 the small Garibaldi halibut fleet caught nearly one-third (32 percent, to be exact) of the Oregon sport halibut harvest.

The halibut fishery out of Depoe Bay, located about mid-way between Newport and Garibaldi, also started to mushroom in 1994, and by the end of the season this tiny port accounted for 11 percent of the state's halibut catch. And to south, a couple of charter operators out of Charleston (Coos Bay) also began running halibut trips in 1994, and by season's end this small fleet caught about seven percent of the halibut taken by Oregon anglers for the year.

In just one season, Newport's share of the Oregon sport halibut catch dropped from over 90 percent to only 50 percent, and anglers along the coast suddenly had choices about where they could try their luck at charter fishing for halibut.

For those looking to know a little more about these "new" halibut hot spots that have no doubt been there all along, just waiting to be discovered, here are the basics (working from north to south):

Garibaldi

The boats go north to fish off the mouth of the Nehalem River in about 28 to 32 fathoms of water. The area features a classic gravel bottom, the kind halibut like and the kind that keeps loss of tackle to a minimum. Part of the beauty is that boats come back to the south, with the tough north wind at

The large, protected harbor at Yaquina Bay makes Newport a natural for Oregon boaters. Lots of off-shore structure attract halibut to within range of charter boats and at least some of the private craft. Limited inshore halibut action is also available.

their backs. There were, at last count, at least a half-dozen charter boats operating out of Garibaldi.

Pacific City (Cape Kawanda)

Anglers who launch their dories in the surf at Cape Kawanda have targeted lingcod and rockfish for decades, but an area about 28 fathoms deep just off the cape also produces fair halibut fishing.

Depoe Bay

Banana Bank is a north-south running reef area that doesn't show on the charts, maybe 18 miles offshore from this tiniest of Oregon ports, and it's here that most of the charters and some of the bigger private boats go for halibut. Like Newport, it also has some near-shore fishing in water of 30 fathoms or so. More than a half-dozen Depoe Bay charter boats are involved in halibut fishing.

Charleston

Halibut boats are still doing a lot of prospecting here, but one of the places that produces fish is Coquille Bank, known locally as the "Blanco High Spot," a reef that comes up from deep water to about 60 fathoms. It's within reach of the charters and the bigger private boats out of Coos Bay and is an excellent halibut-fishing spot. The only problem is that it's southwest out of Charleston, so it's a bumpy ride home against the north wind. Some boats beat the wind by running up to the bank from down at Port Orford, but the problem there is that there is no boat ramp, just a couple of slings. It's closer to the high spot, and you come back with the wind.

South Oregon Coast

This area has halibut and certainly holds great promise for halibut fishing, but there has been little fishing activity or prospecting for halibut here. Brookings would be the logical take-off point for charters or larger private boats in search of productive halibut spots.

There are, according to the Oregon Department of Fish and Wildlife's Jerry Butler, other, untapped halibut-fishing opportunities along the Oregon coast just waiting to be discovered or exploited more fully. Florence, for example, has serious potential, especially for boats running north to fish Heceta Bank. There are boat ramps, but the bar (mouth of the Siuslaw River) is not a particularly friendly one. You would have to pick your days for crossing the bar, then run north to Heceta and come home with the northwest winds.

"Even if a given area doesn't offer an obvious reef or other structure to draw halibut, I think that if you go out and explore in 100 fathoms of water almost anywhere along the coast you're going to find some halibut fishing," says Butler. "That kind of exploration is beginning to happen, but there's still plenty of untapped potential."

CHAPTER 23

California Halibut: Sub-Compact Of The Barn-Door Family

The California halibut doesn't achieve nearly the size of its big cousin to the north, but it's a big hit with anglers from San Francisco Bay to the Mexico border and beyond. What's more, the inshore gillnet ban of earlier this decade seems to be benefitting halibut and halibut anglers, which bodes well for the future of this fishery. Tens of thousands of California anglers are hooked on halibut, and if you aren't one of them, maybe you should be. The following pages will tell you what you need to know to get started...and to be successful.

There is actually a little overlap in the range of the California halibut with that of the Pacific halibut, but for all intents and purposes one fishery begins where the other ends. Seldom will you find hot fishing for California's north of about Bodega Bay on the northern California coast, while Pacifics are rarely encountered by anglers south of Eureka, many miles to the north. Really good fishing opportunity for California halibut— with an occasional exception as noted below—quickly peters out a short distance north of San Francisco Bay.

The California halibut is substantially smaller than its northern relative, but certainly grows large enough to attract the attention of anglers. California regulations require that anglers release all halibut under 22 inches long, and it takes four or five years for the fish to reach this size. The International Game Fish Association lists an impressive 53-pound, four-ouncer, caught near Santa Rosa Island in 1988, as its all-tackle world record, and the official California state record, also caught off Santa Rosa Island, is four ounces heavier at 53 pounds, eight ounces. There are documented reports of fish exceeding 60

The California halibut's affection for shallow sand flats makes it susceptible to a variety of fishing methods. Angelo Cuanang trolled a Bagley plug in eight feet of water near the San Francisco International Airport for this San Francisco Bay flatfish. Bay-area halibut anglers tend to use heavier tackle than that favored by anglers farther south. Abe Cuanang photo.

pounds, and anglers like to talk about a couple over 70 pounds, one caught in the 1970s and another much earlier in the century. The IGFA's list of line-class records documents a number of California halibut over 30 pounds, and fish in the 20- to 30-pound range are common enough to keep things interesting for serious halibut anglers.

Another difference between the two relatives is that the Pacific halibut is a right-eyed flatfish, meaning that in the vast majority of cases the eyes are on the right side of the head. The Californian, on the other hand, is a member of the left-eyed flounder family. The oddest thing about all this is that about half the California halibut caught have the eyes on the right, rather than the left side, so the scientists who call it a left-eyed fish are right only about half the time.

Whatever side of the head its eyes are on, the California halibut is a cooperative, strong and sweet-eating sportfish, one that enjoys great popularity wherever it is found in fishable numbers. Luckily, that includes much of the central and southern California coast and many of the state's offshore islands. Let's take a closer look at where and how they're caught.

NORTH COAST

Although we told you earlier that there is little hot fishing for California halibut north of the San Francisco Bay area, pointing out a recent and very exciting exception may give you some incentive to explore places not traditionally known for their productive halibut fishing.

Humboldt Bay, although it gave up a California halibut now and then, was never considered a halibut hot spot, at least not until the summer of 1994. That's when a combination of factors, including two or three years of warm El Nino currents and good halibut production several years before, resulted in a bumper crop of halibut throughout the bay. Drawn to Humboldt's warm, shallow water, they moved in by the thousands, providing several months of some of the best California halibut action found anywhere in the state. Many of them were just-legal 23- to 24-inchers, and it wasn't unusual for anglers to hook as many as 10 a day. Five-fish limits were common, most of them taken on live anchovies drifted along the edges of shallow-water breaklines. Needless to say, the wild and crazy halibut action drew plenty of angler interest, and left them wondering if the scene will soon be repeated, according to Ron Warner, a fish manager in the California Fish and Game's Eureka office.

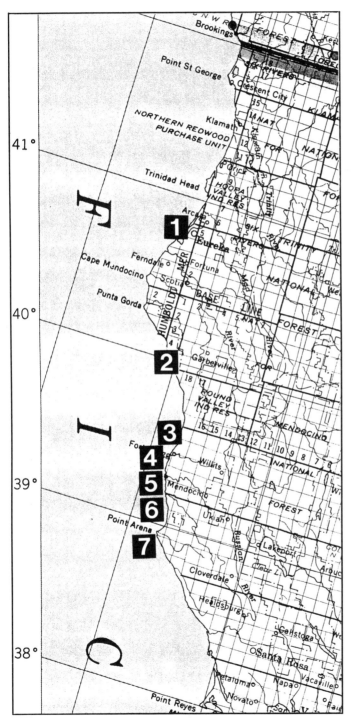

California
North Coast

1. Humboldt Bay
2. Shelter Cove
3. Noyo Bay
4. Mendocino Bay
5. Whitesboro Cove
6. Greenwood Cove
7. Arena Cove

Other North Coast possibilities? Shelter Cove, on the south side of Point Delgada, might be worth a try, as might Noyo Bay, near Fort Bragg. More likely possibilities include Mendocino Bay, Whitesboro Cove, Greenwood Cove and Arena Cove. None of these has a great reputation as a halibut haven, but summertime prospecting with live anchovies might pay off big.

SAN FRANCISCO BAY AREA

The Bay itself offers a number of prime halibut-fishing spots, any one of which might provide an angler with several good fish for a few hours' work.

Among the places worth investigating are the Berkeley Flats off Emeryville, the flats off the south side of Sausalito, Raccoon Strait, the southeast side of Angel Island, the west side of Alcatraz Island, the area off the Alameda Rock Wall, the waters off Oyster Point (South San Francisco), the west end of the Bay Bridge, the flats off San Quentin and the flats off the San Francisco International Airport.

Much of the fishing here is done in eight to 15 feet of water, says Abe Cuanang, Bay-area outdoor writer and long-time halibut enthusiast, and one of the easiest ways to fish those depths is to drift live bait. Many anglers use the same rods, reels and line they use when mooching for salmon, with 20-pound monofilament pretty much standard. As for terminal tackle, tie the main line to a three-way swivel, then use an eight- to 12-inch monofilament dropper to hang a four-ounce bank sinker. A five-foot leader runs from the swivel to the bait, which is usually pinned through the nose with a size 1/0 or 2/0 hook, according to Cuanang.

Another technique that sometimes works is trolling diving plugs that will dig deep enough to tick the bottom as deep as 15 feet.

Rapalas and other long, thin plugs that resemble anchovies often produce the best result, Cuanang says.

Anglers fishing the flats and shallow ledges should use their depthsounders to locate any humps of a foot or two that might jut up from the bottom. These humps often have halibut on or around them.

Anglers fishing San Francisco Bay catch quite a few sub-legal halibut (under 22 inches), but five to eight-pounders are considered average keepers and there are enough fish over 20 pounds to provide a real opportunity for catching a trophy fish.

California
San Francisco Bay Area

8. San Francisco Bay
9. Point Bonita
10. Seal Rock
11. Monterey Bay
12. Morro Bay
13. Port San Luis
14. Pismo Beach

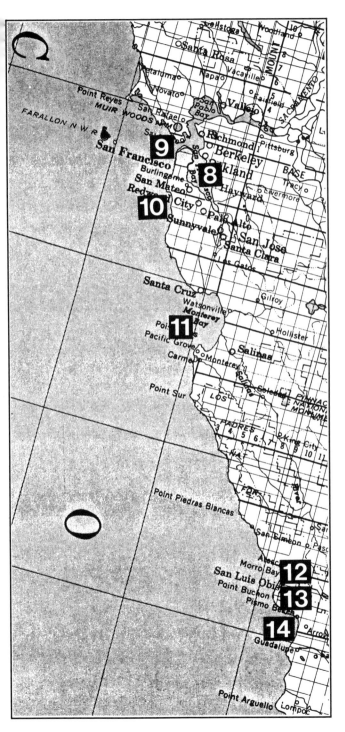

Now and then the Bay gives up a 30-pounder, according to Cuanang.

Several ocean areas around San Francisco are also worth investigating. One of the best is Seal Rock, south of Half Moon Bay, where anglers do especially well from late-June through September. Fishing live bait from about an hour before to an hour after the high tide often produces the best results. Pillar Point Harbor, just north of Half Moon Bay, is another good possibility for ocean anglers. The fishing may be best inside the harbor or in the open ocean just off the harbor entrance, so check out both locations if you're in the area.

Another productive halibut spot is off Point Bonita, at the north entrance to the Golden Gate. Also called North Bar, it's a place where baitfish often congregate. A key to success here is to put out as many baits as possible in order to cover lots of water, says Cuanang.

Speaking of covering lots of water, anglers both along the coast and in San Francisco Bay sometimes troll for their halibut, and the standard trolling rig consists of three plastic squid (hoochies), tied about 10 feet apart and fished behind a dropper line with eight to 16 ounces of lead on the dropper. Blue and silver, green and silver or brown and silver are the top squid colors, and many anglers fish one of each color until one shows signs of being the hot color. Wire line is often used for this type of fishing, so a seven-foot rod with a roller tip and a 4/0 reel are standard.

Monterey Bay to Point Conception

California's southcentral coast provides some good halibut-fishing opportunity, much of it in the major bays where the fish move inshore on their springtime runs into the warmer shallows where even private-boat anglers fishing from small skiffs have a chance to get at them.

Monterey Bay is the scene of a moderate skiff fishery for halibut in the spring and early summer. Drift-fishing with live anchovies accounts for some fish, as does trolling with bait, diving plugs or plastic-squid rigs similar to those used in San Francisco Bay.

Party boats sometimes take halibut along the coast between Monterey Bay and Morro Bay to the south, but most are caught incidentally by anglers in search of lingcod and rockfish. That's not to say, however, that an adventurous angler couldn't find the Mother Lode of halibut action if he were to do some serious looking. Some of the state's biggest commercial halibut catches have come from this vicinity, according to Bob Hardy at the California Fish and Game's Morro Bay office. This stretch of California coastline offers little in the way of protected waters for small-boat anglers to fish, and boat-launch facilities also are few and far between. Beach-launching is a possibility in some areas, and there's also the option of surf fishing. Since California halibut move right up against the surf line in spring and early summer, fishing bait or small leadheads adorned with plastic grub bodies will produce a few flatties for anglers interested in prowling the beaches.

The Morro Bay area, on the other hand, is home to a fairly productive small-boat fishery for halibut. Much of the action is outside Morro Bay itself, on the more open and much larger Estero Bay, where springtime anglers do most of their fishing in 10 to 30 feet of water. Drifting with live bait is productive, but if the bait shops are low on anchovies or if you simply want to avoid the mess and hassle, you might try plastic grubs fished on small leadheads. Just like their northern cousins, the California halibut in these parts often prefer white grubs, but carry a selection of colors, just in case. As for leadheads, you can get by with weights of one-eighth to three-quarters of an ounce in most water conditions. Again, casting from the beach is also a possibility, especially along the long, sandy beach at Morro Bay State Park.

Halibut sometimes move through the narrow channel and into the protected waters of Morro Bay itself, where anglers fishing from small skiffs, even rowboats, can get at them. This is an early summer fishery, and anglers use the same bait and jig rigs they use on the outside.

While the typical halibut from the Morro Bay area might be a fish in the range of just-legal to maybe 10 pounds, the area does produce trophies from time to time. In the fall of 1993, for example, a whopping 52½-pounder was caught just outside the bay.

Farther down the coast, Point San Luis juts southward into the Pacific to create another natural bay where halibut often congregate in good numbers during the spring, summer and early fall. Immediately inside the point at Port San Luis, and farther down the coast around Pismo Beach, anglers drifting live bait across the flats make some good halibut catches. Since the fish here are sometimes caught right up against the beach, in water as shallow as two or three feet, it's another area where surf-fishing is a logical possibility.

CHANNEL ISLANDS

California anglers may find the southern version of a barn door (something over 20 pounds) almost anywhere along the coast, but the odds of doing so improve greatly if you head offshore to any of the big islands scattered along the southern one-third of the California coast. Getting there takes some doing, but if it's big flatties and more of them you're looking for, the trip is well worth it.

The Northern Islands— San Miguel, Santa Rosa and Santa Cruz

San Miguel, Santa Rosa and Santa Cruz have special reputations for their trophy-size halibut, giving up fish over 30 pounds quite regularly and over 40 pounds from time to time. As mentioned earlier, both the official California state record and IGFA all-tackle world record California halibut came from Santa Rosa Island, and Santa Cruz Island produced IGFA line-class records of 38 and 45 pounds.

Captain Fred Benko, skipper of the party boat "Condor" out of Santa Barbara's Sea Landing, specializes in halibut trips to San Miguel, Santa Rosa and Santa Cruz, and, although angling interest is highest from mid-spring to early fall, he says the islands provide year-round halibut-fishing opportunity. The average halibut from these offshore hot spots, he says, runs 10 to 15 pounds.

Most of Benko's clients fish live bait, usually anchovies or sardines, and the tougher squid or even mackerel if they're available. The water is quite clear, so he advises using 12- to 15-pound monofilament and running it straight to the hook without a leader. Using the lightest possible slip-sinker, with a split shot or some other form of sinker-stop a short distance above the bait is standard practice. Depending on the speed of the drift, the bait may be hooked either in the nose (fast drift) or through the collar (slower drift).

Like many other California halibut angling "coaches," Benko preaches his clients to "feed 'em line" whenever a fish first takes the bait. Unlike Pacific halibut, these southern fish may mouth an anchovy or sardine for 15 seconds or more before the hook is deep enough for a good set, and many anglers strike too quickly.

Benko often backs his 88-footer right up against the beach to begin his drift, often fishing only a few feet of water as he starts to parallel the shoreline. He finds halibut from the water's edge to as deep as 100 feet, usually over sand but sometimes over sand-and-gravel bottom. When the usually productive sandy bottoms aren't producing, he'll fish the bases of steep cliffs, the edges of kelp beds, even some cobble humps until he finds action.

Benko says the north face of San Miguel Island is one of his favorite halibut spots, but other areas that produce well include the bay just north of Fraser Point on the west end of Santa Cruz and Skunk Point on the east end of Santa Rosa. The two are only about six miles apart, so it's fairly easy to run from one to the other depending on wind and other variables. As a general rule, he says, Santa Rosa produces the biggest halibut of the season, but San Miguel produces the most.

The southern islands, especially Santa Barbara, Santa Catalina and San Clemente, also provide anglers with a good shot at both large numbers of halibut and trophy-class specimens. Catalina in particular has given up its share of south-coast barn doors, including line-class records of 38½ and 41 pounds, both landed in 1988.

SOUTHERN COAST

There are no doubt more halibut anglers per capita and more halibut-fishing opportunities per angler available along the southern California coast than anywhere else in the state. From Santa Barbara to San Diego, halibut fishing here is serious business.

While there are no major protected bays from Point Conception south to Rincon Point, this stretch of beach produces some good halibut catches, including some very large fish. April, May and June, when waters are warming, provide some of the best action along this section of coast, but fall can also be productive.

Besides drifting with live bait, halibut anglers around Santa Barbara (and out around the northern islands) have perfected another fishing system that works here, one that was stumbled upon by salmon anglers and perfected for halibut fishing. It's a bottom-bouncing trolling technique that the locals call bounce-balling, and it involves pulling a fresh bait or plastic hootchie behind a flasher, which in turn follows a lead-ball sinker heavy enough to stay close to the bottom at trolling speed. Bouncing the lead ball regularly along the bottom is part of the secret, because, like many halibut anglers along the entire coast, bounce-ballers believe that the sound and puff of sand created by that bouncing sinker helps to draw halibut

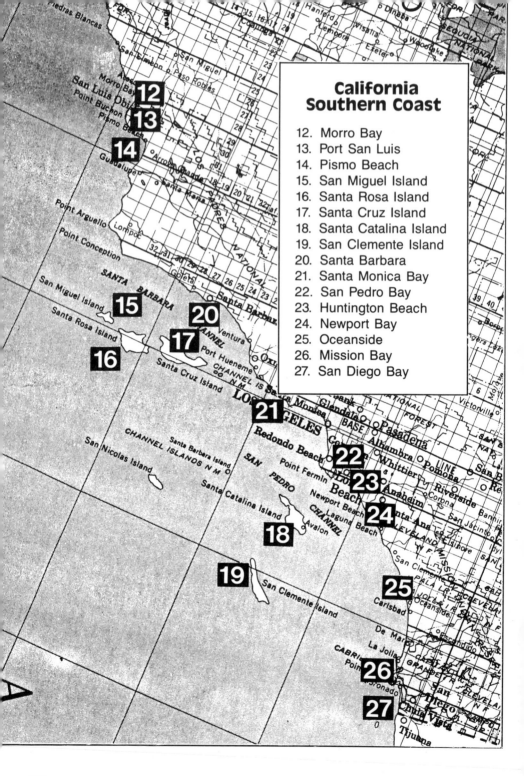

California
Southern Coast

12. Morro Bay
13. Port San Luis
14. Pismo Beach
15. San Miguel Island
16. Santa Rosa Island
17. Santa Cruz Island
18. Santa Catalina Island
19. San Clemente Island
20. Santa Barbara
21. Santa Monica Bay
22. San Pedro Bay
23. Huntington Beach
24. Newport Bay
25. Oceanside
26. Mission Bay
27. San Diego Bay

How to Catch
Trophy Halibut

in for a closer look. It certainly doesn't hurt, because the technique works.

Travel down the coast a little farther and you're in Santa Monica Bay, the first of many top-notch South Coast halibut-fishing spots. March, April and May are the favorite months of most halibut anglers here, since that's when large numbers of flatties move in from deep water and set up temporary residence in the bay to warm their bones after a long winter and to gorge on the many baitfish species available in the bay's shallow waters. The fall months, especially October and November, can also be good, and the consensus is that, while halibut aren't as abundant in the fall, the chances for a barn door of 20 pounds or more are considerably better than in spring.

The protected waters in and around Long Beach Harbor in San Pedro Bay are another good bet, especially for spring halibut fishing. This area features a great deal of soft bottom from sediment deposits, and a key to finding halibut action is locating the hard-bottom areas, using a depth sounder to find the fairly obvious hills of hard-packed sand from dredging and oil-drilling operations and to look for the more subtle deposits of hard sand scattered naturally throughout the bay. Finding the latter sometimes takes well-tuned electronics and careful observation. As in most halibut fishing, good charts will be very helpful in locating the potentially productive spots.

This area can be productive even for the angler who doesn't have a boat. Casting from the beach pays off with some respectable halibut, and a favorite haunt of halibut surf-casters is the Belmont Shore area between Long Beach and Seal Beach.

The gently sloping flats off Huntington Beach are productive from early spring to late fall, with March, April and May providing the fastest action, November and December most likely to provide a shot at a trophy topping 20 pounds. Like many of the halibut fisheries along the southern coast, this is a shallow-water operation, where the majority of fish are hooked in 10 to 20 feet of water.

Farther south, the Newport Bay area is another south coast halibut hot spot. Good numbers of fish move right into the harbor early in the spring, providing small-boat anglers with some excellent opportunities to drift live bait for halibut that may be found in water as shallow as five or six feet. The same technique also works outside the harbor, and if you don't have a boat you can still catch halibut here by surf-casting the final hour of the incoming tide and through the flood.

Continuing down the coast, the flats off Oceanside provide the next major halibut fishery. The hottest fishing here usually occurs in the spring, but halibut are available in decent numbers throughout the summer and well into the fall months. The harbor entrance at the north end of Oceanside is one of the favorite halibut-fishing spots.

Farther south are Del Mar Beach and Torrey Pines State Beach, both of which offer good springtime halibut-fishing opportunities for surf anglers, according to southern California outdoor writer and halibut enthusiast Tom Waters. He recommends scouting these areas during low tide to locate places that may be hot spots when the tide comes in. On flat, sandy beaches, he says, shallow depressions in the sand attract halibut. On rocky stretches of beach, look for small patches of sand around rock piles and rocky points. All of these are areas where a halibut or two can nestle into the sand and wait for an easy meal to pass by.

The next major halibut hot spot along the coast is Mission Bay, immediately north of San Diego. Because of its shallow, warm waters, the bay provides year-round halibut fishing, and its protected waters are well-suited to fishing from small private boats and skiffs. Halibut of five to eight pounds provide much of the action, but 15-pounders are common enough throughout the year to keep things more than interesting. Public beaches throughout the bay even give shorebound anglers an opportunity to cast diving plugs, leadheads with plastic grub bodies or bait rigs, and they, too, make some good halibut catches. One of the favorite halibut spots is right off the popular Sea World marine park, where warm water from the park's outflow seems to draw fish in close. The best fishing here is in water as shallow as 12 feet.

Like Mission Bay, the warm waters of San Diego Bay also draw good numbers of halibut, and this is another fishery that produces year-round results. Drifting the flats in a boat or casting from the beach will take fish, and halibut are also caught from the four major fishing piers around the north and east side of the bay. The flats outside the bay may also be productive, especially in spring. While boat anglers are most effective here, surf-casting from the west side of the narrow "Silver Strand" of beach between Coronado and Imperial Beach also produces halibut.

Fishing techniques and terminal rigs may vary a little from angler to angler, but halibut enthusiasts along the southern

How to Catch
Trophy Halibut

coast from Santa Monica to San Diego employ some more-or-less standard strategies and methods for catching their fish. Novice halibut fishermen need to know these tricks if they are to catch California halibut consistently.

Most anglers locate halibut by drifting with bait or trolling. Unless you have a couple of particular humps or small patches of sand that you expect to hold fish, the more ground you can cover, the better. Standard practice is to drift a live anchovy or other bait along the bottom, using a sinker just heavy enough to keep the bait near bottom but not so heavy that it constantly settles into the sand or hangs in the rocks and gravel. Most anglers use an egg sinker or other style of slip sinker, and many veteran halibut anglers recommend a split shot or some other kind of sinker stop on the line rather than an in-line swivel to keep the sliding sinker above the bait.

Most south-coast halibut anglers will tell you that these fish are line-shy, probably because they're usually found in shallow, clear water. Monofilament as light as four- or six-pound-test is used, but the majority of halibut fishermen go a little heavier in order to cover themselves in case they hook-up with a big fish. Ten- to 15-pound mono is common on south-coast halibut reels.

Those reels, by the way, may be either spinning or revolving-spool casting models, and they're usually attached to rather soft-action rods of seven feet or longer. Many halibut anglers prefer long, fiberglass rods, even fly rod blanks equipped with casting or spinning guides and butts, which are better suited to this close-quarters fishing in shallow water and to the halibut's fighting style of short, strong lunges.

Drift-fishing for halibut with live bait and light line presents a real challenge when it comes to setting the hook. These fish are usually slow and deliberate about taking a bait, sometimes playing with it a minute or more before fully inhaling it. Although many halibut gurus recommend the patient approach to ensure a hook-up, sticking your hook deep in the gullet of a big halibut while you're using six- or eight-pound line almost guarantees that the fish will chew through and break off before you can bring the trophy to the boat. For that reason, some light-line enthusiasts suggest a quicker hook-set to increase your chance of sticking the fish in the outer edge of the mouth, where line damage is less likely. You may have to adapt your hook-setting strategy according to specific conditions.

A size 1 or 2, light-wire hook is commonly used for live-bait halibut fishing, and it's usually stuck through the nose, collar or just ahead of the dorsal fin of an anchovy. Single hooks have long been the favorites of halibut anglers, but in recent years light-wire trebles have become increasingly popular among live-bait halibut fishermen.

While anchovies are by far the most commonly used halibut baits, they are small enough to be fair game for a wide variety of other bottom-dwelling marine fish, several of which can quickly become a pain in the butt for a serious halibut angler. Tomcod and lizardfish are two species commonly found on and around the halibut grounds, and they will pounce on a live anchovy every chance they get.

Using a larger, tougher bait is often the best way to avoid harassment from lizardfish and other pests, so anglers who can get smelt, grunion, sardines, squid, queenfish and mackerel will use these instead of anchovies. These larger baits offer the added advantage of attracting some larger halibut. The problem, of course, is finding these larger baits, and it's not always possible.

An alternative is to use the "pest" fish themselves for bait, and some anglers do just that. Small tomcod, in particular, make an excellent bait for larger halibut. As with other large baits, you'll have to up-size your hooks for this kind of fishing, going to a 2/0 or perhaps as large as a 3/0 hook.

California halibut, like any fish, sometimes get downright lazy about taking a bait, refusing to chase down a live offering or simply swimming over it and settling down on it to pin it against the bottom. If you know or suspect this is happening, try drifting dead rather than live bait. "Lazy" halibut that ignore a moving anchovy might inhale a still bait without hesitation.

If you know of an underwater hump that holds fish, or if you discover one while drifting, you might try anchoring near the top of that underwater hill and casting around it. Work a nose-hooked bait slowly up the sides of the hump, pausing when it gets to the top, where halibut might take their time in deciding to pounce on it. Work the hill from several angles to be sure to cover all the possibilities.

Working a known hump or channel breakline is also a good place to try artificials. Diving, minnow-type plugs that will work deep enough to reach bottom can be effective here, as can leadhead-and-plastic combinations. Use a leadhead that's heavy enough to reach bottom on a slow retrieve, but no heavier than necessary. Most leadhead enthusiasts recommend swimming the jig along bottom rather than actually jigging it. Sometimes a steady retrieve is best, but experiment with a stop-and-go retrieve if slow-and-steady doesn't work. Plastic bodies on those leadheads should be two to five inches long, and the most productive colors are white, smoke, clear, salt-and-pepper, natural greens and blues or combinations of these. Unlike live-bait strikes, when a halibut hits a plug or jig, there's little doubt about what's happening and absolutely no reason to pause before rearing back to set the hook.

About the Author—Chris Batin

As editorial director of Alaska Angler Publications and editor of the bi-monthly journal, The Alaska Angler® , Chris works year-round in keeping anglers up-to-date on new adventures and money-saving ideas that he discovers in Alaska sportfishing and hunting.

He is author of the award-winning books, *How to catch Alaska's Trophy Sportfish*, which has emerged as the classic, must-have guide for knowing the secrets to successfully catching Alaska sportfish; *Fishing Alaska on Dollars a Day*, the best-seller on fishing Alaska inexpensively; *20 Great Alaska Fishing Adventures*, an action-packed book that reveals the best trips he's experienced in 20 years of fishing Alaska; *Hunting in Alaska*, which is Alaska's best-selling hunting book.

He is considered by many of the country's top outdoor writers and fishing authorities as the "foremost expert in Alaska sportfishing."

The outdoor media turns to Chris when they need expert advice on Alaska sportfishing. He has been featured in major newspapers and outdoor magazines across the country and has personally appeared on the covers of 10 outdoor magazines.

There is a reason for this widespread exposure.

Chris has made a 21-year career searching out and studying the best of Alaska sportfishing. He has fished all over the state, and has written about it in over 1,000 columns and features in local and national magzines and newspapers.

Far from being an "armchair outdoor writer", Chris spends about 120 days afield each year. The result of this experience is available to you through his books and publications, and is experience you can't find or buy anywhere else. He has hiked into volcanoes to fish, rafted glacial rivers, driven countless miles of road and climbed wilderness mountains to search out unique and undiscovered sportfishing opportunities. A portion of this knowledge and experience is available to you in this book. Chris works dilligently to keep this wealth of information coming to you year 'round through The Alaska Angler® . Because The Alaska Angler® is not sold on newstands, subscribers are the first and only ones to know about his current findings and research in Alaska sportfishing techniques, lodge and guide reviews, do-it-yourself fishing opportunities and "inside information" on Alaska sportfishing deals and disasters. His readers put this advice to use each year on sportfishing trips based on his recommendations.

When he isn't in the office, he is in great demand for personal instruction and consultation from various lodges and sportfishing businesses around the state. He is now entering his 14th year of teaching the extremely popular Advanced Alaska Fishing Techniques, an intense, eight-hour seminar for anglers who must pre-qualify before being accepted. The secrets he reveals in his class can be used to strip a watershed of its fish. Chris only wants to teach anglers with a solid, ethical foundation. He accepts for instruction only those who understand and accept the responsibilities of what it means...and takes to be truly successful in Alaska sportfishing. There are no exceptions.

Since 1984, he has been a featured speaker at the Great Alaska Sportsman Show, where hundreds of people fill the bleachers to hear his dynamic presentations. He was featured as a celebrity speaker on Alaska fishing and hunting at Ed Rice's International Sportsmens Expositions throughout the Lower 48 states.

In 1984, the International Gamefish Association appointed Chris to be their senior Alaska representative. He helps promote the conservation goals of the organization and assists in verifying world-record fish. He has fished throughout the Lower 48 states, Mexico, southeast Asia, Sweden, Germany, Hawaii, Japan and Russia. He says he has yet to find a place that offers the variety and quality of sportfishing that Alaska offers.

Through his feature articles, journals, books, seminars, media reviews, personal consultation and workshops, Chris Batin has introduced the best of Alaska sportfishing to millions of people around the world. From the best possible do-it-yourself trips or one of his unpublished, secret fishing destinations, Chris can continue to provide you with the advice and information you need to know to make your Alaska fishing trip a success.

Turn to the catalog in the back of this book to see how he can help you now, or write him at:

P.O. Box 83550, Fairbanks, Alaska 99708

About the Author—Terry Rudnick

A life-long Northwesterner who grew up on the banks of Western Washington's Puyallup River, Terry has been an angling fanatic for as long as he can remember. Beginning with pan-size cutthroats and rainbows from neighborhood ponds, then graduating to bass, steelhead and salmon fishing throughout the Puget Sound area, he was an accomplished angler by the time he left home to start college.

His fishing affliction, however, wasn't cured by higher education. Journalism classes at Green River College and the University of Washington only added another dimension to his interest in the outdoors, and he began to dream of following in the footsteps of his childhood heroes Ted Trueblood, A.J. McClane, Ray Bergman and those other fantastically fortunate men who actually got paid for writing tales of their angling adventures.

Terry wrote and sold his first magazine article in 1971, and since the late-seventies he has been one of the Pacific Northwest's most prolific and popular outdoor writers. Hundreds of his feature articles, columns and photographs have appeared in newspapers, national and regional outdoor magazines and general interest publications. The majority of those articles are on Northwest angling subjects, but he also writes about hunting, boating, hunting dogs, camping, RV travel, whitewater boating, conservation and a broad range of other outdoor-related topics.

Those articles and photographs have earned Terry numerous accolades, including 18 Excellence in Craft awards from the Northwest Outdoor Writers Association. He was presented the 1990 National Conservationist of the Year in Communications award from Trout Unlimited and the 1991 Ken McLeod Journalism Award from the King County (Washington) Outdoor Sports Council.

Terry is also in demand as a speaker, and has given angling seminars and slide-show programs for dozens of Northwest sports and civic organizations. Since 1983 he has been a featured speaker at more than three dozen outdoor sports and boating trade shows in the Puget Sound region, Oregon, California, Utah, Colorado and Texas.

As both an author and public speaker, Terry prefers to cover outdoor subjects that he enjoys as an active participant, which is what led him to this, his first book project. An avid saltwater angler and holder of several former and current state and International Game Fish Association world records, he is fascinated with the brute of all North Pacific bottomfish, the Pacific halibut.

"The halibut is one of very few Northwest fish species that grows larger than the people who fish for it, and what could be more exciting than that?" says this die-hard halibut enthusiast. "It's incredible, with hundreds of books about bass and trout fishing, that no one has ever gotten around to writing a book about where and how to catch these big, tough, formidable trophies, and I'm more than happy to be a part of filling that void in angling literature. This is a book that cried out to be written, and I had to be one of the people who helped write it."

Hunting in Alaska
A Comprehensive Guide

By Christopher Batin

''(Hunting in Alaska) is the standard by which other Alaska hunting books will be judged.''
Bob Robb,
Petersen's Hunting

Hunting in Alaska is a rich source of Alaska-tested hunting ideas & strategies that work!
- 416 information-packed pages, 138 photos, many award winning
- 51 maps & illustrations
- Expert advice on hunting sheep, bear, moose, caribou, waterfowl, and more!
- Detailed, where-to-go information and harvest statistics for each species in each Game Management Unit

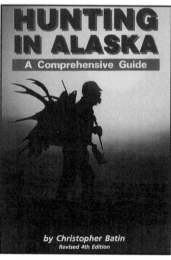

HUNTING IN ALASKA
A Comprehensive Guide

by Christopher Batin
Revised 4th Edition

ISBN 0-916771-11-3

For years, successful guides and hunters have known that it takes scientific knowledge and specific strategies to successfully harvest Alaska's most coveted big game trophies.

Now, for the first time, **Hunting in Alaska: A Comprehensive Guide** offers you over 1,000 of these hunting secrets and tips. Master guides and big game experts provide decades of first-hand experience, ensuring your Alaska hunt is a complete success.

Based on 15 years of Alaska hunting experience and research, ''Hunting in Alaska: A Comprehensive Guide'' **provides you with a wealth of never-before available information on:**
- High Bush and Low Bush Thrashing: Tactics scientifically proven to call in trophy moose.
- Specifics on hunting Kodiak and Alaska Peninsula Brown Bear
- Scientific data on the habits of full-curl Dall sheep, where they're found and how to hunt them, including interviews with guides who regularly take record-book sheep.
- 10-year trends on game populations, hunter statistics and harvest totals that give you pre-hunt knowledge of your chances for success in each of Alaska's 26 Game Management Units.

- Detailed maps and Game Management Unit descriptions that will familiarize you with Alaska's wilderness hunting hotspots and game concentrations.
- Planning a do-it-yourself hunt.
- Secret bear hunting techniques used by one guide who is nearly 100 percent for big brown bear, and who has put several in the record books, including a 30-incher.
- Criteria for choosing an Alaska big game guide.
- Learn secrets of taking wolves along salmon streams
- Understanding seasonal migration habits of big mountain goats and goat hunting methods that have helped one guide bag over 40 trophy goats for his clients.
- Specialized equipment needs for guided, unguided, backpack and float hunts.
- Over 1,000 listings of where you can hunt Alaska's big and small game and waterfowl.
- Care of trophies and meat.
- How to hunt ridges, over bait, berry patches, and tidal flats for trophy black bear.
- Extensive chapters on duck, goose, sea duck and crane hunting, small game, grouse, ptarmigan.
- Four award-winning stories on Alaska Hunting Excitement, Ethics, Camaraderie, and Adventure.
- Big game behavioral and natural history information of special interest to you as a hunter. Historical synopses of Alaska big game species, including transplants and current distribution information.

Hunting in Alaska: A Comprehensive Guide

Softcover....$25.95 (Canada.....$27.95)
Hardcover........$45 (Canada.........$47)

How to catch Alaska's Trophy Sportfish

By Christopher Batin

"Alaska Fishing Book Unparalleled" *Rich Landers Field and Stream magazine*

Over 30,000 anglers around the world have benefited from this advanced guide.

Anyone can catch four-pound rainbows or 12-pound salmon. But if you want to catch 60 to 80-pound Alaska king salmon, 300-pound halibut, 20-pound silvers, 30-inch rainbow trout, trophy grayling and steelhead, **"How to catch Alaska's Trophy Sportfish"** is your must-have, on-stream guide.

How to catch **Alaska's Trophy Sportfish**
by Christopher Batin
Foreword by Homer Circle
Angling Editor of Sports Afield

ISBN 0-916771-04-0

This book is also a must-have volume to fully understand the author's fishing recommendations in "Fishing Alaska on $15 a Day."

"Batin's long time on Alaskan waters (over 30,000 hours) gives his new book singular value. What fisherman wouldn't pay for a decade of experience condensed into plain English? The author's experience shows. No matter what the species being sought, Batin's book is a great place to start." *Joe Bridgman The Anchorage Times.*

This book can make your Alaska fishing trip a success with its:

This Book Gives You A PH.D. Crash Course In Alaska Fish Habits and Biology Necessary for Success

"How to catch Alaska's Trophy Sportfish" translates volumes of biological data into terms every angler can understand and use to catch trophy sportfish.

You'll learn about:
- aggravation responses that catch 70-pound salmon,
- social hierarchies that tell you where to find fish before you reach the water,
- stream equations necessary for catching the largest trout and char.

We show you how each species of Alaska trophy sportfish respond to stimuli, and how you can duplicate those responses through our proven field tips and techniques. If you order NOW, you can have this knowledge today...at your fingertips.

Use this book when you go shopping for flies and tackle.

You receive sixteen full-color pages showing the different sportfish and the best flies and lures you need for success, all of which have earned the highest marks for catching trophy sportfish in 10 years of testing.

With this advice, you'll spend your time catching fish, rather than wondering what to catch them on.

- 368 pages and 120 action-filled photos showing you the fish-catching secrets that has enabled the author to catch and release thousands of sportfish.

- Fly fishing techniques for Alaska's lakes and streams.

- Detailed information, life histories, and feeding habits for all of Alaska's 17 major sportfish species.

- Over 500 specific areas in Alaska where you can catch your trophy sportfish.

- 16 full-color pages identifying Alaska's trophy sportfish plus color charts of the most effective lure and fly patterns.

- Detailed charts and illustrations showing you where to find trophy sportfish.

- Fish-catching secrets of over a dozen guides and biologists.

"If you plan to go to Alaska, or already live there, read this book thoroughly and you fish it better. Chris Batin IS Alaska fishing." *Homer Circle Angling Editor, Sports Afield magazine*

How to catch Alaska's Trophy Sportfish

Softcover....$25.95 (Canada.....$27.95)
Hardcover-Limited Edition.............$45
(Canada..........$47)

Chris Batin's 20 Great
Alaska Fishing Adventures

by Christopher Batin

The greatest adventures in Alaska sportfishing that you can experience today!

Frustrated by shoulder-to-shoulder crowds... mediocre Alaska fishing opportunities...and fish that are small and too few in number?

If so, get ready to fly into a glacial-rimmed volcanic crater and fish nearby streams where you will land 50 salmon a day... a wilderness mountain retreat where you catch 11 different species of sportfish in one week... or discover a remote river where anglers catch several, 10 to 17-pound rainbow trout each day!

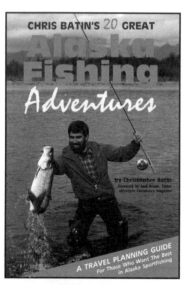

CHRIS BATIN'S 20 GREAT
Alaska Fishing Adventures
by Christopher Batin
Foreword by Jack Brown, Editor
Western Outdoors magazine
A TRAVEL PLANNING GUIDE
For Those Who Want The Best
in Alaska Sportfishing

ISBN 0-916771-09-1

Free information on contacts, charter pilots, lodges, road-access routes, telephone numbers...everything you need to plan your Great Alaska Fishing Adventure THIS YEAR!

It's an adventure book you won't want to put down!

This book is also chock-full of Alaska wilderness fishing adventure stories and anecdotes that not only entertain, but inform. Only a handful of anglers experienced in the world's best fishing have known about many of these areas.

At your fingertips is everything you need to duplicate the author's successes...as well as specific travel details necessary for you to plan one of Alaska's 20 finest fishing adventures NOW.

Many fisheries are so remote, only a handful of anglers visit them each year!

This book has over 150 photos and maps...showing you what you can expect first-hand. See the rivers...country... fish...and the adventure you can expect on each trip!

This book offers you detailed information on where to find fish at each location...forage fish and hatch information...and personal observations on the habits of these sportfish so you can make outstanding catches...and releases... of trophy fish Alaska is famous for.

A comprehensive listing of the most productive flies for each area, based on actual field tests.

''In 20 Great Alaska Fishing Adventures, Chris Batin captures the spirit and excitement of Alaska sportfishing adventure!''

Jack Brown, Western Outdoors magazine

''In recent years, Chris and Adela Batin have become synonymous with and trusted sources for Alaska fishing information.

Twenty Great Alaska Fishing Adventures stresses the best in Alaska sportfishing and details trips that qualify in that 'adventure of a lifetime' category. The book also offers a commendable emphasis on catch-and-release fishing.''

The International Angler

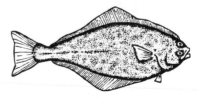

Chris Batin's 20 Great Alaska Fishing Adventures..............$24.95

Fishing Alaska on Dollars a Day

A Comprehensive Guide to Fishing & Hunting in Alaska's National Forests

by Christopher and Adela Batin

A seven-day stay at a premier Alaska fishing lodge will cost over $4,000, a price beyond the financial reach of many anglers.

However, if you can row a boat, cook your own meals and handle cast-after-cast excitement for feisty, fresh-from-the-sea salmon, you can enjoy comparable Alaska sport-fishing for only dollars a day.

Fishing Alaska on Dollars a Day reveals Alaska's best angling hideaways where you can catch trophy steelhead, salmon and trout. The book is the result of years of research and travel to some of Alaska's best fishing hotspots.

All the information you need for planning your trip is in this one book, saving you hundreds of dollars in research time and phone calls.

This 352-page book provides you with:

■ **Specific details on over 200 wilderness cabins,** exact locations, how to get there, free boats for your personal use, free cabins and shelters, and where you'll find the best wilderness sightseeing, wildlife photography and adventuring opportunities, as well as pages of alternate contact sources for more information.

■ **Available for the first time are the names and locations of over 375 Alaska steelhead streams.** Discover where you can average 8 to 12 steelhead per trip; choose from over 200 cutthroat waters, many located in Alaska's finest scenic mountain wilderness, or the best intertidal areas where fly fishermen catch over 20 silver salmon per day!

3rd Edition

Fishing Alaska On Dollar$ A Day

A Comprehensive Guide to Fishing, Hiking & Outdoor Recreation in Alaska's National Forests

By Christopher and Adela Batin

ISBN 0-916771-26-1

■ **Detailed USGS topographic maps and fishing charts** help you pinpoint the best fishing and hunting areas. If purchased separately, these maps alone would cost you over $150. These maps are **FREE** with the book, and are invaluable in helping plan your trip.

■ **Specific advice on flies and lures,** as well as 100 photos to prove these recommendations work!

■ **With this book you'll also learn where you can inex-**pensively hunt for moose, goat, brown and black bear, wolf and Sitka blacktail deer, as well as waterfowl. You'll have the comforts of a wilderness cabin to enjoy at the end of a successful day's hunt.

The book is profusely illustrated with over 150 maps, photographs and charts, When used in conjunction with our award-winning book, *"How to catch Alaska's Trophy Sportfish"*, you have all the information you need to plan a complete and successful Alaska fishing adventure.

"An excellent book that is essential for anyone considering making the trip."
San Francisco Examiner
"If you've dreamed about an Alaska adventure but can't afford the $2,000 to $4,000 price tag for most outfitted trips, this book is the answer."
Allentown Morning Call
"A comprehensive guide destined to become dog-eared by dedicated anglers. Written by Chris Batin, perhaps the best-known fishing authority in Alaska."
Akron Beacon

Fishing Alaska on Dollars a Day....$24.95
Canada............$26.95

Periodicals

The Alaska Angler ®

"a publication for anglers who want the very best in Alaska sportfishing."

Dear Alaska Angling Enthusiast in Search of Adventure:

If you're planning a trip to Alaska this year, be careful.

Alaska sportfishing is not what it used to be.

You stand a 60 percent chance of fishing with an incompetent guide.

A 35 percent chance of fishing on streams with few or no fish.

Perhaps you'll choose one of the state's unsafe air taxi operators, or one of the fishing businesses that "left town" with the entire season's deposits from clients...businesses that are big advertisers in major magazines.

You can take your chances with the 320,000 other people who fish Alaska, and settle for mediocre catches of sportfish, or none at all.

Or you can subscribe to The Alaska Angler ®, where I will be your personal guide to Alaska's best fishing... away from the crowds.

Just ask Rick Sanchez. He had been to Alaska twice. Each time, fishing was poor, despite what the guides promised. With information he obtained from **The Alaska Angler** ®, he decided to make one last trip and fish our recommended stream where he could catch a king salmon on a fly.

A week later, Sanchez had caught 76 king salmon on flies, most from 30 to 60 pounds and set 16 world line-class records in the process. And he didn't see another angler the entire time.

Like Rick Sanchez, you, too, can benefit from **The Alaska Angler** ®. You'll know exactly what to expect before spending hundreds of dollars on a mediocre lodge or poorly-arranged do-it-yourself trip.

Make your next trip a success with information offered in **The Alaska Angler** ®.

Christopher Batin, *Editor*

Our Position: We provide you with unbiased reports based on a stringent rating system. We do not receive any remuneration or benefit from these reviews. We are not booking agents, promoting those lodges and services that offer the best commissions. What The Alaska Angler® does provide is pages of inside information, the kind only anglers experienced in the world's best fishing have access to.

Each Issue of The Alaska Angler® Provides You With 10 Benefits:

Lodge Reviews

You don't need to spend $4,000 to discover if a lodge has a four-star rating or whether it's a fly-by-night operation. We visit the lodges and provide you objective reports on the number of fish you can expect to catch, accommodations and compare it with other lodges. We take the risks, you benefit from our experience.

Do-it-Yourself Alaska Angler

Tired of fishing with the crowds? Receive inside information on affordable trips you can enjoy, both from the road system and fly-out trips. You receive everything necessary to duplicate our successes: names of air taxi services, contacts, detailed maps, what to use and how to fish it: First-hand information because we've been there, and want to share these great fisheries with you!

Advanced Alaska Angling Techniques

With each issue, you become an instant expert with a crash course on a specific angling situation you're likely to encounter while fishing Alaska. You'll be on the cutting edge of the most popular and effective fish-catching techniques as well as field-proven flies, lures and equipment. The result? You'll be catching fish when others are not.

Guide Review

In a recent field survey, over 60 percent of the fishing guides we fished with were judged to be incompetent. Why fish with a guide who will catch you five fish, when you can fish with a guide who can help you catch 20 fish, and larger ones at that? I review the best guides, investigate their success ratios and score them against the industry's best.

Alaska Angler Field Notes

Bringing a loved one to Alaska, or looking for a trip that caters to women? Perhaps a secluded cabin you can rent for dollars a day, away from the crowds but in the thick of the salmon? Or specific technical data on water flow, speed, substrate, forage fish and hatches on streams? I tell you the specifics, and the best patterns you need to catch the big ones. I know because I've been there, having earned more than 30 trophy fish certificates and awards, so that you can benefit from this experience, NOW.

Alaska Angler Field Reports

Read about the successes or failures of other anglers who fish Alaska as they rate the best and worst of Alaska fishing...valuable information that will help in taking home personal experiences of catching and releasing trophy fish...not just stories of the catch someone else made last week.

Short Strikes

Brief news notes on items that will enhance your fishing knowledge, making you a better angler. Some recent topics include "Techniques for finding and catching trophy gray-ling"; "Forage fish preferences of Alaska rainbow trout"; "Three steps to catching 10-pound-plus fish when all else fails"; and "When do fish feed during Alaska's 24 hours of daylight".

Alaska Angler Notebook.

Trip discounts, last-minute fishing closures, and field notes regarding Bush travel, suppliers of inexpensive, quality flies for Alaska fishing, uncharted steelhead fishing and more information on how you can fish Alaska on a shoestring budget.

Custom Trip Consulting

Planning on making a trip soon? Subscribers can take advantage of our low-cost information service on lodges, guides, resorts or areas you plan on visiting in 1991. We'll tell you what to expect, and if you'll be better off going elsewhere! We provide harvest statistics, success ratios, lures, tackle equipment for specific areas and contacts over the telephone if you need them in a hurry or by mail if you want to share them with friends.

Special Reports

Discover the behind-the-scenes story major magazines won't publish, stories that will change how you view so called "blue ribbon" fisheries. In the past, we've covered the problem of Alaska's widespread incompetent guide problem, the demise of the Iliamna watershed fishery, the advertising hype surrounding the Brooks River fishery, and more.

Not Available in Stores!

The Alaska Angler® is available only by subscription...it is not sold on newsstands or to libraries. Thus, our information stays among our close-knit network of subscribers.

If our bi-monthly reports were made available through newspapers, magazines and tv, the good fishing I reveal would cease to exist. But I'm willing to share this information with you, a fellow sportsman who cares about Alaska's fishery resources.

Why You Need to Act Now!

The Alaska Angler® has become the information source for anglers who want the very best in Alaska sport-fishing. Here's what our subscribers have to say:

"Informative, concise, well worth the investment." Dr. R.T., New York, N.Y.

"Excellent information on Alaska sport-fishing. We have planned trips because of articles in The Alaska Angler."
I.H., Anchorage, Alaska

Receive over 60 pages of special reports and information a year...the cost of a couple flies or a fishing lure per issue. And the price includes first-class postage to your home or office.

The Alaska Angler......$69 per year

Best Recipes of Alaska's Fishing Lodges

by Adela Batin

A unique addition to your cookbook collection. This book tells it all...the lodges and accommodations, the cooks and their recipes, photographs of scenic Alaska, fishing and food. Everything you've wanted to know about Alaska's fishing lodges.
An excellent travel planning guide, you'll learn what it's really like to be there!

Best Recipes of Alaska's Fishing Lodges is more than just a cookbook—It's a celebration of a wilderness lifestyle that many of us dream about, but few live.

Best Recipes of Alaska's Fishing Lodges
Adela Batin

ISBN 0-916771-10-5

■ 190 kitchen-tested recipes, home-style to gourmet: Fish, meat, poultry, soups, salads, breads and desserts.

■ Delicious ways to fix your Alaska catch of salmon and halibut, moose or caribou. Plus the perfect accompanying dishes to make a complete meal.

■ 140 photographs showing the food, fishing, accommodations and activities at the lodges.

■ Three-color format, 6'' x 9'', 320 pages, complete recipe index.

Each chapter is seasoned with photos and descriptions of 16 of Alaska's finest lodges, garnished with cooks' profiles and frosted with anecdotes on Alaska that inform as well as entertain.

This book gives you a variety of lodge experiences. Each lodge is unique in its location, the type of fishing it offers, the way meals are prepared, the type of food served, and the ambiance created by owners and personnel.

Each year, thousands of anglers pay up to $4,000 a week to enjoy the services and partake in the sensational meals served at these world-famous lodges.

Best Recipes of Alaska's Fishing Lodges gives you the opportunity to sample the many wonderful flavors of Alaska.

Delight family and friends with this taste-tempting assortment of **190 best recipes** that include: Alaska Sourdough Pizza, Savory Dill Salmon, Smoked Halibut Spread, Kulik Cream Cake, Stuffed Kvichak Chicken, Icy Strait BBQ Halibut and Strawberry Island Bread.

Best Recipes of Alaska's Fishing Lodges, was recently honored as the ''Best Outdoor Book'' by the Northwest Outdoor Writers Association, winning first place in design and editing. It makes the perfect gift for anglers and cooks alike.

Novice and gourmet cooks—as well as anyone interested in Alaskana—will cherish this book.

This book is your link to the Alaska lodge experience. If you've stayed at one of these featured lodges, these recipes may help you savor those memories. If you've never been to Alaska, allow this book to be your guide.

Best Recipes of Alaska's Fishing Lodges (softcover)..........$24.95
(Canada....$26.95)

Bear Heads & Fish Tales

By Alan Liere

Patrick F. McManus, internationally recognized humorist, book author and columnist for Outdoor Life magazine, has this to say in the foreword of Alan Liere's recent book on Alaska outdoor humor entitled, "Bear Heads & Fish Tales":

"What's funny? Nobody knows for sure, but I would venture to say that it's that tiny, gritty bit of truth that produces the pearl of laughter. I do not mean to imply that author Al Liere in any way resembles an oyster. The man is a funny writer, which is the best thing you can say about a humorist. I personally plan to buy a gross of Bear Heads & Fish Tales. If we have another Great Depression, people will need something to cheer them up, and I figure a copy of this book will be as good as gold in the marketplace."

Bear Heads & Fish Tales is a collection of zany outdoor stories written by Alan Liere, Alaska's ambassador of mirth and humor to the funny bone. Learn the techniques for smoking fish, Alaska-style, by burning your neighbors garage; what words to say to your oil pan while sleeping under your car, tips on preparing wilderness gourmet meals such as Chicken Noodle Salmon or Humpy Rainwater Soup, how to stuff a mature bull caribou into the cargo space of a Subaru hatchback and much more.

"This book is for anyone who has ever wielded a fishing rod, a shotgun, or a wiener stick," says Liere. "It's for those who experience deflated air mattresses, rubber rafts, and egos— sometimes all on the same outing. **Bear Heads & Fish Tales** is for anyone who believes in that fine line between tragedy and comedy and knows with all their heart that maturity is highly over-rated."

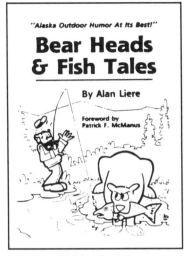

"Alaska Outdoor Humor At Its Best!"

Bear Heads & Fish Tales

By Alan Liere

Foreword by Patrick F. McManus

ISBN 0-916771-05-9

The 13 stories in this 139-page book are based on Liere's real-life personal misadventures and hilarious insights. In "King Tut's Revenge," Liere expounds on his childhood phobia regarding mummy-type sleeping bags. "Thanks, Aunt Judy" reveals tips on how Liere has learned to survive Alaska mosquitoes through such evasive tactics as "The Screamin' Exit" and the liberal use of garlic. And with a humorous eye, he examines that glossy, hope-inducing product of creative writing and adjective overuse known as "The Alaska Outdoor Brochure."

Each story is illustrated by outdoor cartoonist Jeff Schuler. The combined efforts of both author and cartoonist effectively capture the side-splitting antics and foibles of sportsmen in the Alaska outdoors, the Northcountry's grandest comic playhouse.

Bear Heads & Fish Tales $9.95

HOW TO ORDER

FOR IMMEDIATE SHIPMENT—

VISA and Mastercard orders only call:

1-907-455-8000

24 hours a day, 7 days a week

BY MAIL—Detach the handy order form. Please print clearly all necessary information on the order form, and enclose with your remittance in an envelope.

PAYMENT—We accept your personal check, certified check, money order, Visa and Mastercard. For Canada and foreign countries: We accept U.S. Funds only. Make checks payable to:

Alaska Angler Publications

DELIVERY—Allow 4-6 weeks for bookrate, and 1-2 weeks for priority airmail. Express mail on request for 1-2 day delivery.
Canadian and Foreign delivery, extra shipping charges apply. See order form for additional charges.

How to Catch Trophy Halibut:
Proven Tips, Techniques and Strategies of the Experts

How to Catch Trophy **HALIBUT**
Proven Tips, Techniques and Strategies of the Experts
Christopher Batin & Terry Rudnick

BONUS: Includes where-to-go locations for Alaska, British Columbia, Washington, Oregon, and California.

This 400-page book reveals the inside secrets of how to catch trophy halibut from 80 to 400 pounds.

Catching a slab-sided halibut is the dream of every angler...a fish so heavy it takes several people to hoist it onto the scale!

Catching these huge flatfish requires specialized skills and knowledge that takes a lifetime to acquire.

Now, you can obtain this information in hours rather than years.

How to catch Trophy Halibut reveals the success secrets of the experts with decades of on-the-water experience.

This book reveals time-proven bait rigs, specialized techniques, floating jig secrets, drifting methods, flyfishing tips, and world-record strategies that will help you catch trophy halibut wherever you fish along the California, Washington, Oregon, British Columbia and Alaska coastlines.

Whether you fish from your own boat or hire a charter, this book provides the inside information that will give you that added advantage over other anglers in catching trophy halibut.

THIS BOOK REVEALS HUNDREDS OF TIPS FOR HALIBUT SUCCESS:

• A newly discovered, remote area where halibut average 80 to 100 pounds, and the world's best hotspot for 300 to 400-pound "barn-doors."

• How to make super-effective metal jigs in your own home for pennies, and specialized techniques that outfish bait.

• New type of leadhead jig that so closely imitates a crab that it drives big halibut into a feeding frenzy.

• A new floating jig that enhances bait presentation by over 200 percent.

• In-depth research that shows how you can create a powerful scent field that attracts schools of halibut...as recorded on sonar units.

• Specific advice on the new technology lines, hooks, and equipment that will increase both the size and amount of your catch.

• Exact guidelines for identifying 16 prime holding and migration areas favored by slab-sided halibut.

• Secret baits favored by huge halibut. Learn the Injection Effect to triple your catch. Illustrations showing best knots, leaders, rigs, double rigs, and more.

INFORMATION-PACKED CHAPTERS INCLUDE:

SPECIAL TRAVEL SECTION: Over 100 pages of secret hotspots, best charter operators, local secrets and best times to fish Alaska, British Columbia, Washington, Oregon, and California.

AND MUCH MORE: Memorable Halibut Battles • • Halibut Guides Reveal Secrets • For Flyfishers Only: Two Deadly Flies that Catch Halibut in Shallow Water • Photo Guide to Filleting Fish • Money-Saving Tips on Freezing, Packing, Shipping Halibut • Scientific Studies Reveal Preferred Foods of Big Halibut • Making the Record Books with Your Fish • Halibut Recipes • New Seasickness Remedy that Works • And hundreds of additional tips with photos of record catches to prove this information can help you realize your dream of catching huge halibut.

How to Catch Trophy Halibut............$25.95

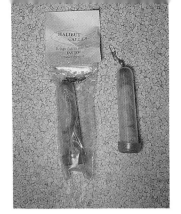

Halibut Caller

Halibut Caller is a new scent-delivery device that attracts trophy halibut to your bait or jig.

Here's how Halibut Caller works: The fluorescent pink wick contains a carefully formulated mix of fish attractants, oils and scents in a special timed-release bonding agent that stays effective for hours.

Commercial longline and sportfishing boat research has shown that halibut follow the scent field created by the caller and strike its accompanying bait or lure, while ignoring herring, squid and salmon belly baits and scents.

Developed by long-time Alaskan fishermen Glen and Mark Graham, and tested extensively by sportfishing author Chris Batin, Halibut Caller creates a super-concentrated scent field as described in Chapter 10 of *How to Catch Trophy Halibut.*

With Halibut Caller, there is no messy scent bottle to handle. Bait thieves can't steal it. Best of all, Halibut Caller lasts through an entire day of fishing. After a few hours use, Halibut Caller can be recapped and fished again at a later time.

Halibut Caller is easy to use. Open the canister, and attach the caller to your mainline swivel, so it doesn't interfere with your bait or lure. The patented, timed-release method of delivery allows the scent to disperse slowly into the current, attracting halibut from great distances. The caller's fluorescent pink wick is highly visible at extreme depths, and acts as a visual "appetizer" once halibut are in close.

Order your season's supply of Halibut Caller today, and eliminate the headache and frustration of trying to create and maintain an effective scent field.

Halibut Caller is available in limited quantities, and not always found in stores.

Halibut Caller

(package of three callers and instructions)
..............................**$12.95 postpaid**

Field-Tested And Approved Halibut Tackle And Scents

The Halibut Bouncer

Halibut Bouncer is a super-effective new halibut lure that will help you catch barn-door halibut like those that appear in this book. This lure will change forever how you fish for trophy halibut.

Halibut Bouncer imitates the octopus and crabs that big halibut search out and eat. Its unique, life-like action in the water and venturi scent-release system surpasses the effectiveness of bait, chunk bait, squid, herring and salmon. It's unlike any other jig on the market, both in terms of appearance and action. You can measure the results for yourself with every hook-set.

How to Catch Trophy Halibut co-author Chris Batin has spent years designing, testing and refining this lure. It is always the first lure he fishes, and usually the only lure he uses during the day for one simple reason: Halibut Bouncer catches BIG halibut. Until now, only participants in Batin's Advanced Alaska Fishing Techniques seminars have known about this amazing big-fish producer.

The Halibut Bouncer has proven itself in trophy halibut waters from Ketchikan to the Bering Sea. When used in conjunction with Halibut Caller, the Bouncer creates a strong scent field that big halibut find irresistible. And there's no messy bait to bother with or replace.

Halibut Bouncer is also effective in catching trophy ling cod and huge yellow-eye rockfish.

Halibut Bouncer is not available in stores. Order today if you want to duplicate the success of the author and others who have landed trophy halibut with this easy-to-fish and effective lure.

"It's the most life-like lure I've seen for halibut."

Glen Graham,
commercial halibut fisherman and
co-creator and designer, Halibut Caller

Halibut Bouncer
One lure, fishing tips fact sheet **$15.95**

BONUS
One lure and Halibut Caller.........**$18.95**

Appendix

Appendix Table 1. Stomach contents of 70 Pacific halibut from the Hecate Strait and Dixon Entrance areas of British Columbia, May 13-22, 1983.

Location	Date	Depth (fms)	Length (cm)	Sex	Food Weight (lbs.)	Stomach Contents
51:44 129:21	5/17	44-51	83	M	0.10	2 sand lance, 2 hermit crabs
51:47 129:22	5/17	45-78	94	F	0.10	1 herring
			82	M	MT	
			84	M	0.80	2 sand lance, 3 herring
			86	M	MT	
52:55 130:48	5/18	22-26	83	F	0.28	1 sand lance, 10 unidentified crabs
53:33 131:09	5/19	20-34	98	M	0.46	3 unidentified flatfish, 1 unidentified crab, 8 clam siphons
			124	F	0.80	20 unidentified crabs
			82	F	0.12	4 unidentified crabs
			144	F	4.10	1 Pacific cod, 8 unidentified crabs
			82	F	0.01	1 sand lance
			87	F	0.38	14 sand lance, 2 unidentified crabs
			82	F	0.30	7 sand lance, 1 herring, 1 hermit crab, 1 clam siphon
			90	F	0.50	1 unidentified flatfish, 1 hermit crab, 6 unidentified crabs, 1 clam siphon
			129	F	0.59	5 sand lance, 1 unidentified crab, 1 Pacific cod
			134	F	0.20	1 unidentified flatfish
			87	F	0.81	1 hermit crab, 5 unidentified crabs
53:31 131:12	5/19	16-36	98	F	0.50	1 butter sole, 1 unidentified rockfish, 1 unidentified flatfish
			84	F	0.25	1 hermit crab, 4 unidentified crabs
			93	F	MT	
			87	M	0.73	1 herring, 1 hermit crab, 13 clam siphons
			96	F	0.80	1 Pacific cod, 4 unidentified crabs
			106	M	0.64	28 sand lance, 1 unidentified flatfish
			106	M	MT	

Table 2. Food items identified in stomachs of adult halibut from northern British Columbia and Gulf of Alaska waters, 1955, 1980, 1981, and 1983. Numbers of stomachs in which each item was observed.

Food Item	Hecate Strait	Masset	WC QCI*	Timbered Islet	Gulf of Alaska	Chirikof Island	Shumagin Island	Total
Octopus	12	5	13	13	1	16	32	92
Crab**	39	22	3	4	6	8	3	85
Pacific herring	16			3	33	1		53
Pacific cod	6	13	5	3	5	5	1	38
Sand lance	34	3			1			38
Arrowtooth flounder		14		1	5			20
Walleye pollock	5				13	1		19
Tanner crab					18			18
Pacific halibut		8		9				17
Rockfish	4		4	3			1	12
Salmonid	4	4		1	1			10
Unidentified eggs	1					2	7	10
Starfish	1	1			1	1	4	8
Sablefish	2	1	2				1	6
Clam siphon	4			1				5
Flathead sole					4			4
Skate	1	2		1				4
Dogfish			2		1	1		4
Hermit crab	4							4
Snail fish	2						1	3
Ratfish		1	1	1				3
Snails			1			1	1	3
Petrale sole		1		1				2
Rex sole	2							2
Sea urchin			2					2
Lingcod			1					1
Rock sole	1							1
Poacher						1		1
Mussel			1					1
Scallop						1		1
Digested flatfish	8	27		20	10	1		66
Digested fish	59	47	11	34	10	54	79	294

*West Coast, Queen Charlotte Islands
**Crabs from British Columbia and S.E. Alaska include at least 6 identifiable species plus unidentified crabs; Chirikof Island had 6 Tanner and 2 unidentified crabs; and Shumagin Islands had 1 rock, 1 hair, and 1 unidentified crab.

Excerpted from Pacific Halibut as Predator and Prey, E.A. Best, Gilbert St. Pierre, 1988. IPHC

Travel Planning Guide To Charter Operators And Services

Whether you're looking for an opportunity to catch a 400-pound halibut or a few flatties for the freezer, the charter operators and services listed in this section can help you achieve your goal.

These businesses will provide additional information on the fishing opportunities available in their region, plus advice on wildlife viewing, salmon fishing and when to plan your trip for optimum success. Be sure to ask about any trip discount or fishing specials they may be offering at the time of your call.

ALASKAN ESCAPES

P.O. Box 69, Point Baker, Alaska 99927. Phone (907) 489-2211. Fax (907) 489-2211 after 5 p.m. Alaska time.

Fish **Prince of Wales Island** for trophy halibut and king salmon aboard the F/V Bold Venture on your exclusive charter, or enjoy private beachfront accommodations, complete with skiff/motor for exploring local waters. **ALASKAN ESCAPES,** it's your choice.

Kim and Sue Betzina, owners.

AWARD CHARTERS

P.O. Box 631, Anchor Point, Alaska 99556. Phone (907) 235-7014. Fax (907) 235-2282. In Alaska (888) 235-7014.

Alaska family business specializing in daily halibut fishing trips aboard twin engine, fully-equipped, high-speed vessel accommodating up to six people. Fishing in the **lower Cook Inlet and Gulf of Alaska** with marine-life viewing every trip. All fishing gear, tackle, bait and fish filleting included.

Robert Ward, owner.

BOARDWALK WILDERNESS LODGE

P.O. Box 19121, Thorne Bay, Alaska 99919. Phone (907) 828-3918. Fax (907) 828-3367.

Fish **PWI** for barndoor flatties in secluded luxury only two hours by plane from Seattle. Maximum of 12 guests with family suites and double-occupancy rooms. Enjoy our outdoor hot tub and gourmet meals. Limit-out on halibut and try our rivers and streams for salmon, cutthroat and Dollies.

Doug and Donna Ibbetson, owners.

CHAZMAN CHARTERS

P.O. Box 2826, Kodiak, Alaska 99615. Phone (907) 486-6930.

Fish **Kodiak** and enjoy Alaska's fishing at its best while out of the rain on our covered fishing deck. Every customized charter includes quality fishing gear, bait, lunch, soda and filleting of your catch *at no additional expense.* We can also arrange all your accommodations. "One call does it all!"

Captain Chaz Glagolich, owner.

CIE JAE CHARTERS

P.O. Box 170, Yakutat, Alaska 99689. Phone and fax (907) 784-3544.

VISIT YAKUTAT for halibut, ling cod, stream and fly out fishing for steelhead, kings, sockeye and silver salmon, glacier tours and lodgings. Where the pristine beauty of Alaska still abounds with breathtaking glaciers and mountains, and excellent uncrowded fishing. Fish Yakutat and you'll be hooked for life.

Chuck and Roberta Crabaugh, owners.

DUTCH HARBOR CHARTERS

P.O. Box 308, Unalaska, Alaska 99685. Phone (907) 581-2226. Fax (907) 581-2268. Reservations (800) 891-1194.

Enjoy Grand Slam fishing and a steaming volcano with it's own glacier, 45 minutes to 1 hour from **Dutch Harbor**. Come join me for jackpot halibut fishing on the charter boat "Grand Aleutian", 32-foot Albin. Comfort is what this boat is all about.

Captain Darryl Dossett, owner.

GOODHAND'S CHARTERS

Summer: P.O. Box 970, Valdez, Alaska 99686. Phone (907) 835-4333. Fax (907) 835-4385. Winter: P.O. Box 218, Ester, Alaska 99725. Phone (907) 479-5562. Fax (907) 479-0395. e-mail: glaciers@alaska.net, Website http://www.alaska.net/—glaciers/

Prince William Sound halibut and salmon fishing. Day trip: 1—8 persons, 7 am—7 pm. Remote long range tours, overnight trip: 1—6 persons, 1—3 days (1—2 nights). Owned and operated by a year-round Alaskan family.

John Goodhand, owner.

THE GRAND ALEUTIAN

P.O. Box 921169, Dutch Harbor, Alaska 99692-1169. Phone (907) 581-3844. Reservations (800) 891-1194.

Best place for trophy halibut. New IGFA world-record halibut, all tackle. 1995 Alaska Angler® Lodge of the Year. Fly-out salmon fishing to secluded Volcano Bay. Luxurious full-service hotel. Complete sportfishing packages for adventurous anglers.

HOMER OCEAN CHARTERS

Box 2543, Homer, Alaska 99603. Phone and fax (907) 235-6212. Toll free phone and fax (800) 426-6212.

Day and multiple day trips from **Homer**, six passenger and larger vessels. Homer Ocean Charters is the pioneer in long-range halibut fishing and vessel-based fishing/hunting combinations. If you want the best, call us toll free.

Captain Roark Brown and Rick Swenson, owners.

LION'S DEN WILDERNESS LODGE

P.O. Box 29, Port Lions, Alaska 99550. Phone and fax (907) 454-2301.

Fish for trophy-sized halibut and five species of Pacific salmon. Enjoy gourmet meals and spacious accommodations. The very best location on **Kodiak Island.** All-inclusive packages or day charters available. Serving the serious angler since 1983.

Kevin and Katy Adkins, owners.

SALTWATER SAFARI COMPANY

410 K Street, Anchorage, Alaska 99501. (Downtown across from the Hotel Captain Cook). Phone (907) 277-3223. Outside Alaska 1-800-382-1564. Fax (907) 274-5977.

Enjoy the ultimate deep-sea fishing experience out of **Seward** aboard either of our 50-foot charter vessels *Legend* and *Legacy.* Fish in the middle of the most productive halibut fishing grounds in the world with the company that pioneered them.

Steve Babinec and Bob Candopolous, owners.

SELDOVIA FISHING ADVENTURES

P.O. Box 121, Seldovia, Alaska 99663. Phone and fax (907) 234-7417.

Fantastic fishing from beautiful remote **Seldovia!** Experienced, successful skipper. Custom built, 30-foot cabin cruiser with twin diesels. The latest in fishing technology. Deluxe packages include transportation, fishing, family-style meals and oceanview lodging. 90 percent repeat clientele— We do it right!

David and Peggy Cloninger, owners.

SILVER SALMON LODGE

These huge halibut (400 and 200 pounds) were caught within one hour on Peter Guttchen's charter boat near Raspberry Island and **Kodiak Island** shores. We fish in protected waters—you will not get seasick. Travel time from the lodge to the fishing grounds is between 5 to 10 minutes. We provide all saltwater fishing equipment as well as packaging and freezing of your catch.

P. O. Box 378, Kodiak, Alaska 99615
Phone and fax (907) 680-2230

Beautiful lodge in remote wilderness setting. Limited to 10 guests. Float plane access. Magnificent scenery and wildlife. Ideal for photographers.
Peter and Baerbel Guttchen, owners.

How to Catch
Trophy Halibut

SILVER SALMON CREEK LODGE

Box 3234, Soldotna, Alaska 99669. Phone (907) 262-4839. Fax (907) 262-4686.

A unique opportunity for uncongested trophy halibut fishing on **Cook Inlet's west side.** Fully-modern lodge, cabins, new fishing gear aboard the M/V "Song of Joanne". Set in picturesque Lake Clark National Park with renowned food service and other attractions including stream fishing and bear viewing. *David Coray, owner.*

SPORTSMAN'S COVE LODGE

P.O. Box 2486, Olympia, WA 98507. Phone (360) 956-3442. Fax (360) 956-0345.

ALASKA'S Sportsman's Cove Lodge on **Prince of Wales Island** features consistently hot salmon and halibut fishing! Why get tossed around in rough waters when you can fish the calm Inside Passage on deluxe 36-foot boats? For a brochure and available dates, call 1-800-962-7889 or fax 360-956-0345. *Jeff McQuarrie.*

TED'S SPORT CENTER

15526 Hwy. 99 N., Lynnwood, WA 98037. Phone (206) 743-9505.

Ted's has one of the **largest selections of halibut tackle** in the Northwest: rods—reels—rod belts—line—lures—leaders—swivels—sinkers—harpoons—hooks—spreaders—bait, etc. Write or call for a catalog. **WE MAIL ORDER ANYWHERE.** *Mike Chamberlain, owner.*

WEST COAST FISHING RESORTS

4680 Cowley Crescent, Richmond, BC V7B 1C1 Canada. Phone toll free (800) 810-TYEE (8933). Fax (604) 278-3120.

Fabulous salmon, halibut and trout fishing in **British Columbia locations—Douglas Channel, Milbanke Sound, Rivers Inlet and Eutsuk Lake (Tweedsmuir Park).** Exclusive fly-in locations, round trip airfare from Vancouver included. All inclusive packages at competitive rates, from $1,395! *Contact Amy Richards.*

Alaska Angler® Information Service

Want to know the best rivers to catch all five species of Pacific salmon? Anxious to discover the Top 10 do-it-yourself trips for wild, 8 to 10-pound rainbow trout? Or a listing of Alaska's five-star lodges that serve you early-morning coffee in bed and at night, place European chocolates on your pillow?

The answers to these and other Alaska sportfishing questions can be answered by calling the **Alaska Angler Information Service**.

The Information Service provides "answers for anglers" who are planning a fishing trip to the 49th state.

"There's a common misconception that Alaska fishing is good year-round, no matter where or when you go," says Chris Batin, editor of **The Alaska Angler®** . "Alaska has over 3 million lakes and 3,000 rivers covering a land mass one-fifth the size of the continental United States. Planning is crucial for success. A miscalculation of several days can have anglers staring at fishless water rather than a stream filled with salmon."

He stressed the information service is not a booking agency.

"Objectivity is the key to the Alaska Angler Information Service," Batin said. "We do not receive any remuneration or benefit from recommending one stream or fishing service over another. This ensures that our customers receive objective information on fishing opportunities, guides and lodges that surpass industry standards for service, quality and professionalism. We can provide all the information anglers need, from the best flies for a particular watershed, water conditions to expect, type of hatches, and even the flora and fauna in the area."

Travel agents and booking agents are often unfamiliar with Alaska's myriad sportfishing options.

"Many travel agents sell a limited selection of trips that offer the best commissions for them," he said. "It's not cost effective for them to recommend quality, inexpensive trips, even though it may be perfect for the angler's needs. The Alaska Angler Information Service provides unbiased information so the angler can personally decide whether to spend $25 or $4,000 for a trip.

The crew of **The Alaska Angler** spends over 180 days a year fishing Alaska, searching out the best do-it-yourself and full-service adventures for the company's information service, periodicals and books.

The cost is **$30** for **15 minutes of consultation**. Before consultation begins, callers provide a Mastercard or Visa credit card number. To expedite matters, have ready your list of questions. To benefit from the Alaska Angler Information Service, call **1-907-455-8000** 10 a.m. to 6 p.m. Alaska Standard Time, Monday—Friday.

How to Catch
Trophy Halibut

Send $1 for your Alaska Angler® Resource Guide that includes our entire selection of Alaska fishing books and periodicals that ensure your success on the water!

Ship to: _____

Address: _____

City _____

State _____ Zip _____

Daytime Phone( ) _____

Send order to:
Alaska Angler® Publications
P.O. Box 83550-TR
Fairbanks, Alaska 99708
Or call (907) 455-8000
24 hours a day, 7 days a week

Quantity	Item	Price	Total
_____	Bear Heads & Fish Tales...	$9.95	_____
_____	Best Recipes of Alaska's Fishing Lodges....................	$24.95	_____
_____	Chris Batin's 20 Great Alaska Fishing Adventures.......	$24.95	_____
_____	Fishing Alaska on Dollar$ a Day..................................	$24.95	_____
_____	How to catch Alaska's Trophy Sportfish, softcover......	$25.95	_____
_____	How to catch Alaska's Trophy Sportfish, Limited Edition, hardcover..	$45	_____
_____	How to catch Trophy Halibut.......................................	$25.95	_____
_____	Hunting in Alaska: A Comprehensive Guide.................	$25.95	_____
_____	The Alaska Hunter® newsletter (one-year subscription).............	$69 ppd	_____
_____	The Alaska Hunter® custom binder.............................	$12 ppd	_____
_____	The Alaska Hunter® ceramic mug (great for the office).............	$12 ppd	
	Circle color: Cobalt blue Black Both have microwaveable gold trim		
_____	The Alaska Angler® newsletter (one-year subscription).............	$69 ppd	_____
_____	The Alaska Angler® custom binder.............................	$12 ppd	_____
_____	The Alaska Angler® Field Staff ceramic mug (great for the office)	$12 ppd	_____
	Circle color: Cobalt blue Black Both have microwaveable gold trim		
_____	"Alaska Angler®" poplin leisure cap, one size fits all...............	$14 ppd	_____
	Circle color: Teal Green Red		
_____	"Alaska Angler®" leisure cap, one size fits all..........................	$16 ppd	_____
	Circle color and fabric: Teal Green Red Corduroy Ripstop Nylon		
_____	Halibut Caller..	$12.95 ppd	_____
_____	Halibut Bouncer...	$15.95	_____
_____	Halibut Caller and Halibut Bouncer..............................	$18.95	_____

Gift Section

Book(s) personalized to: (please print)

Name _____

Title of book(s) _____

_____

Book(s) personalized to:

Name _____

Title of book(s) _____

_____

Book(s) personalized to:

Name _____

Title of book(s) _____

_____

Book Shipping Charges

Priority Mail delivery (1 to 2 weeks)........$6. _____
each additional book Priority Mail.............$3. _____
Newsletters, binders, apparel post paid.....0.
Canada, add to above charges................$3. _____
Foreign countries, Airmail, per book.....$15. _____
Foreign Airmail, per newsletter sub.......$20. _____

ORDER AND SHIPPING TOTAL _____

Payment Method

Enclose your personal check, money order or credit card info.

☐ Check   ☐ Money Order   ☐ VISA   ☐ Mastercard

Card Acct. Number _____

Exp. Date ___ — Signature _____

You can obtain any Alaska Angler® or Alaska Hunter® book in print by ordering directly from the publisher. See the order form on page 367 in the back of this book, or for our complete catalog of books and publications that help ensure your success in the Alaska outdoors, send $1 to:

Alaska Angler Publications
P.O. Box 83550, Dept. TR
Fairbanks, Alaska 99708

Or call (907) 455-8000

Would you like to list your charter service in our travel-planning section? Give us a call at (907) 455-8000 for more information.